WARRIORS OF OUR AGE

The Brutal Clash of Ageless Realities

C.J. Hazard

Raider Publishing International

New York London Cape Town

First Printing

Cover image courtesy istockphoto.com

ISBN: 978-1-61667-083-2

Published By Raider Publishing International
www.RaiderPublishing.com
New York London Cape Town
Printed in the United States of America and the United Kingdom

Dedication

THIS BOOK IS DEDICATED TO THE NOTION THAT IN A WORLD of great change and apparent progress of the human condition, while many things may be changing with ever-greater speed for the better, there are some things that never change, at least in the lifespan of humanity.

There is also much reported as fact, when in reality it is fiction, while much reported as fiction, may well be fact.

When will we also learn the repetitive lessons from history, and live full and good lives in the present while embracing bravely the excitement of the future?

It is the ability to embrace this ethic, to understand and confront these conflicting elements of human experience that are the distinguishing features of the discerning and wise person.

They also remember never to stop asking questions.

Special Thanks and Acknowledgements

I AM INDEBTED TO DAVE WALDRON FOR TIMELY EDITING, objectivity, wise guidance, and unwavering encouragement and humour.

I would also like to thank my family: Louanne, Charlotte, and Bryan, for their patience and many words of encouragement, and Paul Harris, for his faith in me and for his encouragement when I often needed it.

Author's Thanks and Acknowledgements

I WISH TO ACKNOWLEDGE THE KINDNESS AND ASSISTANCE of people of Croatia, Cape Town, Ireland, Boston, Paris, Dubai, the State of Montana in the U.S.A., Rome, Bavaria, Western and Eastern Cape in South Africa, England, and Livingstone in Zambia, who enabled me to experience and understand— a little— these beautiful and fascinating cities and regions of the world. Acknowledgements and references for a story of this nature: there were many other books, references and people that provided invaluable information, facts and insights. I would like to thank and acknowledge the following because, without their knowledge and influence, this book would never have been written.

The Economist	*Opus Dei*, John L. Allen	*sti.nasa.gov*
The Cape Times	DSTV – History Channel	*railfaneurope.net*
The Economist: Technology Quarterly	*Francis of Assisi*, Leonardo Boff	*telegraph.co.uk*
Marine Media, Lloyd's Register	Ideas shared: D. Waldron, P. Harris, C. Laing.	*pilotreport.com*
Mere Christianity, C.S. Lewis	Split Tourist Board, Croatia	*airliner.net*
Writings and papers of	*Collections.*	*southafrica.info*

Prof. David Horsfall	*Masterworks: A Lincoln Tribute*	
World Religions, Myrtle Langley	International Court of Justice, Web Site	*google.co.uk*
The Story of Christianity – 2000 Years of faith, M.A. Price and M. Collins	British Passport	*timesonline.co.uk*
Conversations, Msgr Andrew Borello	Catholic Link	*maritimeconnector.com*
World Atlas – Philips	BP: World Energy Statistics	*en.wikipedia.org*
The Bible	*Gas Utilization Handbook*	*britannia.com*
Croatia Tourist Information	*Adelina*, D.W. Horsfall	*jesuit.org*
		travel.state.mt.us

Foreword

JUST HOW SAFE AND SECURE IS OUR MODERN LIFESTYLES?

This is a chillingly topical and fast moving tale of intrigue that shows how a series of devastating attacks on national infrastructures can leave the world's security services floundering, and the world itself in danger of falling under tyrannical forces again.

Entirely feasible events occur across a global stage— from old-world Europe to a mountain retreat in America, from the Gulf of Arabia to the dusty plains of South Africa, and at sea in the South Atlantic. Key international sporting events determine urgent and dreadful time lines, particularly the Soccer World Cup in 2010 and the London Olympics in 2012.

Ageless forces of good and evil match wits on a technological battlefield, each manipulating innovation to gain an upper hand.

The stark reality of the world's reliance on energy and technology is laid bare as issues such as spirituality and belief, poverty, economics, and the timeless values of justice, integrity, and love are explored.

Find out if indeed you have the qualities to be one of the *warriors of our age*.

WARRIORS OF OUR AGE
The Brutal Clash of Ageless Realities

C.J. Hazard

Contents

Main Characters

Trimbledon Family

MARTHA, *married to Charlie; lives in Boston, Massachusetts, U.S.A.*
JOHN, *married to Mary; lives at Himbledon Grange, England*
THOMAS, *single, lives in Cheltenham, England*
LUKE, *monsignor at Vatican*
TIMOTHY*
PAUL
RUTH
MARK
JOSEPH

Milshner Family

EDWARD*, *married to Hilary**
HANK*
HANK, JR.

Others

LOUISE JONES, *Joseph Trimbledon's Welsh girlfriend, reading law at Oxford*

---

* *deceased*

MICHELLE ADLER, *Hank Milshner's mistress*
TADO JUDAIRE, *Michelle Adler's Japanese lover*
PORTIA CONTADINO, *head of the Contadino family in Tivoli, Italy*
FRANCESCA CONTADINO, *daughter of Portia, a medical doctor and research microbiologist at MIT in Boston*
ACHMED MISANRIE, *friend of Trimbledon family in Dubai*
FRANK HARRIS, *head of County Police Force*
BROTHER PATRICK, *Jesuit Friar, Boston*
FATHER BRENDAN, *Franciscan parish priest, Sulphur Springs*
FREDDIE HARDWICK, *Himbledon Estate gamekeeper and Trimbledon family personal bodyguard*
PAUL HARDWICK, *Freddie's son, family bodyguard to Trimbledon's*
CHARLOTTE HARDWICK, *Freddie's daughter, Mark's girlfriend, and local vet*
BRIAN HARDWICK, *Freddie's son and a first officer, British Navy*
NEVILLE VAN DER WALT, *sheep farmer in Karoo, South Africa*
ROB YEATES, *retired structural engineer, Sulphur Springs, Montana, U.S.A.*
JOE WIESE, *piano tuner, Sulphur Springs*
ENZO ESCARBO, *psychiatrist, Colorado, U.S.A.*
STANLEY, *Hank Milshner's butler and other things*
LISKA, *Russian ballet dancer a friend of Thomas Trimbledon*
CHARLIE, *Martha Trimbledon's husband and commercial airline pilot*

I

How It All Began

1

Paris

A TYPICAL TUESDAY IN PARIS HAD STARTED ORDINARILY with commuters hurrying to work. It was a bright spring day, promising clear blue skies and warm temperatures as the trucks edged their way through the usual early morning traffic. Passengers on the Metro below the bustle and noise above were unaware of the nightmare about to unfold, as too were the drivers hurrying through the road underpasses near Notre Dame Cathedral.

There was nothing unusual about the large concrete transport trucks, with the huge containers on the back slowly turning to keep the cargo of concrete slurry in a liquid form ready to be discharged. They were a regular sight early in the morning in the Paris rush hour making their way to various construction sites around the city.

The modern world that we carelessly take for granted has been created largely with concrete and steel. From high rise buildings, shopping malls, bridges, roads, sporting stadia, and ports; concrete has turned man's urban vision into a reality across the world. There are many different types of concrete for a variety of applications with differing strengths and setting periods. Each type of concrete is carefully produced with a specific formula and combination of essential ingredients of natural aggregates, cement and water. Other ingredients may also be added such as speciality bonding agents, fly ash and ground blast furnace slag. Special bonding and rapid setting agents are added to create exceptionally strong and fast drying concrete.

In liquid form, as slurry, the major concrete producers have perfected fast and efficient delivery systems. Whether to a high-rise building project or for the walls of tunnels deep underground, tons of liquid concrete can be precisely delivered in seconds. Delivery trucks are in a range of sizes, with capacities from as small as one point seven cubic metres up to seven cubic metres. As the economies of delivery have sharpened and competition increased, there has been a trend toward larger transit mixer vehicles.

The Paris Metro, particularly for the long underground tunnels serving the centre of Paris, has various fresh air ducts to the surface. Within these large vertical shafts are mounted huge electrically driven ventilation fans both to provide fresh air from the surface while also extracting the stale air from the tunnels below.

With the inner and outer ring roads serving central and greater Paris there are numerous underpasses and bridges designed to speed traffic around the city. Many of these two-lane underpasses pass under major intersections on the surface with bridges above the underpass.

It had been planned meticulously— every detail for months before. Even the temporary parking permits had been forged with precision to deal with any unwelcome enquiries from the traffic police. In the event, the few passing traffic police never bothered to check, since such construction trucks had become a regular and innocent part of the city landscape. Even for those that had stopped at unlikely locations it was assumed by the odd passing traffic cop and pedestrians to be temporarily broken down.

A single bulk concrete supply depot on the outskirts of Paris has a typical fleet of forty liquid cement delivery trucks and at any one time some thirty-five would be fully operational. A large mixer truck had a single driver who handled everything necessary to drive to a construction site, position the truck, set up the delivery chutes, and discharge the load. Ready-mixed concrete could also be pumped through long pipes and via chutes. The inside of the transit mixer used a simple Archimedes screw to mix and lift the concrete to the delivery chute for highly accurate and rapid delivery. After years of productivity studies and operational refinements to reduce costs, boost efficiency and enlarge profits, such cement supply companies had streamlined every aspect of their operation.

The corpses of the few regular workers on the night shift at the concrete depot had been well concealed and a handful of regular staff, also part of the plot, remained behind to ensure everything appeared normal at the plant. The perpetrators had calmly loaded the thirty-five trucks with the ingredients including the special rapid setting and bonding agents from the bulk mixing hoppers before sunrise on the Tuesday morning. The thirty-five drivers, five regular drivers who had been planted with the company some months before and thirty specially trained impostors, arrived at the depot dressed in overalls and caps with the company livery, clocked through security and took charge of their vehicles as a matter of routine. They departed from the depot at irregular intervals so everything appeared normal.

At 7:30, the first truck was in position, the temporary traffic warning triangles in place on the roadside and the delivery chute positioned above the ventilation shaft. By 7:35, the remaining trucks were similarly positioned, and, at 7:40 a.m. precisely, the chutes were opened, and the diesel engines turning the concrete drum locked onto full power. The concrete poured into ventilation shafts, over the parapets of bridges on to the racing traffic below and onto the tracks of the great railway stations serving the city. Each target site had been fastidiously chosen to wreak the greatest havoc and to bring the city of Paris to a standstill within just a few minutes.

The successful completion of their mission by just ten of the trucks would have secured success for the enterprise. The fact that all thirty-five trucks succeeded completely, or in part, was a bonanza for the perpetrators. Most of the trucks had completely discharged their deadly payloads before anyone nearby realised an inkling of what was going on and was able to clamber onto the trucks and jam the chutes closed. By then it was too late. Urban dwellers also generally prefer to walk on by and ignore any possible disturbance to their daily routines. So it was on that fateful spring morning in Paris.

It was the speed and suddenness that had taken Paris by surprise. By 8 a.m., the perpetrators had already abandoned the trucks, several still running and continuing to pour the few remaining cubic meters of fast-setting concrete slurry. They melted into the population of the city undetected, casually walking away into the crowds of hurrying Parisians on their way to work. The carnage being wrought by these huge cement machines was not apparent for some minutes to those nearest to them since the impact was being felt out of sight, either below bridge parapets or many metres below ground on the Metro.

The most instant impact was felt at the underpass near Notre Dame Cathedral, on the opposite side of the river Seine, on the riverside highway. A school bus carrying students had swerved to avoid the first deluge of concrete slurry from above as it completely obscured the vision of the driver, splashing across the front of the vehicle. There was an instant collision and other vehicles, unable to stop in time, crashed into the side of the stricken bus. Other vehicles followed and within seconds there was a heap of tangled wreckage of cars, buses, trucks and other vehicles in the underpass. The concrete kept pouring, trapping survivors in their vehicles. Quickly, it became an impenetrable wall of twisted steel and fast-setting concrete. In just under two hours, by 9:30, the concrete had set solid, closing the underpass to anything apart from a few pedestrians who were brave enough to climb over the wreckage to find a way through.

Just a few cubic metres of rapidly setting concrete slurry would have wrought major disruption being discharged onto rapidly moving motor traffic during the rush hour, but the full contents of one of the large mixer trucks brought many of these speeding motorists to a sudden and fatal end to their journey.

The first attack being near the Notre Dame Cathedral was entirely deliberate and intended to symbolise, by the perpetrators, a strike at the heart of the traditional Christian world. Notre Dame, one of the great Roman Catholic

Cathedrals in Europe, was a living symbol to be ultimately destroyed.

Scenes of mayhem, injury and death were repeated throughout Paris at strategic road intersections and underpasses. The road system of central Paris had become, in the space of ninety minutes, inoperable. The whole city, by 9:45, was gridlocked. Emergency services and their vehicles had become useless. Many could not even leave their depots due to the gridlocked traffic outside. It was mayhem and no one, apart from the perpetrators, had any idea of the scale and magnitude of what was unfolding in Paris on that morning.

The peripherique, the ring road, was closed completely within twenty minutes of the first load being discharged. Numerous strategic intersections on the auto route, *voie rapide*, grand *itineraire* and *itineraire secondaire* road system throughout Paris had been quickly made inoperable. The inner city road, with various underpasses passing next to the river Seine, was the early target. The auto routes on the outskirts of the city had also been targeted with access to and from the Charles de Gaulle, D'Orly and Du Bourget airports completely cut.

All main line stations in the city had also been brought to a standstill with tonnes of cement rapidly hardening on the tracks and the rail intersections below the road bridges above. There had been several derailments and collisions with passengers trapped in the wreckage. On the western edge of Paris the business district around La Grande Arche was rapidly seizing up with hundreds of office workers and business executives already at their desks in the high-rise office towers. Many were still unaware of the mounting chaos throughout other parts of the city.

The cellular phone network quickly became overloaded, as did other means of communication. Most cell phones became useless. The radio and television networks started to broadcast news about what was happening at around nine fifteen. The initial stories were piecemeal, reporting specific incidents and they were reported as accidents rather than a carefully planned, co-ordinated and executed attack on the whole of

Paris.

Much of the news was confused and the official emergency services and police were unable to take control for many hours due to the total dislocation of the city.

A helicopter TV crew reporting on the morning traffic had only picked up that something was out of the ordinary some minutes after several road underpasses had already become blocked. It was pictures from this helicopter that the various news channels started to beam out a little after nine. By then it was too late, matters were way beyond the control or influence of any of the legitimate city authorities.

By 9:30, some on the ground news crews had managed to get to some of the accident sites, and were busy beaming live coverage back to their news desks. Television monitors around the city and the world were beginning to reveal the horrors of twisted wreckage, lines of stationery traffic on all the roads and highways and the widespread carnage and disruption. There were reports of great bravery and of miraculous escapes as further information began to pour in about the extent of the attack.

Paris is small and compact with a highly efficient integrated transport system. The underground metro rail system is the cornerstone of this transport system in the inner city areas carrying thousands of passengers every day. There are three hundred and seventy stations, with eighty-seven of these being busy interchanges. Ten of the busiest interchanges ceased functioning within fifteen minutes of the first liquid cement being delivered to their targets. Each of these targets had been carefully selected to ensure that within a short time the whole metro system including the four lines that serve the suburbs would be shut down.

Beneath the ground, the Paris Metro underground rail system had come to a complete halt. A series of incidents throughout the inner city network occurring within a short time had triggered automatic safety circuit breakers to be activated. Trains had been derailed, there had been collisions, others trains were simply stationary in the dark tunnels. The power had been shut down, so only the odd emergency light was still functioning.

The hundreds of commuters now trapped in the darkness were panicking, women were screaming and some men were desperately trying to open doors and smash windows in attempts to escape their incarceration. There were many injured people at the scenes of the rail car collisions and derailments.

Some fires had broken out in a few places in the subterranean network. Acrid smoke and fumes billowed along tunnels and into the stationary railcars. Most of the critically important ventilation shafts were now blocked with hardening cement and the vast ventilation fans fell silent. For those commuters who had survived the first onslaught with derailments and railcar collisions, asphyxia awaited.

Rumours began to circulate and panic spread to various parts of the city. Without correct and reliable information about what had taken place people started to make up and circulate their own incredulous stories. Few were as incredulous as what had actually happened that morning in Paris. It took days for the authorities to piece together the whole picture and to grasp just how easy it had been for the perpetrators to inflict such carnage and disruption on one of the world's great cities.

The only means of getting around apart from walking was either in the air with helicopters or on the river Seine with river craft. The river Seine and airspace over the city was to witness intense activities in the weeks ahead as the military brought in dozens of amphibious craft and helicopters to assist with emergency operations.

Emergency hospitals and mortuaries were set up at various sports stadiums and parks around the city in the days that followed. Parc des Princes, Palais Omnisports de Paris-Bercy and the Roland Garros tennis stadium and various other locations quickly became the scene of grim images of the dead and dying.

Other members of the European Union had been quick to provide support with medical, engineering and communications equipment. Dozens of helicopters, heavy lifting machinery, boats and medical emergency equipment were brought to Paris. The clean up operation alone took hundreds of specialist military and private contractors. A special team of mining specialists had been flown in from Johannesburg and the sound of jackhammers could be heard around the city for days afterwards as these and other mining teams carefully cleared the many accident sites. Most of the equipment such as compressors, medical supplies and other materials for the rescue operations had to be flown in and carefully deposited at the various accident sites.

Businesses and residents were evacuated from central Paris and accommodated in huge temporary camps set up near Orly Airport. The impacts were vast and diverse across France and the rest of the world. Stock markets had crashed, many European countries had assumed the highest level of security, air travel was restricted and the U.S.A. had imposed stringent social order controls.

Social unrest had flared initially in the outer suburbs of Paris where many racial minorities live. There was widespread fear, suspicion and violence toward foreign residents. A wave of recriminatory attacks started on the premises of foreign businesses. This violence was also spreading across France and other European countries. Turkey and Morocco began an urgent repatriation of their citizens living in France. The U.N. Security Council was meeting on a permanent basis and the heads of state were appealing for calm.

No one was ever able to provide a precise number of the thousands of fatalities that occurred. Estimates had been painstakingly made over the weeks and months that followed the event, drawing on a multitude of data. Many were simply never accounted for. It took months to restore Paris to anything vaguely similar to what it had been before. Just to systematically clear the city of traffic took several days before the authorities were able to close off central Paris as a huge 'crime scene' and no go area. For several weeks after the attack central Paris looked like a war zone, empty and haunted. The impact on business, social, cultural and the many other aspects of life in Paris was devastating. Still, the full cost remains a carefully guarded secret.

2

Himbledon

"THANK YOU, FATHER." JOHN TRIMBLEDON SAT IN HIS customary armchair amidst the shelves of books, paintings and untidy papers in piles around the room. Calm and welcoming, he smiled, his eyes glinting with life and warmth as he welcomed his young son Joseph to his study.

"So we have reached the day, Joseph," he said, fixing his gaze on his sons face and expression.

"Yes, Father." Joseph replied. "And it is very good of you to have cut short your trip to Australia to be with us all at Himbledon."

The soft warm light and surroundings of the study intensified the differences between the two men. Shadows drew a stark contrast between the fulsome face of youth and the lean, weathered, angular lines of experience and age. Joseph, a young man in his twenties, had just completed his doctoral studies, and distinguished himself as an Oxford Blue, marksman, and other sporting achievements, with his life before him, dark haired and handsome, and aspiring to greatness, wherever that may lie. His father, a man of deep experience, with white hair and penetrating blue eyes, sat relaxed, his arms resting easily on the arms of the chair. John Trimbledon, also a distinguished athlete when younger, now reclining and gentle with his youngest son, did not show his full physical presence being tall, lean and intensely fit for his years. He had an overwhelmingly calm but strong presence in any place, but particularly in his own sanctuary, his study.

Joseph knew full well that this conversation, on this particular evening, to be of special importance.

"Louise is a lovely girl, Joseph. Fine looking, too. Strong willed no doubt, which will serve her well as a barrister," said John, looking ever more intently at Joseph for some response that might provide further insight to this particular relationship. This was no time to betray personal matters of the heart to his father and the question threw him rather off balance, since Trimbledons never normally interfere with each other's personal lives. Such matters are always automatically assumed to be within the individual's own jurisdiction and ability to manage.

After a few seconds, a noticeable pause in the conversation, Joseph replied with an artificial air of casualness, "We have experienced some really happy times together since meeting last year and we share many similar interests and ideas, so I am fortunate to have her as my companion."

"Yes, indeed," John replied, continuing quickly. "Of course, you do not need my approval Joseph, and this is certainly not what this is about." Lifting his brandy glass and holding it in the fingers of both hands before him, he continued, "Just two things Joseph. Firstly, never forget some of the grave errors some Trimbledons have made over matters of the heart and the heavy price some have had to pay, especially their women folk. There is a family vulnerability somehow in these matters. Secondly, you must always protect her now that she has come close to you and this family. Strong as she may be, neither you nor she will yet be aware of the sacrifices that may be exacted of you. Some ladies have the fortitude to live with this, while others do not; if not, it is better to avoid the suffering now. You will already know, Joseph, of the uniqueness of our service and that there may be times in your life when the noble thing to do is to spare further unhappiness, whatever the emotional cost may be to you personally. For the sake of Louise's future happiness, as harsh as it may appear to you here today, I felt the need to remind you of these realities, being who we are. There is also the whole matter of common values Joseph… to have similar interests and ideas is one thing, but remember, as you have always been taught, never fail to look deeper. We are all complex, there are many reasons for who we are and how we behave, and our systems of belief are fundamental to who we actually are. Remember this Joseph in the months ahead."

Suddenly the recent carefree times at Oxford, his orchestrated schooling in various private select establishments around the world, all dimmed in his mind as his father spoke. His mind now became focussed, the music in the distance now silent in his brain as he carefully formulated his answer.

"Yes, Father, I remember some of the broader family history, and how Uncle Thomas failed to adhere to one of our truths and caused great distress to others and himself. But times were also different then, Father, we live in a very different society today where women are more independent, stronger and can take care of themselves..."

John interrupted Joseph abruptly, "You may be right, Joseph, but always remember, some things do not change, but I am sure you will always protect those who come close to you, especially women, and always do the honourable thing by them. We are not like other people, sometimes regretfully so I think, but there it is. You will know what to do Joseph, should the circumstances ever dictate."

Joseph knew perfectly what his father had just raised and that he would from this day forward have a special responsibility to his father to protect Louise from future risk, danger or unhappiness, whatever transpired with their relationship. This was now a given. Joseph also knew that his father's highly attuned insight had enabled him, after the briefest of meetings with her, to know that Louise was special to him.

Joseph knew, with the formalities over, his father wished to quickly come to the point of this brief and intimate conversation in the study. Anyway, the party continued elsewhere in the house and the guests would soon begin to notice their absence.

"Twenty-eight is a young age, Joseph— at least in this family, to receive what I have to say to you tonight. It is just a pity it also has to be when we are celebrating your birthday with your very beautiful girlfriend at the house. I wish it could have been different. Unfortunately, there is no alternative, in view of the grave circumstances being faced." John said to his son, now sitting erect across the coffee table between them. He placed his brandy glass purposefully on the table and continued. "You, like your brothers, have been prepared from a young age to serve, you know this of course, but I would have wished you to have enjoyed a few more years of relative freedom before being called." There was a calm, strong yet sad tone to John Trimbledon's voice as he looked away, permitting himself a momentary lapse to gaze through the high leaded glass windows of the study to the night sky beyond. "Timothy's untimely death in Paris means, Joseph, you must possibly pick up the reigns in his place."

Joseph had suspected his brother's murder and the atrocities that had taken place in Paris a few weeks before would not leave his life untouched, but the suddenness of it, took him by surprise. There was clearly much he did not know despite being fully involved in the anguish of the family at the family Chapel when Tim was buried, some weeks before, and laid to rest in the family mausoleum.

Grief is something not openly displayed by the Trimbledon family, although the mention of Tim again caused that empty, anguished pain to stab him in the pit of his stomach.

"What do you want me to do, Father?" Joseph quickly replied.

Suddenly, the warm and deeply affectionate conversational tone between son and beloved father changed to one of functional efficiency. A job was to be done, as it had across the centuries by the Trimbledons, and Joseph knew today was no different.

John stood, his six-foot-three-inch frame casting a slight shadow over Joseph's face as he walked to the bookcase. "In the limited time we have at our disposal, Joseph, the first thing you need to do is to reflect on your own personal situation. I will try to give you as long as I can to do so, for you to take the decision whether you wish to serve one of the long established traditions of this family, or whether you do not. It has always been an intensely personal matter, and you have the perfect right to say no. Always remember this fact and that you are under no pressure or obligation whatsoever. Indeed, unless you choose of your own free will, your service will be meaningless and ultimately dangerous to yourself and those who share the same creed. You will know precisely what I am talking about Joseph, and you will also know the nature and extent of this service and what may well be required of you in the years that lie ahead, should you decide to dedicate your life to this service."

There was a pause while Joseph looked intently at his father. John looked straight into Joseph's eyes as he continued, "I want you to continue with your trip to Croatia with Louise, in a few weeks time as planned, after you have attended your first board meeting. Life must continue as normal for the immediate future. Anything else will imperil you both, and I do not intend losing another son to these misguided people. But Joseph, from now on you must be vigilant, carry your firearm and remain contactable at all times. I know you will protest, but there will be no further discussion on the matter, I will be sending Freddie, from the Grange, at a distance to ensure you have no troublesome people on your travels."

Joseph understood fully the implications of what his father was telling him and continued to listen intently without interruption.

"I am sorry it has to be this way Joseph, and as I have said, I just wish there were more time, but I will need your decision, no later than a day before the special board meeting. In any event, just come to Himbledon immediately on your return from Croatia and arrange for Louise to return to Oxford, where I have also made discrete arrangements for her protection. You will of course say nothing to her; we would not wish to alarm her. Be sure to brush up on your Arabic and French in the meanwhile. I will provide you with further instructions when necessary. In the meanwhile, it is better that you have no further details of what we will be dealing with."

"Yes, Father," Joseph replied, sensing that the

conversation was shortly to end.

"Congratulations Joseph, on the Doctorate and your birthday today, may God bless and keep you," John said as he moved toward the study door and smiled as Joseph walked toward him. "It is now time for us to rejoin our guests, and for me to give your beautiful Louise a dance."

3
London

AS HE MINGLED WITH THOSE ATTENDING THE BOARD MEETING, Joseph was reminded that much of the world's wealth remains in private ownership. What is not directly owned is controlled and influenced by what is owned. Those who possess this unimaginable wealth are sometimes individuals, often corporate trusts or families. However, for the Trimbledons, such wealth had not only bestowed privilege and an exclusive lifestyle, but also unimaginable responsibilities, service and sacrifice. The family could trace its lineage across many centuries back into ancient times. Throughout this history they were the custodians of knowledge and resources that had a purpose. They had survived many dark experiences, savage attacks, attempted infiltration of the family and other onslaughts. The Trimbledons also never acted alone, they never attempted to glorify themselves, and they always acted in true humility and submission because they fully understood their place and role in the greater scheme of things. Much of what Joseph had been taught was founded on the principle that wealth, power and authority were actually worthless and self-defeating, unless linked to ageless rules of justice, sacrifice and the beatitudes.

He had come to know at an early age that business, profit and success in this life are only part of a much broader tapestry of human history and endeavour. Business success is one thing, to be at peace with oneself, to know your purpose and to have given yourself to the defence of hard won values for future generations is an altogether different reality.

He was only eleven when the concept of parallel realities had been introduced to him by a lady tutor in an exclusive college outside Darling in Australia. She had used the natural universe to illustrate and bring the concept to life. Joseph, with his enquiring nature and retentive memory, had always been a sought-after student by teaching staff. He quickly assimilated the most complex of theories, concepts and formulae, and it rarely took too long before he was making them his own.

As he gazed around the reception area and smiled at various unfamiliar faces, he thought that this reality was so different from the reality of the Oxford Colleges and academic environment he had enjoyed in recent times. Yes, there was competition in the academic world; yes, Dons can be ruthless and self-serving, but in an entirely different way to the rules of this game that he was now entering. Global competitive business was worse than the jungle; it had few rules; success was the only currency to survival, and man was the most cruel and ruthless of all predators. Yet he had been taught over the years that there is a nobler aspect to global commerce and that at times in order to realise this you also have to understand the mind of the corporate predator. Above all else, the words still ringing in his head as he put his empty coffee cup on the table, as his brothers had always drummed into him, business is a means to end, not an end in itself. Be more concerned with the ends of business Joe, than the actual chase.

"You must be Joseph," an unfamiliar male voice jerked him from his thoughts.

"That's right, and you are…?" Joseph asked.

"Hi, I am Neville van der Walt from a bloody long way away. I flew in this morning on the overnight from Cape Town."

"Are you attending the board meeting?" asked Joseph, somewhat surprised by the man's appearance dressed in slacks, large leather boots and a short-sleeved safari jacket.

"Ya, actually looking forward to it. I'm standing in for my old man who had to go for an emergency operation, his second bypass. I phoned my sister on the way from the airport and all is well, he is now in ICU. Guess if I cock up here, though, he will be back for another operation." He said it with a chuckle. Just then the large tall doors of the boardroom opened and everyone gradually made their way to the meeting.

Today's agenda appeared to Joseph to be very brief. With people attending from around the world the whole thing appeared to be a huge waste of time. Listening to his father at the head of the table made it difficult for Joseph to take the whole affair seriously, despite the various support staff moving around in a state of apparent awe. The business was brief and to the point: the appointment of a new head of operations for the marine line in Hong Kong; confirmation of the leveraged buyout of a small group of copper mines in Indonesia; a mandate given to Neville about assistance to Interpol to stop the illegal import of blood diamonds into the European Union; a donation to some undisclosed conduit to support urgent AIDS research; and, then finally, the appointment of Joseph as strategic advisor to the non-executive board of Dandler Global Aggregates in Paris.

For all of those attending the board meeting, only John Trimbledon had an overall understanding of the extent of the family business interests. They were certainly extensive, global in nature and right across a whole range of critical and strategic business entities. From shipping, ports, airlines, infrastructure, energy, information technology, banking, pharmaceuticals, the list was almost as long as the equities listed on the JSE, NYSE, CAC and the many other stock exchanges around the world. Yet this global business network was largely unknown to even those present, and less so to others.

The lunch after the board meeting took place in an adjoining room to the boardroom. It had been carefully orchestrated with seating arrangements prescribed by John himself. Everyone was seated at a replica of the boardroom table they had just vacated. There was no alcohol, only berry juice and iced water during and after the simple meal of salad, fish and pasta. Fresh coffee and Viennese chocolates were served afterwards in the lounge.

Seated next to Joseph at the table was an Italian woman who extended her hand to greet Joseph.

"Hello, I am Portia… you must be John's youngest son, Joseph."

"Yes that's right, I am pleased to meet you," replied Joseph, shaking the lady's hand.

"Have you met Achmed from Dubai?" she asked, turning to a distinguished gentleman seated on the other side of Joseph.

"No," he replied and extended his hand in greeting.

"Our deepest condolences to you Joseph, on Tim's untimely death," Portia said looking into Joseph's eyes. Her dark hair glistened under the down lights above the table, and Joseph felt a deep compassion in her manner. He judged her to be in her late forties, stylishly dressed and with a special poise. "Achmed and I have been working with a small team to address a range of diseases prevalent in Central and North Africa," she said, smiling at Achmed.

"Yes, if only we could get to grips with the widespread corruption in so many of those countries," added Achmed who continued. "We have the medical solutions, the major barrier is getting the various medications properly administered in the field to the needy."

"Surely that should be no problem," responded Joseph. "The World Health Organisation has field operations and distribution arrangements, haven't they, to deal with such matters?"

Laying her hand on Joseph's hand, Portia replied gently, "If that were only the case Joseph, we would not have thousands of young children dying of malaria each year, and many other avoidable deaths and suffering. Sadly, many of these international agencies simply do not function as intended. The reality on the ground is often depressing and frustrating, so we are not only developing the medications, but also investigating new approaches to getting them properly administered." Joseph nodded his understanding. "When you are next in Rome, please come and visit me Joseph," Portia said, sensing that their meeting was soon to end.

"Yes, I certainly will."

An impressive gentleman in a dark suit and black bow tie announced that coffee was now served in the lounge. He was John's butler and managed all the family's business catering. The surprise for Joseph came later over coffee, after everyone had moved to the lounge, sitting in the sumptuous leather armchairs. It was here that John moved around effortlessly doing the real work of the gathering. It was here that the major justification for all of these people coming together, some travelling from the other side of the world, became a little more apparent to Joseph. It was in these informal, unrecorded and unofficial surroundings that other business was now being conducted.

Joseph wondered whether the business at the board meeting was actually real or just some front for all this. Seeing Neville van der Walt eating copious handfuls of the chocolates and alone, Joseph walked across and invited him to join him for some more coffee.

"Sure, thanks, that's great. I will have some more coffee. These sweets are good and much better than the dairy slabs we get in South Africa," said Neville as he sank into a nearby armchair.

"Do you think this is all real, Neville, or am I perhaps dreaming?" asked Joseph.

"It is certainly awesome Joe, but you should know, with that being your old man over there," replied Neville. "All I can tell you my man is that from what I have been told, this is all very real, more real than what's going on outside in the street, or even down the road in your Thread Needle Street or Parliament. It's certainly a lot more real than what's going on in Pretoria, where I come from."

"I meant the business earlier," retorted Joseph.

"Yes, of course it was all real Joe, those are all real businesses and so is Dandler Aggregates where you are off to shortly. You are in for a tough time after what happened in Paris the other week and your old man must have great confidence in you, man. Hell, it was bad what happened there eh, and also to Tim eh, and we are all sorry for your loss Joseph. He was a great guy and we had some good times together up in the Eastern Cape in South Africa some years back. You know we offered Mass as a family for him and your family on the day he was buried, as no doubt many of the others here today did," said Neville. Joseph felt that familiar anguished feeling in his stomach again as he was reminded of Tim, his older brother. They had been close over the years, even though so often many miles apart. Neville looked at Joseph, waiting for some response, but realised that the mention of Tim had cast their conversation into a fresh realm. "Do you reckon Tim was onto something connected to the Paris attack, Joseph?" Neville asked, wishing to break the protracted silence.

"I don't know," replied Joseph. "…But my father will be briefing me fully before I land in Paris."

"I bloody well hope so Joe because the world is in a tailspin just now, and we all need answers," retorted Neville.

Immediately the catering staff had replenished the coffee jugs and chocolate trays, they withdrew, closing the high large doors behind them. Few noticed these happenings, most people being in intense conversation with others, but for Joseph this was a new experience and he wanted to capture it all in his mind. Suddenly his father rose to his feet and cleared his throat and the room fell silent.

"Here we go," chirped Neville to Joseph with a broad smile as he fixed his gaze across the room on John Trimbledon.

Although his address was brief, he took the opportunity to address every person in the room personally to reinforce the message and to relive an age-old practice of their community. Just a few weeks ago a dreadful event had happened and it now transpired it was possibly only the beginning. Civil society, where man can practise his beliefs freely, was again under threat. The fraternity must awaken again to protect, defend and defeat. Each person present had been provided with an encrypted CD with a full briefing. For those present, acting on behalf of a parent, they were asked to kindly deliver the item safely. In ending his remarks John appealed for steadfastness, calm, vigilance, and care for themselves and their families at this time. Their families were now to stand ready to serve as events unfolded and to await further contact. He thanked them all for their presence and ended proceedings with the customary concluding remarks and farewell.

Everyone present knew precisely what John had been referring to, why he or she had come and what they now had to do. There was no need for further discussion, no need for questions, and no need for procedures and managerial processes to be clarified. Although many of the attendees had never met before and would probably never meet again, they were about to walk well-worn paths, re-enact established behaviours and share a common value system that underpinned and directed their actions. The fraternity had already existed for hundreds of years, handed on from one generation to the next, its survival and *modus operandi* perfected over two thousand years and more.

Joseph knew he had no special privileges in these surroundings so quickly gathered his papers. He had no CD to collect since, as his father had told him, he would be briefed when it was time to do so. As he moved to leave the building he touched Neville van der Walt on the arm and said goodbye. He was leaning over putting his papers into his bag and turned sharply to face Joseph.

"Ya, thanks, Joe; it has been good to meet you. Take care of yourself. I am on the overnight back home; otherwise, I would have suggested a beer, but next time perhaps, eh? Watch your back in Paris, and if you have any trouble with wild animals there, call me," he chuckled. "You will be in my prayers Joe and be sure to pray for me too, goodbye." With those words Van der Walt was suddenly gone and Joseph was left standing there waiting to say goodbye to his father.

As Joseph stood waiting, the name Van der Walt persisted in his brain. It was in some vague way familiar, and then it came to him, he remembered someone called Wimpie van der Walt from his childhood who he had been told about many times by his mother. For years when small, Wimpie had been a regular bedtime story. It was a story of bravery and a distinguished military career in the Second World War.

The truth was that these stories were about a Colonel Wimpie van der Walt who had been one of South Africa's outstanding wartime fighter pilots and leaders. He had fought in Abyssinia, the North African desert and in Italy, flying Spitfires. In 1943, Wimpie was appointed deputy leader of one of the South African air force squadrons. His squadrons of Spitfires were engaged in ground attack operations in support of Montgomery's Eighth Army in Italy and the partisans in Yugoslavia. It was at this time that Wimpie led his squadrons on an attack against an enemy landing ground, for which he was awarded one of his many medals with the citation commending him for his 'brave leadership and skill'.

During a distinguished and courageous period of service for the remaining years of the war he was at the forefront of many critical battles. As the ground forces advanced into Abyssinia he flew many sorties over enemy positions and on one occasion he landed behind enemy lines to pick up a fellow pilot who had been shot down. Then during an assault on an enemy airfield he was engaged in a thirty minute running battle with enemy fighters but managed to escape and land his aircraft with several bullet holes.

As the Eighth Army advanced, he and his squadron moved forward in the desert providing support. There were many tales of his exploits, bravery and distinguished leadership. He was awarded many honours and rare distinctions for such a young officer. In the 1950s, he resigned from the South African air force, since he was disillusioned with the local restructuring of the armed forces, which he felt seriously disadvantaged certain sectors of the local population, and he left flying to establish a number of prosperous farms in various parts of Southern Africa.

As Joseph was boarding the train for Oxford, he was still wondering whether there was any connection between Neville and this illustrious character of his childhood.

4
Oxford

WHEN HE ARRIVED AT OXFORD RAILWAY STATION, HE CAUGHT a taxi to his college. As he walked through the archway toward his room, the porter Mr. Hankey called after him, "Dr Trimbledon, excuse me sir, but there is an envelope here for you, your young lady left it here at tea time." Joseph turned, took the envelope and said, "Thank you Hanks, I am very grateful, good evening."

He felt both comfort and a feeling of familiar security being back in Hall again. Yet it was also mixed with a sense of sadness and regret that all this was now coming to an end. It was a warm summer evening with sunset still a few minutes away. He changed his city clothes, showered, and sat to read his messages as he sipped a cup of tea he had made on arriving at his room. Her message was cryptic as ever: 'Love you, party wonderful, your father sexy, your mother a dream— see you at nine at Bunters'.

He laid his head back and gazed at the ceiling. How good in this topsy-turvy world to have an anchor like Louise, bright, beautiful and becoming. It brought a smile to his face after an awkward day in unfamiliar surroundings with a bunch of strangers. As he turned over the last few hours in his mind, again he smiled to himself. *With a name like van der Walt, hardly a prime Catholic candidate for the fraternity,* he thought. Then again, he seemed to be a fine fellow, and someone to look forward to meeting again, perhaps, one day.

The many impressions of the day tumbled through his

mind. Malaria in Africa, blood diamonds, Hong Kong shipping lines and so much more. There was clearly much for him to learn and to do so fast as he faced the transition from this comfortable academic life to a brutal and complex reality that lay beyond. Sipping his tea, he thought that, for now, he would try to relish these last few days in Oxford and leave everything else for tomorrow.

Bunters was its usual bustling self as Joseph edged his way toward the bar. “Hello darling,” she said as he bent forward with a greeting kiss. “Got one in for you already; thought you would be thirsty after smelly hot old London,” she said.

“Thanks, yes; spot on, as usual.”

He took a long drink from the pint glass of ale. It was after 11:30 when they both emerged from the pub, having spent an amiable couple of hours with each other and various college friends, sharing the hospitality of Bunters that evening. They wandered arm in arm along Beaumont Street, into Corn Market, before turning off along Blue Boar Street and Bear Lane to her small apartment on the second floor of the residential block behind her college. He knew the route all too well and her flat, since for the last few weeks he had waited there many nights. Tonight, Louise was hoping for more. After all, having met his parents, been received like a member of the family and everything else that had happened in the last few days, tonight should surely be when they consummate their relationship.

As they wandered along, stopping occasionally to embrace and kiss; they talked animatedly about the previous couple of days. “I thought Himbledon completely over the top, Joe; a sort of throw back to a time and place I thought long gone,” she said, smiling at him.

“Well, being a Welsh Puritan, a lady of little faith that is precisely how you would think,” jibed Joseph in return. “But then your mother and father just bowled me over, so warm and kind and real people, despite Himbledon Grange and all that stuff about your ancestors.”

Louise continued to share her perceptions while at the same time probing gently to learn more about Joseph, this complex gentle, manly companion she was falling in love with.

Joseph was tired after his earlier excursion to London, but he sensed Louise was eager for their relationship to change tonight. After arriving at the apartment, Louise made coffee and then changed into more relaxing attire and a silk dressing gown. Joseph lay on the sofa reading an open copy of the *Legal Digest* that Louise had left earlier, before rushing off to meet him at Bunters. The article's headline had instantly attracted his attention: 'The legal defence of radicalism'. As he read the opening synopsis he noticed that one of the authors was with the World Bank. Louise legs nudged him out of his thoughts as she stood above him with the two cups of coffee.

"Shift up," she said, and moved gracefully to lie beside him.

As a Trimbledon, Joseph had been taught how to properly conduct himself with women. He had experience of the unique mingling of the male and female bodies that Louise could not even imagine. He had been taught disciplines, skills and given knowledge about women, their complexities, needs and emotional characteristics. He knew they were his equal and always to be treated so, and he had also learnt they are essentially different from men, and these differences should be celebrated.

Louise was typical the modern lady, fiercely independent, frank, confident and thinking she knew all there was to know about sexual gratification, particularly her own. How little in fact that she actually knew about Joseph and such matters, was to be revealed in the weeks and months ahead. She had put his reticence and awkwardness about physical intimacy down to inexperience, shyness and his general manliness. Unusually for Louise, on this matter she was wrong, very wrong.

As a teenager, Joseph had spent several weeks during a hot summer vacation from college in Scotland in Sicily. Part of this sojourn in the Mediterranean was also part of his transition from boyhood to manhood.

He had stayed with a trusted friend of the family in a villa, where a family with five daughters and a son, Eduardo, who was two years older than Joseph, embraced him. During those long hot summer days and balmy evenings Eduardo and his father had been Joseph's tutors taking him gradually and gently through several rites de passage. As well as playing tennis with the girls, swimming, diving and sailing along the coastline, Joseph had also been schooled in the skills of shooting with a variety of firearms, whilst also learning how to treat women properly, with respect and care.

Giving pleasure rather than taking it, respect for oneself and others, especially women, and self-control were the essential elements of his tuition during those carefree yet focussed weeks in the sun. It was Joseph's first series of innocent flirtations and moments with local women. Joseph had been taught not only how to handle and use with precision a variety of hand guns, rifles and shot guns, but also how to show self-restraint, treating ladies with charm and dignity.

When he reached his early twenties he locked this knowledge deep within himself. Such gifts came with responsibility, honour and were never to be abused, but only ever to be released with compassion and love. His preparation over the years was always to use whatever power you had at your disposal sparingly and only ever for good. It was better to be perceived as awkward, shy, embarrassed and inexperienced rather than give the slightest hint to anyone, especially women, of what lay beneath.

It was not long after finishing his coffee that his eyelids became heavy and he just managed to put his cup down when he fell into a deep sleep. Louise sighed, but realised that he had had a long and tiring day and although she had wanted to take their relationship to another level, she knew that the time was not yet right. She carefully extracted herself from the sofa, covered him, kissed him gently on his forehead and retreated to her room knowing that when she got up the following morning he would have gone.

As Joseph walked home through the back lanes of Oxford to his college his mind was racing and it was divided. One part of him was still inebriated with her beauty and the desire he felt for her. Yet his rationality, his iron control and pragmatic mind was struggling with other realities of their relationship. Although he was deeply attracted to her, the way she smiled and looked at him, her sharp mind and zest for life, there was also something missing. Her humour, the way she laughed and her powerful physical beauty all intrigued him, but he knew deep down he did not love her, not yet at least. Perhaps this would come later, he thought, but there was also so much to reconcile, somehow. He had a role to fulfil, obligations and dangers to face. He had been prepared, Louise had not. Was it fair and responsible of him to let any woman, however beautiful and talented, into his life? He had convictions born of a certain traditional value system handed down over generations. Louise was a radical, a non-conformer, and an atheist who believed in the prowess of man rather than God. She believed utterly in the liberation of the human condition from religious bigotry. Joseph was a devout Roman Catholic, believed utterly in the Trinity and the spiritual imperative of the role of the church in the world. Louise believed herself to be free, rational, in charge of her life and validated everything with the modern scientific method and evolutionary principles. Joseph knew himself to be free in a joyous way Louise simply could not understand or accept, and that evolution was a mere element of God's greater creation.

Too much tonight to reconcile, Joseph thought, as he walked across the courtyard to his rooms, preferring to return to the warm thoughts of her beauty.

5

An Unexpected Funeral

TIMOTHY'S DEATH HAD BEEN A MYSTERY. HIS BODY had been discovered by his fiancée sitting at his desk in his apartment in the Montmartre district of Paris. For a man of thirty-five who was fit and active to die suddenly would always raise suspicions, but it had only been after the autopsy that the cause of death had been confirmed as poisoning. The precise type of poison had been identified, but little was known as to how it had been administered, despite a very thorough forensic examination of his apartment and clothing. There were no outward marks on his body to indicate any other possibility than ingestion. It had been a slow working poison that could have been administered several hours before Tim died.

Since Tim had been a strategic advisor to Dandler Global Aggregates, a company possibly associated with the Paris atrocity, there was clearly a link between his murder and the subsequent attack on Paris. The precise reason for Tim being in Paris and the work he was doing for the fraternity had been kept a secret and was more sensitive than many members of the fraternity had known. Only John Trimbledon himself had known the full extent of the work being undertaken by Tim and how dangerous it was.

Immediately news came of Tim's death, John had gone personally to Paris, liaised with the police and authorities and made arrangements for Tim's fiancée, Anna, to return to Himbledon without delay. While in Paris he had also carefully examined Tim's apartment and had found various items missing together with some clumsily removed secure files from his laptop computer. This information was never disclosed to the local police and John set in motion his own lines of enquiry and analysis. He discreetly removed Tim's laptop and took it back with him to England.

It had not taken John long to identify Tim's murder as a professional hit. Tim's demise had been at the hands of a skilled practitioner of death who apart from Timothy's identity had probably not known the reason for his murder. The assassin had also probably not known who had ordered this murder, receiving the barest of details and a price in order to undertake the lethal act. It may have been a man or woman, a westerner or someone from another culture, a mere mechanic of death. Such people had operated for centuries. There could be one near you right now, as you live your life unaware of these other realities. A neighbour, the man who maintains your car or the friendly dental nurse smiling over you as your dentist replaces a broken filling.

To outward appearances they are just like the rest of us, leading ordinary lives, making a living and going about their routine lives until a call comes, specifying the person, place and price. With modern air travel, the speed and secrecy of their particular work, has been made easier and their anonymity almost impossible to penetrate. Just like state hangmen, they have a job to do, dispassionately calculating the weight of the victim and the length of drop to ensure a clean and swift death. So, too, these professional practitioners select the appropriate means to suit the purpose. They generally act on commissions from anyone and have no interest in the reasons why. The better they are at their trade, the higher the price they command and many regard themselves as professionals performing a necessary, if rather unusual, service for some distant client. Some even believe that the responsibility for such acts lies not with themselves, but those who give the order.

John knew of these realities all too well, although they were rarely acknowledged or discussed. What was more important now, was to know who had ordered the execution and why. Why had Timothy been silenced at this particular moment in time? John and certain members of his family always lived under the shadow of such dangers and Tim would have been fully aware of such potential threats. He had stepped up to these possible risks when he had willingly assumed his fraternal responsibilities. When facing what may be either evil or simply the misguided antics of extremists, there are always unforeseen risks involved. To stand, or even be seen to be attempting to stand, in the way of such forces, places an individual in extreme danger.

After the local autopsy and various formalities had been completed John Trimbledon arranged for the discreet return of his son's body to Himbledon for a further detailed examination. Following this Tim was buried on the estate.

All the members of the immediate family, many members of the extended Himbledon family, Tim's fiancée and her family and close friends attended the funeral service in the main Chapel at Himbledon. It was a simple Requiem Mass conducted by three members of the religious who were all close to John Himbledon and the family. Joseph and his brothers Paul and Mark together with John, plus two friends of Tim had carried the coffin from the Chapel. Tim's body had been laid over in the Chapel the evening before. It was a sombre affair on the late winter's morning and despite the surroundings a humble, dignified and deeply felt sad farewell to a beloved son in the tradition of the family. Only immediate family members accompanied Tim's body to its final resting place in the family grave. Mary Trimbledon, Tim's mother, carried a single small wreath of local flowers, as did Anna, and both were laid on the coffin after the final prayers and invocations, and Tim was laid to rest.

As they walked through the grounds of Himbledon and along the gravel pathway to the main house, Mary comforted Anna and walked with her arm gently around her shoulder. Anna had been in a state of shock and deep grief since finding Tim's body and having to break the terrible news to John Trimbledon from her cell phone. Ruth, one of John's daughters, had also flown instantly to Paris to be with Anna and she too walked on the other side of Anna. Ruth had accompanied Anna on her journey to Himbledon and had remained at the Grange until today. This was a time for the whole of the immediate family to close ranks, pull together and care for their own.

The log fires burning in the main hall of Himbledon Grange were a welcome respite from the cold and the many mourners talked quietly as they waited patiently for the main family members to return from the final act of farewell to Tim, in this life at least. It was John Trimbledon who spoke first to the assembled mourners who had come from all over the world. He spoke briefly, paid tribute to Tim and the courage of Anna his fiancée and thanked everyone for coming and that he and Mary looked forward to talking with everyone there during the course of the morning. Then Mary spoke, extending a warm welcome to everyone, also paying a deeply touching tribute to her son and asking that Our Lord forgive those who had murdered Tim. She then asked that everyone simply bow their heads for a moment as she gently recited in a crystal clear voice Our Lord's prayer. As Mary commenced with the opening words of "Our Father, who art…" the whole assembled company spontaneously joined in and the prayer resounded around the hall. At the end of the prayer, Mary blessed herself and invited Archbishop Guggar to say Grace before inviting everyone to partake of refreshments.

Such gatherings of so many members of the Trimbledon family were rare and generally only took place on this scale for weddings and funerals. There was a great amount of family contact between various elements of the extended family, however. Many of the ladies would meet periodically for various charity and cultural events. There were also frequent family celebrations for major birthdays and many of the men would participate in various sporting activities together. However, for so many to be together in one place at one time was unusual.

John's elder sister Martha had flown in from Boston the previous day with her husband Charlie and one of their daughters Lucinda, and Luke who was John's younger brother had arrived from Rome two days previously. Uncle Thomas, John's elder brother was also there with his current lady friend who was some years younger than him, a Russian ballet dancer. Thomas had driven up the evening before from Cheltenham and stayed at a nearby pub in the local village. Mary's family were also strongly represented with family members from Scotland, Ireland and Australia all mingling with the other guests. Her brother Edward had only managed to arrive that morning from Sydney with his wife Sarah and they had hardly had time to freshen up after stepping out of the taxi before the funeral. Mary's elderly mother, Annabel, had also come to stay at Himbledon from her home in Edinburgh, soon after receiving the news of Tim's death. She was now in her eighties was a remarkable lady for her age and many took her for being younger with her agile mind, sharp perception and nimble wit.

Among the gathering there were also members of the church: two friars, an archbishop, two dignitaries from Rome and two local parish priests. There was also a Jewish rabbi, Samuel Steinberg, and his daughter, Rebecca, and two Moslem gentlemen, Achmed Misanrie and Mohammed Albour, with their wives. Samuel Steinberg was now elderly and had been a long-time friend of John's father and the Trimbledon family for several decades. Rebecca, now in her early fifties, was at one stage close with Thomas and they continued to remain devoted friends. Achmed and Mohammed are also longstanding and close friends of the family, going back over many years.

The vicar of the local Anglican church, with his wife and the local Methodist and Baptists ministers, were also there, together with two senior members of the County Police Constabulary, the head of the local Salvation Army, and people from various national charity and aid organisations. The Red Cross, Help the Children's Fund and Help the Aged were all represented with many of these people being close and dear friends of Mary and John over the years, through their extensive involvement in numerous inter-church and charity activities, both on a local and international scale. Mary had always been particularly active with such interests and even Uncle Thomas donated generous amounts of his time to various activities for the less fortunate. The role of music in assisting with autism in children was a particular interest of his. Mary had also initiated and served on a local interdenominational group that worked for better understanding and tolerance between different faith groups, particularly among the many different Christian factions. Alcohol and drug abuse, a growing concern even in their largely rural county, especially among younger people, was also a growing concern, especially of Mary's, where she was devoting an increasing amount of her time working closely with local bodies as well as the police.

As was customary on such occasions various female members of the Trimbledon family were busy ensuring that all the religious men present and those guests of other faiths had plenty to eat before offering food and hot drinks to the rest of those present.

Thomas, Martha, Luke, John and Mary Trimbledon moved graciously around the gathering, talking to everyone, enquiring of their families and listening intently to the various guest's news, family developments and conversation. Their role today was to comfort others, to show fortitude and forgiveness. There were several guests who were not Catholics, particularly many of Tim's friends who he had come to know over the years from his school, university, teaching and business activities. The majority, were either believers of other faiths, or non-believers. Mary, Thomas and John felt a particular need to make these guests feel welcome and at ease in what must have been very unfamiliar surroundings. Martha joined in simply because it had always been a Trimbledon family tradition to make absolutely everyone welcome. Her particular bent was the various staff from the estate that she targeted immediately with comments and questions about the estate and its affairs.

Andrew Philips, one of Tim's oldest friends and his wife Lucy had been staying with Tim and Anna in Paris for a few days before Tim's death. Andrew and Tim had been at Winchester together and then continued their friendship when they both went up to Cambridge, Andrew to read medicine and Tim chemistry. He and Tim also had the same fascination with mountaineering and climbing and had both been close to

Uncle Thomas in their younger years, and he had inspired this interest in them both. Seeing Thomas replenishing his coffee cup from the jugs on a nearby table, Andrew excused himself from those around him and taking Lucy by the hand walked over and touched Thomas on the shoulder.

Turning, Thomas's eyes glistened with delight. "Andrew, how are you? Where have you been? It is so good to see you, despite these wretched circumstances." Thomas beamed, as he could see the moisture and deep sorrow in Andrew's eyes.

Without hesitation or a second thought, Thomas stepped forward and put his large arms around Andrew and hugged him. Andrew stood there, his arms limp by his side, gently trembling and trying to avoid embarrassing himself and others with an uncontrollable emotional outburst. Speaking softly only for Andrew to hear, Thomas said, "Don't worry Andrew, there was nothing any of us could have done to save Tim, just one of those things, and rest assured, we will get the bastards." Thomas then stepped back, still holding Andrew by the shoulders, almost like a rag doll, steadied Andrew on his feet and quickly turned to face Lucy, who was standing awkwardly nearby.

"Aren't you going to introduce me, Andrew, to this lovely lady you are with?" enquired Thomas, without the merest hint of his recent exchange with Andrew who suddenly remembered that Thomas had never met Lucy, now his wife, although he had often spoken to her of him and the many happy hours he had spent at Himbledon with Tim and Thomas.

"Er, yes, of course, I am sorry. This is Lucy, my wife. Lucy, this is Uncle Thomas, who I have told you so much about," said Andrew, quickly restoring his composure.

"It is good to meet you at last Thomas," said Lucy looking up into the broad, ruddy face of Thomas and extending her hand.

Detecting a Scandinavian accent, Thomas quickly responded with his hand, "You, too, Lucy. I have a special affection for Nordic ladies." As they looked deeply at each other, they both laughed, laughter to deal with a somewhat tense situation.

Lucy had heard much from Andrew about the

Trimbledons, the special place he had in the family, the adventures he had shared with Uncle Thomas and Tim, their shared passion for climbing that Lucy always considered unnecessarily dangerous, and so much more. At this moment of meeting, Lucy's female intuition told her that Andrew did not completely belong to her, while Thomas also knew this was a different Andrew he was meeting today to the younger man he had known some years before.

After passing quickly through these moments of mutually identified awkwardness, Thomas was quickly getting to know Lucy, like where she was born in Sweden, an area that he knew quite well from his climbing expeditions. They soon also found a mutual interest, music, and there began a rapidly developing warmth between these two strangers.

Thomas, a gifted musician, was an old fashioned charmer. He did not care much for all this nonsense, as he saw it, about fortitude and forgiveness. An eye for an eye and a tooth for a tooth tended to be more his mantra. He had lived his life to the full, led more often by his heart than his mind and he was regarded within the family as the "other" Trimbledon. Despite being a little older than John, he had managed to slip the grasp somewhat of family responsibilities and traditions, particularly after moving to Paris to study music. His two passions in life were music, particularly piano, and mountain climbing. The less charitable members of the family would probably also suggest a third passion of his from a young age had been women. However, with Thomas, one always got straight answers, graciousness, wit and an inexhaustible zest for life. He was also deeply compassionate as well as passionate about those matters that he held dear.

In his younger years he had been immensely strong and although he never wished it to be discussed, he had saved the lives of two of his climbing companions in his mid-twenties on the north face of the Eiger Mountain, when they slipped on a particularly treacherous part of the climb. He had held them both, dangling over certain death, for many minutes, until two other members of their party, climbing from beneath, could reach them with safety ropes. This incident had threatened the musical career of Thomas, when he lost the feeling in his right hand for several weeks after the rope had cut deep into his hand and wrists. Although he would never admit it, it was this accident to his hands that had probably precluded him from becoming one of the great concert pianists of his generation. There were many other acts of bravery and grit ascribed to Thomas by others who knew him, although he would always brush off any such talk. Those who knew him well, however, had come to know that under the affable and lovable exterior lay another person of an entirely different metal, and Andrew had experienced the merest glimpse of this earlier.

In contrast to Thomas, those who only knew his younger brother John casually usually perceived him to be aloof, rather cold and a little pompous. Yet again such impressions can be misleading, but the fact remained that Thomas was always regarded, despite being the rather odd Trimbledon, to be the gregarious one, the Trimbledon who could be despatched from time to time to go anywhere and to meet and befriend almost anyone. Such moves, however, always had an element of risk and unpredictability whenever Thomas was involved, because, while he was always pleased to oblige if he was able to, it was always ultimately done his way.

Through his mountain climbing exploits, although having no interest whatsoever in money or commerce, he had almost by accident made a modest fortune designing a whole range of lightweight climbing equipment that another chum of his, also a climber, had had the wit to properly patent and commercialise. Surprisingly, this financial independence that he gained in his early forties had brought him back to the family after many years of isolation from them. The important thing for Thomas was that it was now on his terms, rather than theirs. Being stubborn and independent, relying entirely on one's self must be in the Trimbledon genes, since all the family men folk share this characteristic. Old family disagreements, particularly between himself and John, had been largely laid to rest, and Mary had been instrumental in these reconciliations. She had always had a soft spot for Thomas, and he for her. For some years now, Thomas had been a regular and welcome guest at Himbledon. Indeed the grand piano was always kept finely tuned, on his personal instruction, and it was the only non-human part of Himbledon that he truly cherished as his own.

Just then Mary and John joined the three of them by the coffee jugs. Ignoring Thomas for the moment, Mary made straight for Andrew, guided by her deeply felt intuition that he needed a cuddle. Mary always regarded Andrew almost a member of her own family, another son needing a mother from the early days when he had visited Himbledon with Tim from Winchester. The premature death of his parents in a motor accident a few years later merely cemented this special relationship when Mary had become Andrew's surrogate mother, confidant, advisor and on some occasions, even protector. He had a special place in her heart and she in his.

"Andrew, come here and give me a hug," Mary said, extending her arms to him.

"Mary, I am so sorry about Tim," he replied enveloping Mary in his arms.

"Yes, yes I know, we will all miss him terribly," responded Mary, momentarily losing her composure, before taking a deep breath and re-focussing her mind. "You will both be staying over, of course, tonight with us; won't you Andrew?" Mary asked as a rhetorical question, as she put an arm around Lucy.

"We are staying in Ashby," Andrew replied before being cut short by Mary.

"We will be hurt if you both do not stay over and anyway it will not be safe for you to drive after dinner." Then, looking mischievously at Thomas, standing nearby, she said, "With Uncle Thomas in the vicinity, no doubt the local constabulary will be out in force just waiting for drunken drivers to emerge from Himbledon." Everyone laughed, including Thomas, and the matter was closed. Andrew was pleased to be embraced by the family again, especially at this sad time, and Lucy was intrigued to know more about Andrew's surrogate parents.

Joseph arrived to also replenish his coffee cup and he and Andrew began to talk about Tim, Paris and recent events. Mary chatted to Lucy briefly about London and knowing Lucy to be an interior designer enquired whether she would be interested in redesigning the interior of the apartment she and John had in Chelsea overlooking the Thames.

Meanwhile John and Thomas were in conversation, John asking Thomas wryly, “How do you do it, Thomas? Where do you find these beautiful, young and talented women, and manage to convince them to befriend a reprobate such as you?”

“Well,” retorted Thomas, “it goes with the territory, not knowing a B major from a B flat, how on earth could you ever understand, or me ever to start to explain.” They both chuckled, betraying the brotherly warmth between them despite differences in earlier times.

“Are we in sight of dealing or being able to help with the situation in Paris, particularly those who murdered Timothy? Just tell me who they are John; you know I will do the rest, without any connection with your fraternal buddies. I am bound for Hell anyway, so what is there to lose?” Thomas asked, instantly changing the tone of their conversation and venting his anger at the loss of such a wonderful and talented life so young, a life that was as close as losing a son of his own.

John thought for a moment, then replied, “That is not the issue, Tom; revenge must never be our motive, and you must never take the law into your own hands; you know that, but yes, I had some revealing information late last night that appears to indicate who the perpetrators may be, and they are not who everyone else is suspecting. We have more work to do before we can be sure, but yes, we are working on it.”

Standing close to each other, Thomas said, “Well, the media and the intelligence services are at a loss and, as we all know, there are all manner of wild accusations being aired in the absence of anyone claiming responsibility.”

“That’s right.” John nodded in agreement.

They both knew this was neither the time nor place for this type of conversation and it was Thomas who interjected, “Let’s talk later when we are alone, John, you are bearing up well, I feel for you and Mary at this time.”

John nodded and gave a small smile as he began to walk

away to talk to more guests. As he did so he turned and took a pace back to Thomas saying, "Now you had better find your beautiful Russian lady friend and stop neglecting her any longer."

"No worry of that, John. She is probably trying to convert some of the religious to atheism, right at this moment," Thomas chuckled as he put his empty coffee cup on the table.

"Oh yes, one more thing, Thomas. Mary and I trust you will be staying at Himbledon tonight, so we have had your usual suite made up in the family quarters."

Now with that little ritual completed, Thomas smiled, saying, "Thanks, John; we will, of course, be delighted to stay."

After two hours most of the friends, staff from Himbledon estate and other non-immediate family guests attending the funeral had conveyed their condolences, talked with John, Mary and other members of the family, bid farewell and departed.

6

Saying Goodbye

THAT NIGHT AT HIMBLEDON, A LARGE INFORMAL DINNER had been arranged at the main house. It included all the immediate family, Mary's mother, brother and wife, Anna and her parents, the various members of the extended family, Andrew and Lucy, and the various religious who were present earlier, apart from one of the officials from Rome who had to return urgently. The Moslem couples and Samuel and Rebecca were also there.

At 6:45, everyone gathered for pre-dinner drinks and an evening to pay tribute to Timothy, to share their grief and loss, and to be joyful at his life before it had been abruptly ended and he was called elsewhere. Lucy, a non-Catholic, did not know what to expect and having had little exposure to church anticipated a sombre and difficult evening. On the contrary, it was an occasion of immense warmth, dignity, humour and several wonderfully touching tributes to Tim.

One of the highlights of the evening was when Thomas and Liska, his lady friend, performed a special tribute to Tim in a way Tom knew he would have appreciated, had he been there in person. First, Thomas played a brief sequence from Swan Lake, and Liska performed the dance of the dying swan. It was intended to recognise death, which it did so, to every person in the room. After a brief pause, Thomas followed on by effortlessly playing haunting pieces by Debussy, D'un cahier d'esquisses from Images and Reverie. These Debussy pieces of music were some of Tim's favourites and ones he always asked Thomas to play whenever they could manage to meet up at Himbledon. They then concluded with Maple Leaf Rag by Scott Joplin, the father of ragtime. The music was suddenly full of life, and Liska danced beautifully with vigour and excitement. This final piece was to signify the resurrection, life after death.

They were rewarded with thunderous applause and appeals to play on. Thomas needed a drink by this stage and Liska needed to change from her dancing costume.

During the course of the evening all the members of the immediate family paid tribute in their own special way to Tim in song, word, poetry, sketches and stories. John and Mary read a brief playlet that Tim had written when in sixth form that had characterised many of those present in the room with humour and a certain precision in identifying so many of their foibles. Further applause followed and there was a toast to Tim's unquestionable writing abilities.

Joseph always hated having to do such performances at family gatherings although by now with the aid of Thomas on piano again, Luke on guitar and Mark on a particularly haunting harmonica, he performed a very touching rendition of "Amazing Grace", to which many in the hall joined in with several encores. He was relieved that Louise was not there since he had also been encouraged by several glasses of the excellent claret during the course of the evening.

Even shy Andrew by this stage had been cajoled by Paul to perform together one of Tim's favourite Peter Cook and Dudley Moore skits from "Beyond the Fringe." Several of the religious also paid their own personal tributes to Timothy, either with stories of humorous experiences with him, or with songs, and Archbishop Guggar told three hilarious stories all involving Tim, various pranks and mischief he had got up to over the years.

One of the most heart stopping tributes was given by Mohammed Albour, who simply stood up at the long table with a glass of water in his hand and read two short, but deeply moving, passages from the Koran that explained the mercy of God, his love of honourable souls, and his welcome for the righteous dead. He then turned to Mary and, with tears in his eyes, told her she was a blessed lady and that Allah felt her pain, before he walked to John, who involuntarily stood up to be kissed by Mohammed on both cheeks.

As John stood, Mohammed said in a dignified voice, “Your suffering is my suffering, your loss is my loss, and we are together in this matter under the will of Allah.”

There was complete silence in the room as he walked slowly back to his place at the table, and his wife smiled gently up at him as he sat down. There was a long period of complete silence, the room fell into a period of sadness and reflection and after several moments Thomas went to the piano and gently played a piece of Bach. Gradually conversation resumed although the dignity of the occasion had returned.

It was late when coffee was served and the port was poured. Lucy had been enthralled by the spontaneity of the whole evening, by the talent, depth and warmth of this very special occasion. As they stumbled up the narrow stairs to their room on the third floor of the Grange, Andrew whispered in her ear, “Darling, I always said they are special people, different and special. See what I mean?”

II

Ancient Traditions in a Secular World

7

A Secret Reality

MARK TRIMBLEDON HAD WORKED LATE INTO THE NIGHT preparing the encrypted CDs for the board meeting. Deep beneath Himbledon Grange there is a secret warren of passages, rooms, kitchen, sleeping quarters, library, bathrooms, communication equipment, a computer centre, a small medical area with operating theatre and a chapel. There is also an extensive network of canals leading to a concealed entrance to the great lake on the estate fed from a small river from the hills beyond. The underground canal system had been built in the late seventeen hundreds by James Brindley, a distinguished engineer of those times, as a special commission for one of John Trimbledon's ancestors. Brindley had created various canal systems for the Duke of Bridgewater including the now derelict coal mine at Worsley with an underground canal system for transporting the coal out of the mine and via canals to Manchester. Coal had been mined in the Worsley area since Roman times.

Few people knew of the existence of what lay beneath Himbledon Grange and its recent historical significance to Britain. It had been a well-kept secret and still today provided a range of unusual functions. Churchill had held secret war cabinet meetings under Himbledon Grange during the darkest days of the Second World War when the Nazis were at the height of their bombing raids over England. It also housed many secret materials and documents related to high security state affairs. All these remnants of the war had been removed many years before and the underground facilities at the Grange forgotten about, apart from the Trimbledons.

Mark was Joseph's elder brother by eighteen months and one of the four sons of John, with Timothy being the eldest and Paul a year younger. Mark was the studious son, enthralled with technology from a young age and the boffin of the family. He had graduated with a Master in Mathematics and was working for his PhD on some obscure abstraction that only he understood, apart from his tutors at Cambridge. His particular responsibility and calling within the family was to provide all the technical, computer and communications support required for the fraternal activities of his father and family members.

It had been here in one of the well-appointed meeting rooms that some weeks earlier a very unusual gathering had taken place. Periodically, under the patronage of John, strategic information discussions took place to keep abreast of world events, developments with rogue governments, major criminal threats and the ever-shifting tide of public behaviour, beliefs and other factors that may be set to threaten the free world. Such meetings were rare since the fraternity never wished to draw attention to their activities and any gatherings of prominent people always risked drawing unwanted attention. All the participants had spent weeks before gathering relevant information and supplying this via the technical support of Mark to provide a distilled set of data and information. The strategic review was completed within a day and none of the participants stayed over at the Grange.

What in years past had taken many days of laborious effort, often by female members of the fraternity, typing and translating documents, manipulating data with abacus, slide rules, manual calculators and even large punch card machines after the Second World War, had now been handled by the plethora of computer hardware, software and communication facilities at Mark's disposal in a matter of hours. As well as being ancient in one sense, the fraternity was also always modern in its acceptance and deployment of current technology. Mark was also a strategic advisor to several hi-tech commercial companies and had played a leading role in the commercialisation of military satellite navigation technology. His particular favourites were the satellite maps available on the web that enthral everyone.

The major objective of this meeting was to prepare a highly secret set of scenarios of possible outcomes from various destabilising developments around the world. This meeting had taken place before the attack on Paris, although the possibility of precisely what happened had been identified earlier. Such information gathering and analysis is not an exact science and the most critical variable is always the timing of such events. The murder of Timothy was linked to the attack and had preceded it; otherwise, the carnage may well have been averted.

History has demonstrated the consistent failure of governments, elected leaders, national security agencies, world organisations such as the United Nations, the World Bank and the International Monetary Fund and various regulators and watchdogs to actually ensure security, justice and freedom. There are many reasons for this, although the fact remains that the fraternity have had to intervene, as an invisible hand over the centuries, to preserve certain values and restore order, due to the failure of public authorities and institutions that the public assume have everything in hand. The reality is very different.

Many times during history the fraternity has wished to step aside and pass these ageless responsibilities to the official organs of state. Sadly, it has only been for brief spells in history when this has been possible while world events have remained calm and ordered. The fraternity has existed and survived for so long precisely because it is so different from the worldly order and the political, military and economic structures that have been created by man to order his affairs.

Fraternal realities, the way it operates, thinks and behaves is entirely different from the conduct of the world at large. It draws from a set of beliefs and values that would simply induce incredulity if ever publicised. Yet these very realities are communicated every day from pulpits around the world in various churches, irrespective of creed. While the activities of the fraternity are certainly secret, of necessity in order to survive and function, the reasons for its work and the matters being defended are certainly not secret. They are there for anyone who has ears to listen and eyes to see. These messages have remained largely consistent for thousands of years, but as history has amply demonstrated, so often, few are listening.

A series of scenarios had been agreed at the meeting based on a diverse range of information gathered from around the world. Since the fraternity worked independently of all regular security and other official institutions, it had developed over many years highly refined and effective information gathering methods, sifted and validated at every level throughout a complex and global network of eyes and ears. It had the ability to laser in on the information that is important and to discard all the welter of irrelevant noise. Those providing the information knew precisely what to look for. They had also developed skills and processes to piece together even the most obscure intelligence to form a larger canvass of useable knowledge.

The way information was evaluated and deployed was also unusual. Various gifted minds were involved using interpretative and evaluative techniques drawn from centuries of wisdom. John himself, a distinguished philosophy, politics and economics academic was just a small part of this total process. Socrates and many other great thinkers and contributors to human knowledge were also involved, if now only in spirit, certainly their intellectual disciplines were at the centre of fraternal processes.

There was always an ever-implicit distinction between information and knowledge and the dispassionate objective assessment of information. Without context, balance and validation just so much information is worthless. It has to be carefully and systematically converted into knowledge that it then becomes useful and actionable. Assumptions are also always dangerous, and so too must be tested to destruction before becoming the foundation for judgements.

Interpretation and the matter of judgement was certainly the most disciplined element of fraternal processes. Many issues adjudged to be long term were handled gently, slowly and painstakingly, enabling all aspects and dimensions to be subject to scrutiny, consultation, and validation before carefully considered and weighed decisions were made. All too often, hasty and poorly thought through decisions had cost lives and human freedom.

Fraternal processes always sifted and scrutinised knowledge in such a manner that short term and urgent issues came to the forefront. These were pinpointed and assigned to relevant members for further scrutiny, investigation, analysis and the formation of option outcomes, timescales and impacts. These were then systematically ranked according to a vigorous set of evaluative criteria and, if they were then judged to be imminent, short term and dangerous, they were notified to senior members of the fraternity.

Prayer was also at the centre of all of their activities and had been from the earliest times. They also followed the liturgical calendar of the church. Such prayers in the fraternal context had three primary purposes; to exalt, to give thanks and pay tribute, and to seek to serve and receive guidance and the necessary discernment to act not in their own strength, but that of God. The abiding belief of them all was to give humble service not to themselves, but to the Trinity of God, the Son and the Holy Spirit.

Over the years they had also subjected all their activities to detailed, vigorous and independent scrutiny by other elements of the fraternity. They operated a learning culture, and still do, one that never flinches from mistakes and understanding how they arose and trying to ensure that such mistakes are avoided in the future. In many cases where there were human errors, corrective measures have been implemented without delay. Where there has been deliberate disobedience, and this is proven, the fraternity has several refined methods of dealing with such matters. Through this process the fraternity has accumulated a wealth of experience, knowledge and wisdom together with a degree of personal responsibility and accountability among its members found nowhere else on Earth.

Many of the failures that the fraternity feel fully culpable for have occurred for the simple reason that so often the recipients of fraternal wisdom and security advice have not been able to recognise the significance of what was being told, and the giving of invaluable information freely, in love and as an act of charity and compassion. Such, is much of the cynical world we live in.

8

A Long History

EVEN THE HUMAN STRUCTURE AND CONDUCT OF THE CHURCH itself was never above fraternal scrutiny, even today. Many times, those wishing to destroy it had infiltrated the church itself. Many times in its long history, some members had lost their way, become distracted, and fallen to wayward sinful ways. The human aspect of the church will always remain vulnerable. The church had always, however, survived, repaired itself, and dealt with the threats from without and within. Never did the fraternity get involved directly in the spiritual life of the church, since this was never to be its place. It did, however, always seek the truth, the honest admission of human failures, restitution and the continued mission of the church in the world, as the founder wished two thousand years ago, and still does today.

The fraternity was an observer before Constantine, the first Christian emperor who, in 311, became a generous patron and protector of the church. During the great persecution, when in Antioch in 298, during pagan sacrifices, the pagan priests accused Christians of upsetting the ceremony, and troops had to intervene. It was the beginning of a period of bloody persecution. Eusebius of Caesarea wrote at the time "So many suffered that the murderous axe was dulled, and the executioners grew weary."

The fraternity witnessed the introduction of monasticism that was spread by St. Benedict of Nursia. As a young man Benedict, who was born in 450, was drawn to prayer and meditation, and for three years he lived in a cave, attracting followers. He set up twelve monasteries before founding one at Monte Cassino, near Naples. Today, the Benedictine order is of great importance to the church.

The fraternity witnessed the fall of the Roman Empire and the fall of Constantinople in 1453 to the Turks. Also the great Christian conversion of Europe between 600 and 1055, and when Western Europe was returned to chaos after Charlemagne's death in 814 and his empire was attacked from all sides. Throughout this period, the Slavs attacked from the east from the plains near the Danube, and the Magyars, originally from central Asia, attacked Europe from the east. The Vikings came from the north, sailing from Scandinavia, and were particularly destructive. Finally, there were the Muslim Saracens who came from the south.

Throughout, the fraternity continued to witness these events, outside and separate from the Catholic church, unseen in defending moral truth and freedom. While things were deteriorating in the West in the 600s, matters in the East were generally peaceful, where the emperor of the East was enjoying a renaissance. It was only by the end of the tenth century they began to take greater interest in the East when political and religious differences with the West began to emerge and serious divisions and schisms arose.

A troubled period for the fraternity was during the Crusades and the Renaissance. They supported the Gregorian Reformers although their role in the Crusades remains shrouded in mystery. The Reformers left the church in a better position than they found it, with greater independence of the powerful and with various distortions rectified. They witnessed the spiritual revival at that time and the start of the Cistercians began in 1098. Unlike Benedictines, who wore black wool habits, Cistercian monks and nuns left theirs white and untreated. They often ate only one vegetarian meal a day, had a disdain for ornament, and founded their monasteries in the wilderness, considering hard manual labour and austerity important. By the eleven hundreds monks were often also priests and were recruited from the better educated. The Cistercians also allowed peasants to become lay brothers, saying certain prayers and working with the community on the great Cistercian estates scattered across Northern Europe. It was a period when the Cistercians provided wise custodianship of monastic farms, woodlands and the communities under their protection.

During the twelfth and thirteenth centuries there was political and economic progress in the West, allied with rapid development in the arts and sciences and the continuing revival of spiritualism. The centuries of invasion were over: Vikings, Saracens and Magyars had been civilized. Towns and cities rapidly grew with improvements in agriculture that had been established by the monastic farmers and with increased trade new wealth was created that in turn helped to fund an explosion in learning and the arts, and led to the glories of the thirteenth century.

By the early thirteenth century, intellectual advance and institutional reform had transformed the church, although these developments had had little impact on the peasants and the poor. The rapidly growing towns and cities presented an ever-growing problem, and church structures created earlier for rural areas, the parish system, were increasingly unable to serve the growing numbers of the poor townsfolk. The friars emerged into this rapidly changing world to serve these new pastoral needs. They were the followers of two particular men.

The first of these was Spanish born St. Dominic Guzman. In 1204, he had converted large numbers of heretics in the south of France and he became convinced that uneducated clergy left their flock open to heresy, so he founded the Order of Preachers, known today as the Dominicans. An associated order of Dominican nuns was also founded, and both the Dominican sisters and the friars became very important as educators and scholars.

The other great order of friars that was founded were the Franciscans, who developed from the witness of St. Francis of Assisi. Born Francesco di Bernadone in 1182, he was the only child of a rich merchant in Assisi in Tuscany, Italy. He was wounded during a battle with a neighbouring town when a young man and returned home to recover and during that time he decided to reject his family inheritance in order to dedicate himself to service of the poor. He evidently sang as he walked into the snow of a Tuscan winter and a band of followers gathered around him, sharing all they had, they devoted themselves to preaching the gospel in simple language and caring for the poor. They nursed the sick, especially lepers, held church services, begged for their food and slept in the open or in crude shelters. In 1212, a friend of Francis, a wealthy young woman of Assisi called Clare, founded a similar order for women.

There are today Dominican and Franciscan men and women preaching, tending the poor and the sick, throughout the world. They are of many different nationalities and one of John's distant relatives continues to practice as a Franciscan parish priest in South Africa to this day.

The fraternity witnessed when Luther rightly criticised the conduct of the church regarding the widespread practice of paying indulgences. When the parish priest and professor, Martin Luther, nailed his 'Ninety-five Thesis' to the door of the castle church in Wittenberg in October 1517, it sent a shock to the centre of papal authority, and launched the reformation. The glories of the Renaissance had led to deplorable excesses in the Western church, such as the sale of indulgences to raise money for many dubious uses. Martin Luther, a devout Catholic and theologian, publicly refuted such practices.

From his translation work as a professor, Luther had developed sola scriptura that the Bible is the final authority for Christians, and sola fide, that salvation comes by faith alone and not by good works. He also believed that the Bible should be available to all people, not just to clergy, and that every Christian is a member of the priesthood. While these propositions ran against more than a thousand years of church tradition, he believed he was doing nothing wrong, simply realigning matters that had strayed. There were many who understood and shared these deep matters of conscience in the fraternity. This dialogue may never have extended beyond academia had Luther also not been a parish priest, living in the world as did the fraternity, experiencing at firsthand some of the unrest at that time, so he spoke out publicly against what he saw as abuses, deficiencies and misunderstandings in the church. Quickly his ideas took root and his knowledge of his work spread through Germany and beyond.

Other reformers followed his example and joined the effort for reform. The Catholic Church refused to listen to any of this, and the unity of Christianity became fractured and divided once more. The Reformation soon engulfed political rulers who sensed the advantages of breaking the church's territorial power and took sides. The splitting of the church and the state had much sympathy among fraternal members and there was much debate and soul searching during these times. The litmus test always to be applied, however, was the preservation of the truth and the moral code taught by the founder of Christianity. Yes, there had been serious need for reform, but not the distortions of these truths, the fragmentation of Christianity and the deep divisions that developed over the centuries that followed. Luther probably never intended such consequences.

Whilst misguided and also not being fully part of this world, the Catholic Church was slow to respond, and by the mid seventeenth century the religious map of Europe had been redrawn. These deep divisions among many Christians led to bloody wars as Catholic and Protestant nations battled with each other. As the Catholic Church had been wrong in its deployment of Christianity for earthly ambitions, the new denominations also started to behave in a similar fashion in the pursuit of similar rewards. This led to conflict and the abandonment of an inclusive church based on community, compassion, forgiveness and love. Judgement became a new force to be reckoned with, the judgement by one man of another. This ethos was foreign to the fraternity since to members there is only one who has the authority to judge and it is certainly no man.

Such earthly judgement— of man by man— was not new. The Catholic Church had misguidedly deployed judgement and the wrath of God for centuries to enslave its flock, particularly the less educated and poor. It had, however, also been the protector of the faith, and a source of widespread and compassionate charity and paternalism towards those in need. The reformation brought much good, it also introduced the spread of Christianity via Catholic missionaries who travelled and preached in the far off lands of Latin America, India, China, Japan and Africa. It also started deeply felt conflicts between so-called Christian and Christian for the following centuries.

For many years, the Catholic Church was under siege, with brief respites and various spiritual renewals. While the reformers such as Luther, Calvin and others were passionate about their beliefs, frequently putting their own safety at risk, they were not prepared to abandon the tenets of the Catholic Church. Others, however, were far less conciliatory. Known as the radical reformers, these Protestant believers firmly rejected the Lutheran position that only those Catholic practices that actually seemed to contradict the Bible should be done away with.

The radical reformers, called Anabaptists from the Greek meaning 'to baptise again', believed that anyone baptised as an infant had as an adult to be re-baptised, to be re-cleansed. They abandoned any doctrine, practice, or ecclesiastical act that was not clearly stated in the Bible. By inference, they also abandoned belief in the intervention of the Holy Spirit in mystical ways since the crucifixion, in providing divine discernment to holy members of the Catholic Church. For the radical reformers they refused to support nationalistic causes such as bearing arms or swearing allegiance whereas even Calvinists, who had similar beliefs in Biblical authority, believed there to be no need to break with these practices.

Resulting from these differences in belief, many Anabaptists were persecuted and killed by the governing authorities, including the Catholic Inquisition. Other Protestant believers also turned on Anabaptists and it was an appalling period of intolerance and injustice with many incidents of kindness and protection afforded to people of all faiths by fraternal members. Nevertheless, extreme and long-lasting dysfunctional value systems were being born on the fringes of these emerging Christian groups, with antipathies that would last for centuries.

Although allied under the "Brotherly Union" adopted at a Synod in 1527, the Anabaptists may best be described with reference to the beliefs of those who organized the different groups. Menno Simons and Jakob Ammann were two early leaders. Born in Holland in 1496, Simons was ordained a Catholic priest in 1524, and his biblical studies, particularly the New Testament, led him to question the authenticity of transubstantiation. In 1536, he converted to Anabaptism and began serving in Groningen and while his ministry was one of moderation, especially when compared to the apocalyptic visions of some other Anabaptist leaders, he was a literalist when interpreting the Bible and he did not accept the term "Trinity" since it does not appear in the Bible. He was the founder of the Mennonite church.

Amman, born in 1644, was a Mennonite elder who lived in Alsace and his extreme attitude towards separation from the rest of the world, was defined in the 'Eighteen Articles of Confession of Faith' adopted by the Mennonites in 1632. In 1693, he broke relations with other Mennonite churches and, with several thousand followers, founded the Amish Mennonites.

It was the apocalyptic Anabaptists, on the fringes of these new churches that had attracted the special attention of the fraternity at these times. Thomas Muntzer, who had once been Luther's friend, came under the influence of the apocalyptic Zwickau Prophets and began demanding political dissent and upheaval. When he moved to Mulhausen in 1524 and set up a theocracy, Catholics and Protestants joined forces to bring an end to his call for civil war, and he was soon captured and executed.

In 1526, while serving as a minister in Stockholm, Melchior Hoffman became obsessed with the end of the world, predicting Christ's return. After joining the Anabaptists in Strasbourg, he preached in various places, and then returned to Strasbourg to await the end of the world. Here he was arrested and imprisoned for life by the authorities. However, he did attract converts, and the Melchiorites survived him as a distinct party among the Anabaptists. One of Hoffman's converts, Jan Mathys, believed that the city of Munster would be the New Jerusalem, and, in 1533, he stormed it with an army of Anabaptists, believing he could take over the world, and he and his supporters were captured, tortured and killed.

Other radical reform leaders, including Felix Manz and Balthasar Hubmaier of the Swiss Brethren, suffered similar fates as they were hunted down and sentenced to death. Even peaceful and well-respected Anabaptists such as Jakob Hutter were brought before the courts. While the Hutterites were pacifists and their abilities as farmers were much respected, even Hutter was finally killed as part of the widespread purges of Anabaptists ordered by King Ferdinand the First. From these early times, many discreet cells of these fringe and extreme beliefs survived and established themselves in various parts of Europe.

In years to come they were to travel to America where there was greater religious tolerance especially for many who wished to escape the persecutions of Europe. Many of the forefathers of the United States, the early colonialists who had settled and made their own various lands in the eastern side of the country, were determined to break lose of the bonds of the established European order.

The fraternity had been there when Galileo Galilei, an Italian mathematician, transformed man's understanding of the heavens in direct disobedience of the church's teaching after he had demonstrated his telescope to friends in Venice in 1609. He went on to demonstrate how the Earth circled the sun, rather than the other way around, and he stood for scientific enlightenment, to the dismay of Catholic priests. The fraternity, always sympathetic to fact rather than fiction, quickly embraced this new understanding

There is one other element of religious history that is necessary for the telling of this story. Established in Rome in about 1515, the Oratory of Divine Love was an early new Catholic brotherhood of the Catholic Reformation. Their aim was to sanctify members by daily prayer and good works and several members of the clergy were enrolled. It was from these ranks that new religious orders rose. Of all the new orders, it was the Jesuit order, first called the Society of Jesus and founded in 1534 by the Spaniard Ignatius of Loyola, which made the greatest impact.

Loyola had lived an austere lifestyle of self-denial, yet, like Luther, he was unable to find inner peace. Instead, he chose to obey the leaders of the church, so, in addition to taking the vows of chastity, obedience and poverty, Jesuits also vowed obedience to the pope. As Luther's faith and conscience had led him to rebellion, Loyola's had led him to obedience.

By 1640, the Jesuits had established hundreds of schools and several seminaries and universities. Many dignitaries who held powerful positions in central Europe were brought back to the church, and Jesuit activities halted the spread of Protestantism. They established themselves in various European countries, where they encouraged a reluctant church to reform, bringing many back to the faith. They travelled also to the east and to South America, particularly Paraguay and Francis Xavier led missions to India and Japan, while Matteo Ricci travelled to China. Frequently these expeditions proved dangerous with several Jesuits being brutally murdered by the indigenous people of these far off lands.

With these developments the stage was set for increasing division between various Christian groups, rising suspicions and ever more diverse groups to conduct their nefarious activities in the name of God in the centuries that lay ahead.

The role of the fraternity over the centuries had always been to act as an astute observer, honed to work in peaceful ways wherever possible, to defend freedom, personal choice and to defeat tyranny. Mass psychosis induced by apocalyptic fanatics had always been viewed as a particular danger and threat to Christianity and civilisation. Even within the Catholic Church, such practices had been condemned over the centuries. While there have been many things beyond their control and influence, being a largely human entity, their invisible hand had often been a stabilising force at critical moments of human history.

If there are forces of evil, of deliberate dysfunction at the hands of misguided men and women, which appears to repeat itself over the centuries, what earthly human forces must there have also been to defeat them? The fraternity is one of these, and, just as there is organised badness on Earth, there is also organised goodness, however imperfect and fragile it may be in practice. Why do we enjoy the freedoms we do today, freedom to practise personal beliefs in a generally ordered society when these very essentials have so often and so consistently been under threat? Surely the question begs a proper answer.

So it was that members of the fraternity had witnessed many shifts, conflicts and reconciliations of human affairs over the centuries. They had observed the ebb and flow of human development, periods of great enlightenment, discernment and prosperity together with the darker times of repression, exploitation, ignorance, war, starvation and suffering. They had learnt from bitter experience to identify the most lethal and destabilising of threats, where they came from and what had borne them.

9

No One Listens

THE FRATERNITY ALWAYS TRIED TO FACILITATE PEACEFUL and honourable outcomes. By various means they had access to world leaders and national and international security organisations without ever disclosing their origins. Rarely did they ever wish to intervene directly to resolve problems, although on some occasions they were compelled to intervene directly. Something that still haunts many of the older fraternal members is the fact that had they intervened and not left matters to the official role players, many atrocities, deaths and suffering could have been averted, especially in the two great world wars in the twentieth century. However, their strict code rarely permitted the fraternity from getting involved, apart from providing precise warnings, specific intelligence, and other clear messages to the authorities. Again, the reality is not what one would expect; so often, those who should have been listening were not, even in recent times.

The Twin Tower atrocity in New York, the tube bombings in central London, the nightclub bombings in Bali, and many more atrocities could probably have been averted. The appearance of many security bodies, the FBI, CIA, Interpol and MI5, for example, outwardly look to be efficient and effective in safeguarding the public. Again, the actual reality is not quite so. The poor record of these security bodies speaks for itself. Each of these bodies suffers from turf disputes, the large egos of senior members, arrogance and the desire to serve one's self rather than others. The CIA and FBI in America have often been accused of hidden agendas under the dictatorial leadership of powerful, ruthless men with little accountability to the U.S. Congress. There is division between and within these security bodies, lack of collaboration and human stubbornness. The United Nations is equally flawed, particularly the composition and processes of the Security Council, as are so many of the institutions established and resourced to safeguard public freedom, safety and security.

The lists of failures are too many to ignore, especially in recent history. There are also too many to document here, although for this story to be accurately told, just a few examples are necessary. It is also of particular relevance to reflect for a moment why these failures have happened, and there are many reasons related to each specific set of circumstances. The matter that must concern us here is that there are different realities colliding, a modern world of science, technology and so-called rational thought that has little space to consider alternative lines of thought. The secular world, despite so often claiming to be objective and open, is often as imprisoned and biased as those mystical thinkers it so quickly condemns. Science has also become a religion, so often misused for dishonourable purposes, as too is the contemporary disregard, so often, for holiness, ancient belief and spiritual value systems.

The failures have so often occurred not because of some deliberate act of sabotage or some clandestine plot, but simply because the wrong paradigms have existed, and ineptitude. When wisdom is ignored, when the secular world and its authorities lack the humility to listen and understand and persists in its blind arrogance that it knows better, mankind is in peril. We also do not appear to learn lessons from history and the profound insights that it provides to human conduct, the great cycles of reform and darkness, of human frailties, and the repetitive abuse of power and the exercise of wickedness.

The horror of genocide in Rwanda, in Africa, in recent times, where thousands were butchered, had been avoidable. It was foreseen, as the dreadful animosity had simmered between the Hutus and Tutsi, the smaller of the tribal groups making up the Bantu-speaking people of the country. Members of the local church and other observers had grown increasingly alarmed at developments, and the customary, fully documented warnings had been given well in time to international peacekeeping authorities and various governments around the world. Even senior members of the small United Nations local peacekeeping force on the ground in the country had fully supported these urgent warnings. However, the international communities were indifferent, or they simply did not understand the urgency or the nature of the messages being conveyed to them. To make matters worse, since these messages were coming from what was regarded as a religious quarter, some officials regarded them with contempt. Those agencies that did have the power to intervene became embroiled in bureaucracy while they pondered these strange reports despite being organs of the modern secular world, supposedly efficient and the beneficiaries of contemporary science and rationality. On this occasion, as with many others, the reality was very different and the result was a tragedy.

Thousands of people had been butchered, many innocent women, children and men. Many Christian missionaries also perished. When the international news crews eventually arrived in the country, the world watched in incredulity the horrendous pictures of rotting corpses strewn across the verdant countryside of a once beautiful country. By the time the outside world began to properly listen and understand, it was too late. As time passed, the Western world and the United Nations and European Union in particular simply set aside any responsibility or personal accountability – just another atrocity in Africa. However, these failures are now coming closer to home, threatening the very underbelly of Western security.

Those external institutions established precisely to address such conflicts also grossly mismanaged the genocide and ethnic cleansing in the Balkans, with murderous leadership of Moslem and Christian militia alike. Through a dreadful disregard for human life, neglect, misinformation, vacillation and self-interest, they all combined to delay a co-ordinated response to bring the conflict to an end. Thankfully, they eventually did, but only after horrendous loss of life, human rights violations, the violent rape of innocent women, and thousands of deaths, particularly children.

Archbishop Guggar had expressly notified and briefed a senior security advisor to the French government about the possibility of certain attacks on Paris some ten days before the atrocity took place. Disbelief, poor communications, ineffective prioritisation and the absence of various key political figures at high profile media events outside France had all contributed to the failure of a proper and prompt response. The source of the information, always a thorn in the side of the French establishment, had also lacked necessary legitimacy that also led to an irresponsible disregard by public officials.

In a world attuned to spin, the sound bite and the careful massaging of so many messages, the simple, straightforward and humble entreaty from a man of the cloth is easily ignored and put aside.

There are many such stories and in these circumstances much work remains for the fraternity to do.

When the American astronauts first reached the moon, one of them had taken with him a Host and a tiny wine container to celebrate Holy Eucharist, in respect and thanksgiving as they circled the moon and he looked back to Earth. NASA never actively publicised this event, although today various shots of the moon landing hang in one of the underground meeting rooms at Himbledon.

Women were admitted to the fraternity many centuries ago. Although not a rigid adherence, many women become members after their child bearing years since fraternal membership may cause conflicts with motherhood and the needs of younger children. Unmarried women, often members of holy orders, those with a vocation to the religious life, have played leading roles within the fraternity. Many laywomen have also played significant roles and in recent history and modern times female members play an equal role of importance to male members.

Passive influence, the watchword of the fraternity for centuries, has also caused regular debates and disagreements between members. Some have wished to always remain in the shadows, leaving events ultimately in the hands of God. Others have sought more direct intervention, and even the use of violence, if essential, to defend against evil. The cardinal principle of acting in love, turning the other cheek, and upholding scriptural teachings has, however, always won the argument. Despite this long and unwavering tradition of the fraternity, there have been times in its existence when certain elements have resorted to arms, in self-defence, rather than die martyrs. So it is today, and any fraternal members who do not turn the other cheek do so according to their own consciences in the full knowledge that ultimately such behaviour will be subject to judgement, as all their actions in this life will be. When these rare circumstances arise, those involved know they will receive no help from other fraternal members; they then stand alone and must face the full consequences of law.

Despite these controversies, the fraternity exists for only two fundamental reasons. They are to protect morality and to ensure it is handed intact from one generation to the next; and, to protect the freedom of all people to choose. For the fraternity, morality is still defined by the seven pivotal virtues identified many centuries ago. Four of these virtues are the primary ones that most civilised people recognise of prudence, temperance, justice and fortitude. The remaining three may be regarded more as theological virtues although they remain as a cornerstone of all fraternal activities. They are Faith, Hope and Charity.

Prudence involves common sense, taking the time and trouble to think through what you are doing and what the consequences are likely to be of actions. Temperance does not mean teetotalism to the fraternity. When it was originally defined, temperance did not refer specifically to drink, but to all pleasures. The intemperate man is one who is excessive in any aspect of life even those who condemn those who enjoy a drink. Justice is the old name for everything we should now call fairness and it includes such matters as honesty, give and take, keeping promises and truthfulness. Fortitude involves courage, facing up to issues, bravery in action, and to stand up for justice, however unpopular this may make one. When combined and the consistent essence of a person, together with faith, hope and charity with genuine compassion and humility, then one begins to come close to an understanding of the nature of the fraternity. It is not at all religious in the usual sense; it is a value system that more importantly is practised rather than being spoken about, visible in men and women's daily behaviour, often irrespective of a particular faith or even regular church attendance.

Some two thousand years ago, a new dispensation was granted. From that time onwards, new men and women appeared. Today, they are all over the Earth and many, but certainly not all, make up the majority of the fraternity. Now and then one will meet one. Their voices and faces are different from ours: they are quieter, happier, stronger and more radiant. They have no need to be needed, having left that temptation way behind. While they may be recognised, you will have to know what to look for.

They will not be outwardly religious or pious and they will certainly not try to convince you of anything. They do not draw attention to themselves and you will tend to think that it is you who is being kind and attentive to them when in fact they are being attentive and kind to you. They love you more than others do, and they love you unconditionally. However, they also need you less and they never judge you as a person. They will appear to have a lot of time just for you, and will be relaxed and calm in this time-driven world. You will probably wonder where all their time comes from and they will appear contented and at peace with themselves and their surroundings, wherever that may be. You will be very much at ease in their company, they will have an openness, be broad minded, often a sharp sense of humour and at ease discussing a wide range of subjects. They are difficult people to surprise and shock; it is as though they have witnessed so much already, both good and bad. Once you have learnt to spot one, it will become easier for you to spot others, but you will still be left wondering whether they are a member of the fraternity or not.

Such individuals also recognise one another instantly and without hesitation or doubt, across the barriers of sex, culture, class, age, colour and even creed. It is, in a sense, as if being on the side of goodness is rather like joining a secret society, but without the need for the clandestine signs and symbols of other secret groups. These people share a common set of values, a shared system of timeless justice, honour, love and obedience.

10

Scenarios of Horror

THE SCENARIOS EMANATING FROM THE FRATERNAL MEETING were broad, yet very specific, covering a range of topics, including health, disease, hunger, social, political, economic, military, environmental, and other elements of global developments. Under the section that attempted to pinpoint threats there was a lengthy section on radicalism. All this information had been carefully encoded by Mark on the encrypted CD for the various fraternal family heads represented at the board meeting.

Radicalism was certainly not new; it had been the primary cause of social, economic and political conflict and other dysfunctions for centuries. Whether it was the radical left with Communism or the radical right with fascism in Europe and the emergence of the Third Reich and the Nazis, the nature of the beast was not new, only the current day forms of such extremism. Moslems are not the only perpetrators of radicalism and extreme intolerance, contrary to much public opinion. There are also radical zealots within the great religions of the West and the East among Christianity, Judaism and Islam on the one hand, and Hunduism, Sikhism, Parsism and Jainism on the other.

Then there are the primal religions where, for some two hundred and fifty million people living today, in many small-scale pre-literate societies, they practice ancient beliefs handed down by word of mouth from one generation to the next. Small-scale ethnic societies are spread across the globe, and include the tribal hill peoples of China, India and parts of south-east Asia, the islanders of Papua New Guinea, the Inuit of Canada and Siberia, the Indians of South and Central America, and the hundreds of ethnic groups spread across the huge continent of Africa.

Intolerance has characterised the monolithic religions of the West more than the great religions of the East, although if one looks closely enough, the distortion of the teachings and beliefs of all these religious traditions has occurred across the centuries by fanatical and misdirected men and women, wishing to challenge the established order either by peaceful or violent means.

The different scenarios had been defined according to a number of possible change variables and likely outcomes. Of particular note were the likely triggers for these developments that had been carefully classified.

Distress in many parts of the world together with various economic, political and military factors were fully documented, particularly the geo-political tensions in Iraq, Iran, Pakistan, Sri Lanka, North Korea and parts of the former U.S.S.R. A list of recent attacks and atrocities by the Taliban was included with a detailed commentary of their persistence particularly in Pakistan, Iraq, Sudan and Afghanistan. Recent rumblings among the IRA and the Protestant Paramilitary groups in Ulster were included together with recent developments with other liberation and revolutionary groups around the world. For each of these there was a detailed description of the security authorities involved, military countermeasures and the steps being taken by the legitimate authorities to deal with these groups. In most cases these hot spots had been troublesome for many years and would continue to be so.

With surveillance satellites and space stations orbiting the Earth sending back a wealth of data, meteorological stations monitoring climate, environmental monitoring, telescopes trained on the heavens, and the myriad of secret military eyes and ears, there is almost data overload. How can such a huge flow of data be consistently and accurately interpreted, correlated with other information, and be reliably deployed to screen out imminent dangers and threats? Surprisingly, most of the time, this network of information gathering and interpretation does work exceedingly well, but sadly not with one hundred percent infallibility. From time to time, nuggets of critical intelligence fail to be picked up or interpreted correctly. As a result perhaps the greatest dangers facing civilization today, as it becomes increasingly sophisticated, is the complacency that all this technology engenders and the inevitable likelihood that there will be a failure to spot a vital nugget of crucial information upon which the modern world's very survival may depend.

Epidemics, potential pandemics and a range of other natural and man made disasters had all been monitored, quantified and assessed. The breadth of information under continuous review included natural disasters and the whole controversial matter of global warming and carbon dioxide emissions. The latest research findings of leading international scientists working in areas as diverse as monitoring volcanic activity, seismic research related to earthquakes and ocean bed movements were all summarised and noted. While such events were beyond the control of man the fraternity always played a profound role silently behind the scenes with rescue missions and the provision of medical and after care. Such natural disasters often struck in the poorer regions of the world and made the swift and effective mobilisation of rescue and relief aid, all the more urgent.

They had monitored the whole debate and research findings about global warming even before it had become such 'hot news'. Indeed, in fraternal archives were historical records of weather conditions across the centuries and concrete evidence of the impact of climate on the living conditions of people in various regions of the world. Early missionaries travelling to far off places had provided a wealth of information about all manner of things, including local climate and seasons. These purveyors of Christianity had travelled to places largely beyond the gaze of Europe and in doing so opened up a window to the world, gathering scientific information and contributing to man's broader understanding of his environment.

For the fraternity, environmentalism, 'space ship earth' and the preservation of species have always been established values and fundamental principles to guide mankind. They passionately believe in the notion of good stewardship of God's creation, a gift to be preserved and protected, to be handed from one generation to the next. Just as morality needed to be preserved from one generation to the next, so too, the richly abundant environment that God has created. We are just passing through and we will leave this earth as we entered it, with no physical possessions.

In the interim, fraternal members believe everyone has a moral obligation, irrespective of creed, to respect and preserve the natural environment. The efficient use of the earth's scarce resources, especially energy, water, productive land and even the thin layer of atmosphere that circles the earth that sustains all terrestrial life, are God given resources to be used properly and equitably. So notions of energy efficiency, conservation and the protection of the environment have always be keystones of fraternal values and behaviour.

The current hysteria about global warming, whether in fact this is true in the greater scheme of things and whether the activities of man are leading to sudden irreversible changes in climate are of equal concern to the fraternity. However, there is scepticism about much of the claimed science behind some of the predictions and claims by politicians and other vested interests that this is all some new way that mankind should start behaving. For the fraternity, mankind should have always behaved in a more responsible and caring manner toward the environment. To them this is a non negotiable, so there is a certain bemusement among those responsible for these matters in fraternal circles. Pollution, a range of emissions from industry, the poisoning of rivers and the oceans are just a few of the terrible symptoms of man's greed, irresponsibility and his very short term perspective on life. Irrespective of whether we are to enter an ice age or large swathes of the earth are to become deserts, the fraternity fully support the need to reduce carbon dioxide and other emissions and finding clean energy solutions. They see this as part of responsible stewardship of the earth rather than some urgent human directed and controlled disaster management exercise.

Their current position on global warming might be that 'the jury is still out' and that man still does not properly understand the full complexity of this issue. Energy is an essential driver of economic growth and the equitable distribution of resources so they view clean energy technologies as a matter requiring urgent attention. Demographics and the growth of global population they view with equal importance to the many theories of global warming. The balance between human demand and what the earth can properly provide while sustaining the environment for future generations is where the fraternity place most of their attention, at the moment, in this area.

All these matters and potential threats are viewed as being medium if not longer term within the various fraternal scenarios that are continually being refined, updated and reviewed. For the moment their attention is focused on more immediate and quantifiable threats to human civilisation.

It was, however, two particular items that were of special concern to John and his son, Mark. First was a lengthy analysis of various apocalyptic cults that were active in various locations across the world, many of them concealed and highly secretive. The second was a review of possible specific threats to the sophisticated infrastructure of many Western developed countries and regions including Europe, the U.S.A., various South American countries, Australia, New Zealand, Japan, Malaysia, large parts of India, Russia, parts of modern China and Scandinavia. All these countries had very similar vulnerabilities.

Human history is littered with the carnage inflicted by dictators and psychotic men and women. Power, from any source, has also corrupted so many. Among these have been a number of zealots, people who have had an obsession about unimaginable things, such as the end of the world, plagues, intervention of supernatural forces, world domination and interference in human affairs by extraterrestrial life. In many cases, such people and their small bands of followers are rightfully regarded merely as crackpots and generally harmless enough. However, in some other instances, such insanity had captured the imagination of large numbers of people, even in recent so-called enlightened times, such as when the Nazis gained sufficient credence and popularity to actually believe themselves to be a master race, with authority to impose their will on the world. Such insanity led to the death of sixty million people in the 1939 to 1945 war, just a few years ago, and the murder of millions of people simply because they were Jewish, mentally slow, travellers or crippled.

The tipping point from being a few harmless crackpots to becoming a destructive force with the potential of threatening modern civilisation had always been one of the critical signs of danger that the fraternity monitored. The item on this topic in the confidential scenario documents alarmed both John and Mark.

There was clear evidence of two particular apocalyptic groups and that their affairs were changing and taking on a very sinister appearance. One particular group was a cult that traced its roots back to the extreme Anabaptists of the fifteen hundreds, under the dictatorial leadership of a reclusive American billionaire that had been successfully recruiting significant numbers of followers on the Internet. Mark had been monitoring various reports of their secret activities and had contributed information to this particular section of the scenario review and he had also expressly drawn his father's attention to this information.

What had disturbed Mark was a series of secret papers, audio tapes and a video recording that had been handed to a Jesuit Friar in Boston in the U.S.A. by a disaffected member of the cult, whose body was subsequently discovered in a drainage ditch in a remote area just off the Interstate Highway. This information had been captured via secure software, encrypted and sent to Mark. It revealed the distorted, obsessive and insane diatribes of an extremely unstable person. There was visual evidence of various rituals and the almost slavish adherence to his commands by a group of about forty members of the cult, who could be seen in the footage. There were grotesque images of both young men and women being ritually mistreated in some twisted form of cleansing ceremony amidst images of long corridors, heavy reinforced doors and many cell doors. Although the soundtrack of the video was of a poor quality, the music appeared repetitive and appeared to be directed toward their leader, it was a chanting sound that mesmerised the assembled followers. A theme that appeared several times in these scraps of information was the fanatical ranting both by the leader and various high ranking followers of some special authority they appeared to believe they had to accelerate the end of the world.

A small group of young saboteurs who had tried to attack the tallest building in Montreal, some years previously, Mark found from his research, had been suspected of being members of this cult. Sadly this was never proved since they all died mysteriously while in captivity after being arrested. Together with the range of secret information about the practices, rituals and teachings of the cult leaders, there was also some video footage of a compound. In the background of some of the shots it was possible to make out large display pin boards in some of the larger rooms with different maps, drawings and other information. On one of these display boards was a map of France with what appeared to be various nuclear power stations clearly marked. Paris had a red circle around it with an arrow pointing into the centre. There were also other plans and materials pinned to various wallboards including what appeared to be electricity transmission diagrams, airport layouts and even an aerial view of what appeared to be the Panama Canal.

The other group that had attracted Mark's attention was a group of fanatical Christian fundamentalists in Japan, a small splinter group that had broken away from a highly respected Protestant community just outside Tokyo. It was the Pastor of this congregation who had alerted their international Chapter with serious misgivings of the activities of this small group, and this had led to their initial identification by the authorities. Two years earlier this small group of extremists had been suspected of a number of computer attacks on some sensitive installations in Japan. None of the suspected offenders were ever brought to justice, largely due to the lack of hard evidence and the highly sophisticated way in which these cyber attacks had been planned and executed. For some months three members of this group had been under close surveillance by the Tokyo special police, but they suddenly vanished and it was suspected they had gone into hiding. They identified themselves in these computer attacks with a highly refined and obscure computer language symbol and this had enabled Mark to link them to the American cult. There was now firm evidence via special Internet monitoring and some of the American cult video footage that in at least one spot on the pin boards this software language sign had been written with a tick alongside. With the assistance of a friend at Cambridge and with the discrete use of a large university computer, Mark had been able to break various obscure computer languages to demonstrate clearly that these two groups were now in regular contact and were collaborating.

John had also recently read a confidential thesis by a distinguished sociologist that postulated certain theories based on a range of evidence about a fracturing of social order in rich countries. It drew attention to a rapidly expanding underclass of poorly educated, often illiterate, people who were frequently unemployed and due to economic and other circumstances living a life ever more on the fringes of society. From a detailed study of this group, that existed in most developed countries, it had been shown that a significant percentage of people who could be described as marginalised were also dependent on state support, many had various degrees of mental disorder ranging from being anti-social, maladjusted to psychotic, and there was an exceptionally high usage of medication and anti-psychotic drugs. Alcohol, combined with street drugs, was frequently abused by large numbers, with violence and criminal behaviour being persistent defining characteristics. There was clear evidence of an ever-expanding number of alienated, poor and often antisocial young people whose needs were being mismanaged by mainstream society and the prosperous.

This report also contained a wealth of statistics and other information describing trends in prescription drug use among very large numbers of the citizens of the rich nations. The figures clearly showed an explosion in the use of what could be described as behavioural medications, uppers and downers, prescribed by doctors faced with a rising barrage of socio-psychological disorders. While there are many genuine mental illnesses that require professional treatment and medication— and these cases were on the increase— what struck John was the huge increase in regular chronic drug use for the non-psychotic disorders such as anxiety, depression, mild obsessions, phobic states, stress and even digestive disorders. Even within that sector of the prosperous population of the world that could be regarded as normal and healthy, there were huge numbers of people regularly taking various forms of mood changing medications simply to get through their day. This usage ranged right across all spectrums of society from the professions such as doctors themselves, dentists, accountants, and engineers to the skilled people working in computing, technicians and trades people. No sectors of the economies of the rich countries were immune from this creeping and often invisible drug use.

John wondered whether some of these continuing trends within rich world societies could perhaps create internal social stresses leading to trouble. Certainly the underclass was already showing itself to be a major problem with increased violence, rape and other antisocial behaviour, particularly in urban areas. However, the use of prescription drugs on such a massive scale was, perhaps, even more worrying. Since the 1980s, the whole world, and especially the developed countries, had enjoyed consistent economic growth and rising levels of prosperity. History had already demonstrated many times that these golden periods also had led to excesses and abuses that in some instances had also been the very ingredients that had catapulted mankind into trouble, conflicts and then long periods of darkness.

What will happen if the global economy goes into a marked recessionary period with rising unemployment, he wondered. *The rich countries also have an ageing population and rapidly rising health care burdens to deal with. Will these medications that appear to be holding much of the fabric of modern society together always be freely available to everyone? What dependencies are being created among millions of citizens? Will some people have access to them and others not, in the future, and what will the social consequences be?* The question in John's mind that was of particular concern was the matter of social shocks and how these people would cope. Physical elements such as steel, wood or concrete, if they are put under sufficient stress, will eventually break. So too with societies, but unlike physical matter, societies are living entities, they are dynamic with many constituents all either working together with some level of cohesion or pulling apart and destroying itself. Society, unlike some physical materials, has the added capability of being able to rapidly self-destruct.

John pondered these disturbing matters that even within the very body of modern society there are many disconcerting elements and trends that could destabilise, pose a threat and destroy.

The thesis for the scenario exercise concluded with dire conclusions that these social trends needed to be addressed without delay; otherwise, hugely disruptive consequences could arise. John had also been struck by the suffering of those people increasingly living on the fringes of mainstream society and the almost callous disregard the majority of people had for their plight. There was also the threat that such an ever-growing army of fringe citizens could present. Although the circumstances and details are different, certain similarities to earlier periods of history were indisputable.

11

Ploughshares to Weapons

THE OTHER ITEM, UNTIL NOW UNRELATED, WAS A REPORT by a utilities engineer in Germany who had studied the inherent security risks of utilities and other infrastructures that are the backbone of civilised and ordered urban life for millions of the world's citizens. He had deliberately chosen to consider a host of things that many take for granted and that are also ordinarily benign yet essential for daily living. His focus adopted a different perspective, an unthinkable yet entirely possible reality. Many things in the modern world have a duality, on the one hand peaceful and constructive; yet, these same things can also be deployed to destroy and kill. This had been perfectly demonstrated when two commercial airliners had been hijacked and instantly converted to weapons of mass destruction bringing down two of the great icons of the modern era, the Twin Towers in lower Manhattan.

Modern urban life is highly dependent on an increasing range of technology and infrastructure that is there to sustain us. Much of this infrastructure is rarely obvious to the general public and has become so reliable that people naturally take it for granted. These aspects of life are also the last place that security authorities would think to look for threats. Yet, millions of those who live in the rich world have come to forget just how fragile this modern world actually is.

Much of this information must for necessity remain secret and confidential. Only a little of its nature may be disclosed here for the purpose of authenticity of this story. Some of this knowledge must certainly never be made available to the general public and certainly not in the form of the full analysis that had been provided for the fraternity. What particularly concerned John and Mark and certain other members of the fraternity was that there is already much of this potentially sensitive information that does not have restricted access. Many of the authorities that are the guardians of this information are also seemingly unaware of the potential risks that exist from the misuse or deliberate disruption of these essential services.

What the fraternity had gone on to do was to collect further intelligence related to this matter, subject it to rigorous analysis and then expose the results to a disciplined probability review. A terrifying range of possibilities had been revealed, even including a number of robust doomsday scenarios for the developed world.

They were in the process of converting this huge amount of information into useable knowledge, and had drawn out some early conclusions just a little time before the Paris atrocity. The French maps showing Paris with a red circle around it in the cults compound is what had led the fraternity to brief Archbishop Guggar to confidentially alert the French authorities that something sinister was afoot. Although at that stage precise intelligence was not available, had the French authorities responded by raising the level of alert among the Paris police and other security agencies, perhaps the attack might have been spotted sooner, the ready mix concrete trucks identified and disarmed and some of the perpetrators caught. Certainly the magnitude of the attack could have been curtailed; the concrete vehicles could have been pulled over by the traffic police immediately when the first suspicions were raised. In the event no one suspected anything, it was just another ordinary spring day in Paris and the surprise factor had played perfectly into the hands of the perpetrators.

High-speed trains travelling at over two hundred kilometres per hour throughout many parts of world; air traffic control systems navigating and guiding thousands of large civilian aircraft over cities twenty-four hours a day;

computerised control systems for traffic speeding along busy motorways; underground rail systems beneath many large cities; water purification and distribution systems to millions of homes; health and safety assurance for much of the food and pharmaceutical products we consume daily; radiation monitoring for radio and other high level transmitters; numerous emissions from factories; agricultural pesticides, especially those sprayed from low-flying aircraft; the dangerous pollutants from petrochemical plants, often located dangerously near to high density urban areas.

These and many more elements of the finely tuned modern world had come under scrutiny.

The accident at the Chernobyl Nuclear plant some years earlier had already alerted the world to the implicit dangers of nuclear power. France, generating much of its electricity from nuclear generation plants, is particularly vulnerable. However, extreme danger lurks in so many places elsewhere. Electricity transmission and distribution networks that stretch over thousands of kilometres unguarded and unprotected are highly vulnerable. With the right knowledge such networks can be swiftly paralysed, aided by the automatic protection devices that shut these systems down, within minutes, to protect them from serious overloading. If planned and executed properly, such attacks can also ensure that these supply networks remain inoperable for long periods. Even when such highly sophisticated technical supply infrastructure "goes down" periodically through normal problems, it can take many hours or even days to synchronise all the power generators to come back safely onto the grid. This manipulation of thousands of volts of electricity across thousands of miles of territory is also ordinarily carried out through an intricate system of remote control devices that are now largely computerised. Take control of these computer networks and you have control of vast power stations, transmission lines and the potentially lethal energy they convey.

Imagine losing the national electricity grids in several countries all at the same time and being without electricity for a sustained period of time. Imagining this nightmare, just briefly, provides a little insight to the type of possible scenarios that John and Mark were now confronted with. Electricity has become essential to modern life and whole towns, cities and countries would simply cease to operate without it. Without electricity there would be no light at night, no hot water, TV, road traffic lights, life support equipment in hospitals, refrigeration plant would stop, whole computer and communication networks would be unable to operate. The list of almost instant impacts is comprehensive and dire. Emergency services, police, hospitals and fire fighting services would be reduced to confusion. Even those special premises with emergency back-up power supplies would only be able to operate at greatly reduced levels. Many emergency back-up systems rely on batteries that are replenished from the national grid. These would quickly dissipate. Those with standby generating plants need fuel to drive them. With no grid electricity at oil refineries, many would be forced to quickly shut down to avoid further perils. Television broadcast would become sporadic and many with television receivers would be unable to receive the signals. Other telecommunication systems would quickly collapse or at best be seriously disrupted. Cell phone networks might still be able to provide a limited service where photovoltaic electricity supplies are being used, although the major transmitters still require large quantities of grid-supplied power. Cellular telephone networks would also rapidly become overloaded, making cell phones useless.

Such dislocation for a day would wreak havoc. However, such dislocation for a week would become a national disaster of huge proportions, with food rotting in warehouses, electric pumps to provide clean water and handle effluent falling silent, and people isolated, alone and afraid in their dark homes. The streets would be dark. There would already be social disorder, the looting of shops, crimes unreported. Mortuaries would cease to be able to operate, as would many hospitals, prisons and other public facilities. The authorities would have few functioning resources with which to attempt to manage a rapidly deteriorating situation.

After just a week, such a situation would be degenerating into total chaos and life threatening, first to the weak and vulnerable and then to the general population. People would start starving to death, unable to get fresh food, sickness would start appearing as proper sanitation completely fails and the survival of the fittest would begin to prevail. If such dislocations occurred in a synchronised way across several developed countries at once, there would be little external help available. Indeed, such sudden upheavals could even destabilise the fragile peace that exists between various nationalities and governments. Countries would laager, feverously attempt to protect their borders and immediately start squabbling over scarce resources. National armies would be withdrawn from the trouble spots around the world to return home to restore order and martial law would be declared.

If these scenarios are bad enough, there are even worse possibilities documented together with how relatively simple such attacks might be. If such a systematic attack was carried out across the developed world, it was estimated that just four hundred and fifty properly trained and equipped fanatics, working in strategically deployed secret cells, could execute such an insane scenario. In a matter of hours, what had taken centuries to build could be brought to its knees. No more would need to be done since towns, cities and whole countries would simply implode on themselves. They would drown, suffocate, starve and tear themselves apart without the essential lifeblood provided by so many essential services.

This self-destructive process could also be accelerated and made even more lethal. If executed in the northern hemisphere in the winter, the freezing temperatures across American, Canada, Scandinavia, Northern Europe, Russia and China could also be leveraged to inflict swift and maximum carnage. The natural cycle of the seasons and the weather together with many other natural phenomena could also play a destructive role. The very things man had come to tame could be unleashed again. If the pumps stopped in parts of Holland, for example, vast areas would become flooded.

Natural gas that is transported in huge quantities through extensive transmission pipelines across whole continents, as with electricity supply, is also vulnerable. Gas supplies can be disrupted via the pressure stations along the length of underground pipelines and the sophisticated remote telemetry that enables the careful control of flow rates and pressures, to those with the necessary technical and computer knowledge. Gas supplies can be rapidly terminated and disabled for weeks by just a few carefully targeted and orchestrated attacks. Many countries around the modern world depend on huge volumes of natural gas every day to heat homes, hospitals, and public buildings and to provide a range of essential thermal energy services. In hotter countries such as Australia and the Middle East, natural gas provides cooling and air conditioning in the hot summer months. This energy infrastructure and the sophisticated technology that it drives provides carefully controlled and comfortable environments for millions of people every month of the year. Without these services many would simply perish, freeze to death or die of heatstroke; first the elderly, the young and the infirm, and then others. Some fifty-five thousand people had perished in France over a few days when there had been a heat wave a few years earlier, so the human devastation from such a scenario is clear to see.

The list of these types of threats appalled John and Mark, especially in view of the confluence of intelligence that was emerging, about the activities of the apocalyptic cults, the threats already existing within the fabric of rich societies with the expanding disaffected underclass, and the ever rising tide of prescription drug use to keep many ordinary people functioning. Any of these individual phenomena could suddenly become a trigger, but, when combined, they could send uncontrollable thunderbolts ricocheting around the world. Through the information analysis and interpretation process of the fraternity they had begun to join up the dots and see a bigger, terrifying picture emerge. Not only had they perhaps spotted where such terror may be born and gestated, but they had also started to imagine a whole range of deadly weapons that lay easily within the grasp of such destructive forces. These possible weapons of destruction were also ironically the very lifeblood of the carefully provided secure, convenient and comfortable rich world. They were also the last place our official organs of protection would ever wish to look and take precautions. Could they become the exposed flank of civilisation to unimaginable horrors, John wondered.

III

Life, Love, and Pressing Realities

12

Croatia

JOSEPH HAD MANAGED TO FIND A CONVENIENT FLIGHT for them both from Gatwick, south of London, directly to Zagreb, arriving in the late afternoon. As Louise drove them from Oxford to the airport, one or the other of them would periodically interrupt their conversation by suddenly remembering something or someone they had forgotten to deal with before leaving Oxford. The last forty-eight hours before they left had suddenly become frantically busy. Although it was now late summer and they had enjoyed a break from formal college activities, being research scholars in their disciplines, there still had been plenty to do. Louise had just managed to tie up the remaining arrangements for her final year of academic activity with various professors, and she had also acted as host to her younger brother from Wales for a week, who was looking for accommodation and making other arrangements for when he returned in late August to commence his studies at the university. He had only left the previous day to return to Wales.

Joseph, meanwhile, had also been busy wrapping up various affairs before his final departure from Oxford, planned for a few days after returning from Croatia. When they finally relaxed into their seats on the small Airbus, a favourite with Croatia Airlines, their minds relaxed and they finally knew they were on their way. After putting his seatbelt on, Joseph sat with his mind rapidly slowing as a wave of tiredness passed through his body. At that moment he wanted to relax, think of nothing in particular and aimlessly watch the flight attendants busying themselves with preparing the aircraft for take off. On his lap he had a small travel wallet with his tickets, money, passport and various other bits and pieces and he casually opened it, more to pass the time than anything else, and started to flick through the contents. Something anyone rarely does is to look at his or her own passport, but, there in his hand, lay his open passport. He took a quick look at his photograph, the various stamps of the many destinations he had visited in recent years, and then he read the declaration inside the front cover. It read:

Her Britannic Majesty's secretary of state requests and requires, in the Name of Her Majesty, all those whom it may concern to allow the bearer to pass freely without let or hindrance, and to afford the bearer such assistance and protection as may be necessary.

In all the years he had travelled with his British Passport in his possession, this was the first time he could recall having ever read this declaration. It struck him as quaint, of a past era when Royal Navy gunboats would have sought to retrieve British citizens in peril in foreign lands. It was also rather touching and personal in the sense that this entreaty to allow him to pass freely, without hindrance, was from Her Britannic Majesty herself, and that the secretary of state was a mere servant carrying out her instructions. As a linguist he was struck by the language and as a historian intrigued by days past.

He was shaken out of his ponderous thoughts by Louise who, placing her hand on his knee, suddenly asked, "Joe, what time do we arrive in Zagreb?"

"It's only a short flight, so we should land at four thirty," he replied.

Louise smiled and went back to her magazine.

It was a warm afternoon when they finally emerged from Zagreb airport, following the intensified security checks in place, pushing their baggage trolley and calling for a taxi. Twenty minutes later, through the rush hour traffic, they arrived at the Dubrovnik Hotel situated in the central square just beneath the old town. Joseph knew the city well, having visited a number of times previously, but for Louise it was her first visit to the country. Although she had promised herself an opportunity to read up on the country earlier, she had now arrived having failed to do so, and had only various vague ideas about its history and culture. Joseph was in charge on this occasion, even though Louise never openly admitted the fact.

The holiday plan was to spend the text ten days relaxing and being together, to explore and to share a country with a rich history, friendly people, wonderful architecture, good food and one of the most enchanting coastlines in the whole of the Mediterranean. They would spend the first three days in Zagreb before taking a hire car and diving to Split and then taking a boat to the island town of Hvar, which is one of the sunniest spots on the Adriatic coast. After exploring the island, Joseph then wanted to sail down the coast to the island of Mljet, which he remembered as a place of enchanting beauty with sandy beaches, lakes in a national park and pinewoods. A local legend claims that Mljet was where the beautiful nymph Calypso lived and in Homer's Odyssey seduced Ulysses and held him prisoner for seven years in a cave on the island. There are hundreds of small islands on the Adriatic coast off Croatia, many uninhabited, and Joseph had sailed these waters before with friends, always promising himself a return visit. The last three days of their trip were to be spent in Dubrovnik staying at a luxury hotel where Elizabeth Taylor and Richard Burton had stayed.

After their time in Dubrovnik they were to fly together to Gatwick and on arrival Louise would return directly to Oxford and Joseph to Himbledon Grange for a meeting with his father. The precise arrangements for him going to Paris to assume his responsibilities with Dandler Aggregates had yet to be confirmed, but he anticipated it would be soon after his return to England and final farewell to Oxford.

Zagreb is both old and new with much of the historical old part of the city being the Upper Town— Gornji Grad— and the modern city being in the Lower Town— Donji Grad. Gornji Grad is the site of the original town built in the eleventh century and it has a market place where local farmers sell fresh produce and on the steps leading up to square there are fresh flower sellers. Most of the traders were packing up their stalls when Joseph and Louise arrived. Having eaten on the flight they decided to freshen up and take a walk around the old town. Louise was particularly interested to discover the impact of some thirty-five years of communist rule in a predominantly Catholic country under Tito when it had been Yugoslavia. In 1945, Yugoslavia was established as a Communist state under Tito, with Croatia one of six separate republics.

As they walked among the many old churches, pavement cafés, past the bustle of people hurrying too and fro, Joseph noticed Freddie reading an English newspaper seated in the open air Kamenita Vrata, a popular pizzeria, and they just glanced at each other momentarily, with no further contact as Joseph strolled past arm in arm with Louise. He had noticed Freddie on the same flight into Zagreb, seated at the back, when he rose to open the baggage locker on landing. How had his father known which flight they were on, he wondered, and then realised that Mark had probably set up Freddie's travel itinerary having tracked Joseph's online travel bookings. How had he also managed to get here so quickly and to get through the increased security at the airport carrying a side arm so easily? Seeing Freddie again was both comforting and disconcerting, since it brought back, in a flash, his father's conversation of a few weeks earlier. In the rush before leaving he had also forgotten to take his father's advice to carry his side arm that now remained locked safely in his safe in his Oxford quarters.

There was one particular place that Joseph wanted to show Louise on this initial walk through the old town. It was the church established many centuries before by the Jesuit's that stands today just around the corner from the Croatian parliamentary building that flies the flag of the European Union that they hope to join shortly. Walking past the statue of St. George slaying the Dragon and up though the Kamenita Vrata— Stone Gate— passing the shrine where pilgrims still light candles, they emerged into the square in front of the church.

"This is all so beautiful and quaint," said Louise squeezing Joseph's arm against her body as they entered the small cobbled square.

"Yes, it's a lovely town with so much character and history, but just take a look at this church Louise," replied Joseph as he pushed open the large heavy door and held it for her to enter beside him.

They stepped into a large entrance area and then through more doors into the front of the church. Everything was suddenly silent and it took her a few moments to adjust her eyes to the sudden lack of bright light as she stood looking down the isle with dark wooden stalls on each side, to the altar beyond. It was breathtaking as she stared at the murals, the light streaming in through the stained glass windows, the statues and the huge cross with Jesus nailed to it beside the altar. Joseph and Louise had now become separated within their own thoughts as they wandered around the interior of the empty church. Joseph had blessed himself with the sign of the Cross on entering the church and had walked gently up the aisle to the front of the altar, where he had kneeled leaning on the altar rail, and was praying, occasionally looking up at the Tabernacle.

Standing now in the middle of the church behind Joseph, Louise kept glancing at him, now some distance away, to see what he was up to and she felt strange and rather alone at that moment in such unfamiliar surroundings. Having rarely been inside a church, to suddenly be standing under a painting of John the Baptist in this cool, quiet place, she found rather unnerving. Under her feet she could feel the smoothness of the floor tiles that had in places been worn down by years of worshipping congregations. As she looked up at the stained glass windows, each with pictures of significant people and events, her head began to swim. She leant forward, took hold of one of the pews and gently stepped in and sat down. In comparison with the warmth and bustle moments before outside, by walking through those large heavy church doors, she had been transported in seconds to another world, a very different, almost timeless world containing all these relics and an eerie stillness.

As she sat in the coolness she could see a stream of light falling onto the altar from the stained glass windows high above. She could see a large Bible on a lectern beside the marble altar and candlesticks everywhere. The light also was illuminating the top of Joseph's head and his back as he continued to pray, a solitary figure beneath all this splendour, and she knew instinctively that he was now far away from her, in another world that she did not understand, something she had always scorned. She felt alone looking at Joseph by the altar, that he was different from anyone she had ever known before and a feeling of inadequacy started deep with herself for the first time in her life.

Joseph then stood up, stepped back and genuflected and turned to find Louise. As he walked down the isle toward her, she felt an increasing reassurance as he approached, smiled and sat down next to her. Joseph was surprised when Louise pushed both her hands into his and snuggled up to him silently looking toward the altar. They did not speak and sat in silence. Joseph could feel her body giving the occasional shiver and he sensed her vulnerability.

After a few moments Joseph whispered, "Come on, let's go and warm up outside."

He took her by the hand and walked slowly to the back of the church. Leaving her for a moment he touched the font and blessed himself again and as he turned to reach for her hand again he saw for the first time, a beautiful young woman whose self-assurance and confidence had vanished, she stood looking bewildered and almost afraid. He gently took her hand and escorted her out into the bright evening warmth and they strolled silently across the square, not exchanging a word as he put an arm around her waist. They walked through St. Mark's Square, passed the president's official residence, remaining silent.

"Let's have a drink Louise and rest our legs for a while," Joseph said, calmly guiding them into one of the pavement cafés.

After the waiter had served Joseph a beer and Louise a glass of wine, they continued to sit quietly, Louise deep in thought. Joseph knew this was not the time to be talking as he enjoyed the local beer, and Louise again moved close to him and held his hand. The light was beginning to fade and Joseph reflected on the last hour and what had happened. Coming to Croatia was always to be an opportunity for them to get to know each other, away from a very different life they had enjoyed in Oxford together. This was more Joseph's world than Oxford had ever been and he always enjoyed a feeling of peace and continuity whenever he visited Croatia, despite its recent troubled past. Little had he realised that such a personal exploration of each other would have started so soon.

As they walked back to their hotel gas lamps were being lighted in the age-old manner by a lamp lighter. In their copper frames, the gas lamps gave a gentle, warm light that reflected from the stone walls of the old buildings. It was an enchanting and romantic environment, yet there was a strange distance between them. Louise had become almost sullen and withdrawn, saying little, but continually seeking physical warmth and reassurance from Joseph. On returning to their hotel, they had a light supper of cold meats and local breads that had been left in their suite. Tired after a long and busy day, they retired to bed, and fell asleep in each other's arms.

Sitting facing each other over breakfast, Louise was her happy and confident self again. Joseph did not ask her directly about her behaviour and change of mood the previous evening, but approached it by asking what she thought of the old town. Then as the conversation flowed he asked, "What did you think of the church we went to?"

"It was interesting Joseph, in a fairy tale sort of way, of little relevance to us today, but I can see how it enthralled the uneducated for hundreds of years," Louise replied curtly, her manner becoming defensive.

Joseph nodded and smiled, and thought that perhaps this was not a line of conversation to pursue right now. "Come on then, Louise, if you do not want any more coffee, let's get our things; there is a wonderful bookshop I want to show you."

Underneath the hotel Dubrovnik there is a long established bookshop and they indulged themselves for a long time paging through various editions of this and that. Louise bought an inexpensive travel guide to Croatia since she felt the need to quickly catch up with Joseph's knowledge of the place and at least have some influence on the next nine days. Beneath the old town is a bustling modern city with large department stores, fashion shops and ice cream sellers on every corner. After leaving the bookstore they wandered among the modern shops, dodging the trams as they crossed to explore more and more shop windows.

"Come, I need to buy a new swimsuit for the islands," Louise said as she noticed a ladies fashion shop.

"Oh, all right. What, in here?" enquired Joseph, as Louise took his hand and led him through the circular doors.

The next hour was spent with Louise investigating a range of ladies fashions. She touched and felt the texture of all manner of clothes, not just swimwear. After the initial few minutes Joseph realised this was not to be a quick activity and had patiently taken to sit in a deep armchair to respond periodically with Louise asking him his opinion about various colours, styles, what suited her and what did not. He opened the latest edition of *The Economist* he had bought at the bookshop and occupied himself with some recent news from around the world.

Louise then appeared again with a handful of clothing.

"Come, Joseph, I want to try these on, come and tell me what you think," Louise enquired looking at the sales assistant who had a knowing smile.

"Will that be all right, men in the ladies changing rooms?" retorted Joseph.

"Yes, of course it is," replied Louise, handing some of the clothes to Joseph.

Everything Louise had selected looked perfect on her. She had a figure that flattered everything she wore. Gradually they worked through various dresses, slacks and other apparel with Louise turning and adjusting each garment as she stared at herself in the long wall mirrors. The changing booths were large with doors with a bolt. Each had an armchair and single chair. Joseph had been placed in the armchair for his opinion. Among the possible purchases, Louise had also picked out some footwear and some high-heeled shoes. Two sets of clothes were being selected, those items that would be purchased were hung on one of the wall hooks and another bunch of clothes being systematically rejected and placed over the back of the armchair where Joseph was sitting.

So far so good, thought Joseph, who was now becoming a little eager to move on from ladies fashions to other interesting sites in Zagreb.

Louise had deliberately kept the best to the end as she now turned to a small pile of swimsuits and the high-heeled shoes she had selected.

"Thanks, Joe for being so patient, not much longer," Louise said as she slipped from the summer dress she had just tried on and by mutual agreement discarded over the back of his chair. She then slipped from her underwear and stood naked, without any hint of embarrassment, and with her back to Joseph slipped off her walking shoes. Joseph looked up at her and he admired her beauty. Her blond hair fell about her shoulders, dishevelled from putting on so many clothes. She appeared strong, fit and alluring before him. Slipping on a pair of high-heeled shoes she then tried on various costumes ranging from full swimming costumes to skimpy bikinis, and as she did so with every change she was becoming more teasing and provocative. They were both giggling and a swimsuit, a dark blue bikini, was selected since it suited her perfectly.

Just then there was a loud knock on the cubicle door from the saleslady, there had been a sudden rush of customers and other ladies were waiting to try on garments and the cubicle was needed. The second knock on the door brought Joseph and Louise to their senses and they looked at each other sheepishly and burst out laughing. Turning, Louise looked up at Joseph and kissed him on the cheek.

"Come darling, this is hardly the place to be naughty, someone might come in," Louise said, giggling, but in a matter-of-fact way. Joseph stood there wondering what had just happened and how natural and unashamed it had been.

With a clutch of shopping bags between them they wandered back to the hotel with a renewed air of closeness between them. They deposited the shopping in their suite and as it was now early afternoon decided to have a light meal in the hotel bistro on the second floor looking out over the square below. They checked their cell phones that had been charging, cleared their various messages and then sat in the lounge reading. Louise became more fascinated as she read about the history of Croatia in her guidebook. She had never really understood the dreadful conflicts that had recently taken place in this region and had this fixed idea that it was all because of religion and ethnic conflicts. This was partly true, but she was curious about the relationship particularly between Communism and Catholicism since Croatia evidently remained a predominantly Roman Catholic country, at least among the ethnic Croats.

Louise had been brought up by her free thinking Welsh parents in the small town of Aberystwyth on the west coast of Wales. Her father was a professor of law at the university college, one of four colleges that made up the University of Wales. The college dominated the life of the small town. Her mother, also an academic, was a fiercely independent free spirit who had dabbled in several alternative belief systems and various New Age philosophies. As Louise had grown older she had gradually come to know of the openness of her parent's relationship and the discreet promiscuity of her mother. Her father, embroiled in his world of academia, was an acknowledged and distinguished writer, lecturer, tutor and consultant on legal matters. He was some years older than Louise's mother and was a rather reclusive and self-absorbed person. It was natural in these circumstances for Louise to have been heavily influenced by her mother. Notions of free will, lack of guilt, female independence, self-fulfilment, personal pleasure and the pursuit of amorous affairs largely defined her mother. A few months before going up to Oxford, Louise had also discovered that her mother had also a proclivity for lesbian as well as heterosexual affairs.

Both of Louise parents were atheists; they rejected all notions of a superior being regarding all religious practices as fairy tales created by man over the centuries. They mixed with other non-believers and so-called free thinkers, embroiled in a world of what they regarded as rational modern thought. Her mother, a sociologist, could fully explain and justify her contempt for religious beliefs and could talk at length about various human conflicts and suffering that had resulted from religious bigotry. Guilt was a favourite topic, how various churches had enslaved their members with completely false and damaging feelings of personal guilt among followers. No one should feel guilt was the maxim, unless it related to the deliberate damage of others or the destruction of the environment. Personal freedom, the right to choose and pacifism were also important matters and they believed in libertarian notions of conscience.

Perhaps, Louise thought for a moment, she could find something here in Croatia to counter such arguments that she had been exposed to since her earliest childhood. There had been little influence in her life until meeting Joseph to make her seriously question the ideas and beliefs she had learnt at the feet of her parents.

Reading about Croatia she discovered that near Zagreb evidence of early man had been discovered in caves dated circa 30,000 B.C. In the sixth century trading had taken place in Hvar and in 305 A.D. the Roman Emperor, Diocietan, had completed his palace at Split. Then in the seventh century Slav tribes from Poland and the Ukraine migrated to the Balkans and a group known as the Croats settled in Dalmatia and Slavonia. In more recent times, since Croatia declared independence from Yugoslavia in 1991, there had been dreadful conflicts in the region. Croatian Serbs established the Republic of the Serbian Krajina and drove many Croats from their villages with the assistance of the Yugoslav army. The first mention of ethnic cleansing originated at this time and conflicts broke out with bloody sieges of Vukovar and Dubrovnik. In 1995, the Erdut Agreement ended the war with Serbia following Operation Storm when Serbian rebels were evicted and there was a massive exodus of refugees into Bosnia and Serbia.

Louise suddenly shuddered to think that even Dubrovnik, where they were going in just a few days, was under bloody siege just a few very short years earlier. *How we take our freedom so much for granted*, she thought. *A given that will always be there with thoughts that, while there may be conflict elsewhere in the world, most of Europe, and particularly Britain, remains immune, secure and away from it all.*

Joseph was well through a book he had brought from Oxford. It had lain amongst his papers for weeks and he had never managed to get the time to open it, much less to explore its contents. It was an unusual book, quite rare, since it promised an expose of *Opus Dei*, the religious organisation of the Catholic Church, an organisation apparently shrouded in secrecy and mystery. Since Joseph's uncle Luke, who lived in Rome, was a member of *Opus Dei* and Joseph, although not a member, knew quite a lot about the organisation, he was intrigued to know how such a book would read. There had been much speculation, controversy and incorrect information about the organisation for years in the popular press. They appeared to have become associated also with other misrepresented aspects of Roman Catholicism.

Opus Dei in Latin simply means 'the work of God', and, although the organisation is influential within the church and it is discreet about its activities, it is certainly not secret. Members do have to be obedient to certain practices, and dedicate themselves to the teachings of Christ. This spiritual organisation was started in Spain in 1928 by Saint Josemaria Escriva, who focussed on the sanctification of work and the belief that people can find God through their daily work, whatever it may be. Lawyers, engineers, clerks and road sweepers can all lead spiritual lives providing their work is undertaken with the correct spirit and offered to God. To achieve this, members undergo intensive doctrinal and spiritual formation and lead highly disciplined lives saying the Rosary, visiting the Blessed Sacrament and other acts of worship every day.

Opus Dei has been accused of being overly traditional and conservative yet it has members who are liberal in their views. Despite the core observances by *Opus Dei* members, it has grown to become a large organisation with tens of thousands of followers and houses across the world, and it contains many divergent opinions among its members. Some *Opus Dei* members, a minority, still wear the 'cilice', a barbed chain, around their thigh for two hours a day and the organisation still refuses to divulge details of members. These aspects plus the accusation by some that Opus Dei is a secret organisation obsessed with power and secrecy, has become dangerously misleading and has obscured the real purpose of the organisation. This is simply the practice of a belief that redemption of humanity must come largely through laymen and women sanctifying their daily work and reforming the secular world from inside. A holy life is, therefore, not the special domain of the religious, but is there for everyone to exemplify through work and daily relationships with others. Thus, ordinary activities and relationships take on an entirely different meaning and significance to members of *Opus Dei*, eternal qualities far removed from the secular world we all experience. It is a profound and very powerful reality to those who belong to this organisation and its members live among us, tending our towns, doing our tax submissions and even fixing our teeth.

Joseph was jolted from his reading by a text message on his cell phone. It was from his elder brother Paul who had been competing in one of the major tennis tournaments in the U.S.A., asking Joseph to phone him. Paul was now nearing the end of his professional tennis career since he had been on the international circuit for some years. He had won a number of clay court tournaments in Europe and the U.S.A., but had always failed to get closer than the quarters of Roland Garos and Wimbledon. He was also regarded as the mystery man of tennis and the media had long since given up trying to report on him, apart from his tennis. He had become adept at brushing aside those incidents when strangers recognised him by graciously responding, "Yes, I know I look like him, he is my double, and you know we all have one."

Joseph rose from his chair and walked into an empty area of the hotel and phoned Paul.

"Hi Paul, how are you," Joseph asked.

"Hi there, Joe. I am great, thanks. So how is Croatia? I believe you are there with this new lady friend of yours," replied Paul.

"It is great to be back here Paul and the weather is good. Yeah, Louise is her name and we met at Oxford. We are having a great time and it is good to be away for a while," replied Joseph.

"Yeah, I can quite imagine that with all this trouble in Paris. I did not even bother to go there this year since Roland Garos was cancelled of course, so came straight to the States. I should be finishing up here in a few days and will then be back in London. When will you be at Himbledon again, Joe? Mother didn't quite know when I spoke to her earlier. Thought it time we have some golf together," said Paul.

"It should be in nine days time when we get back from Croatia. I am going straight to Himbledon for a meeting with Father, so perhaps we can get together then; what do you think?" asked Joseph.

"Yeah that sounds a strong possibility, I will call you again nearer the time and confirm. Take care of yourselves over there and God bless," Paul responded, now bringing the conversation to a close.

"You too Paul and thanks for the call," Joseph clicked the End Call button on his phone.

As he walked back into the lounge, Louise uncurled herself from the armchair, stood up and stretched and yawned. "Come on Joseph, we had better get ready for supper, it's getting late. Who was that on the phone?" she asked.

"Yeah, okay. It was Paul, my brother who is in the States, about a game of golf sometime," replied Joseph as they strolled hand in hand through the lounge into the hotel lobby and waited for the lift.

It was another glorious evening in Zagreb as they strolled up into the upper town, across the marketplace and into the square in front of the Cathedral. Joseph gently led Louise as they walked and talked together up stairs, in between market stalls, around corners, down cobbled lanes and then into the square. Just on the left there was an entrance under an archway that lead to Baltazar, a traditional restaurant in a lovely courtyard. As they were led to a table tucked away under the vines by the waiter Louise was enchanted with the place. They talked late into the evening as Louise disclosed much about herself, her family, life in a small Welsh seaside town before going up to Oxford, and her passion for her law research that she had inherited from her father. In the meantime, Joseph had shared many humorous stories about the family and himself. It was an intimate, gentle yet exciting evening as they explored each other.

Next morning after breakfast standing outside the hotel Joseph hailed a taxi.

"Where are we going?" enquired Louise.

"You will see, just wait a little while longer. Anyway, if I tell you, you will not wish to go," replied Joseph.

The taxi journey did not take long as it climbed the hills above the city. Suddenly they had arrived beside a high wall with green cupolas on top and the Mirogoj Cemetery. Joseph paid the taxi driver and he led Louise by the hand as they walked across to the impressive entrance, into yet another world, peaceful and still apart from the many tourists walking quietly around. Just inside the main gates there were long arcades on either side with statues, tombs and many impressive monuments to the earlier generations of Croatia. The cemetery had been designed by Hermann Bolle, who had also been involved with the impressive Cathedral situated opposite where Joseph and Louise had eaten the evening before. In the grounds of the cemetery there are many tombstones with Catholic, Orthodox, Muslim and Jewish graves side by side. There are also some tombstones with the five-point Communist star that, altogether with the others, provide an eclectic statement about the inescapable reality of death, whoever you may be. While not the most cheerful of tourist sites, Joseph had wanted Louise to at least come and see this place, to experience the peace within and the fascinating monuments.

As they walked gently around the cemetery reading various inscriptions on the graves, Joseph often translated them for Louise. As their time there progressed Louise became quieter and increasingly sad. In contrast, Joseph regarded all this as a mere reality of living and in no way depressing. Without death there can be no life and death is never to be feared, these were deeply held beliefs of Joseph, so for him a visit to this place was completely natural and in no way alarming. In contrast, faced with so much black stone, silent statues, rotting flowers and the warm silence, Louise was unable to easily witness these many tombstones.

Joseph noticed tears on Louise's cheeks as she stood silently beside him as he translated an inscription on a child's tombstone. He instantly realised that Louise was vulnerable again, she reached with both of her hands his hands and asked if they could leave now. She was demure, clearly afraid and troubled. They walked toward the gates and Louise nuzzled her head under Joseph's arm on his chest as he held her around the waist. They were soon outside again into the bustle of tourist buses and taxi's and Joseph asked her if they should walk back down to the town below and she agreed.

It was early the next morning as Joseph drove the hire car out of Zagreb to pick up the highway to Karlovac and then onto Split when Louise started to talk again. She felt she owed Joseph an explanation for her behaviour the previous evening when she had refused to go with him to a local jazz club for their final night in Zagreb. They had spent the evening apart, Louise reading in the hotel room and Joseph had gone to evening Mass at the Cathedral. After Mass he had spoken to the celebrating priest and asked if he knew anyone at Split to hire a sailing boat or to get a couple of berths to sail between the islands. As coincidence would have things sometimes, this priest's younger brother, Franjo, lived in Hvar and was involved with boat charters and would certainly assist Joseph if he made contact on arrival. Joseph took Franjo's contact details and thanked the priest before wandering back to the hotel. By the time he had returned, Louise was asleep

As he carefully avoided the tramways and trams in the early morning traffic bustle of Zagreb he sensed that Louise was troubled and he made it easy for her to talk, saying there was no need to apologise and he had also been tired and anyway had also been happy to retire early.

"Stop being so nice and charming all the time, Joe; you have it all so bloody together all the time, I sometimes wonder if you are actually human," blurted Louise.

Joseph knew something of the sort was coming, but had

been taken aback by the suddenness of her outburst. Louise then started to cry and sob uncontrollably, so Joseph immediately pulled over and guided the car into an empty bay in front of a dreary apartment block on the outskirts of Zagreb.

"What is the matter, Louise; why have I upset you? I am sorry; please do not cry," said Joseph, leaning over and putting an arm around her shoulders as he wiped away the tears from her face.

Louise pushed his hand away, embarrassed by this uncontrollable collapse of her protective public face. "I am all right Joseph, don't fuss," she replied tersely. "It is just that I do not often think of death and I don't know why you had to take me to that graveyard yesterday. It was so depressing and we are supposed to be on holiday. You seem to enjoy all these morbid things, rather like that church you took me into on our first night here, and that silly Bible you read so often, it is all nonsense Joe, silly superstitions, once we are dead we are dead and that is that and I do not want to be continually reminded. There is no one looking after us apart from ourselves, there is also no scientific proof for all these fairy tales and I would have thought an intelligent man like you would know that."

Louise suddenly stopped talking, wiped the tears from her eyes and looked imploringly into Joseph's eyes. Joseph was struck how the torrent of words had seemed somehow to be trying to reassure Louise herself, rather than challenge him. For the first time since he had met her, Joseph could see real fear in her face, an anguish and confusion. He leant forward again and smiled gently, quickly gathering his thoughts. He knew this was not an attack on him personally, but a response by Louise to perhaps having to confront issues that many just wish to forget about, leave until another day or simply dispute.

He felt a deep sense of sympathy for Louise in her vulnerable state of mind as she fumbled to reach for his hand that lay by her side and sought some sort of physical reassurance that she had not hurt him in any way by her outburst. There was a torrent of information flowing backwards and forwards between them and much of it was unspoken.

Joseph remained calm, caring and silent, waiting patiently for Louise to calm herself and stop crying. Then he said reassuringly, "That's all right Louise, don't worry, I am not going anywhere and I am sorry to have been so thoughtless – yes, I suppose you are right, viewed in a certain way those places are not the happiest of spots to go to on holiday. But you know darling, you must not be fearful of death, and let's trust that it is anyway far off for both of us. I promise no more cemeteries for the rest of the time we are here, I promise."

There was a short period of silence as they hugged each other and Louise straightened herself in the car seat, smiled awkwardly, and busied herself with her handbag.

It was some minutes later when they had left Zagreb far behind that Louise started to speak again. "You're not angry with me, are you, Joseph?" she asked.

"No, not at all; don't be silly. I am just trying to make sure we don't get lost before getting to the highway," he chuckled, making light of the earlier incident.

"Shall we listen to the radio?" she asked.

"Yes, what a good idea," replied Joseph, and Louise turned the car radio knob until she settled it on a popular music channel. Although the announcements were unintelligible to her, most of the music was familiar Western pop tunes.

As the miles glided past, and the jolly music filled the car, Louise began to sing along to some of the more familiar numbers. She felt silly and stupid at her earlier outburst, and a little guilty at her tirade in the car, and she wondered what he would be thinking of her. She tried to dismiss it from her mind. *Anyway, all that life after death stuff is nonsense*, she thought, trying to move herself beyond what had happened. Hard as she tried, the deeper realities and her troubled doubts had bubbled to the surface, and these thoughts would not leave her mind easily.

Joseph continued to concentrate on the highway ahead while turning over in his mind the recent events. It was now clear to Joseph that underneath the confident and happy exterior of his beautiful companion lay another person, fearful, not knowing, alone and with a limited compass with which to guide and live her life. Everything was here and now, instant, living for the moment with little concept of either the past or the future, particularly her own. He was also suddenly conscious of Louise's impulsiveness rather than what he had taken as pure spontaneity and that she relied greatly on her physical beauty and sensuousness to manage situations where she felt uncomfortable. Yes, Louise had a sparkling career ahead of her in any branch of the law that she chose to follow. Yes, Louise was very beautiful and could have almost any man of her choice. She was well educated and very intelligent, with many talents, but, for all that, the last two days had also revealed emptiness within her. There was a lack of true self-assurance, insecurity about herself and who she truly was.

The conversation about her family, parents and years before coming to Oxford over dinner in Zagreb had given Joseph further insights into who this lady is. It is rarely enough simply to take on the values of our parents without some independent and personal commitment. Her openness and honesty were immensely refreshing for Joseph and it made her especially vulnerable when her defences were down. Despite her sophistication and cleverness there was a real innocence about so many aspects of her life. It was as though there were serious issues that concerned her that she was not properly equipped to deal with within her existing human self alone. While the humanistic behaviour might have always served her well at home in Wales and among her university friends, it had come crashing down around her when confronted with this extraordinary gentleman beside her. As she hummed to the radio, she knew it and so did Joseph.

They arrived near Karlovac by mid morning and stopped at a modern highway garage and restaurant and had coffee and a sandwich before continuing on their journey. Once back on the highway Louise turned to Joseph and asked him why he thought the Catholic Church was still so predominant in Croatia after more than thirty years of Communism. They debated at length various facets of this topic and Joseph pointed out that Tito had led a moderate form of communism, less extreme than other parts of the USSR, where the church had been tolerated. Although the state frequently introduced laws and rules that hindered the practise of Catholicism, they never outlawed the church. Joseph had firm views on why the church had survived and continues to do so, although he confined his remarks to the more prosaic reasons for its longevity during their discussion. Had he started to explain the more spiritual and biblical evidence, he knew Louise would not have readily accepted and therefore understood it. He had come to understand that we all see life through a complex prism of highly personal reference points, prejudices, earlier life experiences, acculturation and the impacts of years of socialisation in various environments. He had discovered that few had the ability to simply listen, understand and accept information without imposing a complex range of judgements, many of which are even unrecognised to the individual concerned. It is a rare human mind that is disposed to understand certain matters objectively and calmly, simply in the context of the associated evidence being presented.

There was no value judgement of Louise in his thoughts, he certainly did not think her in any way inferior to himself, quite the contrary, he regarded her as his equal in all things and with some matters, more intelligent, creative and decisive than himself. No, it was more a matter of having a common language with which to share ideas and arguments. He could not for example sustain a lengthy discussion with a skilled car mechanic because he had absolutely no appreciation of the technicalities of the modern combustion engine. He also rarely had discussions with Mark, his brother, about his computer work and mathematics because firstly they did not share a common vocabulary on such matters and also Joseph's very brain had almost a different structure with which to engage the reality of his world with that of Mark's. Although simplistic, these analogies go some way in describing the dilemma Joseph was turning over in his mind, and the deeper rift that existed between Joseph and Louise as they chatted in the car speeding toward Benkovac, Skradia and Split.

It was a long drive between Karlovac and Benkovac and after passing through a road tunnel they emerged to a different and rather barren landscape. As they continued to descend towards the coast they continued talking about all manner of things.

"Do you want a drink, Joe?" Louise enquired as she reached over to the back seat to grab a water bottle.

"Yes, please," he answered and Louise took the top off and carefully handed the full bottle to him. She then took a long drink from the bottle and, having noticed his Bible lying on the backseat, asked him why he carried such an old tattered volume around with him all the time. Joseph answered by referring to the actual Bible, which his mother had given him many years before. What Louise was actually referring to was more about him reading it periodically, and why he did so.

"No, darling, I meant why is it so important to you?" she asked, thinking he was being obtuse.

"Well," he replied with a long pause. "There are many reasons."

"Such as?" probed Louise.

After what had happened earlier in Zagreb, Joseph wondered why Louise was wishing to raise this sensitive topic between them again. He tried to dismiss the matter at first because he was beginning to feel a little weary, having been at the wheel for some hours, but Louise persisted. He asked her if she had ever read the Bible and she replied with an emphatic no. He thought for a few moments, and decided to explain what the Bible was rather than its spiritual, religious and mystical significance. He used the analogy of a library, since he thought this would appeal to her legal mind.

Over the course of the next hour or so Joseph gripped Louise's imagination as he painstakingly and patiently described the well-worn book on the back seat of the car. By now, Louise had come to experience another aspect of Joseph, that whenever he spoke about something he knew and clearly loved he was a captivating speaker, precise, with a wonderful use of words yet humble. She loved just to sit and listen to him. He spoke without ever trying to convince one of anything, but just laid everything out with humour and an engaging, gentle manner.

He explained that the word 'Bible' comes from the Greek '*biblos*', meaning 'book', and that was precisely what it is: a book containing many books, all within one cover rather like a library. In fact, it contains, in total, seventy-three books, with twenty-seven of these making up the New Testament, and forty-six making up the Old Testament. Within this array of writings, there are also many different types of writings ranging with legal books such as Leviticus and Numbers, novels such as Jonah, travel in Tobit, poetry in Psalms, and philosophy in Wisdom. In the New Testament there are also the gospels, letters and even coded messages in Apocalypse.

"But when was all this written, and who wrote it all?" enquired Louise.

Joseph suddenly felt sad that Louise had clearly never been exposed to the Bible or ever given an opportunity to explore it. He felt that he was gradually opening a magical treasure trove to her.

"Well, it was written by many different people, living in different times over hundreds of years," Joseph answered. He went on to explain that the actual writing of the various books began around 1000 B.C., that the writing of the Bible was completed by the end of the first century A.D., and that the Bible was written in various languages such as Hebrew, Aramaic and Greek. The Old Testament, written by the Jews, divides these particular books into three groups; the law under the Torah, which is the first five books of the Bible, the Prophets in Nebiim from Joseph to 2 Kings, and all the other prophets such as Isaiah to Malachi, and then the Writings of the Kethubim, which includes Psalms, Proverbs, Job, Song of Songs, Ruth, Lamentations, Ecclesiastes, Esther, Daniel and a few others. Joseph continued by describing the New Testament particularly the four gospels of Mark, Mathew, Luke and John. All the time Louise was asking questions and Joseph was providing clear, precise answers. The Pauline letters particularly fascinated Louise after Joseph had explained about the origins of Paul and how he had travelled spreading these teachings.

Split was probably another hour from where they had

reached and Louise suggested they stop and stretch themselves.

As they stood by the car looking out over the countryside and a beautiful river estuary beneath, Louise looked at Joseph and said "Goodness, Joe, I thought I was the legal one of us; how do you remember all that stuff? But I must say you explain it really well and I enjoyed listening to you." Joseph just smiled and raised his arms above his head to stretch, stifling a yawn as he did so.

13
Social Disorder

FOLLOWING THE ATROCITY IN PARIS, RETRIBUTION had started with ugly scenes repeated in many parts of Europe. Wild stories had circulated, starting first in France and then spreading particularly via Internet chat rooms to other parts of the world. No one had claimed responsibility for the attack. There were no clues as to who the perpetrators were and why they had done it. The local police and international security agencies were becalmed, they had no leads, little reliable intelligence and were frankly at a loss, groping in the dark in their investigations while their political masters were becoming increasingly intolerant of their lack of answers.

Various ethnic minority groups were the first targets and some of the outrageous attacks on them were violent and vicious. In a few cases, the police even stood by while angry mobs looted and burned shops belonging to foreigners, particularly those from India and Pakistan. Some mosques had been attacked and this had caused outrage in the Muslim community. It had become so treacherous in certain European cities that those even with a darker skin to the local population stopped going out on their own, and certainly not after dusk. The sense of widespread anger, fear and suspicion was mounting and spreading, and this was further inflamed by the vacuum of reliable information about who had inflicted such carnage on Paris.

Few had even come near to understanding that this first major attack on a major European city may have been a mere rehearsal, a test and trial exercise to measure a range of factors, particularly the broader repercussions that would always be difficult to postulate without practical experience and evidence. Such a cynical, ruthless scenario by the perpetrators was not even in the minds of highly experienced security advisors who were busy at work trying to shed light on recent events in Paris.

The media had been in a feeding frenzy once it had awakened to the magnitude of the atrocity. The TV media especially, without culprits to report on, had started to become innovative and speculative about whom the possible perpetrators could have been. Various special reports had been hurriedly put together, all speculative and invariably following up mere hunches by news editors. Prime time news programmes had to be filled and the various television news channels vied with each other for ratings. Paris, the emergency work, the temporary accommodation camps, the death toll, on the scene reports, the views of a selection of experts, all dominated the news coverage. The rest of the world almost ceased to exist during the weeks that followed the attack.

Dandler Global Aggregates did not produce or supply ready mix concrete, but they focussed on the supply of the aggregates to the concrete companies. They operated quarries around the world and the logistics of bulk handling and transportation of these materials. They had also diversified in recent years into the development and supply of various additives to enhance different types of concrete for a number of arduous applications. The company from where the cement mixer trucks had come from that demolished Paris was a client of Dandler's and was part of an international concrete and cement company. John, as the Chairman of Dandler, had resisted pressure in recent years to sell the company to these international concrete companies, preferring to specialise in the wholesale supply of materials to them.

The senior management team of Dandler Aggregates had been interviewed by a special team of police and other specialists set up soon after the attack in Paris. They were particularly interested in the human resources records of all the employees and any possible connections with ParisCrete and their employees. Despite detailed investigations they turned up nothing worth following through.

What had particularly disappointed the Paris police was that not a shred of evidence was ever found in any of the thirty-five ready mix trucks used for the attack. No fingerprints, no scraps of evidence left behind in a hurry, no eyewitnesses who could describe the drivers. It was a complete blank.

Mary Trimbledon was sitting at her desk at the Grange when the phone rang and Charlie Harris, the chief superintendent of the local county police force, called.

"Hello Mary, how are you?" he asked.

"Well, Charlie. How is the family?"

"Well, thanks Mary. Listen, I am sorry to bother you, but could we perhaps meet as a matter of urgency, please? There are some sensitive things I would welcome your opinion about," Charlie asked with a tone of urgency in his voice.

"Of course; if it is very urgent, why not pop over tonight for supper? John is away in London on business today, and I am not expecting him back until late. How about 7:30 here at Himbledon; how would that suit you?" she asked.

"That will be fine; thank you so much, Mary; look forward to seeing you at 7:30 then," he said, and they hung up.

Mary greeted Charlie in the personal quarters at the Grange, a homely suite of rooms on one side of the great house. Among other things it had a large kitchen with a cosy dining area at one side and Mary had prepared a simple supper for the two of them. Charlie was in his early fifties and had made his way up through the ranks of the local police force starting as an ordinary copper on the beat. There were times when he felt a little out of his depth in the present day hi-tech police force. Mary had known Charlie and his family for some years, and she admired his simple but practical approach to policing that had been acquired over many years of practical experience. He was a humble man, and always weighed matters up very carefully before coming to a decision. He was also a member of the local Anglican Church, a member of the choir, and Mary could testify to his lovely tenor voice, having attended various services at the local church. Matins in the early summer evenings were often a favourite with both her and John after a long walk in the countryside back to the Grange. Charlie had been decorated several times for bravery and he was highly respected and popular with members of his force. He still played soccer for the police veterans and did much valuable work among the youth in the town where he lived.

After supper they settled down in the armchairs in the kitchen as the late summer sun set slowly behind the hills beyond. With talk of their families and other matters of mutual interest now complete, it was time to hear what had been so urgent. It transpired that the home secretary had called an urgent meeting of all chief superintendents to take place the day after tomorrow outside London to review public order and to agree on measures to urgently address the situation. There was growing alarm at the rising social disorder in various parts of the country and the many racial attacks that had taken place on minority groups since the devastation of Paris. Charlie knew he could speak with Mary in absolute confidence and he greatly valued her opinion on such matters. He never enjoyed these high level meetings, especially at the home office, and needed to get his thinking and ideas sorted out before attending. He had already consulted with his senior officers and various other specialists in his force, but wanted an outside view. Charlie asked her what she thought about the ways things were deteriorating, particularly in some of the large urban areas of Britain and what could be done to address the situation. Bradford, Birmingham, parts of Manchester, Bristol, the home counties and London had all witnessed a sudden surge in inter-group violence and intimidation. There had been a number of deaths and in many cases innocent bystanders had been injured. The Moslem community and various other groups such as Pakistan shopkeepers had been particular targets as too had been some Polish immigrants.

Mary thought for a moment, looked at Charlie, and quickly dispensed with all the obvious things that the police would be doing anyway. She raised the issue of troublemakers, ringleaders, and that they needed to be isolated in some way, but with extreme care not to further inflame the situation. There needed to be firm control, but not a major crackdown, since this would only further inflame the situation.

"Above all else we must appeal to the leaders of all these communities, black, coloured and white, those with legitimacy and local community influence to stand together and to condemn these attacks. There must be a display of unity that everyone relies on everyone else, and that living in Britain involves respecting the freedom of others." As Mary spoke gently and in a considered manner, Charlie took notes in a small police notebook. Mary also repeated several times the maxim of liberty that every individual irrespective of colour, culture and creed is innocent until proven guilty. Indiscriminate acts of intimidation were simply not to be tolerated by the various multi-cultural communities themselves and that stability will have to be sought from within these communities rather than simply attempting to impose it from outside. They agreed about the many worrying signs that this ugly situation was rapidly escalating and feeding on itself.

Mary suggested that he call a meeting of all the religious leaders in the county and that they all meet together as a matter of urgency to thrash out mutually agreed and owned solutions that they would each be held accountable for. Similar meetings should be held with head teachers, and the senior managers of the local large employers and other relevant people in positions of authority to ensure firm yet sympathetic leadership at this time.

There should also be clearly understood statements issued by the home office and the prime minister briefly describing the types of behaviour that will not be tolerated, such as inciting others to violence, hate speech, carrying of dangerous weapons and so forth. In these cases the police must act swiftly, make arrests and bring people to the courts. Mary suggested that Charlie also ask the home secretary that in these currently very difficult conditions that the backlog of trivial cases clogging up magistrates' courts up and down the country be postponed so they can swiftly ensure justice is done and seen by the population at large, with the inevitable increase in arrests that there will be.

Mary also spoke about caring for the victims and the need for the Social Welfare people to move quickly to support those who suffer together with their families. The churches, in particular, must be galvanised into helping whoever is in need due to these problems. She also spoke about the need to pray and that special church services should be arranged. As they looked at each other, they both knew that prayer was perhaps the most important thing of all to be doing right now.

It had been nearly two hours that Mary had been speaking, with the odd question from Charlie. It was now late in the evening when the headlights of John's car could be seen approaching. Shortly after the car lights dimmed, John came in through the kitchen door with two briefcases.

"Hello, Charlie; how are you?" he asked as he put down his baggage on the long kitchen table and walked over and kissed Mary. "How about a night cap for both of you? I could certainly do with one, what a day it has been."

Mary noticed that he looked tired and drawn. "Come on Charlie, just a small brandy, you have had only one glass of wine much earlier, that will be perfectly safe," added Mary.

John slumped into the armchair, sipped his brandy and listened to Charlie talk about the local soccer team. At 11:30, Charlie briskly stood up and said, "Thank you both. Thanks for the fine brandy and thank you Mary as always for your wise counsel." He walked over and gave Mary a kiss on the cheek and shook John's hand in farewell.

As John and Mary walked upstairs to bed, Mary turned to John and said, "John, I am very concerned about Anna and think I should go to London tomorrow."

Weary after an exhausting day, John replied, "Is there anything I can do? Tomorrow I will be at Himbledon all day; Mark and I have some work to do."

"No, nothing at this stage, thanks John. I will catch the 8:30 train tomorrow that should get me into Ruth's by 10:30, all being well."

John was already asleep.

The next day Mary had an uneventful journey into central

London and she was soon at the house of Ruth just off Kensington High Street. As Mary was getting out of the taxi Ruth was there standing in the open door way ready to greet her.

"Hello, Mother; how was your journey?" Ruth asked as she closed the door behind her mother.

"A bit crowded nearer to London, but, apart from that, it was fine," answered Mary.

"Come on through and I will make some tea," Ruth said as she ushered her mother into a comfortable lounge at the front of the house.

In due course they were chatting and drinking tea and Mary enquired about Anna, who was still staying with Ruth in London since Timothy's funeral. Ruth was a practising behavioural psychologist, was on the part-time teaching staff at Birkbeck College, part of London University and consulted to various local and international organisations. She also had a small number of personal clients.

Mary and Ruth had been talking regularly about Anna since the funeral and it had been Mary who suggested to Ruth that she invite Anna to stay on in London and not return to Paris for a while. Anna had clearly taken Tim's murder very badly and was suffering more than mere grief.

"Frankly, Mother, I am very concerned about Anna, particularly in the last few days. I think she is having a nervous breakdown. I think she has suffered a deep trauma and is wrestling with all manner of demons, and this is why she is in this state. Putting it simply, she is suffering extreme guilt about something, and all manner of weird delusions. She is not sleeping properly, is becoming increasingly disturbed, and I think she may even be a danger to herself."

"Oh, dear Anna, and you, my dear, having to deal with all this since Tim's death," answered Mary.

Ruth continued, "There is no need to worry about me, Mother, and, as far as Anna is concerned, she is in the best possible place right now. I arranged with a friend of mine, a psychiatrist, to see Anna two days ago and he has prescribed various medications to make her more comfortable. She is sleeping now, since she was up several times during the night."

"Is there anything I can do, Ruth?" asked Mary.

"No, absolutely nothing, Mother, apart from being a sounding board for me in relation to family matters and Anna," replied Ruth firmly. "I just thought you needed to know of these developments and I would rather you do not tell Father about any of this just at the moment until we can get to the bottom of things," Ruth continued.

"What do you mean, Ruth, get to the bottom of this? Surely the poor girl is suffering these problems because of the shock of Tim's death and grief," Mary enquired with a sudden intuitive feeling that there was much more to this situation than Ruth was disclosing right now.

"Oh, nothing, Mother, it meant nothing," Ruth responded, looking away.

"I know you're not telling me everything, Ruth; you could never keep secrets from me, but, be that as it may, I will ask you no more about it," answered Mary.

It was lunchtime when Anna appeared, dishevelled in one of Ruth's dressing gowns. This pretty young lady, a geologist with a French oil company, looked dreadful; she was clearly heavily sedated and spoke with a slight slur in her voice.

"How are you, my dear?" enquired Mary; Anna did not appear to understand and did not respond. "Don't worry, Anna," Mary said, standing and putting an arm around her shoulder. "We will get you well again, won't we, Ruth?" she said, looking anxiously across to Ruth seated nearby.

It was mid afternoon when Mary's taxi arrived to take her to the station. When she arrived back at Himbledon, she was troubled and concerned about Anna, but could not share any of the day's awfully upsetting experience with John. After parking her car, she entered the Grange and there was no sign of John or Mark. Mary put the kettle on and put the hello code word into the laptop on the kitchen counter. Immediately the screen flickered to life and there she could see John and Mark busy at work below.

"How about a cup of tea?" she asked into the tiny microphone.

"Sure, Mother; oh, hello there," said Mark, with his mind elsewhere. "Coming right up."

14
Adriatic

THEY ARRIVED LATE IN THE AFTERNOON IN SPLIT, and on entering the town after turning off the highway, they drove down to the old town located by the waterfront through rows of tall residential blocks erected during the Communist period. They were characterless, ugly and drab places built to house working class families. Louise thought it a dreadful place; graffiti was scrawled everywhere, there were broken bottles and litter lying around, and unkempt little gardens in front of each block.

So this is Split; what a place, she thought, and smiled to herself as a more descriptive name for the place flashed through her mind, as they continued to descend through the busy early evening traffic.

They arrived at their hotel, a large two-star establishment that had clearly been popular in the Communist period and before the war when Yugoslavia had been a popular tourist destination. The drab hotel that had seen better days and was being refurbished, was half empty and overlooked a small harbour with expensive yachts. They booked in and despite a request from a surly gentleman at reception to leave their passports, Joseph declined and after an onslaught of charm from him, in a novel version of the local language, the hotel official handed the passports back, smiling.

Local knowledge is everything, Louise thought after they had showered and changed in their large yet drab room, handed in their room key at reception and walked hand in hand across to the old town to the ruins of Diocletian's Palace. As they walked Louise read from her tourist guide.

"Did you know, Joe, that Diocletion was born in 85 A.D., and he was the son of a slave, yet rose to become one of the emperor's of Rome? I think I would have liked this man; he evidently persecuted Christians and put them to death." She giggled, then continued, "He was quite a chap, he started the division of the Roman Empire into the Eastern and Western domains which later became the Orthodox and Catholic spheres of influence before he lived here in this place until he died."

"I am not sure you would have liked this fellow Louise," interjected Joseph. "He later converted to Christianity and, full of guilt for his barbarous behaviour towards Christians earlier, he committed suicide here." Instantly, it struck Joseph that he may have said the wrong thing.

However, then Louise said, still trying to retain some little ascendancy by reading from her guidebook, "We should enter the palace through the Bronze Gate on the waterfront that leads into the underground vaults that lead up into the palace. Oh, he is buried in a mausoleum in there. I think we should give that a miss Joe."

After wandering around the stalls, monuments, squares, churches and the wonderful mixture of architecture that had been created over the centuries all jumbled together, Joseph took Louise to Varos, a tavern in an old stone house. They enjoyed a Hvar Island special of boiled lamb, stuffed peppers and fried anchovies with plentiful glasses of red wine. It was a fascinating evening for them both, especially Louise, to be together in this cosmopolitan atmosphere, among the alleyways, cobbled streets and an abundance of interesting shops and galleries. At one stage in the evening two young men dressed as Roman Centurions walked past with their pikes in hand and Louise insisted on taking a photograph of them standing either side of Joseph in front of a large sphinx that, evidently, Diocletion had transported from Egypt, hundreds of years earlier.

They were both tired after a long day, but they were happy. There was a single, but very large, bed in the room they were sharing at the hotel, and Louise, who had become more subdued in the tender company of Joseph, joked with him as to whether or not it was safe for them to sleep so close together. Joseph, who was tired after driving all day, just smiled and lay on the bed with just his pyjama shorts on. It was a warm night with a gentle breeze cooling the bedroom and in the darkness they could see the lights of small ships glinting on the ceiling and walls. Louise lay alongside Joseph and he put an arm over her side, with his other arm behind his head. The energy in his body felt as though it had ebbed away, he felt heavy and sleepy. Louise played and pulled gently the hairs on his chest and laid her head on the front of his reclining shoulder as they lay there in silence recounting the day in their minds before drifting off to sleep.

Joseph was the first to wake the next morning. He got up, showered and emerged with just a towel wrapped around his waist and sat on the bed next to her sleeping body. He kissed her gently on her lips as she lay on her side and then on her cheek. Louise stirred and lifted her head slightly and held her body up on one arm and Joseph was able to put an arm around her. They stayed like this for several moments as Joseph gently kissed her until she was fully awake. There was now a trust and natural ease between them, and no longer the need to play sexual games or compete with one another. Neither felt in any way intimidated by the other, they just wanted to touch, feel and be as one, and doing what came naturally. They laughed and giggled about the silliest of things, spontaneously embraced each other at every opportunity and were becoming increasingly oblivious of their surroundings, completely wrapped up in their own intimate world. There was nothing about their physical bodies they needed to hide or feel self-conscious about; all inhibitions had vanished.

They had breakfast in a hurry and Louise hardly took her eyes off Joe for a moment. The stern waitresses in the large empty dinning hall in their black uniforms were even touched by this beautiful and elegant young couple so in love, certainly the blonde young thing who kept reaching for his hand. They settled their account, booked out, handed in the car keys for the hire car to be collected and carrying their bags they walked briskly to the small harbour in front of the old town. They just managed to get there in time to buy a ticket and boarded the ferry for Hvar. On arrival after making enquiries they found Franjo, the brother of the priest in Zagreb and enquired about yacht hire and available berths on sailing boats going south to the island of Miljet and then onto Dubrovnik.

"Yes, there is a small schooner that was due in later that will have two spare berths that will be leaving the next day to sail south and Franjo was able to take the booking and passage fee, but they should book now to be sure. This yacht has a crew of three including the skipper and there will be two other couples occupying the other two small cabins, they are Americans."

Joseph looked at Louise and she could see the excitement in his eyes, "Yes, let's book and pay now Joe, it sounds perfect."

So the deal was struck.

They spent the rest of the day exploring the island, swimming and relaxing in a small cove just near the town. Then in the middle of the afternoon they went in search of their small hotel for the night. It was a medium-sized villa, well appointed high above the town overlooking the harbour. It had a lovely garden with a clay tennis court that had recently been refurbished with a new net and neatly painted white lines. As they looked down from their bedroom window looking out over the harbour and sea beyond, Louise invited Joseph to have a game with her. After finally raising the stoutly proprietor and with her guidance, rummaging around in a store cupboard, they found two tennis racquets in reasonable condition and some balls. The next thing they were standing either side of the net warming up with a cool breeze blowing from the sea. It was a magical setting and early evening.

Louise considered herself to be a good all-round sports lady and she was quietly confident that she would be able to beat Joseph, especially at a game like tennis. She had excelled in swimming at school with numerous cups and trophies, was the captain of one of the Oxford University's better hockey teams; and had been the tennis captain of one of her schools sixth form teams that won the interschool championships before she went up to Oxford. As they warmed up Louise noticed, however, how agile Joseph was around the court, light on his feet despite his height and strong physique and naturally positioning himself to return her rallies. They played two sets; the first Louise won with a reasonable margin, six to four, although the second set was an altogether different affair. For every game Louise won, Joseph won another almost effortlessly. When he took the second set it was now dusk and both of them were hot, sweaty and happy with their own performance. It had been a good hard last set and they had both managed to execute some powerful serves, lengthy rallies from the back of the court together with some nimble work up close to the net. As they walked to join each other, they shook hands as is customary and thanked each other for the game.

"Where on earth did you learn to play such good tennis, Joe?" Louise enquired as they walked slowly up the steps back to the villa.

When they got back to their room, they showered together in the small en suite shower room, soaping and washing each other's bodies. Louise particularly enjoyed it when Joseph washed her long hair and gently rinsed her head. They dried each other and lay with towels around themselves before getting dressed for supper. It had been another exquisite day.

The following morning they arrived at the harbour early with their bags looking for the yacht they were to be travelling on. After wandering up and down the waterfront, they saw a young man, probably early thirties, sitting on a small deck chair beside a large yacht moored to the large bollards on the quayside.

He looked up at them over his book and over the top of his sunglasses. "You must be Joseph and Louise from England?" he enquired.

"Yes, that's right," said Joseph, and so their sea voyage was secure.

He introduced himself as Eric Nicholson, the skipper and a South African from Cape Town. Within a few minutes they had deposited their bags in a small cabin with two wooden bunks, one above the other in the forward part of the bow. It had a small porthole and a dark brown wooden door with a brass handle to open and close the door that one had to step over a wooden ledge at the bottom to enter. They soon met the other members of the crew; Lisa, another blonde haired young lady from Durban, also in South Africa, who was the cook; and Eddie, the general deckhand from Poland. The three crewmembers appeared competent, relaxed and happy with each other as Joseph and Louise glanced at each other and smiled in anticipation of the sailing before them. This would be a first for Louise, although for Joseph he was an accomplished sailor, having skippered a slightly larger boat just two years earlier in these same waters.

"Where are the other passengers?" asked Louise.

Eric answered, "They have gone to do some more looking around the town and we are expecting them back later before we push off at noon. In the meanwhile make yourselves at home. There is fresh coffee in the galley."

Sure enough, at 11:55, there were the four Americans standing on the harbour side. By this time, Louise, Joseph, Eric, Eddie and Lisa were lazing on the aft deck under a large awning to protect themselves from the hot midday sun. They had come to like and know something of each other remarkably quickly, and Eric had realised that Joseph knew a few things about sailing and these waters, despite his modesty, humour and self-deprecation about such matters. Louise again noticed that Joseph never set out to impress, he always stood back and was always rather unassuming. Sailors speak their own language, and even Eddie had learnt a few things from the conversation, especially when Joseph occasionally translated technical words via French so he could understand. As well as speaking Polish, Eddie also had fluent French and a little Afrikaans that he had learnt from Lisa. He was a music student from Warsaw taking a working holiday with Eric and Lisa.

The Americans came onto the boat, noisily, full of wholesome friendliness and introductions. There was Elaine and Jay, a couple about to be married in the late "fall" after they had returned to the States and they were probably in their mid thirties; and, Andy and Celine, a little younger, who were already married just for a year. They had no children and Andy was undergoing medical tests to see whether his sperm count was sufficient for Celine to fall pregnant. They were sleeping in the rear two cabins and Elaine had plenty of ointment for the mosquitoes and pills for runny tummy should anyone on board need them. Louise found the four charming as did Joseph, but she was always amused when meeting many Americans that within minutes one knows so much about them, and often personal information.

Had they been English, in contrast, she thought, *we would not have got beyond their Christian names by this early stage in the trip together.*

There was no wind as they edged away from the quayside and Eric idled the two large outboard motors to propel them gently through the harbour out to sea. It was not long before the harbour was in the distance and they settled down to a light lunch, prepared by Lisa, of fish and salads and an endless supply of wine for those who felt so inclined. After helping Lisa clear away the lunch plates and glasses, Louise stationed herself in her blue bikini on the forward deck, continuing to read her guide to Croatia, lying under a large sun hat to keep the sun out of her eyes. Joseph was on the stern sitting in the wheel well chatting to Eric. Jay and Celine remained in the dinning area talking while Andy and Elaine had gone to their cabins for an afternoon nap. In the meanwhile, Eddie was fiddling about with various pieces of rigging high above their heads.

The next few hours were spent intermittently under light sail or the outboard motors as they moved across the still waters of the Adriatic. For Louise the sound of the waves gently brushing the side of the keel, the sea gulls popping in to stand on the railings, and the open sea ahead was magical. She turned periodically to ensure she did not burn in the hot afternoon sun and to get a balanced tan all over her body.

Over the next hours everyone got on remarkably well in the rather cramped quarters and everyone had found their little piece of solitude and a place of their own. Quickly and instinctively people come to know which territory belongs to which person, where each person may be found at a particular time and unless really necessary to leave them alone. Whenever they neared islands, after lengthy discussions between Joseph and Eric, they would drop anchor near to the shoreline, swim, dive and catch fish off the boat. The weather was glorious and it was proving to be a magical few days, lazy, free and companionable with new vistas continually appearing of clear blue water, waves, blue sky and beautiful islands.

After the first day Louise even persuaded Celine to also sunbath topless on the fore deck to the slight consternation of Andy, who seemed to think such behaviour rather improper, particularly by his wife.

"Ah, but what the heck, when in Rome and all that," he had been heard to say as he groped his way to the rear of the boat from where Louise and Celine were laying on their backs with sun hats over their faces, talking to each other.

Apart from Eric, who would occasionally give Lisa an affectionate gesture, everyone had just taken her for granted, wearing just a small pair of shorts and moving around the boat sometimes bare breasted. When it was time to eat, she put on a sari to ensure her breasts never interfered with the food. It was hot in the small galley and the door was always open, held back on itself with a brass catch. There was always music playing from inside and an endless supply of coffee, cold beer and other cool refreshments.

On their first evening, Jay had rather put his foot in it, unwittingly, at least for him, when in a jovial way he had enquired of Lisa as she served supper, "Do you still have wild animals like lions where you come from in Africa, missy?"

It was probably his reference to her as "missy" rather than his belief that she has wild elephants in her garden back home that suddenly upset her.

Lisa was serving a hot fish soup and turned to face Jay with her eyes blazing. "My name is Lisa not 'missy', Jay, and no we don't have wild animals roaming the streets in Durban where I am from. It is a big city," she replied angrily, not at all amused by his question.

Everyone fell silent and looked away and Joseph, sensing the awkwardness of the situation interjected, "You do have some wild people over there though, Lisa."

The atmosphere began to ease and Lisa relented and smiled at Joseph. Meanwhile, Jay was busy wiping the hot soup off his upper bare legs that had splashed on him when Lisa sloshed a portion of the hot contents of the bowl wrapped under her left arm off the ladle into his soup plate.

A little after supper Elaine went below and emerged with a handful of creams and sprays and started what was to become a nightly ritual while they travelled together. She generously offered everyone the use of her mosquito deterrent spray and special skin cream to be applied after sunbathing. Some willingly accepted these kind gifts and thoughtfulness while others politely declined. Joseph always took a little of the spray since rather than mosquito's, he knew the small flies that emerge early evening when moored close in shore could be irritating. He also took a little cream for his nose that had the habit of peeling when sailing.

In the four nights afloat, Joseph and Louise never slept below deck preferring to sleep topside. Joseph had rigged up two hammocks, strung between some rigging and the stainless steel rails on the prow of the boat. The first night they slept beside one another although for much of the night Louise insisted on sleeping with Joseph in his hammock. The next evening Joseph put the two hammocks together, one in side the other so they would take their combined weight and they slept in each others arms, half naked, on the foredeck for the remainder of the voyage. They were in their own world at the front of the boat, left alone by the rest and they watched spectacular sunsets, the stars at night and the glistening lights from the shore across the open sea. They awoke to breathtaking sunrises and the dawning of each day in the warmth and security of each other's bodies. They shared many hilarious moments, talked, laughed and lay for long periods of silence in awe of their surroundings.

Louise always managed to clamber free in the mornings, gently extracting her limbs from Joseph as he continued to doze. She was full of excitement and expectation at the first chinks of light appearing in the early dawn across the sea and islands in the distance and would go to the galley, put the coffee on and bring back two steaming mugs to enjoy together as they sat, legs dangling over the edge of the hammocks, to watch together the sunrise. Then, hand in hand, they would plunge into the warm sea and swim together, frolicking and splashing each other before clambering back onto the boat. Joseph always went aboard first, turning and extending an arm to pull Louise effortlessly onto the deck. They dried each others glistening browning bodies, hugged and kissed. It was as though they were one.

They sailed to the islands of Vis and then across to Korcula and then onto Mljet and for Louise it felt as though they been here for an eternity. Time stood still, she felt so happy and complete, with feelings so strong that she had never felt before in her life and knew it was not just the beautiful surroundings. She was becoming more and more consumed with Joseph, living and being so close to him, watching his broad smile, looking into his large generous eyes, holding his hands, listening to his stories, his humour and his generous lips on hers. Already, she could not bear the thought of this ending, being separated from him and being apart. When these thoughts rose in her mind she thrust them away, they caused her discomfort and an anguished feeling in her stomach. Occasionally when lying lazily near him, discreetly watching him reading, and when these unsettling thoughts entered her mind, she tried to console herself with the thought of travelling back to England together and then being able to be with him again in Oxford after a few days. She was on a roller coaster of emotions and had lost herself completely to Joseph, her whole world was turning upside down and she knew she was no longer in control.

When they arrived at Mljet it proved to be the enchanting island Joseph had described earlier. The legend about Ulysses being held captive for seven years in a cave by the nymph Calypso seemed entirely feasible to Louise as she gazed at the island from the boat. It was so beautiful and enchanting.

If only it were so, she imagined, and that I could keep Joseph here in a cave for seven years, we would be so happy together.

She smiled to herself as her practical legal brain asserted

itself. As they approached the island, everyone stood on the side of the yacht along the rail looking across to the island apart from Eric who was still at the wheel guiding them ever closer. Joseph began to persuade everyone that they should circumnavigate the island and to extend their journey by an extra day. He called over to Eric who said that there would be no problem if they all agreed. Having already become the deputy skipper and having the confidence of everyone, they all readily agreed.

Mijet is an exquisite island with coves, small isolated sandy beaches that can only be reached from the sea, pine groves, lush vegetation and lakes in the interior of the island. They explored the rocks beneath the clear water, swam, sunbathed, ate, talked and consumed generous quantities of wine. Eddie played his guitar in the evening after supper and sang Polish folk and love songs as they lay offshore beside the island. During the day they made an expedition into the interior of the island clambering up through forests and looking down on glistening lakes below. Returning to the boat in the early afternoon they felt strangely safe again and they swam and relaxed. Joseph even persuaded Louise to accompany him up the main mast, at least half way up before losing her nerve. When she had returned safely to the deck, Joseph dived into the sea from the rigging high above them all, to applause and yelps from the Americans. Peering over the edge of the boat he did not come to the surface for what to Louise appeared a long time and she became worried he had hurt himself. When he eventually bobbed up and stretched out to swim back to the boat, Louise jumped up and down, yelped herself and then helped him aboard for hugs, kisses and a dry towel.

When they eventually reached Dubrovnik late in the afternoon the following day they had enjoyed some wonderful sailing since some wind and stout sea breezes had come perfectly on time to blow them down to their final destination. For some hours Eric had passed the skippers job over to Joseph, who masterfully controlled the yacht, and Eddie for some enthralling sailing. Eric was suffering somewhat from too much wine the evening before when they had partied late into the night. He emerged later from his bunk as Dubrovnik came into sight, slurped down a strong cup of coffee dutifully provided by Lisa, took over the wheel from Joseph and sailed them safely into the harbour at Dubrovnik.

Eric was picking up more passengers the following day, but now only had a matter of hours to ready the boat again for fresh guests, so, after docking, he and Lisa got busy offloading soiled stores, tidying the boat up, and arranging for fresh supplies to be taken aboard. There are two major harbours in Dubrovnik, one where the huge ocean liners berth and the old harbour under the walls of the old city. It was here Eric had moored the boat and soon everyone was saying their farewells, exchanging contact details, promising to write and send photographs, hugging and kissing. It was a moment of sadness as they all went their separate ways.

Joseph and Louise, carrying their bags, walked through the old town and out through the west gate into the bustle of Dubrovnik. They caught a single deck bus across to their hotel and as they sat opposite each other in the crowded interior. Louise felt dazed and disorientated at this abrupt change of surroundings and already she felt Joseph beginning to slip away from her. They soon arrived at the Grand Villa Argentina, an elegant hotel with clifftop villas overlooking a private beach and the sea. It had been where Richard Burton and Elizabeth Taylor stayed and a popular destination for other film stars and important people. Being Welsh and sharing the same country as Richard Burton and being a fan of his films, Joseph had booked this accommodation as a special treat to happily end their holiday together. Sadly, it was not to be.

As a rather unkempt Joseph and Louise walked into the hotel in shorts, t-shirts and sneakers, looking tanned and sea swept, they looked rather out of place in such grandeur. Booking in, Joseph asked if their booking of a villa overlooking the sea was still in order and apologised for arriving a day late. After a flurry of activity among the reception staff the matter was quickly resolved and they were escorted to their accommodation. Louise was just pleased to have her bags wheeled along ahead of them and to be able to rest her aching arms.

After tipping the hotel porter and closing the door behind

him, Joseph called to Louise, “So what do you think, darling?”

By this time, Louise had thrown back the large drapes over the double doors leading out to their own private terrace overlooking the sea, opened the door and was standing looking out with her hands on the ornate railing.

Joseph walked through and stood behind her, putting his arms around her waist. “So, what do you think?” he asked again.

“It is wonderful, Joe, something out of a fairy tale,” she replied, looking around.

“I thought you did not believe in fairy tales?” Joseph joked.

Louise turned around and jabbed him in the side, smiling.

They unpacked, showered, lay reading in the warm early evening air and ordered supper to enjoy on their very own terrace. After the rather basic conditions on the yacht they kept moving around and sitting in different chairs, armchairs and stretching out on the large bed, relishing all this luxury.

When the knock came on the door with their dinner, Joseph jumped up to open the door, but he was half naked. After the last few days, it had not occurred to him, until Louise said, “Joe, darling you had better make yourself decent before opening the door.”

He grabbed a fleecy white dressing gown hanging in the bathroom and let in the hotel staff, a waiter and another gentleman carrying the wine, water, coolers and various glasses. After responding to a question by the waiter as to where they should serve dinner, Joseph suggested on the terrace. In just a few minutes the table was laid and everything ready to eat from various dishes with warmers on the elaborate trolley.

It was a sumptuous meal and they were both hungry and as Louise served each course impeccably, they talked, laughed, agreed they would certainly contact Eric and Lisa again and debated what to do the next day, their last full day in Croatia. Joseph told her that there was just one particular place he wanted to show her the next morning, and that it was not a church, but a monastery, and that they would also have to walk along the top of the Dubrovnik city walls. They agreed to be up early in the morning to get down to the old town early and they decided that they would return to the hotel for a light lunch the following day before deciding what to do on their last night before returning to England.

The next morning was slightly overcast, but it was still warm and comfortable as they strolled down to the town at just after eight. They entered the old city through the Pile Gate and walked across the glistening white stone of the Stradun to the front of the Franciscan Monastery – Franjevacki Samostan.

"Come Louise, this is the special place I wanted to show you," and they entered into the monastery and walked around the cloisters with a garden in the centre. After turning left and then right along the cloisters they came to this special place that Joseph had been so insistent on showing her.

It was the former monastic dispensary that was first established in the early thirteen hundreds. Joseph just walked through the doors and let this remarkable place speak for itself. Louise walked quietly beside Joseph and they stood in front of a section with rows of bottles, trestle tables, pistol and mortars and various artefacts dating back nearly six hundred years.

"You know Louise," Joseph whispered, "there are two remarkable things about this monastery and the Dominican Monastery on the other side of the old town. Firstly, they still dispense medicine to this day from here, just over there," and Joseph pointed to the new dispensary at the end of the cloister. "The other thing," he continued, "Is that this Franciscan dispensary was established to serve the poor of Dubrovnik and to serve them in the tradition of St. Francis. The Dominican Monastery that is near the other gate, the Ploce gate, particularly served the rich of the local community. Between them they were providing the best available medical care of those times to everyone in Dubrovnik. I think the National Health Service could perhaps learn a few lessons from all this, don't you think?" he chuckled.

Louise, who had been listening intently to Joseph and just staring and studying everything around her, was fascinated by the place, the history and Joseph, especially his enthusiasm.

After looking at a series of display cases that contained religious relics near the old dispensary, Louise looked up and saw what looked like two holes in the wall of the gallery they were in.

"What's that, Joe?" she asked, looking upwards.

"Oh yes," he replied. "They are two shell holes, of Serbian shells, look there, from the war in 1991. Dubrovnik has had many attacks over the years, including these monasteries, but they are still here and this one is still dispensing. That must tell us something, don't you think?" he enquired.

Louise just smiled, a little overawed by all this history, and Joseph's obvious relish of it all. Tourists were now beginning to flood into the monastery and Louise realised why Joseph had wanted to make an early start. They wandered around looking at other parts of the monastery and then left, walking out into what was now a bright sunny day.

"Fancy an interesting walk, Louise?" Joseph asked as they stood beneath the steps that led up the top of the city walls. Soon they were walking along the top of one of the most spectacular two kilometre walks in the Mediterranean. Looking down on the old city, from the medieval walls is a fascinating experience and provides a panoramic view across the rooftops and church domes, private gardens, cloisters and thoroughfares below. Looking beyond the city there is the glistening sea and a small island just offshore.

They strolled arm in arm, stopping regularly to look and discuss various sights and things of interest. Regularly Louise would pull Joseph to a stop and position him somewhere and take photographs. She had no hesitation to ask passers by to take pictures of them together and then retrieving her camera with profuse thanks. Louise remarked several times about how beautiful the roofs all looked under their clay tiles.

"Yes, a beautiful contrast to all the white stone of the buildings and the blue sea beyond," responded Joseph, continuing. "Many of these roof tiles are new, following the Serbian attacks on the city in the early nineties when most of these lovely old houses were hit by shells fired from up there on the hill," and he turned and pointed to the old fort, now defunct, high above them behind Dubrovnik. Louise just looked around, smiled at Joseph, and thought how dreadful it must have been for everyone involved.

After descending into the old city again, where no cars are allowed, they ambled, arm in arm, down the streets and alleyways peeking into shops, galleries and listened to a small group of Croatian young men singing Klapa folk songs. Knowing Louise's sensitivities about churches, Joseph decided to avoid the many wonderful churches in old Dubrovnik, and they browsed in various shops. Famous for ties and cravats, Louise bought Joseph a bright red cravat and slipped it discreetly into her bag. In the meanwhile he had found a postcard of Dubrovnik that included a picture of their hotel that showed the villas on the clifftop.

It was now mid day and they were getting tired and thirsty so decided to wander back to the hotel. As they turned a corner to make their way out of the old city, there across the large courtyard they were walking through, Joseph saw Freddie eating an ice cream, standing in large baggy shorts with a camera over his shoulder, looking the typical tourist.

How does this man do it, wondered Joseph. Since they had left Zagreb, Joseph had forgotten about Freddie and these other realities. Yet unbeknown to him, they were soon to invade his life again.

They arrived back at the Grand Villa Argentina, picked up their room key and wandered to their villa. They ordered a light lunch and quickly positioned the wrought iron table on the terrace in the shade, ready to eat. They checked their cell phones that had been charging in the bedroom and Joseph had received a text message from his father to please call soon. Just then the knock on the door signalled lunch, he put down his phone and went to let in the waitress with their lunch tray. Louise was in the bathroom and Joseph called to her that lunch was here, and what did she want to drink.

"Thanks love, a glass of wine please," she called back.

After the waitress had left, Joseph quickly arranged the lunch table and got a bottle of wine from the fridge, opened it and placed it on the table in readiness.

Louise emerged onto the terrace wearing just a light white shirt and her blue bikini bottom and Joseph could see the outline of her breasts through the thin fabric.

"Come let's have lunch," Joseph said excitedly with one hand behind his back.

Louise was also concealing something and, before sitting, she walked around to Joseph, stood in front of him, and rather sheepishly said, "I bought you a little something, Joe, as a keepsake." She placed the red cravat around his neck and tied it gently beneath his chin and laughed. "Red suits you, Joe. It goes with your dark hair."

"Thank you, Louise," Joseph responded, putting his arms around her with a hug.

As Louise sat down, Joseph waved his arm in a flourish and held before her the postcard he had bought earlier. "And I have a little something for you, too, and it has a picture of where we are right now," exclaimed Joseph, smiling.

They laughed and, after Joseph sat and served the wine, Louise got up and moved her chair around the table to sit next to him. They ate, laughed, fed each other pieces of food, and were, again, in their own private world.

It was now mid-afternoon, and the time had passed so quickly; they were feeling lazy and happy after their lunch when Joseph suddenly remembered the cell phone message from his father.

"I must phone Father, Louise. I had a message earlier on my phone," Joseph said as he rose from the table. He appeared again in a few moments wearing a tracksuit bottom and a sports shirt and plimsolls with his cell phone in his hand. "Would you excuse me, let me just see what Father wants, I won't be a moment. You must also decide what you want to do this evening, it's our last night in Croatia."

He walked to the end of their terrace, down some steps through a small gate into the large garden of the hotel that sloped down to the cove and sea beyond. As he did so his cell phone vibrated in his tracksuit pocket and he looked to see a message from Achmed Misarnie, also asking him to call.

Joseph's parting comment about it being their last night together was like a sudden hammer blow that Louise felt deep within herself. She looked at Joseph walking away in the distance and could not take her eyes off him as he came to stand at the bottom of the garden before a further set of steps leading down to the cove below. She could not hear him talking on the phone, but she could clearly see him, a hand in one of his tracksuit pockets, and the other holding the phone to his ear.

He spoke to his father first; the conversation was brief and terse. John Himbledon spoke in a way that Joseph would understand, but few others would; he told of new business information that had emerged, and said that Joseph should go straight to Dubai as soon as possible, and that he should meet with Achmed, who he had met at the board meeting. Fred would continue his journey, from a distance, with Joseph, and he had arranged that Louise would be discreetly taken care of from the time she reached Gatwick the following day by Paul, Freddie's son.

"You will be in Dubai for two nights, Joseph, and then come straight to Himbledon, let me know your ETA, I will arrange for you to picked up at the airport," John said in closing.

Joseph clicked his phone off and just stood looking out to sea with his back to the hotel. The lazy lunch had vanished, he had now been propelled into another world, another reality. He then returned Achmed's earlier call, and they spoke briefly and he asked Joseph simply to text message his flight number and to take a taxi to an address that he would text message to Joseph shortly.

"Looking forward to seeing you Joseph," Achmed said and then he was gone.

As Joseph walked slowly back up through the garden he could smell the sea behind him even though he was deep in thought. This was his last night with Louise before they were to return to England together so he did not want this sudden change of plans to spoil the end of a great holiday. Louise had continued to watch him below make the calls and she studied him intently as he walked up to join her. She instinctively knew that suddenly their carefree holiday together had come to a premature end even before Joseph arrived back and placed his cell phone gently on the table and smiled.

He sat down slowly and sighed. "Louise, that was my father, some important business has arisen and I must go directly to Dubai tomorrow so will be unable to fly back with you to Gatwick, I am afraid. I am sorry, but not to worry, I will see you soon in Oxford once I have had the meeting at Himbeldon," he said, trying to make light of these changes.

Louise had put out of her mind any thought of going back to Oxford, of all this ending, thoughts of normal life again and especially of being separated from Joseph. In the last few days all those horrible things she had thought can be dealt with later. Her private Heaven on Earth had now been suddenly threatened. Many thoughts tumbled through her mind and sensations through her body, many of them irrational, silly and uncontrollable. Her brain was racing, she struggled to remain calm and then somehow, in a moment not too soon, another part of her came to the rescue. The dissonance in her brain had induced her to default to safer ground, to conceal her true feelings, and her legal training came to save her from an uncontrollable emotional outburst.

Louise knew without any doubt that she had fallen deeply in love with Joseph, an ecstatic, all-embracing love, a love felt in the pit of her stomach, a love that filled her with inexplicable happiness merely being near him. Just the sound of his voice thrilled her, a glance from his eyes gave her contentment, and the smell of his body excited her. Yes, it was sensual; yes, it was a magnetic physical attraction, but it was now so much more. She loved him so completely, felt so secure when together, felt his gentle manliness, and was fascinated by his ideas and knowledge about so many things she did not understand. His modesty and his humour just drew her ever closer to him, as did his graciousness and kindness.

Although a biologically liberated woman of the modern era, she was experiencing ageless emotions. She had come to see and was beginning to understand that she was a woman, in the classical sense, and that Joseph was a man. They were different yet complementary, one without the other was in some way incomplete, unable to reach their full potential either as a man or a woman. Of course she was independent, certainly intellectually and economically and he had no legal power over her. However, this new reality she was grappling with was entirely different; it was mystical and deeply emotional, and she just knew she would never be complete without him.

She also knew she was experiencing feelings, emotions and deep longings toward Joseph that she was unable to control, for the first time in her young and highly successful life. Until now she had always been in control, able to keep the various departments of her life in separate and tidy boxes, everything under the orderly orchestration of her mind and cool logic. This had all changed, her heart was now the predominant force within her, and it was unleashing forces she never thought existed from deep within. This was all so new and frightening. There had already been a number of men in her life, various romances and even sexual encounters, so she knew this was not a temporary infatuation induced by their enchanting surroundings, she was mature and experienced enough to know that. They could have been anywhere and she knew she would be feeling the same. There had simply never been anyone like Joseph before; he had enraptured her so completely she shuddered at the mere thought of being away from him, even for a moment.

There are many forms of human love, and real love strikes arbitrarily. It consumes, is possessive and arrives with its own needs and demands. It also often involves sacrifice and personal pain. While Joseph had become the anchor of Louise's existence she also never wished him to be unhappy or to suffer in any way. Her needs must now always be secondary to his and he must never feel encumbered by her feelings or longings toward him. Louise knew love could also destroy as well as create, it could stifle as well as enliven and it could imprison as well as liberate. Her intuition, sensitivity to such things and her sharp mind made these realities inescapable to her. She also knew from within her heart that Joseph, as kind, intimate and caring as he is toward her, did not have reciprocal feelings for her.

"Are you all right, Louise?" Joseph asked, concerned at the vacant look in her face as she stared out to sea.

"Yes, yes I am fine Joe, just sorry you will not be with me tomorrow when I fly back," she replied, desperately trying to mask her true feelings. "Not to worry Joseph, all good things have to come to an end. Now what would you like to do tonight before you rush off for your business in Dubai?" Louise continued with a gentle shrug of her shoulders and a rueful smile.

Joseph's mind had already switched to another gear, thrown into overdrive by his father's remarks on the cell phone. He was suddenly thinking very clearly, especially about Louise. He sensed he had to act quickly, take control of the situation, think for them both for a moment and look after her. He had to make their parting tomorrow as painless as possible for Louise, and she needed to be distracted right now, and not left to dwell on this upset.

"Why don't we get dressed up a little later, walk down to town, have a good supper and find somewhere to dance together," Joseph suggested. As ever he had said the right thing, the thought of being able to dance together immediately started to cheer Louise up a little, and she again pushed all her negative thoughts to the back of her mind.

"Ok, Joseph, that sounds great," replied Louise, rising from her chair with a flurry, also trying to raise her spirits.

As Joseph walked with Louise later, arm in arm, she looked beautiful in one of her new dresses she had bought earlier in Zagreb. It suited her perfectly and hugged her shapely hips. With her blonde hair flowing and a pair of high-heeled shoes, she and Joseph looked as though they had been made for one another. He tall, broad shouldered, dark haired and very handsome, and Louise looking like some Nordic princess, even though she was born in Aberystwyth. As they walked along in step with each other there was a rhythm and harmony to their movement and passers by looked at them and just naturally smiled at this handsome young couple together, so natural and content in each other's company.

They found a bustling restaurant with a live band facing the harbour where Eric had deposited them the day before. It could have been the perfect spot had circumstances been different. Louise vainly looked out at the boats looking for

Eric and the boat of yesterday and just saw another boat moored where they had landed. Eric, Lisa and Eddie with his guitar had of course already left the day before, she reminded herself, with new passengers and were by now probably far away. It brought another rush of uncontrollable sadness that Eric and the yacht on which she had enjoyed such bliss was now gone, a part of her history now only ever a memory. It was as though her mind, insightful and attuned to seeking legal clarity, precision in the use of words and thoughts, was now punishing her. She felt everything so acutely.

Louise left most of her dinner even though the food was delicious. Joseph had also lost his appetite and found himself also falling into a state of lethargy and growing concern for the sadness he could see in Louise. They danced a little to some rave music, but their hearts were not in it. Louise was trying to be cheerful, but was simply unable to completely conceal how she was really feeling. Joseph also knew there was little he could do to help matters and even when he was particularly caring, it appeared to make matters worse. There were long awkward moments of silence and the easy intimacy between them had fled.

The tempo of the music had changed and the band was now playing a set of slow romantic musical numbers. In an almost last desperate attempt to improve matters, Joseph rose from the table walked around to Louise and extended his hand for a dance, smiling at her and they walked onto the dance floor together. Louise immediately reached for Joseph put her arms around him and nuzzled her face by his. He could feel her body pressing hard against him, almost as though she was urgently trying to get inside him. He could feel her total submission, the giving of herself to him, her longing in every sinew of her body as she held on to him. They danced slowly, just holding each other as tightly as they could, for several minutes. The applause from the assembled crowd for the band at the end of the set broke them from this trance, they looked around and they were the only couple left on the floor. Joseph looked down at Louise, she was silently crying, the tears glistening on her cheeks. This feeling of impending loss had overwhelmed her again; she could not empty her mind of thoughts of sitting in her Oxford apartment, this time tomorrow night on her own, without him.

As he hugged her close to his body, they walked back to the hotel, oblivious to all that was around them. Back in the villa, they just stood there together, not saying a word, holding each other's bodies. Louise fought to regain herself, to stop behaving so stupidly, to resist these waves of emotion that kept pouring over her. However, try as hard as she could, she found it impossible. She felt like a little girl again, helpless, being tossed around by her uncontrollable longings and fears.

They undressed and lay semi naked beside each other with their bodies pressed closely together in the elegant bed. There was no sexual arousal, just absolute tenderness and Louise insisted that a small bed side lamp remain on so she could look at Joseph, drink him into her, look into his eyes, touch his mouth and ensure he was still there close to her. Eventually they fell asleep, Joseph first coiled around her body. Louise had a poor night's sleep, she woke many times and just lay there motionless looking at Joseph sleeping peacefully beside her.

The next morning Joseph was up early, had sorted out his flights to Dubai on his laptop computer and had ordered breakfast for them both in the villa. When Louise woke as the breakfast arrived the sun was already high in the sky. Everything had become functional, they had to pack, get to the airport on time and check cell phone messages. Louise had an urgent message to call one of her professors at Oxford who had just woken up to something she had been reminding him about for weeks, and they had to check their travel papers. Then they were dressed and ready to go, Louise to catch the 11:30 Croatia Airlines flight from Dubrovnik directly to Gatwick, and Joseph to fly to Zagreb before catching his flight to Dubai on Emirates Airline later in the afternoon.

In their few remaining private moments together in the villa overlooking the Adriatic, they stood looking smart in their town clothes. They were both holding back, Louise more than Joseph, whose mind was now largely elsewhere.

It was Louise who made the spontaneous move, as ever,

and she walked up close to Joseph, placed her arms around his neck and looking into his eyes said, "You know, Joe, don't you, that I have fallen deeply in love with you? I have never felt like this ever before about anyone, and it is an extraordinary rather scary feeling. I just want to be with you all the time and dread going back to Oxford without you. I am sorry my darling, to be all intense like this when you have more important things on your mind, but I had to tell you, I could not bear the thought of you not knowing how I feel about you. Don't feel awkward Joe and you do not need to say anything. The last few days have been the happiest days of my life, you have made me alive in so many ways, it has been wonderful. I have so much to cherish and thank you for, you cannot ever imagine." Louise stopped talking, stepped back releasing Joseph, smiled and turned slightly away from him.

After a pause she continued, "I know you don't feel the same way and that you cannot help it Joe, I just long for the day when perhaps you will feel a little as I do for you, for me. Until then I know you have important things to attend to. Please keep safe Joe; I will simply die if anything were ever to happen to you. I'm sorry for my silly antics last night, it was hardly what you deserved, for our last evening together after such a wonderful time together. I will be waiting for you in Oxford," and she stepped forward, hugged and kissed him.

Joseph just stood there speechless, thinking how strong and protective of him Louise was being. He was now the defenceless one, being protected by her courage and fortitude. Joseph looked lost and sad, unable to say the words he so desperately wanted to be able to say to her at that moment. He reached out for her and pulled her close as they hugged, kissed, squeezed each other's bodies, there was an almost angry passion between them as the minutes ticked by when suddenly the phone rang. It was reception saying their taxi for the airport had arrived at the hotel.

The flight departure call for Louise's flight came agonisingly quickly once they had gone through the elaborate security checks, Passport Control and other airport procedures. Joseph had an hour to wait after Louise's flight had gone for his flight to Zagreb.

As they stood holding each other in front of the departure gate, Louise looked up at Joseph and asked "Joe, may I ask you a very special favour, and don't be shocked?"

"Yes, of course; what is it?" Joseph replied.

Louise looked into his eyes and smiled and said, "May I borrow your Bible? I will keep it safe for you until you get back to Oxford, and I know how special it is to you. I also bought you a new Bible in Zagreb that you can take to Dubai; it is about the same size; would you mind?"

Joseph was surprised by her request, and he was deeply touched by her gesture that he knew meant so much to them both. "Yes of course," he said, reaching into his carry on bag and retrieving the worn Bible and handed it to Louise.

She smiled and handed him her special gift to him. "Must go my love," she said cheerily, giving him a final kiss on his lips. "See you in a few days in Oxford, and be careful," were her last words as she turned and left.

He watched her walk through the gate, her elegant body moving toward the bus waiting outside, she never looked back fearful she would cry again seeing him standing alone. The bus moved off and she was gone and Joseph stood almost paralyzed with the Bible in his left hand watching the steps being withdrawn from her plane. He still stood in the same spot looking out through the large windows until he saw her flight take off and disappear into the horizon. It was only then that he looked down to see something blue protruding from his bag and leaning down he opened it and there was Louise's blue bikini. Stuck to the front of the Bible she had handed him was a small yellow sticker that he then noticed with Louise's distinctive handwriting. It read "Wanted you to have something to keep me close when we are apart, Love you always, Louise."

Joseph ambled aimlessly across the departure hall and sat down on a metal bench staring into the distance. His heart was heavy, and he continued to feel sad. How could he have been so blind, so stupid, not to have seen what was happening these last few days? How could he have so underestimated her, been so casual about matters that can be so powerful especially with someone of Louise's intellect and sensitivities? How could he have been so careless with her, causing her unhappiness? It was then the words of his father came back to him from the conversation they had just a few weeks earlier at Himbledon. It was precisely this type of situation, and the possible suffering of others, particularly ladies who get close to us, that his father had been referring to.

Just then he looked ahead and focussed on a tourist poster promoting Dubrovnik and there was a picture of the Grand Villa Argentina and he remembered that he had forgotten to tell Louise of the Richard Burton connection after all, in the emotionally charged remaining time they had had together. He reached into his jacket pocket and reached for something to awkwardly wipe a tear from his eye.

As he continued his journey to Dubai his mind remained in two places, firstly with Louise, the happy yet troubled time they had enjoyed travelling together, how they had become so very close, the particular responsibility he now had toward her, to protect and care for her whatever circumstances arose in the future. He yearned to love her, to be able to reciprocate some of her feelings, but it was simply not there. She had a special place in his heart, but, sadly, it was not love.

The other thoughts that he pondered were what may lie ahead. He had little idea why he was actually going to Dubai, what was so important and urgent. He thought about Tim's death, Dandler Aggregates and Paris, and that he would soon need to be focussing on very different things to cruising in the Adriatic.

After arriving in Zagreb he had a four-hour wait in the airport before boarding the Emirates flight to Dubai. As he was about to board the flight his cell phone sounded and there on the screen was a message from Louise.

"Back in Oxford, raining, be careful, talk to me soon, love you, Louise."

As he walked to the boarding gate he tapped out his reply, "Just boarding, thanks, bikini made me smile, I'll be in touch, take care Joseph."

Within just a few minutes he too, was miles away, flying south over the Mediterranean, Egypt and onward to the Gulf.

15

Dubai

ON ARRIVING AT DUBAI AIRPORT, JOSEPH WENT QUICKLY into the baggage hall, through the various procedures and catching a yellow cab to the address Achmed had sent on his cell phone. It was now late at night and he was wide-awake, and talked from the rear seat of the large Toyota taxi to the driver, in a uniform in the front seat.

"Where are you from, and how long have you been here?" asked Joseph.

"I am from Pakistan, and have lived here for twenty-seven years," answered the driver with a friendly and courteous manner.

"Are your family here or still in Pakistan?" continued Joseph.

"They are in Pakistan, but I go home regularly; it's only a short flight from here," continued the driver.

"You must like it here; twenty-seven years is a long," said Joseph.

"Yes I do, very much, for three reasons," the driver continued and Joseph waited for him to continue. "It is orderly and very safe in Dubai, one is free to live one's life and practice your beliefs, and there is regular work with money."

Joseph thought for a moment, and then said, "Yes, they are good reasons, and I can see why you have stayed for so long."

The driver, looking in the rear view mirror, smiled at

Joseph and nodded. They then remained silent as Joseph looked out at all the lights and deserted streets of this new modern city created in the desert.

It was a swift journey and they soon pulled up outside large wooden doors set in a high wall. As Joseph paid the taxi driver and bade him farewell, lights came on either side of the large wooden doors and one of them opened and there stood Achmed. As Joseph got out of the air-conditioned taxi, the heat hit him, even though it was now after midnight it was still oppressively hot.

"Joseph, welcome and come inside," said Achmed reaching forward and shaking Joseph's hand.

They walked through the half-open wooden door under an archway and into a large courtyard with flowers, shrubs and various outside lights showing a large garden area, terrace and residence beyond. They walked across the courtyard up steps and into a large entrance hallway, through more doors into a large airy lounge.

"Would you like some tea or a drink, Joseph?" Achmed asked.

"Some tea would be great, thanks," replied Joseph.

Within a short time Achmed placed a tray with a teapot, two cups, milk and white sugar cubes with some biscuits on the low table by the large suite of comfortable chairs. Achmed asked if Joseph took milk, and then poured two cups of tea, with milk in Joseph's cup, but none in his own. They sat stirring their teacups gently, and talked.

Achmed thanked Joseph for changing his travel plans and coming to Dubai so promptly. After asking Joseph about his journey and his holiday in Croatia, he went on to begin to explain the purpose of his urgent visit. He explained that Joseph's father thought it best for them to meet in view of some recent developments and information they had received related to the Paris attack. Also Portia, the lady Joseph had met with Achmed at the London board meeting, has a daughter Francesca who was routing via Dubai the next day on her way to Rome from the United States to meet with them both. Francesca is a microbiologist, like her mother, and is doing groundbreaking research at MIT in Boston and will be bringing some further confidential information that they think may also be connected with what happened in Paris some four months earlier. The intention was to fully brief Joseph before he returned to Himbledon for a meeting with his father and Mark.

"But that is enough for the moment," said Achmed continuing. "You must be tired, let me show you to your room, I will call you at 6:30 in the morning; we have a busy day tomorrow." With that, Achmed rose and ushered Joseph through the lounge and up a large staircase, along various passages to his bedroom and said goodnight.

It was a very large bedroom, well appointed with expensive furniture and a large en suite bathroom and after unpacking a few things Joseph ran himself a bath. Lying in the bath, his mind was clear yet he could not focus for too long on anything. He suddenly missed Louise next to him, seeing her body nearby and he felt a touch of loneliness despite Achmed's warm welcome and hospitality. He leant over and looked at his watch by the hand basin, and it was one thirty in the morning, so it would be midnight in Oxford, too late to give Louise a call. He suddenly drew himself up in the bath and realised he had to stop this daydreaming and get to bed. Back in the bedroom and in bed he noticed a large flat screen TV opposite, and after fiddling with the remote control, eventually got it to flicker to life. He flicked between channels looking for the BBC news that he could not find, so came to rest on CNN. As he settled his eyes on the screen he could hear a low drumming sound above his head and realised these must be the powerful air-conditioning units keeping it so cool and pleasant. Again, he involuntarily put out his hand, unthinkingly, to reach for Louise beside him, but just found emptiness. *I must stop this*, he thought again. *It is ridiculous, and there is work to do.*

As he started to pay attention to the news on the screen, he was shocked. It now had his full attention. They were reporting in detail the loss of four passenger planes without trace that had gone missing at about the same time three days previously. Each aircraft was from a different airline, and they had all gone down far out to sea, one mid Atlantic, another in the Indian Ocean, another in the Pacific and the fourth in the South China Sea. According to the CNN news report there had been no bad weather conditions at any of these locations and all of the aircraft were new with perfect maintenance records. Two of them were Airbuses and the other two were Boeing 747s. The death toll had been high and there were pictures of distraught relatives and friends at various airports around the world. Rescue and search vessels were scouring the oceans to try to recover the black boxes to find out what had happened. Some strange evidence was already beginning to emerge, each of these particular aircraft losing radio contact with air traffic control at precisely four and a half minutes before they disappeared, and all the captains of the aircraft reporting, precisely four hours after take off to various ground control centres around the world, that they were experiencing minor problems with onboard electronic and computer systems. All this shocking news had partly eclipsed the flood of reporting on the Paris atrocity although there was some coverage reporting that there were no fresh leads, and the French government were continuing with their enquiries.

Joseph just lay there; he turned down the sound with just the flickering screen remaining on. Having been away and at sea in recent days, he had seen no news so all this came as a shock, and he had an eerie feeling all this ugly news was connected. For a moment he gave into further self-indulgence when the thought went through his mind that if only Louise could have imprisoned him on Mljet for seven years, he could have perhaps missed all this growing horror.

Next day he had breakfast with Achmed, who introduced Joseph to his wife and three sons, about to go to school. They were a very gracious and warm family and they were clearly devoted to each other. Joseph and Achmed then crossed the courtyard behind the large residence he had slept in, to another attractive building that had offices, what looked like laboratories and some meeting rooms, all set within the compound. As he walked outside the heat was like a weight on his shoulders and he was relieved to get inside again. Unlocking the door to a large well-appointed office, Achmed ushered Joseph to a large leather suite set near a large impressive desk and he began to talk.

He explained that Dandler Aggregates and some of their leading engineers were part of the consortium that created the Palms, and that Achmed would take Joseph later and show him this extraordinary town with luxury houses and hotels stretching far out into the Arabian Gulf. More importantly, Achmed with some trusted local friends and family members had been doing some of their own discreet investigations since the board meeting in London. They had turned up some potentially interesting information linked to the Paris attack. With the rapid and huge expansion of Dubai in recent years and the massive construction activities, managed and controlled largely by two major construction groups all associated with the ruling family, Achmed had privileged access to all manner of otherwise confidential information. Emirates Airline had also been an invaluable source of information, as had the security police in the Emirates. It seemed likely that fifteen of the drivers of the ready mix vehicles that had been used in the Paris attack were from Dubai.

There is a floating population of construction workers who work around the world on big projects. Dubai attracts thousands of these people, mainly younger men, who come and work long hours, make and save money and then take periods away from the busy and dangerous construction sites. It had become a way of life for thousands and these people often tended to specialise in certain trades and activities. At one time, Dubai had a third of all the high-rise cranes in the world; such was the intensity of local construction. Another interesting and relevant facet of life in Dubai is that unless you have a job or are a tourist, you are required to leave if not a national of the country. If you lose your job then you have to leave, often having to return to your home country.

As a result of Achmed's enquiries with various airline-booking systems they had discovered a list of potential suspects who had all flown to Paris, just forty-eight hours before the attack took place. The Emirates authorities are diligent about record keeping and fastidious about compliance with a range of sensible rules and regulations, particularly in the construction sector. By cross matching the airline passenger information they had discovered that this list of fifteen suspects had all worked in concrete supply activities to construction sites. With further enquiries, clear evidence had also emerged, that several of them were authorised to drive the large ready mix trucks, and that eight of these young men were American. Achmed opened his laptop computer, flicked it on, and touched the mouse locating a certain file, opened it and then turned the computer around on the coffee table between them to show Joseph a listing of the fifteen suspects.

There was a detailed listing showing their age, nationality, date entered and registered with the Emirates authorities to work in the country, their employer, their recent flight movements and a range of other information. There were also passport-sized photographs of each of them.

"Do you notice anything interesting from this list, Joseph?" asked Achmed, smiling at him over the top of the computer screen.

Joseph looked intently at the screen running, his eyes down the various columns and information before him. After a few moments he replied with a little excitement, "Yes I do, firstly all these people returned to Dubai within two days of the attack from various airports in Northern Europe, I see Brussels and Heathrow appear a lot. They are also all white, mainly American with two Brit's and various other West European nationals."

"That's right, Joseph." Achmed smiled.

"It gets even more interesting, however," continued Achmed, leaning over and placing the curser on two of the names before him and highlighting their information on the computer, before continuing to explain matters to Joseph.

Some ten days ago, the two characters highlighted on the computer, both American men in their early thirties, had been arrested for carrying liquor in their car without a licence. While alcohol is widely consumed in Dubai among many of the expatriates living and working in the city, it is carefully controlled and there are strict rules and laws regarding its purchase, conveyance and consumption. As a result of this, they had been automatically fired from their construction jobs and would ordinarily have been routinely deported, both back to the U.S.A.. Through a contact in the special Dubai police, who Achmed had asked to keep a lookout for anything suspicious, the policeman had contacted Achmed who instantly saw an opportunity to further his enquiries. Dubai jails are not the most welcoming of places and, under some tough cross examination, the younger of the two men had become nervous and afraid, especially about any suggestion of deportation back to America. With information quickly provided discreetly by Achmed about their recent travel movements, the questioning had broadened beyond the liquor misdemeanour, to a severe interrogation as to why they had gone to Paris for such a brief period exactly at the time of the atrocity.

The two men had been moved to a high security prison and had been kept apart while the interrogation continued. Four days ago, the younger man cracked, pleaded with the prison staff not to deport him to the U.S.A. and admitted that he had driven one of the trucks in the Paris attack, and would co-operate if the police kept his arrest a secret and permitted him to remain in Dubai. He claimed he had been blackmailed, but would not say who by, and added that his girlfriend, who was still in America, was in great danger if information of their arrest, especially for carrying alcohol, ever got back to certain people. He was very frightened and appeared unable to grasp the seriousness of the situation or the dreadful carnage he had inflicted a few months earlier in Paris.

Achmed leant back in the leather chair and looked straight at Joseph saying, "You know Joseph, we are dealing with something extremely sinister here. This young man appears to have a complete disconnect between what he carried out in Paris, the mass murder he committed, and he feels no remorse or responsibility. He remembers going there, driving the truck and flying back, but little else. Listening to the interrogation audiotapes it is as though he was operating under some sort of autopilot and that he was living in some other sort of bizarre reality, when he travelled to Paris. It is all very strange and perplexing. It is also the same with the other suspect."

"Anyway," continued Achmed. "We are very fortunate to

have stumbled on these two characters, and this latest information is beginning to reveal a whole new range of dimensions to the Paris atrocity. I want you to please take this information back with you and give it to your father at Himebledon."

Joseph was just beginning to grasp the enormity of what he was getting involved with. It was like a horror movie, something out of a spy thriller yet it was all so real and immediate. There were several times when he had to recalibrate his brain to all this, just to be sure he was not having a nightmare.

Achmed turned his laptop computer around again and quickly transferred various encrypted files onto a computer memory stick, removed it from the side of his personal computer and handed it to Joseph.

"Keep it safe Joseph," he said, and smiled.

It was now late morning, and Achmed stood and, looking down at Joseph, said, "Francesca will be arriving shortly, Joseph, and we must go and meet her at the airport."

"Oh yes, of course," replied Joseph, who had completely forgotten about this lady arriving today from Boston.

As Achmed drove to the airport with Joseph beside him, Joseph turned and said, "Tell me something about Francesca, please. I have never met her, and did not know Portia had a daughter."

As he recalled his meeting with Portia, who he now realised must be some years older than he had thought, Achmed proceeded to describe Francesca to Joseph. She was a qualified medical doctor and post-doctoral researcher currently working at MIT in Boston in biochemistry, and was collaborating with Achmed with various humanitarian health projects, as is her mother. Francesca was almost thirty-one years of age, bright and talented, with a quite amazing mind, and rarely had Achmed had the privilege of working with someone so young yet so exceptional. She was also very beautiful. Her father had been a wealthy Italian businessman, owning property and various business interests in Europe and South America. He was also a dedicated legal advocate and it was this that had probably led to him being gunned down outside the law courts in Palermo more than twenty years ago, since he had persistently tried to bring various high ranking men in the mafia to justice.

Achmed smiled and said, “It is not only Islam that can be violent Joseph.”

“Yes, I know,” replied Joseph nodding his head.

Portia had inherited the family fortune and was now the head of the family and one day, many years from now Achmed hoped this wealth and responsibility would pass to Francesca and her younger brother. Joseph sensed that Achmed and Portia had a very special relationship from the manner in which he spoke whenever he referred to her. They were now nearing the airport and Achmed turned the large Mercedes into the parking garage.

As they were getting out of the car Achmed turned and looked at Joseph and said, “Oh yes, there is just one other thing you may wish to know about Francesca, I think she is also a member of *Opus Dei*, although I cannot be certain about that.”

As they walked across to the airport terminal building Joseph asked Achmed what he made of these recent air disasters and whether they may in some way be connected to what they were involved with investigating. Achmed responded in such a manner that Joseph realised this not a question to be discussing while walking in the open in earshot of others, and Achmed merely looked at Joseph and said, “In all likelihood, yes,” in a manner clearly indicating that he would be drawn no further in on the subject.

Joseph stood next to Achmed in the entrance hall of the airport and watched as the various passengers pushed their trolleys laden with baggage wearily toward the waiting relatives, friends, chauffeurs and expectant porters.

“There she is,” said Achmed as a tall, smartly dressed lady with jet-black hair walked toward them with a broad warm smile. She was carrying just a small carry on bag hanging from her shoulder, a handbag and a laptop computer. *Surely this woman has not just stepped off a long-haul flight from the other side of the world,* thought Joseph. She looked so well groomed and different from the rest of the arriving passengers, more like an airhostess than a passenger.

After greetings and introductions they were soon travelling back to the compound and Francesca sat in the back of the car and Joseph in the front next to Achmed. Francesca and Achmed talked together animatedly, often exchanging information that made little sense to Joseph. They used various terms and words specific to their common interest, of working toward the eradication of diseases and infections that took the lives of millions of people every year. Occasionally she would lean forward to sit with her head between the front seats, looking at Achmed, to clarify specific matters in their conversation and Joseph detected her perfume, a gentle fresh flagrance that took his mind back to the flowers in the garden of the villa at Hvar.

Immediately they arrived at the compound and entered the main residence, Achmed offered Francesca the opportunity to shower and rest, but she declined, preferring to have their confidential discussion without further delay, so they walked through to Achmed's office. Walking behind them, Joseph could see Francesca from various angles; she was wearing a pencil skirt with a small slit just behind her knees, a ladies jacket and medium-heeled sensible shoes. Her black hair was long and she had obviously brushed it recently because it lay like a glistening black mane between her shoulders. Although tall, she was well proportioned and smiled back at Joseph whenever he followed her though doors, while continuing her rather intense conversation with Achmed. They clearly knew each other very well and were at ease in each other's company.

On entering Achmed's office, Francesca immediately put her bags down on one of the leather sofas and walked to the water dispenser and filled a long glass with cold fresh water. From her behaviour she also knew this office well and proceeded to pick up her laptop computer and went to an outlet socket and plugged in the computer cable.

"I must recharge my batteries after the flight," she said, slightly tossing her head back to throw her hair away from her face. She then plugged another lead into a device that would show her data on a screen in the office. Joseph had gone back to where he had sat earlier where his computer lay on the seat. Francesca undid her jacket, removing it swiftly and laid it over the back of the chair near her bags, and proceeded to sit down opposite Joseph. She was self-assured, gracious and warm, but clearly had a purpose.

The three of them chatted a little about the flight, how she was looking forward to being in Rome shortly with her mother, and she thanked Achmed and Joseph for being so accommodating and arranging this meeting at such short notice. She knew Joseph had just come from being on holiday in Croatia with his girlfriend Louise and asked him about her, their holiday together and how his mother and father were. Once they had settled she then looked at Joseph with an expression of sympathy and said how upset she had been at the news and circumstances of Tim's death. Although she did not know him well, she had met him on a few occasions and said she had taken an instant liking to him particularly his sense of humour. Joseph was surprised just how much this stranger already knew about him and how genuinely concerned she was about him and the family.

Francesca then proceeded to explain why her mother, Portia, had suggested she re-route via Dubai for this meeting and she referred to the meeting that Joseph and her mother had at the board meeting. She said that an important reason was that she wanted to meet Joseph and that she had heard much about him, and this seemed an ideal opportunity to do so. She spoke with a slight glint in her eye, and looked straight at Joseph without a moment's hesitation or affectation. Francesca knew Paul and he had spoken about his younger brother Joseph, so she was curious. Such frankness embarrassed Joseph, who could feel a blush spreading across his face.

"Don't be embarrassed Joseph, it is the truth and we do not have much time," she said with a laugh and broad smile. "But now to the other reason," she said promptly, and she leant forward, as her hair fell forward either side of her face, and she activated the mouse on her computer and opened a file.

The face of a handsome young man appeared on the screen and Francesca, speaking with perfect English in her soft voice, started to speak. "This man, John Holmes, a master's student at MIT in straight chemistry, has been pursuing me for the last ten months. He is charming, entertaining, has plenty of money from rich parents, or so he claims, is probably fantastic between the sheets and is very sweet. A girl's dream guy, as the Americans might say. He has attempted, rather clumsily, may I add, to try to sexually seduce me a few times, particularly in recent weeks. He must be wondering by now whether I am sexually inclined the other way." She laughed, looking straight at Joseph before continuing. "He is also an evangelist, of sorts, full of good-sounding words and ideas, helping the poor, quotes odd scriptures from time to time from the Old Testament and as well as earnestly wanting to sleep with me, he has also been trying to recruit me and some of my work to help the less fortunate through some rich family trust he claims to have." She paused for a moment to let this information register with them both, particularly Joseph who she knew was new to all this.

She then continued, "Sounds good, but I am afraid a little too good!" She touched her computer again and there was a picture of a body being recovered from beneath a large wooden wharf, in some run-down part of a city, and Francesca continued. "Six weeks ago I discovered via a close friend on the academic staff, who incidentally is a man that I am very fond of, just to put your mind at ease Joseph, that this John Holmes might be an impostor. I made some further confidential enquiries, talked with a senior man in the FBI and was in touch with Mark at Himbledon and working together we discovered that John Holmes is, or was, certainly a post-master's student registered with MIT until his decaying body was hauled from a local river from under this jetty, a month ago. I got the confidential autopsy report and from dental records and a few other tests they ran, the corpse is definitely the proper John Holmes. Came from out of state, and has no family, and something of a loner, so presumably no one has missed his disappearance, until now. Working with Mark via our secure intranet, I completed various questionnaires from my experience of this man, and sent the data back to

Himbledon. Mark ran some data analysis and he say's this impostor fits a whole range of personality and other behavioural profiles that would appear to associate him with a certain cult in the United States. The Bible verses, his methods, the sexual seduction and a few other aspects of this man's *modus operandi*, all strongly suggest there is a connection."

She then paused again and stood up and walked to the water cooler to replenish her glass with cold water. With her back to them both she remarked, "I always dehydrate so quickly whenever I land in Dubai, forgive me gentlemen."

Achmed smiled at Joseph and raised his eyebrows slightly as though to say, 'see what I meant about this lady?'. Joseph smiled back with a slight nod.

Francesca walked purposefully across the room and the light from the window shone on her white embroidered shirt and her tight knee length skirt hugging her body as she sat down again opposite Joseph, with her knees and dark shoes lying together, but slightly to one side before him. "Do you have any questions, Joseph, before I continue?" she asked, appearing to treat Achmed as a casual bystander.

"Where is this impostor now?" asked Joseph.

Francesca sensed a concern in him for her safety.

"I will come back to him in a moment, Joseph." She smiled. "There are two other matters I wish to raise first, and now we start getting into some tortuous areas," she said.

Joseph involuntarily raised his eyebrows as the thought went through his mind that matters appeared to him to already be very tortuous and dangerous. Francesca sensed this immediately, looked straight into his eyes and slightly furrowed her brow showing Joseph that he must please pay attention and keep his mind focussed on what she was telling him. "There are a number of issues," she continued and explained that the cult was probably trying to get their hands on certain bacterial strains that could be rapidly replicated in significant volumes to possibly be used to infect food, water and even bulk milk supplies. While this would be relatively easy, it was the drug resistant bacteria and viral strains that could not be readily countered with antibiotics and other available drugs that they appeared to be particularly interested in. This was also one of her research specialities and why they had probably tried to target her. If they got their hands on these particularly nasty bugs, explained Francesca, pandemics would rapidly become unstoppable plagues.

Francesca then briefly mentioned, to avoid any misunderstanding in Joseph's mind, as to what they were potentially dealing with and how devastating such a pandemic could be, asked him, "Do you know how many people the Spanish flu pandemic killed toward the end of the first World War, Joseph?" He looked at her and said that he did not know, and she continued. "Although exact numbers are not known, it is estimated reliably that it killed over a hundred million people, actually more than those who lost their lives in the war. Many of those who died were young, healthy people and it is believed it started in an army camp in Northern France. It spread throughout Europe and across American within weeks and there was nothing anyone could do to prevent it. These bacteria and viruses are still around and are mutating all the time."

At this moment Achmed spoke, "Without wishing to embarrass Francesca, may I add at this point, that she is one of a tiny handful of medical scientists around the world who is coming up with substantive answers in this sphere of microbiology. Fran is one of the leaders and is making the most extraordinary advances in this field." Joseph heard clearly what Achmed had just said and noticed the affectionate manner in which he had used her shortened name.

Francesca took another mouthful of water, placed her glass on the table and continued, "Yes, you may be right Achmed and this is why they were probably intent on taking some risks in trying to recruit me. But let me return to the impostor that you asked about Joseph. He is still at large and unaware that the authorities have found the real John Holmes, and that we know about him. I want it to stay this way since he could be an invaluable source of information about this highly secret and reclusive cult that none of us, including the authorities, know much about. We have got to quickly discover who they are, how they operate and what dangerous intentions they may have. I will, therefore, act as bait, and try to get closer in the days ahead—"

Joseph suddenly interrupted, "Surely that will be far too dangerous; we must have other methods without having to put you at such risk?"

"We are afraid not, Joseph," interjected Achmed. "And anyway, Francesca knows fully what risks she is facing, and, apart from our young men in the Dubai prison, Francesca is just about all we have at the moment."

Francesca was touched by Joseph's concern for her and turning her head slightly to one side, she smiled affectionately at him. She then straightened herself up in the leather chair and started to speak again. "The last and most sensitive thing I must raise, and I do stress it is still highly speculative and far from certain, is that it just may be that Tim's murder was facilitated by someone very close to him. This could mean that this cult or, perhaps others, have in some way infiltrated us, particularly the Trimbledons."

Joseph was numbed by these remarks, he did not know how to respond and it was so sudden and personal. If true then he and his family are in danger, they have already murdered his brother. His head raced, and he immediately pressed Francesca for further details of her suspicions, but she would not be drawn any further on the matter.

"Just be careful Joseph and listen to your father when he warns you about being careful."

Francesca then turned to Achmed, smiled and asked whether he had managed to book a table for them this evening at the new French restaurant at the Burj Tower because she thought Joseph would enjoy the fountains. Achmed laughed softly and confirmed that he had. It was clear that their meeting was now drawing to a close and Francesca closed her computer and left it to charge.

As she rose to her feet and leant over to collect her jacket she said, "How is Anna, Joseph? I understand she was terribly shocked and upset about it all?"

"She is with Ruth, my sister in London, the last I heard, and yes, she is evidently grieving hard at her loss," replied Joseph.

Francesca stood close to Joseph now, placing her hand softly on his forearm and asked, "Please keep me advised, Joseph, about Anna, once you get home, and especially once you get to Paris."

He was reminded of her mother and sensing it would be fruitless to ask further questions about this matter he replied, "Yes, of course I will, of course."

Francesca turned away from Joseph, gathered up her things, and asked Achmed, "Am I in my usual room?"

"Yes, of course," he replied.

Then, facing them both, she said, "Well, if you will both please excuse me, I am going to have a rest, and I will see you both for dinner later."

Achmed moved to open the office door for her, and she left.

After Francesca had left the room, Joseph turned to Achmed and asked, "Does Francesca come and stay here often?"

"Oh yes, she has her own room in the house and some of her things here, remember her mother, Francesca and I are also working on various health projects together so we all tend to travel regularly between here, Rome, London and the U.S.A.," he replied. Slowly things were falling into place in Joseph's mind about a whole new world and people that he needed to fully understand, and quickly.

In his bedroom before changing to meet Achmed and Francesca for dinner later, Joseph reviewed the secret computer files Achmed and Francesca had loaded on his memory stick and he added a brief covering email and sent them to Mark at Himbledon via their secure intranet. He wanted Mark and his father to have this vital information urgently to add to the other intelligence they were reviewing. It proved so important that John Trimbledon had phoned the prime minister's personal secretary later the same evening, requesting an urgent confidential meeting with him and the home secretary.

16

Dinner By the Fountains

JOSEPH MET ACHMED AGAIN IN THE LARGE, COOL, airy lounge of the main house and walked to a small bar in the corner of the room where Achmed was reading a document.

"Would you like something to drink, Joseph?" enquired Achmed.

"Just some cold water please," Joseph replied, and Achmed turned and filled a tall glass from the cold water dispenser behind him. "Do you drink alcohol, Achmed?" Joseph asked.

"No, I don't," replied Achmed, smiling. "We have alcohol, though, whatever you may like; we keep it for guests. We are more liberal here in Dubai than in some of the other states nearby, although, as I mentioned earlier, there are certain rules here that some people from overseas still find rather strict."

Just then, Joseph heard the sound of high heels and he turned to see Francesca coming down the marble staircase. He and Achmed turned to greet her again as she walked to the bottom of the stairs and walked smiling across the room toward them both. She looked entirely different from the person Joseph had met and talked with earlier and moved with an effortless grace. She had put her hair up into an attractive arrangement that fully revealed her face and her long neck, her high cheek bones, full mouth and large eyes set broadly in her face with a classical beauty. She was wearing a strapless black dress to just below her knees. The dress had markings of gold and her shoes matched, she carried a small black handbag and was modestly wearing some jewellery and she stood now beside them both, upright, with her hands close together at her waist.

She could have been a fashion model by the manner in which she deported herself, although she was fuller in the body than many models and the low-cut dress revealed an intriguing cleavage. As they talked and Joseph glanced at her from time to time he noticed that she not only looked very different from earlier, her behaviour was also very different. Francesca let them lead the conversation, the earlier assertiveness had gone, she was now gentle, very feminine, listening attentively and following everything they were saying with a range of gentle facial and body gestures. She had glistening white teeth and had just a touch of makeup on her face with a little lipstick on her generous lips and a small gold chain around her tanned upper chest and one small gold ring on her right hand. When she turned to listen or answer his questions, Francesca looked straight at Joseph, into his eyes and her whole body was attentive just to him and he felt at these moments a strange intensity between them. When in conversation with her he felt he had her total attention, and that she was there just for him and no one else, listening, smiling, slightly furrowing her brow with serious matters and laughing freely at his humour.

"If you are both ready then, we should go," said Achmed, sensing the chemistry between them that often the perceptive onlooker can see long before those who are directly involved do. Within twenty minutes Achmed's Mercedes and his personal driver pulled up outside one of the modern complexes that characterise the modern Dubai. Achmed instructed his driver quietly to return, just after ten, to collect him while Joseph talked with Francesca and they then walked through an arcade of small shops and into a new restaurant on the edge of what looked like a small lake. It was a very warm evening as waiters seated them at their table on a terrace overlooking the water.

It was an exclusive French restaurant that had not been open for long, and after ordering dinner Achmed described some of the history of Dubai and how it had been a trading centre for hundreds of years around the creek where merchandise was sailed to all the countries of the Gulf and beyond, in the many small dhows that still sail these waters. When oil was discovered, the ruling family wisely used the revenues to lay down important infrastructure on which today's modern city is built. They had the wisdom to know that the oil would eventually run out and that Dubai would have to have other attractions to become a world-class competitive city. There were strong ties between this principality and the British, since the Crown had provided protection before independence. The British Embassy still occupies a prestigious site in the centre of the new Dubai and it was from these earlier times that his family had first worked with the Trimbledons on various matters.

Joseph had many questions for Achmed that he answered fully and graciously. Yes as a Muslim country there were many stringent rules, despite Dubai being the most open and liberal of the states in the Gulf. All were welcome in Dubai, especially those with skills and capital to help collaborate and build a mutually prosperous future. The rules of the state are clear, there for all to see and observe, and providing one abides by them there is a good life to be enjoyed in Dubai. However, disregard them or disrespect the culture and beliefs of the local people and you will become unwelcome. Westerners were honoured guests in Dubai, but, all the same, Joseph felt, they always remained guests. This all seemed to Joseph to be entirely reasonable and despite many strange media reports about the place, he thought many other societies in the West could well learn from this example.

They also spoke about Croatia and Joseph's recent travels including his love of sailing. They asked about Louise, and Francesca watched Joseph intently as he spoke of her, his facial expressions and the way he referred to her, this unknown lady in his affections. Francesca spoke about Boston, how she missed Europe and how she looked forward to finishing up her work at MIT and returning to work with her mother in Rome. This was clearly where her heart was. As they talked they were interrupted periodically by spectacular water and light shows in the middle of the lake just beyond the terrace where they were dining. To a range of enchanting music and special lighting affects the water danced, shot up in the air, cascaded across acres of water, there were huge fountains, running trails of water darting backwards and forwards, precisely in harmony with the various music being played, and after every performance they could feel a fine spray on their faces as the waters fell back to the lake below. Loud clapping and hoots of appreciation from the other diners followed each interlude. It was a wonderful setting and atmosphere, and Joseph had been involuntarily transported yet again to another reality, a world of privilege, wealth and Arabian delight.

It was now a little before ten as Achmed gently pushed a set of keys across the table towards Joseph saying, "Well, it is getting late and if you will excuse me, Francesca you know the way home, and Joseph, there will be taxis outside all night, take care of her and I will see you both in the morning," he rose and as he did so Francesca stood up and so did Joseph, surprised by Achmed's imminent departure. Achmed and Francisca kissed each other on both cheeks and then Achmed extended a warm hand to say good night to Joseph. Within a moment, this tall man walked across the restaurant to leave and Joseph noticed that he stopped momentarily and spoke to the headwaiter, and then he was gone, leaving them both alone.

As though on cue, another musical interlude started and the fountains burst into life again to the accompaniment of Andrea Bocelli singing *Liberta*. As it played, Francesca put both her bare arms forward on the table, looked down and placed her hands together and she rotated her dessert fork between her fingers. She was not looking at the water display, but deep within her own thoughts. Joseph watched the dancing waters with Francesca fully in his field of vision so he was able to look at her face and shoulders as she continued to look down, listening to the music, but with the dancing waters behind her. She was exquisite, almost hypnotically beautiful, he thought, with her long, dark eyelashes lowered over her eyes, her mouth still and deep, and her long fingers slowly turning the desert fork as she sat calmly composed, waiting for the music to stop. When the spray engulfed them, she raised her eyes, looked straight at Joseph, and smiled.

There was a momentary silence between them and Francesca was the first to speak. "Achmed is such a dear man, and so clever, our families have worked together since my grandparents, he is like a second father to me."

Joseph looked at her and could not believe it was the same forthright person in the business suit he had first met earlier. She sensed his slight awkwardness and smiled, putting the dessert fork to one side.

"Would you like some more wine, Joseph, or something more to eat? The desserts here are something special."

"No thanks, not unless you would like something else, Francesca," he answered.

Her beautiful eyes glinted slightly under the low lights and, at this moment, she appeared to him not as a distinguished doctor and microbiologist, but a fulsome woman, demure and respectful of him as a man, and it also appeared that she was instinctively behaving as a highly feminine woman does when in the company of a young handsome man.

There was already, so soon, a mutual respect developing between them and an understanding of the different, yet complementary roles they would have whenever together. As well as her great beauty and charm, she also had a natural dignity and despite her friendliness and warmth toward Joseph, he could only guess as to the full depth of her character. There was also an intoxicating mystery about her.

"Let's share a dessert together Joseph, one of those rich cakes or something that I can never finish on my own," she said, breaking the tension between them.

She looked to the waiter nearby who came immediately, and she asked him to recite the desserts and they chose a lemon concoction that was served a few moments later with two spoons.

"I would also like some coffee; how about you, Joseph?"

The headwaiter came with two other waiters and the coffee was served.

"Would Madame like a cognac or something else?" he asked.

"No thank you, but do you have any small cigars?" she enquired, much to Joseph's surprise.

"Would you like anything, sir?" the waiter enquired.

"No, thank you," Joseph replied, knowing that there was half a bottle of exquisite red wine still on the table.

Before leaving them alone the headwaiter returned once more and enquired whether there was anything else they might require as Francesca lighted her small cigar from the candle on the table.

"No, that is fine," answered Joseph.

Before turning to walk away, the headwaiter looked at Joseph and said, "Please do not hesitate to ask me if there is anything more you would like, Sheik Misanrie asked me to take special care of you both tonight."

Joseph glanced across at Francesca and exclaimed, "Sheik Misanria? Is Achmed local royalty or something?"

Francesca laughed at his surprise, and explained how Achmed, related to the ruling family, was a very powerful man, particularly in Dubai, although you would rarely think so from his modest behaviour.

"I am so pleased we can be together like this, Joseph," Francesca said, changing the tone of them now sitting alone. She continued to talk about her family, the death of her father when she was just nine, her younger brother, how she worried about her mother who insisted on working long and punishing hours with her work; and, how she and Joseph had so much in common. They had both chosen to serve, were of a similar age, would have to assume ever greater service as they grew older and their parents aged, and that it was for this reason she had been eager to meet him and have this opportunity to talk together. She also implied strongly that this was why Achmed had left early, knowing of these realities, to leave them some time alone to talk.

Once more Joseph recalibrated his thinking, Francesca's gentle flirting earlier had been simply that, feminine friendliness, and there was nothing more to it than that.

"Whether we like it or not, we will probably have to spend time together in the years ahead in various ways, in service, Joseph, so it is important we know each other."

Now with this clarification and understanding about the real purpose of this dinner, Joseph spoke freely about himself, his research at Oxford, his love of opera, an interest they shared, his family and the home he loved so dearly at Himbledon.

Francesca then asked Joseph about Louise and whether they had spoken since he had left Croatia and she had flown back to England. Joseph suddenly remembered he had left his cell phone back in his bedroom at the residence and he had not used it the whole day and that Louise will have left messages.

He was distracted for a moment when Francesca said, looking into his face, “Louise loves you very deeply, doesn't she?”

Again, Joseph was surprised by this forthright and insightful comment, but did not know how to answer.

Francesca reached across the table and placed her hand gently on his hands, lying together on the white tablecloth, and continued, “Do not be alarmed or embarrassed by my remarks, Joseph. I do not wish to pry, but we will need to know much of each other as time passes; our very lives may depend on it. We must also come to trust each other implicitly, as our families have done for hundreds of years.” She paused and slowly withdrew her hand while watching Joseph for his response.

Although he was feeling a little tired, he also felt an excitement being with Francesca, there was something about her that drew him closer.

“Forgive me Francesca, much of all this is rather new to me and since deciding to serve, I have been on an almost vertical learning curve, so excuse my slowness in grasping things,” Joseph said.

Francesca sat back in her chair, turning the small cigar between the fingers of her left hand and she raised it to her lips, drew some smoke into her mouth and gently exhaled. The aroma of the cigar smoke, her faint perfume and the wine Joseph was continuing to drink were all combining to lower his reserve and shyness and he suddenly said, “Yes, you are right, Louise does love me, and we had a wonderful time together in

Croatia."

There was a brief period of silence as they looked closely at each other and then Francesca leant forward and, looking sympathetically at Joseph, said, "But something tells me that you are not sure Joseph, whether you love her in return."

Again, Joseph was almost dumbfounded at her directness and accuracy.

"How could you know such things, Francesca? Yes, you are right, and it concerns me greatly, but how could you know?" he asked in a slightly imploring way.

Without a smile and looking serious, Francesca answered, "Female intuition, I suppose, is how I know, together with your pain I observe whenever you speak of her. Friendships, and especially love, are always demanding of us, particularly when we are unable to fully respond to those who love us so intensely. I know because I have been where you are now, Joseph, and it is so hard; a broken heart in someone we care for deeply can be devastating."

Francesca paused briefly as though wishing to reach out to Joseph, to give him support and encouragement with these perplexing concerns he had.

She continued, "But you know, Joseph, just being there for her, showing you do care, and giving what you can of yourself to her, now that you know how she feels for you, is something you simply must always do. Louise has a wonderful career ahead of her and, although it is perhaps a compromise, there are many ways to be intimate, trusting and close with a person without marriage and sexual union. Lack of compromise, the inability to give of ourselves, and to share, causes so much pain in human relationships. There are many forms of love and many ways you will be able to make her happy and avoid breaking her heart."

Francesca smiled gently at Joseph and briefly looked away to allow him time to reflect on what she had said and she then looked back at him, his strong shoulders and his handsome face looking sad before her.

She knew she had to lift him out of his sadness, so she said, "I really look forward to meeting Louise soon, she sounds like a wonderful person, Joseph, and you are blessed to have her as such a dear friend. She will know probably that you do not love her in the same way, we women just know such things, but we are also resilient creatures and can adapt to what we are given. Many never ever experience even what you both have together, as imperfect as it may be, in their entire lives. Just always be truthful, kind and careful with her."

Joseph, who had been listening intently to the calm and caring words, watching Francesca's lips as she spoke, then replied, "Thank you Francesca, you are very kind and it does help to have a woman's perspective on such matters. I will, of course, always try to be careful with her. I could not live with myself if I were ever to carelessly break her heart."

Careless or not, thought Francesca, *Louise no doubt already has a damaged heart*. She was then confronted with a question from Joseph, because he never wished himself to be the centre of attention for too long.

"Have you ever loved anyone so intensely, Francesca?" he asked, also feeling that he could now speak to her about anything, ask her any question, however personal or intimate, without fear of rebuttal.

"Apart from some infatuations when younger, no, sadly I haven't," she replied. "My work tends to consume most of my energies these days, although one day I do hope I will experience true love with a man."

Joseph felt that because of who he was, the special connection between their families, and their fraternal membership, that this was why Francesca had let him into her life in such an urgent and intimate way. Very rarely would others ever be allowed such a privilege. They continued to talk, exchanging many personal aspects of themselves, and Joseph again raised his concern for her with the impostor John Holmes. She shrugged it off and told him not to worry, she would not take any unnecessary risks. Joseph knew that from this day forward they would always be able to come together so easily whenever meeting again. Francesca had had a deep and lasting impact on him so quickly and so unexpectedly. Although it was never mentioned, Joseph had also left something special with Francesca.

When Joseph had returned to his room he immediately checked his cell phone and there were four text messages from Louise, each getting more imploring and worried as they had proceeded during the day. The last read “Going to bed, didn’t sleep well last night, missing you, please text u safe, Love Louise.” He instantly tapped out his reply, “Sorry darling, all well here, v busy, will phone tomorrow once home, Joe.”

* * *

THE NEXT MORNING, AFTER BREAKFAST, ACHMED TOOK THEM both for a tour of the Palms and Joseph was impressed by the scale of this man-made town with luxury houses, apartments and hotels that extended far out into the sea. There were long fingers of land with many fine, large houses each with their own exclusive sea front, lagoons and the final stages of a light railway that was under construction. Achmed explained how they had created all this land, how it had been a major heavy construction enterprise, shifting millions and millions of tons of stone, heavy materials and aggregates dropped systematically into the sea from big ships to gradually construct the whole area. Massive dredgers, heavy lifting equipment and quarries many miles away had all played their special role to make the whole place a living reality and Dandler Aggregates had also played a large part in its success.

Francesca’s flight to Rome was to leave at noon and Joseph was flying directly to Heathrow, London, departing at 3:30. They were soon at the airport, and Achmed, Joseph and Francesca walked through to the place where they would have to say goodbye. Achmed gave Francesca the customary kiss on both cheeks and she looked up at him smiling and thanked him warmly for his hospitality, and said she looked forward to seeing him again in Rome in a few days.

She then turned to Joseph and extended her hand. As he stepped forward to say goodbye, he could feel her firm grip.

“Goodbye Joseph, it has been wonderful to spend time with you, perhaps longer next time, I hope. Look after Louise and have a good trip home. I will keep in touch about things in Boston. Be careful, Joseph, and may God bless and keep you," she said.

Joseph reciprocated with similar wishes and then she turned and disappeared.

It was a while later, just before midnight, that Joseph finally arrived back at Himbledon. He had been met at Heathrow, and with little traffic at that late hour was soon home. There was no one about, so he went straight to bed, but, before he fell asleep, he sent another text message to Louise, saying he was back safely at the Grange.

17

Psychotic Delusions

THERE WAS A SOMBRE MOOD THE NEXT MORNING when Joseph had breakfast with his parents and Mark. They talked about his holiday in Croatia, his trip to Dubai, and Mark mentioned Francesca, saying that "She is quite a dazzler eh Joe," gently teasing him.

John looked rather tired, but was as focussed as ever, and he, Mark and Joseph agreed to start their meeting at eight, below, in a particularly well-appointed and equipped meeting room that had a large window that looked out over a section of the underground canal which, with the special lighting, was a peaceful and serene atmosphere in which to work.

It was now the dying days of summer in England and the days were beginning to draw in. Before joining his father and Mark for the meeting, Joseph walked to the study and lifted the phone to speak to Louise. As he dialled the number he looked out through the high windows to the gardens and meadows of the Grange that lay beneath the great house. It was a clear day with a blue sky, but a touch of early morning haze was still rising from the damp fields and the hedgerows, across the beautiful vista that lay before him.

Just then he heard her voice, "Hello, Louise Jones," and there was a pause before Joseph spoke.

"Hello darling, how are you?" he enquired.

"Hi, Joe. Okay, I suppose, my darling, but how are you?" Her voice instantly conveyed her delight at hearing his voice, yet she also sounded tired.

“I am pleased to be back at Himbledon, although there appears much for us to do here and my father, Mark and I will be meeting shortly, and I must also start getting myself up to speed about this job in Paris. The trip to Dubai was interesting and I think you would like it; we must visit there sometime, together. How are things in Oxford?” Joseph asked.

Louise immediately asked with urgency, “When will you be back in Oxford, Joe? I so want to see you; I have missed you terribly.” She made no mention of her work.

“Not sure exactly, but in the next few days, once I have sorted out things here,” he replied, sensing her longing and then continued. “Listen, Louise, things do not normally get going there for a couple of weeks yet, so why don’t you come to Himbledon and we can return together to Oxford, before I go to Paris?”

There was a slight pause before Louise answered with the weight in her voice suddenly gone, “That’s a good idea Joe, and how thoughtful of you, let me see what I can do from this end and I will phone you later. I do have various faculty meetings and other commitments, but I am sure they don’t need me at all these meetings. Let me phone you this evening, my love.”

“Okay, phone about 6:30 if you can, before we have supper, I will expect your call.”

She replied cheerfully, “Okay Joe, I will call you later, have a good day,” and they hung up.

Joseph walked to the heavy wooden door and proceeded to push it open and walk down the broad steps to the labyrinth of rooms below. On entering the meeting room he could see evidence everywhere; piles of computer print outs, handwritten information on flip charts and various other things, all evidence of many hours of intense work by his father and brother. Having all the information from Achmed and Francesca with his computer, he plugged his laptop into an electricity supply.

His father looked across the large table at Joseph, smiled and said, “It is really good to have you home and you look terrific, Joseph. You must tell me more about how you got on with Louise and how the sailing was later, perhaps after supper if you are not busy with anything."

"Yes, that sounds great, Father," answered Joseph.

John then clicked his computer, and on the screen there was an outline list of topics for their day's discussions together.

"Goodness me," exclaimed Joseph. "You have both been busy."

"Yes," replied Mark. "While you were enjoying yourself in the Adriatic with a naked blonde," he teased.

They all laughed and began to work.

John and Mark, with the assistance of various pictorial material on the screen, began to explain to Joseph some of the fruits of their recent labour. They started by revealing what they had learnt about the suspicious cult in America. Its leader was a fellow by the name of Hank Milshner, and they estimated he was in his late fifties. The Milshner family had made a fortune during the industrial development of America in railroads, steel, oil, mining and property. Little was known directly about Hank, the only son of Edward Milshner, who had been an active philanthropist during his life, including being a benefactor of the Amish community. After the death of his wife Hilary, Hank's mother, in a tragic riding accident on their ranch in Montana, Edward Milshner had become a recluse and was rarely ever seen again by the outside world. His life, and that of his son, had always been shrouded in intrigue since that time. Edward was devoted to his wife, and her death had deeply affected him.

The FBI had various files on the family from the time Edward's brother, also named Hank, had been implicated in an embezzlement fraud on the West coast. He had turned state witness and had achieved the lengthy imprisonment of several known felons at the time who had been involved in racketeering, prostitution and various tax frauds. Since these times, many years earlier, the FBI had lost contact with the Milshner family, and had stopped any surveillance and information gathering about them.

Edward Milshner inherited a vast fortune from his father, Harry Milshner, who in turn had inherited massive wealth from the founder of the Milshner business wealth. They were always a secretive family and just as is the situation with the extensive and broad Trimbledon commercial interests, few had any idea of the full extent of the Milshner business empire today. Harry and Edward had also inherited the Milshner genius for making money, with each generation greatly increasing the scale of this wealth. Edward had diversified the family fortune by investing shrewdly and gaining control of a diverse range of global commercial interests. When his brother Hank was murdered some years after the death of his beloved wife Hilary, he went into a rapid decline and died when Hank junior was in early adolescence. The Milshner fortune and business interests were in trust until Hank attained the age of twenty-five, and he was brought up by various trustees named in his father's will.

The young Hank was a difficult, rebellious teenager and had several brushes with the law for drinking, drug abuse and various other violations. When he was twenty-two he had been arrested and jailed for four days pending charges to be brought forward in the local courthouse. It was in connection with a fire that had destroyed a roadside bar and restaurant outside Colorado. He was implicated with two others. Gustav Onker, who subsequently committed suicide by jumping off a high-rise building some years later in Chicago. He fell into busy rush hour traffic, in an apparent personal sacrifice and warning of things to come. From examinations of his remains, he must have also been semi-delirious from large amounts of heroin found in his body. There were also a number of bizarre and apocalyptic warnings tattooed on his torso. The other person was Michelle Adler who was Hank's mistress at the time. None of them were brought to trial, and according to some local evidence it was suspected that the owner of the roadhouse and local police had been paid off by a Milshner lawyer to drop the case. Since there was no homicide involved, the case was easy to drop and that was some three decades ago. Since that time Hank had appeared to drop out of sight.

Matters, in terms of the historical information trail, may well have ended there had it not been for an Enzo Oscarbo, a local psychiatrist of Portuguese descent, who examined

Milshner as part of the roadhouse fire investigation. He diagnosed Milshner as being a psychopath with divergent personalities and to be a potentially very unstable and dangerous individual. Within Milshner's psychological make up there were also acute obsessive and paranoid traits. During interviews and conversations over many hours, Oscarbo had found on some occasions that Milshner would lapse into a mental state when he appeared to be completely disconnected from reality, although he appeared rational. He also displayed some delusional traits about who he thought himself to be. He spoke of hidden forces, the need to continually cleanse oneself from temptations and attack by secret elements, especially those from the Catholic Church.

Oscarbo had also undertaken detailed conversations with Michelle Adler that revealed she had been raised within a highly dysfunctional family with a puritanical father and a highly submissive mother. It was a repressive upbringing of a highly intelligent and precocious young woman and Oscarbo even suspected some incestuous relationship that may have been forced on her by her father, who had a drinking problem and would hit his wife and threatened her with the wrath of God over even trivial matters. It was a poor household, and Michelle had run away as an adolescent and, from this time onwards, Oscarbo learnt of her of various sexual affairs she had enjoyed, generally with men some years older than herself. She was intelligent, manipulative and had an extremely powerful sexual libido that even Oscarbo had felt at moments during their conversations in the jailhouse. She was very attractive with a beautiful face and body to match. She had met Hank Milshner about eighteen months earlier while hitchhiking and he had picked her up. They had remained together since and were inseparable.

Michelle displayed various pathological traits including a highly manipulative personality and a hypnotic charisma linked to her extreme sexuality that also extended to other women with whom she had been intimate. While she had a better grasp on reality than Hank, she appeared to Oscarbo to also be dangerous, especially since she had a marked interest in sadomasochistic activities and had some scars on her upper arms.

At no time before in his extensive career had Oscarbo ever come across such a lethal cocktail of behavioural characteristics as he had diagnosed in those few days in the county jailhouse outside Colorado. Following what had been something of a traumatic experience, even for him, a psychiatrist with many years experience of dealing with deeply disturbed and psychotic patients, he believed Milshner and Adler to be a very dangerous couple, particularly Hank Milshner. Oscarbo had made further enquiries about Hank and when he discovered the fortune shortly to come within Milshner's grasp, had decided to personally track media reports and other scraps of information that came his way about him. He kept an ongoing personal record of all news reports; the attempted attack in Canada, word of mouth reports he was able to pick up and other information. This was the crucial information source that Mark now had at his disposal and from which he had prepared the confidential information he was laying out before his father and Joseph. Two years before his death at the age of eighty-six, Oscarbo had passed this detailed and confidential dossier on Milshner to the same Jesuit Friar in Boston, who had conveyed the earlier information about the cult to Mark.

Hank Milshner had a multitude of hideaways since his virtual disappearance from public view some thirty years earlier. With Michelle Adler by his side, in the intervening years, working together they had established various small groups of followers to indulge their fantasies. Then some twenty years ago it appears Milshner became convinced, after visiting Europe and having meetings with certain extreme anarchic Christian groups in Germany, that he had a calling to use his wealth to found a new order, an extreme order of total obedience by its members to himself and various visions that Michelle claimed she received when sleeping. He developed an obsessive interest in the Melchiorites of the sixteenth century and swore vengeance to all those he believed had persecuted them then and since. Working together, Hank and Michelle had also employed a team of highly skilled professional legal, financial and other business experts to systematically restructure the Milshner global business empire whereby Michelle had increasing control while Hank retained ownership of variously strategically placed companies and international corporations. Behind perfectly legitimate business enterprise operating throughout the world, lay more sinister interests.

Mark had pulled together a small and trusted team of collaborators to piece together the Milshner puzzle. Mark's colleagues in this task never met face to face. They were a virtual team, collaborating with great speed and precision via the secure intranet that Mark had set up for this purpose.

A specialisation of Hank and Michelle that they had refined over the years was the enslavement of followers through a well-tried and tested process. It started by recruiting followers with a twisted mixture of evangelism and personal glorification for those who had 'special gifts', at least, according to accomplished practitioners of cult activities. These were then combined with flattery and playing upon the pride and vanity of each individual. Each would be assigned a skilled member of the cult who would befriend them and start a subtle and, at first, gentle process of indoctrination that at this introductory level appeared harmless and also skilfully attuned to many of the concerns that younger people had about the world in which they lived. There would be gifts, kindness and ever more embracing activities with other local cult members that imperceptibly started to alienate the individual from the real world around them. All this took place where the individual was studying or working and never anywhere near the various cult compounds where only the truly indoctrinated were ever permitted to be.

No one outside the cult had any idea of the total membership of the cult or where the many secret compounds operated. From his research, Mark had, however, managed to produce some rough estimates, and they indicated there could well be thousands, even many thousands, of members in various stages of this process. He was certain there were dozens of compounds in America and elsewhere in the world. There had also been a subtle blending of some of the cult practices with some of the commercial activities of the

Milshner business empire.

The cult kept detailed information, personality and skill profiles on all their members. Those with particular aptitudes, skills and even dangerous proclivities were of special value, and these were often those who were then selected for further indoctrination into the ways of the cult. Within a short time, the cult practitioners would have learnt of each of the new member's weaknesses, the things that tempted them and made them vulnerable, and they would then have started to play on these. They would falsely flatter them and enable them to do almost anything they desired to indulge themselves. These behaviours more often than not were innocent, but sometimes they were also bizarre and shocking and were recorded for insurance purposes. The use of drugs was not uncommon together with rich privileges lavished on the more favoured. Gradually, these indoctrinees, as they were referred to within the cult, would soon be ensnared, passively going along with each step in this process until they had nowhere else to turn, apart from the cult and fellow members.

It was alleged that there were many more sinister techniques deployed by the cult to posses, control and direct members. The higher one rose through this rigid hierarchical cult structure the more one would be exposed to a form of brain washing that further inculcated an obsessive obedience to the two cult leaders and their commands. There was also a rigid, strictly enforced and often vicious set of rules and penalties for any failures on the part of middle and senior ranking members. There was a clear contract implicit within all of these activities: obedience by members of the cult on the one hand and pleasure, luxury and protection on the other from the cult. Any failure or any hint of disobedience resulted in long periods of solitary confinement, or cleansing, as they claimed, humiliation at the hands of senior cult figures and even death. Personal punishment at the hands of Michelle Adler was always particularly feared. Blackmail was also used with precision and video recorded indulgences of members as they had risen through the ranks were frequently shown to members with explicit threats that if they did not adhere strictly to rules and commands emanating from their revered leaders, then this damning information would be used against them.

Using these methods it appeared that Hank and Michelle had created an inner group of around forty devotees and delegated tasks to them related to the individual's skills and talents. Michelle personally trained all the female members of this inner cabal in an armoury of seductive skills, and a crucial selection criterion for these women was their physical beauty, their sexual appetite and their allure to others. Many were highly cultured, well educated and spoke a number of languages. Many of this upper echelon of the cult were also addictive personalities whether to drugs, alcohol, obsessive behaviours and various sexual practices and perversions. They were also vain, outwardly strong, but weak beneath, with some secrets they wished to conceal. They all enjoyed the power their positions and knowledge of the cult gave them over the mainly younger, gullible and often beautiful and manly interns.

All the men were trained in a range of weaponry, how to influence and control other members of the cult and they, too, were personally trained by Michelle in seductive techniques. Both the men and women also acted as highly skilful trainers of subordinates in the cult who then also cascaded such training and indoctrination practices down through the ranks. It had long since lost the faintest resemblance to a decent and worthy body of people and these processes had been going on silently in a number of cult camps located across the world for at least the last ten years. A picture emerged of a supreme leader of the cult, with Michelle always at his side and his commands always being obeyed without hesitation or question.

Although insane, Milshner always retained a high level of functioning normality and spoke with a numbing conviction and oratory style that hypnotised his followers. He was also a man with an extremely domineering manner, even with Michelle at times, who had learnt over the years how to deal with his tantrums. On his own, the cult would probably have remained small and largely ineffective, but with Michelle, who had captivated Hank from the first time they met, she was probably the deadlier of the two. It was to become yet again a perfect historical example of how power corrupts, and corrupts utterly.

Oscarbo had recorded evidence of cult compounds all across America, and then towards the end of his life he had recorded scraps of information that indicated that they were also beginning to appear in other countries. It looked likely that there were other compounds in various European countries, the Middle and Far East, Japan, Indonesia and Australia. Africa appeared not to have been touched, at least up to the time of Oscarbo's death. These compounds were always remote and in very inhospitable territory and combined with mining, oil exploration, mineral processing, logging or some other heavy industrial activity where the presence of other activities could be readily concealed. It was for this reason that aerial satellites had never picked them up, since they would always appear simply as large sheds, industrial housing for workers and other innocent elements of an industrial or mining complex. They also had properties in most large cities in America where junior members lived and they recruited fresh followers. These were usually in areas of cities and towns where there were universities and colleges, ideal for their recruitment activities and where students typically experiment with new ideas, questioning the purpose of life and other 'rites of passage', regarded as normal and healthy by the secular world. Rarely had any serious suspicions been raised as they had systematically gone about their tasks.

Although it was extremely hard to trace, it appeared to a forensic auditor working in Mark's team that Milshner owned many strategically placed companies via various offshore and other holding companies. Through trustees, nominees and other public faces of this empire he probably also had the power to have directors removed, his own people put in places of inordinate responsibility and influence, to change company policies and much more, merely by picking up a telephone. According to the auditor he believed, although he stressed he was unable to prove it, that Milshner probably had secret control of ParisCrete, the ready mix company whose trucks had devastated Paris in the spring. Other commercial interests controlled by Milshner included a range of highly specialised and competitive subcontractors to various energy utilities, rail companies, and a host of computer software companies whose software was in use in various sectors including telecommunications, aviation and other potentially sensitive areas.

Something that was of particular interest to John was the way the Milshner people had fully exploited the whole recent trend of outsourcing, quickly buying up sensitive service providers that often gave them an increased global reach. Venture capitalism geared to maximising financial returns had also played into their hands since the sudden takeover of even global steel makers, aerospace industries and other business interests were considered the norm and to be applauded. The final icing on the cake for Milshner, as his minions in the global financial and legal sector did his bidding without ever knowing his true purpose, had been the lie of self-regulation and governance. Although deeply flawed, while the world appeared to be getting richer, governments enjoying ever-rising tax revenues, there were few to ever raise an objection to vast industries running themselves without interference. The dangers of this carelessness were now becoming frighteningly real to John, as he listened to Mark.

Nearing the end of his presentation Mark sensed that his father and Joseph needed time to reflect and have a break from such worrying and depressing information, so he switched off his computer and said, "Quite a story eh, if we are just half right about this man and woman we must act quickly and carefully. But let's have a break and resume again after some personal time and after lunch."

With that Joseph re-focussed his eyes and ambled out from the room and along the illuminated underground canal bank.

His father was quick to follow him and called to his son saying, "Do you remember when we used to walk the roof of the old mining tunnels, Joseph, when you were children? Perhaps we should try it again some time?"

Joseph, deep in thought, turned and, looking at his father, replied, "Yes, why not, Father; it would be better than all this horrendous information that we are working with."

As Joseph and his father walked through the Grange into the kitchen, Mary called to John, "It is the prime minister's secretary wishing to speak to you urgently, John."

She handed the phone to him and there was a brief conversation and he replaced the phone.

"I have to go to London immediately, and it looks as though I will be gone for a couple of days, Mary."

"When will you have to leave?" asked Mary.

He replied, "Almost immediately, I am afraid; there is to be a breakfast meeting tomorrow morning with the PM and home secretary, and they have asked if I can be available the following day as well."

It was now 3:30 in the afternoon, and Mary continued, "First have something to eat, John, and I will run you to the station; you should make the 5:30 train comfortably."

"Yes, all right." He nodded, visibly collecting his thoughts. He then turned and walked back downstairs to the rooms below to collect various computer files from Mark.

After he had left, Mary looked across at Joseph, with her hands on the back of a chair by the kitchen table and said, "A dreadful business all this, I just pray it can be brought to an end soon."

"Yes, indeed," answered Joseph as Mary busied herself to put food on the table for them.

It was not long before John, his two sons and Mary were seated, eating at the large kitchen table.

"Sorry about this Joseph, but it will mean you staying on at Himbledon for a few more days I am afraid, because the three of us will need to meet again when I get back. I also need to brief you fully about Dandler and the arrangements for Paris,"

"That's all right, Father cannot be avoided and Louise may be coming to Himbledon tomorrow; she is phoning later to let me know. There is also no pressure in Oxford; I can say my farewells whenever we are finished here," replied Joseph.

"Anyway," interjected Mark, "there is still plenty for us to be doing here, Joseph, while father is away in London."

John smiled, and Mary sighed slightly before looking at the kitchen clock and reminding John of the time.

As he rose from the table, he looked at Mark and said, "Oh yes, will you please give the draft of my address for the Oxford economics faculty to Joseph for his comments, I have to submit it to the Dean by the end of next week. If you will excuse me, I will see you both in a couple of days." With that both John and Mary left and Joseph and Mark were left talking at the table.

IV

Modern Travel, Politics and Country Life

18

The Wonders of Rail

JOHN AND MARY KNEW THE LOCAL RAILWAY STATION WELL, having used it on so many occasions over the years. It was brighter since privatisation, after years under the management of British Rail, only a memory to the rail traveller of today. It had been refurbished, provided with clean and bright facilities for the many passengers now increasingly using the rail network, rather than suffer the frustration and stress of driving on the crowded roads and motorways. Several different commercial rail companies now operated services through the busy station that was on a major rail artery running north-south down the vertebrae of England. John could remember the great steam trains that used to thunder through the station during his boyhood, non-stop on their way to and from London and Edinburgh. They had romantic and evocative names like the Flying Scotsman, which was also a mail train and used to pick up mailbags on the length of its journey with clever scoops as it hurtled past. The train had long carriages that were mail-sorting rooms where rows of postal workers sorted the mail. As well as collect mail, the overnight mail trains used to also drop off sorted bags of mail as it sped through sleeping towns and villages, ready for delivery the next morning into household and business letter boxes.

As John looked through the large train window while it sped toward London, he watched the countryside pass before him for a few minutes, before he turned to his papers, as he warmly remembered the old steam trains, now items of fascination and awe for younger people either in museums or on preserved tourist lines. Speed, convenience and efficiency, the cumulative currency of the modern world, had saved rail travel from extinction particularly with the emergence of high-speed rail travel. Just as with other aspects of human activity, transport had witnessed the ebb and flow of different methods of conveying people and goods. The movement of goods by canal had been superseded by rail and then rail had been cast into the doldrums by air and road transport, and now with road travel becoming less convenient, slower and unpredictable due to increasing congestion, it too is being gradually superseded by rapid rail in many countries, particularly throughout Europe and Japan.

It was the bullet train, the Shinkansen, travelling at speeds of two hundred and sixty kilometres per hour between Tokyo and Osaka on the Tokaido high-speed line, covering a distance of five hundred kilometres, which was opened in 1964 for the Tokyo Olympics that first caught the world's imagination for rail again. Today, the technology of high-speed rail transport has become highly sophisticated, with speed records being regularly broken. The speed record in Japan is over four hundred and forty kilometres per hour, which is almost a staggering two hundred and seventy miles per hour. In France and other European countries, countless high-speed trains travel at speeds of a hundred and eighty and two hundred and twenty miles per hour. In many places, new modern continuous railway tracks have been built to cater for high-speed trains, whereas, in others, special swivelling bogies enable the trains to tilt at high speeds and remain on the track going around corners. Some high-speed train systems no longer used conventional wheels, but ride on an electromagnetic field, and modern high-speed rail travel had now become a full citizen of the modern technological age. The huge train sets are pulled by electric, diesel or even gas turbine locomotives that move the long serpents of carriages with passengers travelling in silent luxury in hermitically sealed compartments.

Within the locomotives there is a welter of modern technology, including computer control and monitoring systems, state of the art communication and satellite tracking, and a host of telemetry. Outside the trains, along the length of the railway tracks, there are an equally impressive range of technology carefully monitoring the speed and progress of the trains as they hurtle across thousands of miles. There are electronic signals, sensing devices, closed circuit television monitors, and the critically important rail traffic control centres carefully orchestrating the movement of these powerful monsters as they almost danced together, elegantly, across borders and whole continents. The French railways have hundreds of high-speed train sets in daily operation with hundreds more in Germany, Spain and across other European countries. Germany and France are among world leaders in high-speed rail, and exported their technology all over the world. There are many high-speed rail projects now being planned, built or newly opened.

High-speed rail is generally regarded as trains travelling at operational speeds of two hundred kilometres an hour, or a hundred and twenty-five miles per hour or more, although many high-speed trains now run regularly at speed of three hundred kilometres per hour. For trains to travel safely at speeds of around two hundred miles per hour, dedicated tracks have to be used, with special banking on bends and other high-speed line features. This elite high-speed rail sector of rail travel is carrying more and more passengers every year. In Japan and France alone, high-speed rail networks carry over seven billion passengers a year. The global fleet of around twenty-three thousand commercial aircraft only carries just in excess of two billion passenger journeys annually. It is now faster to travel by train between the centre of London and Paris than to fly, and the Euro tunnel under the English Channel enables passengers to travel under the ocean between Folkestone and Calais, a distance of thirty-one miles, in just a few short minutes. The Channel is a modern engineering marvel, consisting of two main traffic tunnels and a service tunnel in the middle. It carries high-speed passenger trains, huge vehicle transporters and freight trains and in a typical year will handle eighteen million passengers and sixteen million tonnes of freight. On the Paris to Lyon high-speed line, even double-decker train sets operate, to meet the ever-rising level of passenger demand, travelling at over a hundred and eighty miles per hour.

Despite the size and speed of these juggernauts, high-speed rail has a remarkably good safety record. It was in Germany some twenty years earlier when an Inter City Express travelling at around a hundred and twenty-five miles per hour, considered slow these days, collided with a bridge, causing a major derailment, jack knifing of the carriages, the death of more than a hundred people, and the injury of many more. It had occurred on the main Hanover to Hamburg rail line and led to various safety design refinements for subsequent high-speed trains. In France, the design of many of the modern trains avoids jack knifing of carriages since they are joined together; instrumentation and computer control systems have also been refined to improve reliability and safety. At such high-speeds these trains have to be controlled by computers since everything happens in microseconds and the human reactions of the old fashioned engine driver are now too slow for them to be in complete command. The high-speed train drivers of today are computer operators, no longer train drivers.

John had dozed the last few miles of his journey into central London and other passengers moving in his compartment preparing to get off the train woke him. He awoke refreshed and ready to call a taxi to the apartment to finish up some work, relax and sleep, before his early morning meeting with the prime minister the next day.

Meanwhile, back at Himbeldon, it was around seven o'clock as Joseph sat in his room reading the unfinished book on *Opus Dei*, when Louise phoned. She explained that she was unable to visit Himbledon until tomorrow late in the afternoon, and would only be able to stay a couple of nights because the head of the faculty had brought a whole series of meetings forward in the diary that she must attend. When Joseph suggested that with such work pressures, perhaps she should stay in Oxford, she insisted on driving to Himbledon the next day, so it was agreed. After putting the phone down, Louise felt the greatest calm and happiness she had felt since that last awful afternoon at the Villa Grand Argentina, when the sadness had first gripped her

Since the first night she had returned to Oxford from Croatia, she had been unable to sleep and had tossed and turned all night with so much on her mind. She overslept on her first morning home and had arrived late at a faculty meeting, which was most unusual for her. During the day she had found it difficult to focus and pay attention to the debates going on around her. The next night, her unsettled emotions continued to trouble her, so she had three glasses of wine in the hope they would help her sleep and escape this continual feeling of anguish. Still, she could not sleep and, turning on her bedside light at 3:20 in the morning, she had seen Joseph's old Bible lying on her dressing table. In an act of desperation, she had taken it in her arms and in an almost involuntary movement, hugged it to her chest longing for Joseph to be there with her and returned to bed. She fell asleep and slept soundly until her alarm rang at 7:45 the next morning.

The next night immediately she had cleared her few supper things, she walked to her bedroom and reached for the old Bible again and sat with it close to her on the sofa in her small lounge while reading various academic and other papers. With the Bible near to her, she felt a strange calmness, but dismissed any thoughts that there could be any connection between the old worn volume and this feeling of relief and peacefulness.

I am just being silly and irrational, she thought.

After showering and getting into her sleeping clothes she went to bed, switched off the light and tried to sleep. It was not long before the feelings of anguish returned and she started to toss and turn. She felt alone and the more the thought that Joseph did not love her, raced through her mind, the more fretful she became. It became so bad that she turned the light on, got up and made herself a cup of tea and sat in the quiet of the night holding her tea mug in both hands resting on her knees before her in her lounge. She then saw the Bible again and reached for it, placed her tea on the side table and gently opened the Bible and started to read. She read fast and her comprehension was finely attuned to the written word and as she read she felt herself becoming calm and filled with a sort of peace from the words before her, reaching into her from centuries before. She read for more than an hour before falling asleep to be woken the next morning, refreshed, by the sound of her alarm in her bedroom.

It was only some time later, after the rush of getting dressed, having breakfast and getting ready to leave, that as she walked to her first appointment that she began to recall precisely what had happened the evening before. Again she started to talk to herself saying how silly she was being; that she was imagining things and that how can words supposedly written centuries ago, have any effect on us today?

How can an old Bible and its words do such things? They certainly will not make Joseph love me, she thought as she knocked on the study door of the professor she was to meet that morning.

* * *

IT WAS A LITTLE WHILE AFTER TALKING WITH LOUISE that Joseph heard his mother arrive back from dropping his father at the railway station. He walked along the passage to his parent's bedroom and knocked on the door.

"Who is it?" enquired Mary.

"It's Joseph mother; can I come in?"

"Of course," she replied.

Joseph entered and sat on the side of the large bed as his mother took off her few rings and placed them safely in the drawer of her dressing table.

"Your father is tired, Joseph, you know, and all this is a great strain on him. He is also not getting any younger," Mary said in an unusual display of concern for her husband.

"Yes, I know, Mother; I noticed how tired he looked when I saw him at breakfast. But he is remarkably fit for his age, and still strong, and has such a good intellect; he can handle it."

"Yes I know all that Joseph," interjected Mary with a sound of insistence. "It is not the workload or the complexity Joseph, it is the needless suffering of others that drains him emotionally. You children do not see much of this side of your father, because he conceals it. He is also grieving deeply at Tim's death; they were very close you know. But let's not dwell on this any further, I didn't mean to burden you with such things right now, but always remember, Joseph, your father loves you and your brothers and sister very deeply, even though often he may not show it."

There was a pause as Joseph reflected on his mother's touching words and how easily we can be blind to the needs of others. After a few moments, Joseph moved around to the other side of the bed and sat close to his mother.

"Yes, I know, Mother; do not worry; we will look after him; we also love him, you know." The matter was closed.

Joseph told his mother that Louise was arriving the next evening and this news lifted the mood between them. Mary had taken a liking to Louise at Joseph's birthday party at the Grange, and she always enjoyed welcoming the children's friends to stay.

"Are you falling in love with Louise, Joseph?" she asked with a slight smile.

He was surprised by his mother's sudden directness, and did not know how to answer.

"We had a wonderful time in Croatia together, she is funny, loves life and very intelligent," he answered, almost without thinking.

"That is not what I asked Joseph. Why are you being evasive?" she replied, already knowing the answer to her own question and she continued. "Never mind, Joseph, just make sure you do not hurt her."

Joseph blushed, remembering Francesca's words just a few days earlier in Dubai, and Mary now had complete confirmation of her doubts. Almost without a pause she continued, "Joseph there is something confidential that I wish to discuss with you while we are alone and without your father,"

"What is it?" enquired Joseph, now curious at his mother's furtive tone.

Mary proceeded to confide in Joseph about her visit to Ruth in London, the dreadful state that Anna had been in, and that Ruth had asked her not to say anything to her father. Poor Anna had continued to be unwell, had even attempted to take her own life. Ruth had now arranged for her to have twenty-four nursing at her house in Kensington, where she continued to be looked after.

"Is there anything I can do?" asked Joseph.

"No thank you, Joseph; Ruth says she has everything in hand. It is just that I think there is something else concerning Ruth about Anna that she is not telling me, and I have a suspicion it is also related to Tim's murder."

Then Joseph remembered Francesca's remarks in Dubai and wanting to be kept informed about Anna, but did not say anything, wishing to avoid any further worry for his mother.

"Will you please go to London when you can, Joseph, and see Ruth and Anna? But please, do not mention any of this to your father. Ring Ruth and let her know when you will be able to visit, will you please?" Mary continued in a rather insistent manner, awaiting his response.

"Yes, Mother, of course I will, as soon as I can. Now you must stop worrying, I am sure it is nothing too serious and I will keep you fully informed about Anna."

Mary smiled, she felt a slight sense of relief having shared it with someone she knew she could trust and rely on, and the matter was closed, for the moment.

"Let's go and have supper, will you please call Mark?" asked Mary.

"Yes, all right, Mother," Joseph replied, and they both made their way from the bedroom to downstairs.

The light was fading fast and Mary put the lights on in the kitchen as she entered. A member of the day staff had kindly laid the table in the kitchen with four places and put a casserole in the large Aga stove, cooking slowly in readiness for the family to eat later. Mary removed the place setting for John and she looked at the clock on the wall and thought of him arriving later at the apartment overlooking the Thames. Just then Mark and Joseph arrived, ready to eat.

As she lifted the lid from the heavy casserole dish, and with her back to them both, Mary asked, "How did you get on with Francesca when you met her in Dubai, Joseph?"

As he moved to sit at the table Joseph answered, "Very well, she is an interesting lady."

"Yes she is, and also very beautiful, so like her mother when Portia was younger, they are such a lovely family. It was dreadful what happened to Giovanni, Francesca's father," she said.

"Yes, Achmed Misarnie mentioned to me that he had been shot when Francesca was quite young. Francesca regards Achmed as her second father, she told me," Joseph replied.

"He was a wonderful horseman, I remember, and your father and I had some very happy times with Giovanni and Portia in Italy when we were first married. He was also, like many Italians, a very good cook and always so charming."

Mark and Joseph listened as their mother shared with them her memories of Giovanni and Portia Contadino and as she spoke they both sensed her sadness at Portia being widowed at such a young age. It was Mark who asked why she had never remarried, and Mary said that there was never any shortage of suitors, but it was obviously not meant to be, and, anyway, Portia had been very much in love with Giovanni, and probably no other man could ever fill her emotions as he had. Mary then went on to say that after Giovanni's death, Portia had immersed herself in her work, and to this day it is probably what helps her to deal with her loss and loneliness. Both Mark and Joseph were puzzled by their mother's use of the word loneliness, how could such a lady, a distinguished scientist with so much going on in her life, ever be lonely? Mary smiled slightly, thinking, *the innocence of youth*. Then she said that, however successful or busy one is, there can still be emptiness without a true soul mate there to share the intimacies of it all.

She then added two further perspectives about Portia, that her faith had also been a vital comfort to her, and that had things been different, perhaps there was just one other man who may have filled her emotions after Giovanni had died. They looked at each other, and then at their mother, waiting patiently for her to continue, but there was a long, frustrating pause. Eventually, when Mary did speak again, it was to say that she had probably already said too much so had better leave the matter there. Neither of her sons was to be put off so easily and they worked together, with a subtle persuasiveness, to tease the intriguing information from their mother. When Mary finally relented and told them, they were astonished by the revelation. It was Luke, their father's brother, a member of the religious in Rome, and while they were really surprised, after a few moments reflection, they could understand why it could never be.

It was now getting late in the evening and as Mark poured them all coffee, Mary's cell phone bleeped and she rose, walked across to the welsh dresser and picked it up.

"It's a message from your father, he is safely in Chelsea and says goodnight to you both."

Mary tapped out a similar greeting from the three of them before saying, "Be careful; love you, Mary."

As they cleared the supper things, Mary reminded them both about the service for victims of both disasters being held at the Anglican Cathedral in the county town the following evening and that with their father being away, she trusted they would accompany her so there would be a good family representation. Joseph, who had been previously invited to attend by his mother, had completely forgotten and now he had Louise arriving the next afternoon from Oxford. As he smiled and nodded at his mother, he thought, *oh well, we can all go.*

19

The Prime Minister

JOHN HAD RISEN EARLY THE FOLLOWING MORNING, fixed himself some coffee and toast and caught a taxi to Downing Street. As the taxi travelled along the Embankment, into Parliament Square and along to the entrance of Downing Street it was a pleasant September morning, dry and bright, but with a chill in the air. The security police officers went through the customary checks, asked for proof of identity, checked their records, phoned the main house and then let John proceed through the high ornate gates to walk up the short distance to number ten. There were no media people on the opposite side of the street at this early hour of the morning although the railings were left ready for the next invasion of cameras, microphones, lights and reporters, and as he approached, the large door opened enough to let him enter. The doorman was clearly highly skilled at judging the time between the policeman's call from the gates and the arrival of guests at his door.

John was ushered into a medium-sized room, tastefully furnished with landscape paintings, a small bookcase, a few decorative vases and another door that was closed. The lower floors of Ten Downing Street are meeting rooms, offices, toilets, kitchens, security and other facilities necessary to support the prime minister and his staff to perform their governmental duties. The living quarters of prime ministers and their families are on the upper levels of the great house. John stood as he waited for the PM to join him, and he looked at his watch, it was seven thirty-five and a minute later, the home secretary walked in, a lady of medium height and build, who introduced herself. They had no time to converse before the door opened and in walked the prime minister, without his jacket, but with a shirt and tie on, and clutching a folder full of papers.

"Good morning, Professor Trimbledon; thank you for coming down to London. I see you have met the home secretary. What would you like for breakfast?" he asked.

The door opened and a waiter appeared, in a rather worn uniform, and proceeded to offer coffee, tea, toast, muesli, fresh fruit and eggs.

"However, you may wish to have them, Professor." Time was clearly at a premium, so the prime minister got straight down to business.

"Thank you, Professor, for the information on your suspicions regarding the Panama Canal and other information you passed to us, our security people are reviewing it and have notified all the relevant agencies overseas. Additional security has been established there and at Suez. We have also taken your other advice and notified the overseas agencies to proceed with extreme caution. I just wish we knew who these people are." He wondered as he spoke where on earth Trimbledon had got this information.

John sat quietly, respectfully waiting for the PM to stop talking, and aware of his responsibility of only ever pointing fingers when they were sure of their facts. The PM continued, "Also, just a pity the French did not listen to some warning they got from a bishop or somebody there in the Catholic church a few days before that attack, my security advisors tell me."

The PM was a rather unctuous, medium-sized man originally from Birmingham and had retained something of the local accent. Had he kept the full accent of those parts rather than try to lose it, he would probably not have grated on John as he continued to speak with the words pouring from his chubby mouth. He looked tired, with bags under his eyes, and he had more grey hair John thought, than on the only previous occasion when they had met briefly, at a charity function in the City of London. John never normally had any direct dealings with politicians, or ever wished to, but the circumstances that now prevailed made this meeting unavoidable. The home secretary sat listening and nodding as the prime minister spoke and dominated proceedings.

The prime minister continued to address John across the breakfast table, as he ate his breakfast with speed and ease without choking while continuing to speak. "We are facing the most calamitous situation for decades, Professor Trimbledon. Since the attack in Paris, in less than six months, the global economy has gone into a serious recession, I have had to pump billions into our collapsing banks, unemployment is rapidly increasing, people are losing their homes, and I will have to insist, via Parliament, of course..." he hesitated briefly to admit to himself that he was not quite yet running the country single-handedly, before continuing, "...to drastically cut public spending just when we are needing more police to manage worsening public order, and nurses to treat the rising number of violent assault and injury cases," the PM said, quickly continuing. "To make matters worse my security advisors remain at a loss as to who is behind this mayhem. Even the extreme Imams have been humbled and fallen noticeably silent since Paris, no doubt fearing for their own safety, like the rest of us. But the public assumption that Moslem terrorists are behind all this, is also threatening social stability throughout Europe, and also here. The recent loss of these commercial aircraft, in highly suspicious circumstances, is also just inflaming public fear, and the appearance that those of us in government have lost complete control of the situation." The prime minister then took his coffee cup in his right hand, drank some, put it back on the saucer and looked almost menacingly across at John and said, "I do hope, Professor, that you have some good news for us this morning?"

"Unfortunately, the news is not good; on the contrary, it is grave," John said, immediately wishing to sensitise them both to the gravity of the situation, and that matters could get worse.

He described his suspicions about the cult in America, who

they are and how they appear to operate, the evidence of the Japanese collaboration and some outline details of the Milshner global business empire. He spoke about the arrests in Dubai and that perhaps the British security authorities may wish to liaise with the Dubai special police as a matter of urgency.

"Where are these Milshner and Adler characters so we can catch them, and put an end to these atrocities?" inquired the PM.

"We don't know, they could be anywhere, and I must stress, Prime Minister, that until we have both firm evidence to connect them to these events, and furthermore, a coordinated counter plan properly developed, any careless move at the moment, if our fears are correct, could precipitate even more carnage across the world. We must bring these people to justice, if they are the ones responsible, with extreme care and swift efficiency," John said calmly and purposefully.

As the prime minister listened, he could not help feeling John's directness and precision in the way he spoke. He also kept wondering how Professor Trimbledon knew these things, when his own official high-powered organs of national security, were at their wits end.

"But why can we not act now, Professor? Although we may not know where these leaders are, we can surely shut down their organisation? The FBI in America and other agencies could move quickly and arrest them, close these compounds you talk about, and all this could be stopped?" the PM asked, sensing a swift end to the global terror crisis, and some political capital into the bargain.

Again, John patiently explained that it appeared that they had autonomous cells all over the world, secretly embedded within communities and various enterprises, and that once they were triggered in some way, these cult members instantly moved into action, executing well planned and rehearsed destructive outrages. John sat forward and leant on the table to give greater emphasis to what he was about to say.

"You see, Prime Minister and Home Secretary, we fear that they may have been creating this international network of highly trained fanatics for the last decade, often through legitimate enterprises. This is an apocalyptic cult, Prime Minister, led by zealots and a band of completely dedicated followers who carry out the commands of Milshner without question or hesitation, all dedicated to the end of the world. We also suspect they have a grand plan to achieve this insane purpose, Prime Minister," John paused as he could see the incredulity in the PM's eyes and continued. "Yes, the end of human civilisation, sir. These are very different people to the terrorists on everyone's mind since Nine Eleven, Prime Minister, these people may well be wishing to completely destroy mankind, given the chance, and we must also understand that through unbridled capitalism, particularly in recent years, Milshner now has at his disposal a global business empire, larger in resource terms, than some countries. We think there is a high probability that he may well be ready to deploy this business empire and the concealed cells to deliver a cataclysmic event across the developed world. If we are right, then Paris may just be the beginning."

As John sat back in his chair and placed his hands calmly in his lap, he could see that the colour had drained from the home secretary's face, and the prime minister was silent and sullen.

There was a long silence as John and the prime minister just looked at each other, before John added, "We also do not know how many of these autonomous cells exist, where they are, or how they are triggered and, until we know this, Prime Minister, I would suggest we are impotent."

Again, there was a short silence, and it was the home secretary who then spoke, coincidentally asking the question that had been on the PM's mind earlier.

"Professor Trimbledon, may I ask the source of your information and how reliable it is?" she asked with a sudden feminine assertiveness.

John paused for a moment, leant forward placing his hands on the table, he smiled slightly and looking into her eyes replied, "Madam Home Secretary, in answer to your first question, I am sorry, but I am not at liberty to disclose my sources, except to say that they are honourable and reliable.

In answer to your second question regarding reliability, I believe the information I have placed before you both today is reliable and should be embraced with the various activities that I know your security bodies will be busy with. Perhaps I should also just add, as you will no doubt know, the majority of those crimes that are successfully solved by either the police or other security services, are solved with the aid of information from persons outside the police force or MI5, often by anonymous tip offs, key eyewitness statements, protected witnesses and insiders. While we are certainly not insiders, the information I have provided to you today, I believe, should be received with equal seriousness; otherwise, I would not be here, wasting your precious time."

At first, the home secretary did not know if John was wishing to put her in her place with his final statement about precious time, but then, as she looked more closely at him, she could see there was no malice or other combative intent, and he probably did regard their time as precious. She was unfamiliar with such direct, honest and gracious conversation having been shaped by the cruel and cynical political arena for so long where words and sincere gestures mean little, but often rather a personal attack or sarcasm.

What an unusual man, she thought. *And, if he is right, then everyone has been looking in the wrong direction, and this new avenue of investigation must now become our number one priority.*

"Quite so, Professor," the prime minister said, who had been provided with the customary briefing on John Trimbledon by his office between the time of John's telephone request for the meeting, and now facing him across the breakfast table. It had provided a brief resume of John and included such information that he was a distinguished economist, had held a professorship at Oxford, lived at Himbledon Grange, had no police record or any known political affiliations, he travelled extensively, was married to Mary Trimbledon, had four sons and a daughter and that Timothy, the eldest son, had died under mysterious circumstances in Paris in January. The briefing also highlighted that John Trimbledon had extensive business interests at home and abroad although it had been impossible to trace and quantify what these were. He also had significant wealth and owned much land across the world and was a philanthropist. In a Britain, that now prides itself on its open secular society, there was no mention that John Trimbledon is also a devout Roman Catholic. There was also another section that briefly described his adherence to prudent economic theories and practices, that he had never criticised the government, although his views were likely to be at odds with those practised by the PM and his government during the last fourteen years. There was also a single sentence mentioning that John had been awarded two citations for bravery, although no further details were given.

This prior briefing, plus the confidential information received earlier from him related to the atrocities, had quickly convinced the prime minister that John Trimbledon was a substantive person, not to be trifled with, that he could possibly be politically useful, all making the meeting this morning necessary.

The prime minister then asked, "What are your recommendations, what would you have us do, to combat this terror, Professor?"

John sensed that time was now limited before these two leaders of British government had to depart for other commitments, so he was brief and said, "I am not a security specialist, Prime Minister, and would not claim to know how to bring these threats to an end," he said, before continuing to suggest that the various security bodies, here and abroad, must instantly share their skills and resources, particularly the intelligence they have and are collecting related to the attacks. There appeared to be very limited information on the Japanese extremists, who they are, how they operate and what role they have in all this. There should be a special international task team established, and the Americans must learn not to dominate, since this experience has demonstrated serious failures in the past. The French must also not conceal critical information or the Japanese let pride inhibit them from sharing intelligence. Self-interest and silly political game playing will inevitably put the world at great risk at this time, he emphasised, saying it is now time for unselfish cooperation and generous leadership. The task team must be a joint collaborative undertaking with no country wishing to impose themselves on the others. The best available brains must be called upon, information must be gathered, collated and interpreted quickly and objectively and firm evidence must be established. In parallel, various countermeasures must be carefully formulated and tested in readiness for the right moment to act. Once the connection, between the atrocities and the cult, has been firmly established and the necessary knowledge about how the cells are triggered and where they are, then co-ordinated and pre-emptive counter measures will have to be enacted, Milshner and Adler must be captured and brought to trial.

If it was only that simple, thought the prime minister.

The home secretary looked at her notes that she had taken throughout the discussions. John then continued by firmly suggesting that there be a media liaison team put together to work with the press and TV editors. The media must start playing a more responsible role and assist with giving truthful and fully substantiated news, rather than much of the recent speculative material that was merely making matters worse. In times such as these, the media has a crucial role to play in keeping the public advised and reassured that the government is doing all it can to protect them, and that it is making progress. John concluded his remarks by saying that the countermeasures may well require the co-operation of the international media; so the sooner these collaborative liaison channels are established, the better.

John finally said, "When the relevant authorities are ready to act, I cannot stress enough, Prime Minister, it will have to be a coordinated effort across many countries all at the same time. Miss just one of these autonomous cells, or fail to completely break the triggering system, and there could be further devastation. I will personally ensure that should we have any more relevant information on this whole matter, you will be informed immediately, Prime Minister. May I thank you both for meeting with me today, and let us pray that this nightmare can be brought to a speedy resolution without the loss of further life." John calmly rose from his chair and, standing opposite the politicians, waited graciously for the home secretary to rise before he shook her hand.

The prime minister, who remained seated, suddenly felt irritated by John's behaviour, since it was normally he who terminated meetings, and this innocent act had merely reinforced the fact that Trimbledon was completely his own man. He was independent of any political interest or patronage, and that, if truth be told, he, the prime minister, desperately needed John Trimbledon, whereas the converse was now blatantly not so. Rarely did people ever really make the prime minister pause for thought or truly listen, although he had become adept at feigning such behaviours over the years. On this particular morning, however, he had paused, listened, and been deeply affected, not only by the information that had been provided and the courteous, patient and precise manner in which it had been given, but also by the person who had sat opposite him, slowly eating his breakfast.

Standing next to the breakfast table, the prime minister looked at the home secretary and asked her to prepare for an emergency cabinet meeting that he would call immediately, and then said something that took John completely by surprise. "Will you also arrange for Professor Trimbledon to have the highest level of security clearance and afford him all reasonable assistance in working with us to end this?" He then turned to John, asked for his mobile phone number, inserted it into his phone, and said, "I believe you have kindly agreed to remain in London tonight and tomorrow, Professor, should we need to talk further?"

"Yes, that's right, Prime Minister, and I will keep my phone open. Thank you also for breakfast."

They said goodbye.

After leaving Downing Street, John had hailed a taxi and had gone to the offices where Joseph had attended the board meeting some weeks previously. It was here that a small staff of accountants, lawyers, statisticians and other business professionals managed the vast Trimbledon global business interests. As he sat in the back of the taxi in heavy city traffic, he thought that the PM's claim that the Paris attack had created the recession was both political and economic nonsense; it was well under way long before these terrible events had taken place. The economic recession was also the result of macro and micro economic mismanagement and carelessness on a devastating scale by his British government and the Republican president in the U.S.A.. What is indisputable, however, is that the attacks had removed any remaining business confidence and had driven many sectors of the global economy, particularly international trade into, 'free fall'.

Poor man, thought John. *He has enough to deal with, without all this madness.*

The Trimbledon family, through trusts and other legitimate legal entities, owned many of the companies, while others were partly owned through large blocks of shares and other long-term investments. The work performed at this small group of offices was, in simple terms, twofold; firstly reporting the activities and performance of these many businesses and, secondly, strategic and policy related matters. All the companies and enterprises within this vast portfolio were separate and autonomous companies with their own management boards and they were left to operate their business activities without interference.

There were certain policy matters, that had to be adhered to, particularly by those companies that were fully owned, and influence was brought to bear in the other companies through shareholder meetings and representation on the company boards. The Trimbledons had been operating ethical and honourable business practices for centuries, long before such matters had become fashionable and worthy of special mention by the business community. There were certain types of business activities that they were never involved with such as armaments, certain media groups, the diamond or gold industries and the tobacco companies. Many of the companies within the group also had benefited from organic growth, reinvesting moderate annual profits to expand or improve the business. Borrowings were low and this had helped protect all the group business interests from the ravages of the recession and the limited liquidity due to the banking crisis. These companies also invested heavily in the development and welfare of staff with extensive bursary, health care, housing and other benefits for all their employees. While each of these companies operated in competitive markets and operated at the highest levels of efficiency, sound stewardship rather than just the maximisation of profits, was part of the value system that underpinned this extensive network of businesses.

Each of the fully owned companies and the numerous trust boards that managed this business empire also discreetly gave away millions upon millions every year to charities, educational foundations, medical research and to those in need. An independent board of trustees, that John himself chaired, coordinated all this giving. Although it had been raised from time to time that they should perhaps employ a press officer to provide suitable publicity for this generosity, it had always been given short shrift. Such giving had always to remain secret despite there being many public charitable faces for administrative purposes, the origins of this regular stream of funds was never to be divulged.

After speaking with two of his most senior colleagues, John went to his office and started to clear a neatly prepared in tray of papers that had been put to one side for his attention or information. Among these papers he pulled out a brief press release saying that the Vatican was again in the red although the situation had improved marginally on the year before. He sat back in his chair and reflected for a moment about the huge retroviral drug programme that the Vatican was the first to institute, long before the World Health Organisation and other international bodies had got involved. He wondered if there was any further assistance that he or his business interests should be giving to assist with this global war against HIV Aids. As far as the Vatican being in the red, he smiled to himself and thought it not unusual; it had been that way, on and off, for centuries and, anyway, it was not a bank, and its founder had told his followers two centuries earlier to give away all that they owned and to trust in the charity of others.

As well as this business domain, the Trimbledons also

owned significant areas of land and John had always been brought up to regard this as true wealth, together with knowledge, family and wisdom, rather than the money, shares, futures, debentures, derivatives and all the other paraphernalia that characterise the modern financial world. Land ownership also bestowed special responsibilities that the Trimbeldons had obediently served over the centuries and this whole sphere was an activity of special interest to John. Good stewardship, the proper and responsible use of land whether producing crops, preserving unique aspects of the natural environment or providing land for homes, new towns and hospitals, all fell within this purview. He was not a sentimentalist when it came to land, wishing to retain some rural idyll of thatched cottages and content cattle grazing nearby, but rather the sustainable use of land, a love for it with all its diversity and the plants, animals and people who lived on it and derived their existence from it.

20

Meeting an Old Friend

JOSEPH HAD ALSO RISEN EARLY AND, HAVING BEEN SITTING on aeroplanes and in meetings in recent days, felt the urgent need for some proper exercise. After a light breakfast he had gone to the small gym that had been created in one of the converted stable blocks at the back of the Grange. The gym had been upgraded a few years earlier for Paul as part of his training routines when he visited Himbledon. Joseph and Mark had agreed the evening before after supper that they both deserved some free time this morning and would meet again at ten thirty in the meeting room below. After a lengthy workout on the various machines and a shower, Joseph dressed and put on his walking boots and set off over the countryside to visit an old friend.

There was a distinct chill in the air although the day was clear and bright as he enjoyed the leaves under his feet as he walked along the path through Chopley Copse, a long wooded area that ran along the ridge of the hill behind the Grange. After crossing two medium sized meadows, one with dairy cattle and the other with two large bulls grazing, he stepped over the style and down the small embankment onto the tar of the narrow lane that led up a hill to a row of cottages. As he got closer to the stone wall around the cottages two dogs emerged from the broad gateway and came toward him.

"Hi there Josie," Joseph said as he leant forward to stroke and pat an elderly foxhound bitch just before a Basset Hound arrived and rested against his leg. "Hi there Jonah, good to see you too," Joseph said to the low, squat dog with short legs.

He stood up and walked on with the dogs walking beside him as he walked into the large yard toward a stone out building behind a double garage with the door open with an old Land Rover and a shiny new Toyota Corolla, the property of the lady of the house.

Just then, Freddie's face appeared at the open doorway.

"Hello Joseph, come inside, I am just cleaning some traps. Get down Jonah," he barked, and immediately the dogs were outside, he closed the door so they would not bother them any longer.

"Listen Joseph," Freddie said with a chuckle, "while I enjoyed Croatia, don't go to Dubai again in a hurry please, the heat nearly killed me."

They both laughed and Joseph thanked him for watching out for him on his recent travels.

"How are Ann and the lads, Freddie," Joseph asked and Freddie, putting one of several iron contraptions down on the bench looked up, leant his back on the bench and folded his strong arms across his chest.

"They are all fine thanks Joseph, Ann is inside and she will want to see you. Brian is out in the Gulf somewhere and David is adjusting to civilian life rather well."

"And how is Charlotte?" Joseph continued.

"Yeah," Freddie nodded. "She is also very well, and she and Mark popped in for some tea with Ann the other day while we were away."

They then chatted and laughed and Freddie was happy that Joseph had called by and invited him into the house.

Ann was there and embraced him and immediately put the kettle on.

"You should see this young lady that Joseph was with in Croatia, Ann, what a beauty," Freddie said as they all sat around the kitchen table and talked.

Joseph attempted to conceal his embarrassment and deflect the conversation on to other matters.

"I am not going to ask you Freddie how you manage to be so nimble when we travel and how you managed to arrive in Zagreb before us the other day?" said Joseph as Ann poured the tea.

Freddie, who was sitting at the head of the table, asked Joseph to pass the sugar and then replied, "Tricks of the trade Joseph, tricks of the trade," and he returned the sugar to Joseph and would be drawn no further on the matter.

They sat talking, exchanging news about people and happenings at Himbledon, and the dreadful events of recent days were never raised, as they sought some time together, just to be themselves.

Freddie Hardwick and his father and grandfather before him had been with the Trimbledons for years, back to the Middle Ages. Freddie and his son David were gamekeepers on the estate and farms in the district keeping various vermin under control. Freddie had two sons, David who had just finished a period in the British Army and Brian, the eldest who was an officer with the Royal Navy. Charlotte their daughter, a strong-willed pretty brunette, had gone away to veterinary college, and had now returned to work with the local elderly vet, who was nearing retirement, serving local farmers and those with small pets. Charlotte also wished to specialise with horses so had also been thrilled to have been offered the position as assistant vet at the Himbledon Stud to learn from Liam Flatley, a distinguished horse specialist in the county. David, who was a few years older than Joseph, now lived next door to Freddie and Ann with his wife and small daughter.

A less well-known responsibility of Freddie, and now his son David, was as family bodyguard to the immediate Trimbledon family members. They would act as chauffeurs, waiters, golf caddies and even tourists, whatever it took, to remain close to the particular Trimbledon or others they were asked to protect. Freddie handled shotguns and rifles as a daily part of his work and shooting was a mutual interest he shared with Joseph. There was a very special relationship between Joseph and Freddie; they had spent many hours together when Joseph was younger walking the fields, woods and hills of the district. Freddie and Ann Hardwick regarded Joseph as a third son and he treated the Hardwicks as his second family. They had fished together, tickled fish in the many farm ponds, watched young birds hatch from their shells in the spring and Joseph had been taught how to prepare rabbit, pheasant and a variety of other dead creatures for the pot. Brian and David used to accompany them, and the four of them had learnt many countryman skills from their father. Freddie had served in the British army like his father before him, and had also seen action in the Falklands. He had been trained in hand-to-hand combat and a diverse range of skills that had equipped him perfectly to be a private bodyguard and continue this family tradition with the Trimbledons.

Freddie and Ann Hardwick, together with Amos Hargreaves, the head gardener who lived in the end cottage with his ageing mother, together with various other local people were all part of a substantial extended Trimbledon family. It was a real community where everyone cared for each other, worked together with a mutual respect for the other's role in maintaining the fabric of Himbledon. Although John Trimbledon was the head of Himbledon, he was no feudal master being served by a group of peasants, indeed the opposite was nearer the truth. Everyone at Himbledon had their well-established roles and areas of expertise and when on the estate, John Trimbledon was more often told what needed doing than he commanding others. There was a trust, respect and deep affection between the Trimbledons and everyone living on the estate with John and Mary Trimbledon acting more like parents than modern employers. There was an interest and knowledge of each other, of the children, their education, the frailties and problems of the different families including the Trimbledons, how the elderly were getting on with the new kitchen in the frail care centre, how much Professor John had to spend to help the local Anglican vicar fix the damage to his church steeple and so on.

People's physical needs rarely went unnoticed or unsatisfied for long in Himbeldon, whether it was a new wheelchair, an upgraded central heating boiler in one of the cottages, a bursary for a bright youngster, or a new barn door, they were promptly noted and the relevant person dealt with the matter. Perhaps of greater significance is that the other needs of people, such as belonging, being known and being cherished were also a natural part of daily life at Himbledon. Yes there were disputes, gossip and difficulties that arose from time to time, where either John or Mary had to personally intervene to resolve matters, but these things never lasted long. Compromise, compassion and forgiveness always showed themselves to be of greater importance than contracts and individual rights in settling such disputes.

It was probably this type of agrarian lifestyle that contrasted so starkly with the increasingly alienated lifestyle of the growing industrial cities in the eighteen hundreds of Birmingham and Manchester that had influenced the writers of literature about such changes, at these times. Max Weber the German philosopher and observer of social trends wrote about society and community as he witnessed the spread of industrialisation and the rise of the protestant ethic throughout Northern Europe and a new value system that distinguished the new order from the old. With communities he noted, people are regarded and treated as an end in themselves, holistic beings with needs and obligations living in a network of reciprocal relationships with others. In contrast he described that in society, that increasingly characterised the drab poor industrial cities, people were regarded as a means to an end, elements along with land and capital as means of production, productive resources to be deployed for the creation of goods and riches for those who controlled these assets.

During the eighteenth century, as industrialisation propelled the rich world into a new era and laid the foundations for what was to follow, the ruthless commercial exploitation of men, women and children in mines and factories devalued human beings and led to the alienation of millions.

Notions of fairness, compassion, humility and simple kindness were often replaced by ruthless competitiveness, efficiency, and commercial growth and acquisitiveness and the contemporary protestant work ethic enabled such changes and another phase in the perpetual cycle of man's tyranny against his fellow man, the heartless judgement of man by man.

Among this new industrial tyranny and heartlessness there

was notable kindness and compassion for the disadvantaged among many Protestants, with men like Rowntree and some of the other industrial barons of Britain who built decent housing and provided elementary schooling for their workers.

It was in 1867 when Karl Marx published *Das Kapital* about the relentless and global nature of capitalism. Years earlier, his friend and patron, Friedrich Engels, had written an anti-capitalist text, *The Condition of the Working Class in England*, a scathing attack on capitalism and an unsparing description of the inhumanity of modern methods of production based on his experience as a textile baron in Manchester. It was in the 1840s that Marx and Engels travelled throughout Europe visiting the revolutionary activities of the time. It was in the following century that the dogma of Marxist philosophy was to fully enslave Russia and vast swathes of the world's population suffering under another tyranny.

The two great world wars of the twentieth century also wrought huge devastation across the world and levelled British society, enabling socialism and justice for the common man to prevail after World War II when the electorate dismissed Churchill and a labour government was retuned to power.

Although the grounds of the Grange were now smaller than they had been in the past, and to the stranger this was just another pretty series of farms, old houses, small villages and old churches that make up large parts of the English countryside, closer inspection would reveal something entirely different. Himbledon is a large country estate set in the middle of England and it has been there for centuries and just a mile away are the ruins of a Cistercian Abbey, now under the management of the National Trust. John Trimbledon, as his father before him, was the steward of the estate that had farms, small villages, parishes, a prestigious race horse stud, two public houses, two large dairy herds, community facilities such as a small cottage hospital, an elderly persons home, junior schools, some lakes and rivers and several large woodlands. The buildings, many of them built many years earlier, have a similar attractive natural style, there is a harmony and gentleness to everything, the result of countless generations living and working together with the land. All the Himbledon properties are well maintained, the gardens gently changing in time with the seasons, farm hedgerows neatly cut and the latest farm equipment can be heard in far off fields ploughing in readiness for the next crops to be planted in early spring. It was the earthly anchor of the Trimbledon family, always had been, and would always remain so.

Joseph suddenly noticed the clock on the wall of the kitchen.

"Sorry, I must go, had no idea it was so late, I am supposed to be meeting Mark at ten thirty," said Joseph with a start.

"No need to fuss Joseph, come on I will run you back to the Grange," insisted Freddie.

As they clambered into the Land Rover and closed the sturdy square doors, Freddie remarked, "I think we could have a frost tonight Joseph, I think we are in for a hard winter this year."

It was just a few minutes later that the Land Rover heaved to a halt near the kitchen door at the Grange.

"Thanks Freddie, take care, see you soon," shouted Joseph as he jumped out and briskly walked across the gravel to the entrance lobby, hanging up his coat, untying his laces and kicking off his boots. He hurried to his room, put on some casual shoes and picked up his papers before hurrying down below to meet Mark, already busy working on his computer.

"Sorry I am late Mark, I popped over to Freddie and lost track of time. By the way how are things with you and Charlotte?"

Mark looked over the top of his computer screen and stared at Joseph, obviously thinking about something, "Sorry, what did you say Joseph?" he asked.

"Oh never mind Mark. Now, what must we do?"

After a pause Mark replied, "I think we need to consolidate all this information, make a list of the facts that we know are substantive and then list what we do not know, and how we might be able to fill in the missing blanks. Oh, yes and here is Father's draft paper for Oxford that he asked me to give you," and Mark handed a bunch of papers to Joseph.

They worked well together, each taking tasks that complemented the other and it was not long before there were several flip chart sheets full of notes, arrows, diagrams, numbers and various other relevant facts. On one that Mark had kept to one side he had written up, what to him at least, were important facts; they were all numbers and related to dates of the atrocities and various quantitative features of each. A series of red question marks appeared near descriptive words about the Japanese collaborators, the number of cells, the triggering system, the location of Milshner and Adler and other critical intelligence they urgently needed.

Unlike Joseph, Mark was the stay-at-home son of the family. He was very clever, a little awkward, shy and with a wonderful sharp, dry sense of humour. Numbers, Charlotte and Himbeldon were all he wanted from life, and he certainly never wished to compete with Paul and Joseph, who to him were the bright stars of the remaining Trimbledon brothers. Mark always looked up to Tim, who acted as his second mother when he was young, looking after him and protecting him from Paul and even Joseph at times. He also had one other great talent of relevance at this time: he had a cool objectivity and, despite his nerdishness, he was always able to shine a different insightful perspective on everything. He could imagine and envision what many others never could.

Mark sat down in his chair at the conference table and pushed his laptop to one side, emptied the table before him and looked at Joseph.

"Come sit down Joseph, we need to talk about the Japanese and how little we know about them." He smiled.

Joseph finished up what he was doing and sat down across the table from his brother.

"I have also been working with Ruth to get some insights into what might make all these people tick, Joseph, and if some of these ideas are correct then there could be real fireworks. Trouble is, while we can speculate on how Milshner and Adler may behave, given the detailed Oscarbo information, we just have a blank as far as the Japanese are concerned," continued Mark.

They then discussed various ideas on how they might find

out more about the Japanese. Mark suggested that Francesca could possibly assist via the impostor John Holmes, but Joseph felt this too dangerous and felt that, as an idea, this should be dropped. Ruth had postulated that if these Americans were set on trying to destroy the world, although they are highly secretive, at some stage they would wish to seek some form of public recognition of their power and greatness. Mark used the Nazis to illustrate this notion by saying that although much of their activities were on the one hand secret, they also had this pathological need to be glorified, famous and revered. It is part of the profile of such people he explained, and it had repeated itself from the times of the first heretics and that people like Napoleon, Hitler and Mussolini and their actions had simply replicated a persistent characteristic of certain human natures.

"Although the circumstances are different, the superficial motives different and the weapons of this conflict are very different, why should these other fundamental human characteristics of these possible perpetrators be any different?" Mark asked Joseph.

This was not a casual conversation these two young men were having, but rather a systematic submission of evidence, and then the brutal and systematic testing of propositions, sifting of evidence, frank admission of matters that were not known and understood, and the careful drawing out of useful knowledge. A matter that perplexed Mark about this whole affair is that he could see no pattern, no element of logic that he could identify and then use to possibly predict where, when and how further attacks may take place. If the end of the world is their aim, then this will probably be announced in some way by the cult, but when might this be, and how might this horrendous possibility and date be communicated? Having been in regular communication with Ruth and engaging in a similar conversational process, Mark did, however, have some possible theories that he tested with Joseph.

Ruth and Mark believed that at some stage, if this whole nightmare were to be allowed to run its full course, that at some point in time there would be an event or action by Milshner and Adler revealing themselves, their power and that the end of the world is about to happen on their command. This revelation would be accompanied probably with all manner of symbols and anger directed at those they also wished to destroy, such as the church, and an appeal to everyone to undertake some bizarre practices to prepare for death. What interested Mark was the possible timing of this revelation in relation to the final cataclysmic act, and how this revelation might take place. He was less interested in the detail than the relationship between places, events and methods since this is where he believed the key to defeating these mad people lay.

Joseph listened, questioned, added information, clarified precisely what Mark was saying, disagreed and agreed throughout this rapid exchange and refinement of knowledge between them.

"Any thoughts on where and how such revelations will be made, Mark?" Joseph asked.

"Not sure," replied Mark. "This is all just speculation at this stage, Joseph, and needs careful verification, but I can tell you what I believe may happen if this thing continues." Mark then went on to describe a number of scenarios and he then highlighted the one he thought most likely and continued to share it with Joseph.

"There will be a series of continued attacks, with an apparent randomness, for the moment. There must be an end date in these people's minds; it could be 2012, since there are ancient prophecies that this will be the end of the current age before something else replaces it. The cult leaders will continue to enjoy exercising their power, tantalising and agonising the world with atrocities, displaying in their arrogance the devastating power they have over human affairs. Every successful atrocity will reinforce their own greatness to themselves, and will further embolden them to greater horrors. This is probably all planned, and they may well be following a timetable, with each act symbolising and accomplishing some part of their twisted personal agenda. These could be as trivial as destroying an old adversary, fulfilling some paranoid fantasy or systematically testing and validating various destructive methods and routines, and measuring the consequences. Adler would probably be particularly relishing the pain and suffering being caused, her control over life and death and watching frightened humans behave like scared animals in a maze."

"There may be important predictive information within the nature of future attacks and how they are carried out." Mark also believed that Milshner and Adler would manipulate the media to make their horrendous revelations known suddenly and starkly, probably when the attention of the world would be focussed on some global matter of interest such as a major sporting event, death of a pop star or some other world media feast.

Mark then concluded by saying, "It will then be a matter of hours, days or weeks, but will be unlikely to be months, before they blow the final whistle and fry everyone," he said with a deliberate touch of black humour.

"This is almost unreal, you know Mark. If it were not for Tim, Paris and Francesca, I would think I am having a bad dream," said Joseph.

"Oh yes," interjected Mark. "Something I need to clear up before we break for some lunch. You asked about Charlotte earlier Joseph, well she is very well and particularly enjoying the stud and she will be joining us tonight for the service. I assume that was what you were asking about earlier Joseph?" With a heavy touch of irony in his voice telling Joseph not to enquire any further about any more personal aspects of his long standing relationship with Charlotte, he continued. "I detected a great deal more than mere professional interest by you in Francesca when we spoke of her earlier. At this time Joseph, we must be careful not to let our emotions cloud our judgement and what may be best for the greater good, you know."

They looked at each other without expression as Mark rose from the table and, again looking at Joseph, said, "I just wish we knew more about the Japanese and what their particular role is, in all this." He started to leave the room and walk upstairs for something to eat.

Mark walked to the fridge and took out some cheese, cold meats and other food and put them on the kitchen table. His mother was in town and would be returning shortly so he laid three places at the table. He put pickle, salad and various other fresh produce on the table from the large larder and was just reaching to get a beer glass from the Welsh dresser when Joseph appeared.

“What do you want to drink Joseph, I am having a beer,” Mark asked.

“Is there any white wine open?” replied Joseph, and Mark lifted a tall wine glass from the shelf and placed it on the table.

“Yes I think so, in the bottom of the fridge.” Joseph was hungry after his earlier exercise and walk, while Mark was thirsty having done so much talking earlier and they just sat at the table attending to their needs in silence.

21

Another Horror

IT WAS A LITTLE AFTER ONE O'CLOCK WHEN MARY EMERGED through the kitchen door unusually flustered.

As she put her bags on one of the armchairs in the kitchen and removing her coat she said excitedly, "Have either of you seen the news? There has been a bad rail crash in Germany, Ted at the garage told me as I was filling up."

Joseph was the first to reach the TV controls and switched on the flat screen on the wall of the kitchen.

"Do either of you want tea?" asked Mary as she hurriedly put the kettle on and Mark and Joseph looking at the TV answered no thanks, they were having beer and wine. They then watched in silence, Mark still sitting at the table and Joseph standing with the TV controls in his hand.

It was now one fifteen on the kitchen clock as all the news channels were reporting a crash of a high-speed train in Germany on the high-speed rail line between Berlin and Hanover. The early pictures were mainly from private citizens using their mobile phones and the train had evidently been travelling at around a hundred and thirty miles per hour when it left the track and ploughed through an oncoming train, across the other track and over an embankment destroying houses and buildings in a town below. There was debris far away from the railway line and a picture of the locomotive with what was left of its aerodynamic nose lying on its side under the twisted wreckage of a petrol station where it had eventually come to rest. It was mayhem and the emergency services had just arrived at the scene. There were bodies lying everywhere and injured people walking around dazed, bleeding and confused.

There was also mayhem in the newsrooms of CNN, Sky, BBC and the other news channels. As Joseph flicked between the different channels, the same story was being told and then on BBC, the news reader stopped reading his prepared script and then awkwardly said there appears to be a further report of a rail crash near Madrid in Spain, also possibly the derailment of a high-speed train. All the news channels were asking viewers to stay with them as they brought this latest breaking news to the screen.

"Come Joseph, we must put this on downstairs and record some of this information," Mark said rising from his seat at the table.

"You don't think this is connected to Paris, do you Mark?" Mary asked, looking concerned.

"It looks likely, I am afraid, Mother. Will you excuse us? We will be down stairs if you need us."

Within a short time Mark and Joseph were sitting at the conference table in the meeting room below, watching the unfolding news on the large TV screen and jotting down key pieces of information as the various newsreaders reported the grim details of the accidents.

The accident in Spain had a similar profile to the one in Germany, a high-speed train derailment that had occurred in such a way it had created the greatest possible destruction and death. The train had derailed on an embankment ensuring the locomotive and front few carriages of the train acted like projectiles fired from a huge canon. They had flown across rooftops according to some initial eyewitness accounts and had crashed into the midst of a town demolishing apartments, shops and a large warehouse. Joseph and Mark just sat stunned by the horrendous pictures now being beamed across the world of men staggering half naked, children being carried away from the scene by blood stained screaming mothers, bodies thrown like rag dolls into the unlikeliest of places and positions. Joseph and Mark's emotions were being brutalised by these images and they both felt anger at such wilful and evil destruction of life and property. It was just too shocking, so utterly unimaginable that people could inflict such carnage on others.

Joseph was about to suggest they switch off the TV for a while and to focus on their work and the need to calmly think through what these fresh attacks might mean, when suddenly further news was announced of a further high-speed train crash, near Washington at seven in the morning local time. There are few high-speed railways in America, although there are some new services being planned, and the derailment had occurred with the Acela Express that runs on existing tracks at speeds of up to two hundred and forty kilometres per hour on tilting undercarriages between Washington, New York and Boston, at the height of the morning rush hour.

Just then Mark stood up and, walking to a flip chart, reaffirmed with a question to Joseph the time when these three crashes had happened, and he started to write numbers on the chart. It was now three fifteen in the meeting room next to the tranquil canal and gentle underground lighting, when yet another train derailment began to be reported. In China, near Shenyang, a high-speed train had left the rails and many deaths and injuries were being reported. Again Mark wrote numbers on the flip chart as Joseph walked to the large world map and started to insert red pins into the four locations where these accidents had been reported. He felt numb and had long since shut his emotions down to try to comprehend calmly this dramatic news pouring off the TV screen. Mark was looking something up on his laptop computer and then going back to the flip chart, writing up still further numbers.

Many parts of the world had come to a standstill, people standing on the street mesmerised by the pictures on TV screens in shop windows, busy bars and shopping centres had fallen silent as people stood, sat and just watched. Women were crying, shopping bags lay abandoned, taxi drivers refused to take fares as they too watched. There was incredulity, shock and fear. Business meetings had just ended, abandoned as staff gathered around TV sets. In the city of London, financial markets began to dip as brokers were inundated with instructions to sell and the oil price began to rise.

Had it been a single accident or crash then viewers would probably have reacted as they usually do to the daily stories of suicide bombers, starvation in the Sudan and riots in far away places, with their usual half-bored reactions. This was dramatically and frighteningly different, however; there were so many serious derailments happening all at once; these were not random accidents, but orchestrated destruction being inflicted by some unknown force, and it was happening all over the world. Suddenly, as this reality dawned on people, it all became horribly close to them; it all had a shocking immediacy that could not be easily shrugged away. It was also the precise impact the perpetrators had intended.

All the news channels were running a continual stream of information dedicated to the crash sites and had rescheduled all other news including sporting, financial and political news. The world was beginning to tremble under this sustained and ever more ruthless series of attacks, and people were now not just thinking the words, they were beginning to utter them, "First Paris, then four aeroplanes fall out of the sky and now this… when will we be next?"

Mark now busy doing a series of calculations both on his large fancy electronic calculator and on his laptop computer while Joseph sat, motionless, watching the ever-grim images on the TV screen.

Mark stood up in an almost unthinking involuntary movement and blurted out, "Joseph if I am right, just a hunch mind you, but if I am right there will be news of a further rail attack in a few minutes, somewhere in the eastern part of the world. It appears to be a differential time series and all these attacks, I think we will find, occurred at noon, GMT, London time. Look at these times on the board."

Mark explained to Joseph, pointing at the numbers he had written on the flip chart, that the German and Spanish rail attacks had happened at 11 a.m. local time this morning, which was noon in London. Then the attack in China took place at 7 p.m. local time, which again would have been noon here. Finally, the derailment on the line into Washington occurred at 7 a.m. today, during their morning rush hour.

Seven a.m. in Washington is noon here in London; we are five hours ahead of them.

Before Mark could continue, the TV news reader said, with a shocked look on his face and a slight tremble in his voice, "We are interrupting this bulletin from Washington to bring you further breaking news of another high-speed rail incident in Japan." Mark slumped back into his chair and rested his chin on his hand and stared at the television.

A bullet train travelling at two hundred and sixty kilometres per hour on the high-speed rail line between Kokura and Hiroshima had derailed at 8 p.m. local time, and had left the tracks and collided with a similar high-speed train travelling in the opposite direction, according to reports being received from Japanese television networks. The Japanese work long hours, and 8 p.m. is peak rush hour, so the trains were full to capacity.

Mark said with a heavy voice and fatalistic manner, "You see Joseph, 8 p.m. there, local time in Japan, would have been noon here in London. While we sat here earlier Joseph, discussing Milshner and the Japanese, at midday precisely, each of these five high-speed rail attacks all happened at the same time." He paused for a moment and then continued. "We are facing a formidable and evil enemy, they are going to be difficult to stop and we have very little time to do so."

Sky News had created a train crash and fatality visual chart that they repeated every fifteen minutes and the numbers were mounting. In total, some seven high-speed trains had either been derailed or impacted by these attacks, two in Germany and now two in Japan. In the Washington derailment the train left the tracks as it was passing through a station and had destroyed two other trains on adjoining lines, one a local passenger train and the other a large freight train. This now brought the total number of passenger trains involved to eight. The Spanish attack did not appear to have involved any other train and further news was awaited from China. Although they were estimates since in the panic, debris and confusion no one had any idea of the number of dead, they based their estimates on the typical carrying capacity of the trains. The cumulative total was already showing tens of thousands potentially dead and even this huge number had not come close to describing the grim reality emerging across the world.

Just then Mary walked through the door of the room with two mugs of hot coffee and, walking to the table, placed one in front of Mark before handing the other to Joseph, who was now standing by the map of the world looking to insert a fifth red pin near Hiroshima in Japan.

Trying to insert an element of normality into the intensity within the room Mary asked, “What time will Louise be arriving, Joseph?”

Joseph suddenly remembered that it was this evening that she was arriving by road from Oxford.

“I am not sure, Mother; Louise said late afternoon.” He looked at his watch, which now showed it to be just before four, and continued, “I will call her shortly just to check.”

Mary said, “Thanks Joseph, we can have supper together at six because the service starts at seven forty-five.”

“Have you spoken with Father this afternoon, Mother?” enquired Mark.

“Yes, about half an hour ago at the office. Evidently, the prime minister called him earlier, and they are to meet again tonight and possibly tomorrow, so he has to stay down again tonight. He said that the prime minister may go on national television perhaps later tonight or tomorrow sometime.”

Joseph felt he had to have a break from all this for a little while and switched off the television and the room fell into silence for several minutes as they all remained within their own thoughts.

Then Joseph said, “I am going for a walk in the garden for some fresh air Mark, I will not be long. Will you both excuse me?”

“Yes, of course,” answered Mark, and Mary nodded and smiled sadly.

There was a chill breeze as Joseph walked down to the lake through the garden, along a gravel path that crunched under his feet. The neat lawns and flowerbeds with the bright variety of colours now fading with early autumn, he felt a sense of reassurance in contrast to the appalling news he had been watching a little earlier. As he approached the stone wall and pushed open the gate and walked down across the broad lawn towards the small boathouse, he retrieved his mobile phone from his jacket pocket and phoned Louise. His phone rang for some minutes and there was no reply and he began to wonder where Louise might be.

It was some minutes later as he leant on the corner of the old wooden boathouse, looking out over the lake and watching some swans in the distance, when his phone sounded in his pocket, it was Louise.

"Sorry about that Joe, I just had to find a safe place to stop and have pulled off at a service station on the motorway. Isn't this news about these train accidents awful? I have been listening to it on the radio. Anyway how are you darling?"

"I'm fine thanks Louise; just taking an evening stroll by the lake. What time do you think you will be here?" he asked.

"In about forty-five minutes, I think. I will soon be at the Beasly off ramp, and then it is cross-country, and this tracking thing is great. Just a minute, let me see; yes, it says fifty minutes to destination. What are we doing tonight?"

Joseph smiled at Louise's matter-of-fact way and her confident ability to deal with everything, and answered, "We will have supper at the Grange once you arrive and then we have been invited to a special church service at the Anglican Cathedral with Mother, Mark and his girlfriend. It is a special service for the victims of the Paris atrocity and the plane crashes, and I suppose we must now add everyone who died today in these rail crashes. Father is away in London. We should be back at Himbledon by about ten."

There was a momentary pause and Louise said, "Oh, all right Joe, I will see you shortly then darling, I had better go," and Joseph clicked off his mobile phone.

As he stood by the calm water with the cool breeze on his face, it felt good to be in the open air, in this beautiful place with the calm of the surrounding countryside. However, he could not stop thinking about the horror of the train derailments, people trapped injured and dying, the frantic efforts of the emergency crews hunting for survivors, and the anxiety of family and friend's awaiting news of their loved ones. He looked at his watch and it was just before five so he thought he had better wander back and check with his mother where Louise would be sleeping tonight before washing up for supper and welcoming her. He turned and as he walked back across the rich green lawns he looked up at the Grange standing silent and strong before him, and a grim determination entered his mind as he thought, *we must catch these people, put an end to this madness, and bring them to justice*.

As he walked through the open gate and walked up the steps onto the gravel garden path, a voice suddenly roused him from his thoughts, "Good evening, Joseph; it's a fine, fresh evening."

Joseph looked across. "Hello, Amos. I did not see you there earlier. How are you, and how is your mother keeping?"

Amos had been attending to something in one of the large flowerbeds and stood up and walked toward Joseph with a broad smile on his face.

"I am well, thank you, Joseph, and so is my mother. She complains about her arthritis when the weather begins to turn like this, you know, but, otherwise, she is cheerful enough. How long are you home for, Joseph?"

"Oh a couple more nights and then I must go to Oxford briefly before going to Paris. Isn't it time you packed up, Amos? It's almost five."

The middle-aged head gardener shrugged and with a chuckle replied, "I don't have a watch, Joseph. Anyway, I would rather be out here on such a fine evening than indoors."

"Well, I had better go Amos, take care of yourself, and the gardens are looking lovely as ever. Good evening to you, and please remember me to your mother,"

They nodded at each other as Joseph continued to walk back to the Grange.

After leaving Amos several paces behind, Joseph thought, *I suspect Amos will only find out about the international rail horror when he gets home and watches the evening news with his mother. In the meanwhile he has been oblivious of it all having been in amongst the flowers, plants and lawns all day.*

Then, for a moment, Joseph felt he would gladly exchange

roles with Amos, if it were ever possible, just to be able to escape from these other realities.

Mark was still downstairs working when Joseph arrived back at the meeting room, and he said to Joseph that there was no doubt in his mind, these were a carefully orchestrated and mounting assault on innocent people and cities.

He then spoke slowly and clearly, "If I am right, taking the date of the Paris attack, the loss of the four passenger planes over the sea and now these five rail attacks and the time at which each of these incidents occurred, there is a time series involved. If I am right there will be further attacks. There may be another major one four months from now, and then further attacks at defined intervals and then it will stop because we will have reached the zero point of the series. I need to check my calculations and I would like someone else to validate my logic, but these attacks appear to have a multiple purpose, one being a numerical warning followed by an end state, and I will leave you to conjecture what that might be," and he put his pen down on the table and sat back in his chair looking straight at Joseph.

"Are you saying, Mark, that this is some sort of cynical set of warnings that then proceed to some major apocalyptic end event?"

After a brief pause Mark answered, "Yes, I am afraid it could very well mean just that. What's more, I think I am beginning to understand where the Japanese extremists may fit into the picture, they could well be cyber terrorists of an extremely high and as yet unseen calibre. While you were out, Father phoned again and he is having a further confidential meeting with the prime minister and some other people tonight, but indirectly he also advised me that they have found one of the black boxes from one of the missing aircraft. From the little Father could say in doublespeak on the phone, I think he was trying to tell me that this particular aircraft received some peculiar data from a navigational satellite."

"So what does all this mean, Mark?" Joseph interrupted, rather impatiently with time getting on.

"Well, Joseph, it could mean a number of things, but it could mean they brought these planes down by interfering in some way with the onboard computer intelligence systems between the pilots and the control of the aircraft, and crashed them. They may well have done something similar with the high-speed trains."

Joseph was finding it hard to grasp the seriousness of what was being suggested and since Mark always spoke quietly in a matter-of-fact manner, it all felt unreal as he stood by his older brother.

"Come Mark, we must pack up and get ready for dinner and the service tonight with Mother, we can get back to all this first thing in the morning. Anyway, you look as though you need a break. I am going upstairs now and suggest you do the same," said Joseph as he closed his laptop computer on the conference table.

As Joseph walked along the passage to the kitchen Mary called out, "Is that you, Joseph?"

"Yes, Mother," he replied.

"Louise is arriving and she will be here in a moment."

Joseph walked out through the kitchen and around to the front of the house, where he stood looking down toward the gatehouse and large gates, and he could see Louise's car making its way up the long drive toward the house. As she rounded the last incline into the large area before the front of the main house, Joseph smiled and signalled to Louise to drive around to the side of the house to the family parking area. By the time he had briskly walked to where she had parked, Louise was standing by her car, stretching and breathing in deeply.

"Hello Louise, and welcome. I am pleased you made it safely," Joseph said as he gave her a hug and kiss.

"It is so lovely to be in the countryside and to see you darling," she said and Joseph noticed under her tan and flowing blonde hair that she looked a little tired.

"Come inside, and let me help you with that," Joseph said as he took a small travel bag and her laptop computer from her. As he did so, Louise thrust her hand and arm under Joseph's arm, and they walked together to the kitchen door.

As they entered with Joseph following Louise, he heard his mother welcoming her and giving her a kiss as he closed the outer door. Joseph stood behind them both for a few moments as they talked, and he thought how elegant Louise looked in her beige slacks and blue high neck jumper, while they continued talking about the journey and his mother said how the colour of Louise's jumper suited her. Joseph walked around them and up to a guest bedroom on the floor above where his own room was situated, and put Louise's belongings on the bed and returned to the kitchen where his mother and Louise were now sitting together at the kitchen table talking and having a cup of tea. Just then Mark walked into the kitchen and seeing Louise, immediately walked over and greeted her with a kiss on the cheek.

"Excuse me, Mother, what time are we having supper and when do we have to leave? I must let Charlotte know," enquired Mark.

Looking up from her conversation with Louise, Mary replied, "I have fixed supper for just after six and if we can all leave at just before seven that should give us enough time to be there for the service at 7:45. Shall I also lay a place for Charlotte?"

"Yes please, Mother, thanks. I am going to have a shower," said Mark and left.

"You would probably like to get settled in before supper Louise, we can continue our conversation later. Joseph will you please show Louise to her room," Mary said and Louise reached for Joseph's hand for him to show her the way.

During dinner Mark offered to drive providing Charlotte did not offer any suggestions, either about his driving or any short cuts. Being a local vet, Charlotte knew the district very well and she was also a very competent driver. Freddie her father had insisted that she also take an advanced drivers course since she spent many hours travelling on her own, and often not on the best of roads in travelling to the farms of the district. At one stage during dinner, Joseph and Mark felt somewhat irrelevant since the three ladies were talking so much to each other. Louise had met Charlotte at Joseph's birthday party and they had taken an instant liking to each other and had plenty to talk about.

Travelling in the large Range Rover with the three ladies

in the back and Joseph sitting next to Mark driving, they made the journey in remarkably good time. There was little traffic and everywhere was surprisingly quiet for this time of the week, and then it was Charlotte who suggested that these rail accidents had really shocked so many people so terribly, that many had probably decided to remain at home. Yes probably getting more depressed watching the wall to wall news coverage, added Mark, and they all smiled and fell into silence with their own thoughts. When they reached the county town, it too was unusually quiet, except around the Cathedral where all the car parks were full and there were people hurrying to the service. Mark eventually found an empty bay on the street and swiftly manoeuvred the Land Rover and parked.

As they all clambered out Joseph looked at Charlotte with a grin and said, "I notice Mark's driving ability and coordination has improved tremendously under your influence, Charlotte."

"Of course, what else would you expect, Joseph?" she asked and laughed.

Mark groaned and said, "Be careful Joseph," as he glanced at him and everyone laughed.

They quickly walked across the street and in through a stone gateway and along an old pathway through beautiful grounds and past some medieval buildings before coming to the magnificent cathedral entrance. As they neared this imposing structure they could hear the organ playing and there were people standing outside in huddles. A number of clergymen were in the doorway attending to various people, and to one side there was a large group of young choristers. As they got close to the doorway a distinguished and slightly portly gentleman, with a dog collar, stepped toward Mary.

"Hello Mary, thank you so much for coming. Is John not with you?"

"No, I am afraid not, Bishop; he had to go to London at very short notice and sends his apologies." Mary introduced Charlotte and Louise to the bishop, who then turned to Mark and Joseph, shook their hands, said hello again, and welcomed them.

As they entered the huge building and walked down the central nave, a priest came over and whispered a welcome to Mary, shook Joseph's and Mark's hands, smiled at the young ladies, and disappeared to get ready for the service. Two other religious men came over and spoke softly to Mary before she signalled to her sons and their companions that there was room for them in the front part of the cathedral, about ten rows back from the altar. As they made their way to these seats, Charlie, the chief constable, turned from where he was sitting, and signalled to Mary that he would speak to her after the service. The cathedral was already full and the service was only scheduled to start in a few minutes. Joseph and Mark were making eye contact with several people they knew and were nodding and smiling. Joseph moved the kneeling cushion to one side to make room for his legs after sitting down, as he was sitting back he turned and smiled at Louise and she smiled back. He noticed she looked rather stunned and her eyes were wide open as she looked around the interior of the cathedral. She held Joseph's hand and pulled it in between their seated hips. The organist, playing Bach, was filling the church with glorious sound and this, together with the hallowed surroundings, meant that most people were sitting silently, waiting for the service to start.

Charlotte, once she had sat down and put her bag beside her on the pew, unhooked the kneeling cushion and placed it on the old stone floor and then knelt forward, lowered her head and resting on the pew in front, prayed for a few minutes. The organist had stopped playing for a moment and the whole congregation began to fall silent. Just as Charlotte had sat back next to Mark, there was a sudden cacophony of sound filling the whole building as the organ started to play the entrance anthem, people stood up and started to turn around to watch a procession enter the cathedral with alter servers, the choir that consisted mainly of boys dressed in red cassocks with white collars, deacons, guest religious from other churches, including the Catholic priest who had spoken to Mary earlier, various others and then the local vicars and the bishop at the end, and he was carrying a large ornate shepherds crook. It took a little while before the choir and everyone else had assembled beneath the altar and at the front of the church. There was then another brief pause with the organ music silent as the choir conductor briefly fussed with his music and he then looked up to the organist and again the organ burst to life for a few moments before the choir started to sing "O Praise Ye The Lord." No one else in the church sang; they just listened to the enchanting voices and organ echo around the high vaulted roof of the cathedral, and Louise felt bathed in this exquisite sound and unexpected place.

A cathedral is a church containing a cathedra, the throne of a bishop and as such is the main central church of a diocese. If a building does not contain the seat of a bishop then it is either a parish church or abbey. Westminster Abbey, the scene of many great state occasions, is not a cathedral because it is not the seat of a bishop. England has some forty Anglican cathedrals with more than half this number being ancient cathedrals dating back to when Christianity first came to the country. This particular cathedral dated back nineteen hundred years, when Papal authority created a monastery and abbey. The oldest part of the structure is the Crypt and one of the largest of its period in England and dates back to ten eight six. The Quire has beautiful stained glass windows and had a number of notable shrines until they were demolished and removed during the protestant reformation by order of Henry VIII. The Nave is a spectacular example of gothic architecture with tall columns rising to a great height supporting the delicate and ornate vaulted arches beneath the splendid roof.

The cathedrals of Britain are an integral part of its cultural and spiritual heritage. They were constructed to inspire people and to attempt to reflect the glory of God in stone, pillars, ornamentation and glass. In the Middle Ages they were centres of worship, learning and charity and often the focus of pilgrims who travelled many miles on foot to visit the shrines of the saints. On many pilgrimages men, women and children from all sectors of life, good and bad, rich and poor, distinguished and humble, would often travel together. It was a time to share, to tell stories, to share food and possessions, and to give and receive support with the travails and joys of life.

So it was the same tonight, in this great cathedral that had witnessed almost two thousand years of English history, as people squeezed up together to accommodate the hundreds of local people who had come to the service. They were fearful, perplexed and desperately needed the reassurance of being with others, trying to live normally in a suddenly very abnormal world around them. To many of those sitting and staring from the pews, the spiritual significance of their surroundings, what everything meant in this vast building and the ceremony happening before them, was largely unintelligible. These great cathedrals, apart from a dwindling number of Anglican church goers, like many of the other traditional Christian churches in England and Europe, had become little more than historical tourist attractions, particularly in the last thirty years. God and these great relics were viewed as old fashioned, unfathomable and irrelevant to so many, yet, as the stability of the modern world rocked and appeared to be approaching some precipice at the hands of the unknown, people across Europe were flocking to churches, holy shrines and religious people, seeking reassurance and answers.

It was a dignified service at which the Anglican bishop read from scripture, as did the local Catholic priest, a Methodist minister and an Anglican vicar. There were entreaties to people to remain calm, to have fortitude, to forgive and to trust in God. There were prayers asking God to show mercy to the victims, the dead and the dying, and that He might also forgive and heal those misguided people who had committed these crimes. There were wonderful hymns that the choir led and the congregation sang. Mary did not even need the hymn sheet when they sang *When I survey the Wondrous Cross* and *Abide with me*. The final hymn, *Onward Christian Soldiers*, even Louise joined in with full voice, reading from her hymn sheet and vaguely remembering it from her school days.

After the service one of the cathedral vicars gently moved among the congregants and made his way to Mary and invited her with her sons and their lady friends to please join the bishop for some tea and coffee before driving home. Mary graciously accepted, thanked him and then passed the message quietly via Mark to Joseph and the girls, and Charlotte looked at Louise and smiled. Mary calmly led the way, out through a side door of the cathedral, down a long cloister and into a large room with oak beams high above their heads. There were already about twenty people standing in small groups talking with cups and saucers in their hands as Mary and her group entered.

It was Charlie, dressed in his police uniform, who first saw Mary and her sons arrive and he instantly excused himself from the people he was talking with and walked across and said hello to Mary and gave her a kiss on the cheek.

"Hello Joseph, Mark, good to see you both again and thank you for coming tonight. How are you both?" he asked, extending a hand first to Joseph and then Mark and shook their hands. Louise and Charlotte stood behind and looked around the large room.

Mary said, "You know Charlotte, of course, Charlie. But let me introduce Louise, a friend of Joseph's from Oxford."

Charlie greeted the two young, attractive ladies. Meanwhile, Mark had managed to carry three cups of coffee back with brown sugar cubes in each saucer and he handed one first to his mother and then Louise and Charlotte.

"Thanks, Markie," Charlotte said as she plopped two of the cubes into the cup and started to stir the cup with one hand while holding the saucer in the other. Just then, a large man with a ruddy face came over.

"Hello Miss Hardwick, what a pleasant surprise. When are you coming over to Gabriel's to check my bull? Did your father give you my message?" and they quickly became engrossed in conversation.

Louise, who was standing between Joseph and Mark, glanced over at Mary, who was now in conversation with Charlie. Mary had asked him about the meeting with the home office, and Charlie was explaining that it had gone better than he had expected, and that they had taken their suggestion about clearing magistrates' courts of mundane matters positively, but that many parts of the country were in a very worrying situation. Many of the big cities were suffering a big rise in social disorder, troublesome youngsters now with a perfect excuse to cause trouble, and there was more and more inter cultural conflict. Doctors were also being inundated with anxiety, depression and various other psychological disorders and many people were staying away from work. Charlie said confidentially, that there had even been some discussion that should the situation continue to deteriorate, the government may be forced to consider severe emergency measures and even possibly the suspension of Parliament, and setting up an interim emergency coalition government. Things were looking really bad economically as well and they were sure to get worse after today's events.

Just then, one of the Anglican vicars at the cathedral came over and greeted Joseph and after introducing Louise they began to talk about the service. Mark went off to rescue Charlotte from the local farmer and on the way the bishop stopped him and enquired after his father and Ruth. This left Joseph, with Louise on his arm, talking to the vicar who he had known years before when they were boys. The vicar asked them both if they had read in the newspaper recently about a survey one of the British Universities had carried out about the Bible in Britain today. The survey had reported that the Bible is viewed as old fashioned and irrelevant and that some humorous opinions had been reported. One of the people surveyed said David and Goliath was the name of a ship while another thought that Daniel, who survived being thrown into the Lion's den, was the Lion King. They all laughed and Joseph said he thought such attitudes among young people very sad, and that it was a poor reflection on our religious education in schools and homes. Louise listened and nodded politely.

Then the young vicar continued to say things that she found very unsettling. He said everyone should recognise that the Bible is the foundation of the society upon which the whole British culture has been based. In order to properly live in this country an understanding of the Bible was essential. He said that the packed cathedral tonight showed that within so many people there appeared to be a yearning for something that the secular world was unable to provide, and it was often only when there is a crisis, when people are made to think about their own mortality, that they instinctively turn to the church for spiritual reassurance.

Yes, she thought with a small smile. *He is right; I have been experiencing a little of this since being in Croatia with Joseph*. Her honesty and frankness, with herself as well as others, made her instantly recognise these realities, even in her own life.

It was, however, his final comment that brought this whole conversation almost brutally into her personal consciousness when he told them that, evidently, the campaign officer of the British Humanist Association, an atheist organisation, had commented that the fact that people had little knowledge of the Bible perhaps suggested that it was becoming less and less relevant to people in the twenty-first century. It was this type of remark she had heard so often before from her parents and it now seemed to her to be so utterly fatuous and misleading. Her own clear logic and her legal training suddenly shouted at her, within her head, that such statements were a distortion of the truth and plainly dishonest. Before a person can judge the relevance of anything even in a court of law they are required, indeed entitled, to have some knowledge of the matter under judgement, but if young people are being denied any exposure to the Bible, as she had been, the use of words like relevance are irrelevant. They were being denied a choice, the right to freely choose for themselves based on the facts. No wonder so many people today feel a deep sense of bewilderment about religion and take up the secular view that it is all fairy tales and bigotry. A sudden sense of neglect and then indignity began to sweep into her mind. Then the word betrayal came to her and it persisted in her thoughts, despite her polite nods and smiles.

Just then, Mary caught Joseph's eye from across the crowded room and there was an instant unspoken understanding between them.

"Well it has been good to see you again and thank you for a fascinating conversation. You must come over to Himbledon some time and we must keep in touch," Joseph said, extending his hand to the young vicar.

They said goodbye to one another and Joseph led Louise by the arm to where the bishop was standing surrounded by people in conversation. Mary was already there and Mark and Charlotte appeared behind her.

The bishop, seeing Mary approach, stepped aside of the group he was with and took Mary's hand and asked, “Do you have to go so soon, Mary? We have not had a chance to talk yet.”

“Yes, I am sorry we have to go. I must phone John in London when I get home, but why don’t you come for dinner soon, and we can catch up properly? Ask your secretary to phone me, and we can fix a date when you and John are free,” she said.

“That’s a splendid idea, I will do that. Please give my warmest wishes to John when you speak to him later and thank you so much for coming tonight, goodbye Mary.” Then everyone else said goodbye to the bishop and Joseph thanked him for the coffee.

As they walked to the car Joseph asked Louise why she had been so quiet earlier and she looked at Joseph, smiled and said that she had been listening and thinking about what the young curate had been saying about the Bible and personal choice, and anyway, she was feeling a little tired. On the return journey they changed around and Joseph sat in the back with his mother and Louise and Charlotte sat next to Mark in the front. They were all quiet, within their own thoughts as the headlights shone a path through the dark country lanes towards Himbledon, and Louise laid her head on Joseph’s shoulder.

22

Downing Street

THE SAME EVENING IN LONDON, JOHN HAD RECEIVED a special invitation from the prime minister's office to attend an urgent and confidential meeting again at Downing Street and they had sent a car to collect him from his office. He noticed that he was driven to the back entrance of Downing Street where there was no media presence and he was quickly escorted inside and to a large meeting room where there were twelve other people either standing in small groups talking or sitting at the large conference table reading papers or looking at their laptop computers. The invitation had said that he had been invited as an observer, acting as a special advisor to the prime minister and that he should remain after the meeting for further discussions with the PM.

There were some military chiefs, two foreign delegates, one a woman and the other a man and then various other people mainly from the security and intelligence services. The home secretary, foreign secretary and secretary of defence were also present. Immediately the prime minister entered the room, everyone came to order, and those standing sat at the table as he sat in the middle of the table. After a few grave opening remarks he outlined four topics that he wished to review; firstly, any new intelligence related to the attacks, particularly the rail attacks; secondly, the special task team he had suggested to the UN Security Council and the necessary arrangements for a major British contribution to this; thirdly, the deteriorating security situation in Britain; and finally, his public announcement that had been scheduled for the following morning.

John found the meeting to be highly organised, orderly and to the point. One of the high-ranking intelligence people provided a brief overview of new intelligence and that this related mainly to one of the black boxes that had been retrieved from the sea. Although it was still being investigated, there was evidence that the aircraft had received some unusual digital code information some four and a half minutes before the recorder stopped functioning. There was a brief discussion as to whether such digital information could have been related to the loss of the planes and after a further brief discussion it was confirmed by two at the table that if it had interfered with the aircraft's on board flight systems, there may well be some connection. It was also confirmed that due to the location of the aircraft far out to sea that these electronic signals must have come from orbiting communication satellites.

With regard to the high-speed train crashes, various theories were described as to how they could have been derailed although the five crash sites were still under intense investigation and nothing unusual had yet been uncovered. Since the rail attacks, the foreign office had clearly been the scene of intense activity, with all manner of communiqués from foreign governments, requests for assistance, proposed countermeasures, and several requests for cooperative security activities. Some confidential information from China and the U.S.A. that was reported made the prime minister reiterate that all nations must now work together, and any unilateral actions, however well meaning they may be, could imperil the whole world. He instructed the foreign secretary to communicate this statement as a matter of urgency to these governments and to the British ambassador at the United Nations in New York. The European Union was also busy setting up inter governmental task teams for the deteriorating security situation.

One of the ladies present, a senior member of a British intelligence agency, then provided a brief presentation on potential suspects and there were some strange suggestions on her list that included Islamic terrorists, Iran, North Korea and then some fanatical terrorist groups. John was interested in the small listing of these particular suspects that included Milshner, he was pleased to see and then he heard some highly relevant intelligence about the Japanese extremists who it was suspected had joined forces with the Milshner cult. The leader of the Japanese group was an anarchist by the name of Tado Judaire who had changed his name to Hisoka Takumi Genkei that means in Japanese, if a literal translation is possible, 'Hisoka'— meaning secretive— 'Takumi'— meaning pioneer— and '*Genkei*'— source of reverence. Taken together, these names left little to the imagination as to who this man now regarded himself to be, a secretive pioneer who should be revered.

Judaire was of mixed parentage, with a Japanese mother and a French European father who were both deceased and he would now be aged in his forties. Although little was known about him in recent years, from investigations made by the Japanese special police some years earlier, when he was suspected of a clever cyber attack in Japan, information had been gathered about his schooling and his early teenage years. Being of mixed parentage he was taller than many of his school peers and being different was ridiculed at school. He was an awkward child, withdrawn, but very clever, and he spoke fluent French, English and Japanese from a young age. His extremely high intelligence also alienated him from the other children he grew up with and two of his teachers in secondary school reported that he was more that just intelligent, but had qualities of genius. At the age of thirteen he had submitted a computer simulation game that he had developed with two of his cyber friends for a school science competition and it had created a mild sensation. It was many years ahead of anything similar; it used highly sophisticated computer code and the quality of animation was exceptional even with the limited hardware available at the time. A software company in the U.S.A. had subsequently bought the software package from him and the money was put into a trust for when he became an adult.

From other information gained by the local police, who had gained access to his bedroom after he disappeared, it became clear that for some years he had interacted via the early Internet with other young people of a similar inclination and intelligence. He was described as easily bored and often simply withdrew from those around him into his own thoughts. He was also an only child, and his parents were very protective of him, and his father, a diplomat for the French government in Japan, had lavished material things on him, probably to compensate for his son's apparent loneliness.

It was only during this presentation that John wrote any notes during the whole meeting. This intelligence, although now dated, that the lady was reporting about Genkei was providing vital clues that needed to be brought back to Mark and his virtual team at Himbeldon. As the lady spoke, it also became clear that this young computer genius was certainly not lonely, but existed in a virtual reality that was vivid to him, but to few of those around him, via his computer. He had a small group of young cyber friends who could relate to him, share and understand his ideas, and even join him in his fantasies and delusions. For Genkei, it appeared to John, the end result was probably less important than the adrenaline rush of being able to do such fantastic things, and to be so ahead of everyone else.

The Japanese police had followed up all the computer intelligence they had gathered some twenty years earlier and had tried to interview everyone that had been connected with him. Apart from a few dead ends, most of those who appeared to know him had also disappeared at the same time as he had. One could only conjecture what had been taking place in the intervening years, especially with the rapid development of the Internet since the first email was sent in 1971 between Ray Tomlinson, an engineer in Boston, and Newman in Cambridge. Working with many of these cyber friends conceiving and developing new software and technologies, and in more recent times with the commercial might of the Milshner business empire, John shuddered to think what lay out there, concealed, ready to kill and maim.

The two and a half hour meeting finished sharp at ten o'clock and the prime minister asked the foreign secretary, the home secretary and John to remain for a few minutes and to join him in a small lounge on the second floor. After offering everyone a drink, the four of them seated in armchairs, the prime minister asked if they had an opportunity to read the draft of his public announcement to be made the next day. They all said they had and that it was all he could say at this stage and it had their support. He then said that he had instructed the minister of defence to clarify with the military heads of staff that if these terrorists can bring down four civilian aircraft what might they be able to do with military aircraft and other military hardware, most of which these days are influenced or even controlled by computer systems? No one said anything; they just looked at each other while John wondered whether this horrendous prospect might just be lying ahead.

Then the PM said something quite unexpectedly, which he had received via the foreign secretary, who he smiled at. It was a copy of an email that had been received by the British Consul in Delhi, which, although garbled, appeared to be suggesting that the recent cyber attacks on the Pentagon and various network systems in some Balkan countries and elsewhere, were not the work of Russia or even North Korea, but a group of private individuals, and he mentioned that they should look at a certain cyber game that could be downloaded from the Internet. The PM had passed this information to his security people, but he also wanted John to have it for scrutiny, and to let him know if, it had any significance to catching these people.

Then the prime minister said he was worried about the Americans who wanted to raid and arrest the occupants of all the known cult compounds, particularly in the U.S.A.. He also said that he had spoken personally to the president and they had agreed this not to be the moment to be doing anything rash that may precipitate further attacks. However, there were elements in various security bodies in the U.S.A. who appeared to have inordinate independent power, so all in the room needed to be aware of this danger. The Chinese were also an unknown factor now in this broadening global crisis and how they may react. The prime minister asked John if he had any access or way to find out two critical questions.

Firstly, how these attacks were ordered or triggered and secondly, who gives the order? John replied that he did not have any means of obtaining this information, although any new intelligence that may come into his possession would be communicated immediately with the PM. John asked if he would be required the following day, since he was intending to return to Himbledon and the PM said this was in order, and anyway they could talk if necessary via a secure land line that he had instigated between his office and Himbledon, when John had received security clearance.

The prime minister looked tired as he walked with John to the rear of Downing Street and he thanked him for his assistance and half suggested that had it not been for the information provided, he did not know where they would be now in trying to deal with the situation. John took this as a touching appreciation of the help provided, and they stood for a few moments before the official car arrived at the door to collect John. As they stood, the PM said it was the damnedest thing that no one had any idea of where, when and what, in terms of the next attack. He said in an irritated manner that it was impossible to ground all passenger aircraft or to close rail networks, life had to carry on.

"If only we could find these madmen," the prime minister kept saying.

John calmly replied that this was not going to be easy, that there were many wanted people still at large and in hiding, particularly the most notorious twenty-first century terrorist of them all, who was still at liberty. After a brief pause, the PM sighed and agreed. Just then the car arrived, they shook hands and the PM returned to his meeting with his two cabinet ministers, and John was driven to the apartment by the Thames.

When John arrived at the apartment there were several messages on the answering machine and after calling Mary and saying he would be at Himbledon the next day, he dialled the number of his brother Thomas, who had left a message asking him to call. The conversation was friendly and brief; John was tired and needed to get some sleep. Thomas had been invited to go to Boston to accompany Liska, who was to perform with her dance company in the city, and Thomas wondered if there was anything he could do while there to assist with getting to the bottom of these attacks. He was planning to stay with Martha, their sister, and be there for probably ten days. Without thinking, John said there was just one thing he could do, but he must be careful, he could go and see a certain Jesuit Friar, and convey John's personal thanks for his help in recent months and John said he would get Mark to provide the necessary contact details. It was late and after making a few more urgent telephone calls, John went to bed.

23

Methods of Mass Murder

IT WAS DARK AS JOSEPH WAS AWAKENED BY THE SMELL of Louise and hot coffee and as he opened his eyes there she stood by his bed, whispering for him to turn on the bedside lamp. They sat together, Joseph still in bed and Louise beside him sitting with her legs stretched out on top of the bedclothes, drinking their coffee as they talked about the Adriatic and sailing between the islands. On this autumn morning in England, all that seemed far away, as Louise shared recent happenings in her academic life with Joseph and then asked when he would be returning to Oxford before going to Paris. Joseph could just as easily have pulled her into the bed with him and remained in her arms, with the blinds drawn all day, but other responsibilities lay downstairs.

During breakfast Mary said that she and Louise would be back by early afternoon after they had done some shopping and had had lunch together. Joseph was ignorant of these arrangements as his mother spoke and he looked across to see Louise smiling over the top of her breakfast cup. They had clearly sorted all these arrangements out earlier, well out of earshot of Joseph. Louise asked Joseph if he would be free at four for a jog around Himbledon and the time was agreed. Mary, telling everyone to leave the kitchen dishes, reminded her sons that their father would be arriving late afternoon from London so everyone could have dinner together at the Grange tonight, and that they should entertain Louise somewhere else, apart from the kitchen, before she returned to Oxford the next day. Mark said he would pick up his father from the station and, since it was going to be a 'dinner dinner', he would invite Charlotte. Louise found it touching how so much naturally fell into place when these family members were together and she could see where Joseph had inherited his easy and warm style: his mother. Then the large table in the kitchen was abandoned as the two men went one way and the ladies another.

It was eight fifteen when Mark switched on the underground lights and they both walked down the stairway to the meeting rooms and canals below. Mark and Joseph quickly set the room up for another days work, trying to piece together different evidence to try to move closer to being able to apprehend the culprits and put an end to the horror. Joseph switched on the television set and lowered the sound and switched gently between news channels. They were all carrying pictures, special stories, facts and figures on the five high-speed rail crashes of the day before. The death toll on Sky had risen dramatically since yesterday and after just a few minutes Mark suggested, since there appeared to be nothing about how these accidents had happened, switching off the harrowing pictures and for them to focus on other matters and some other work he had prepared.

After returning from the remembrance service at the cathedral and saying goodnight to Charlotte the previous evening, Mark had returned to the underground meeting room and had worked late into the night trying to postulate how the aircraft and the high-speed rail trains may have been destroyed. He had managed to piece together a wide range of information and had hurriedly put a brief presentation together to share with Joseph when they met again in the morning. It was this that Mark was now beginning to show to Joseph, as he carefully narrated the terrifying details.

Fly by wire computer technology is used in all modern passenger aircraft and it is a very reliable and safe technology. All planes have multiple systems, so if one fails another takes over and in all cases the pilot can override the computer control systems. All aircraft also rely on sophisticated navigational and other technology to guide the plane both in terms of its position and its height from the ground. Planes also have onboard radar systems that the pilots use for visual guidance, especially for monitoring other aircraft in the vicinity and weather conditions. When the radar shows a bad storm ahead, pilots will change course and avoid extreme weather conditions by as much as ten miles. Then there are the flight control centres throughout the world that maintain regular contact and guide the thousands of planes that are in the air at any single moment in time. There is therefore a constant flow of data passing from the plane to the ground, and from various transmitters on the ground and in navigational satellites orbiting the Earth, being received by electronic receivers on the plane. This constant two-way communication is what enables thousands of aircraft to continually move through the skies above us and to reach their destinations safely.

Autopilots do most of the flying, apart from takeoff and landing, the busiest periods in any commercial airline pilot's flight routine. The autopilots, or fly by wire, operate the aircraft at optimum speed and altitude and when these electronic systems, which deploy computer intelligence, are in operation they fly the aircraft. They control all the critical functions within an envelope of optimum flying parameters.

According to Mark, a distinct likelihood, in order to bring four aircraft down with such precision, is that there was some external electronic communication with these planes that instructed the autopilots to crash them into the sea. With the planes going down mid ocean, these signals in all probability came from navigational satellites and somehow they were able to take complete control of the aircraft, probably despite desperate attempts in the last few moments by the pilots to avert disaster, and then crash them. If this was the case, then they would probably also have blocked any outward radio transmissions from these aircraft, which would explain why there had been no mayday calls or any other messages about problems and the loss of radio contact a few minutes before they disappeared. Furthermore, the minor problems reported by the pilots four hours into each of these particular flights and the strange events just four and a half minutes before they disappeared could have been the onboard electronic systems "booting up" with this rogue digital data being transmitted to the onboard systems. Since aircraft have duplex and multiplex systems, for reliability and safety purposes, these would possibly have all been primed to submit to a single chosen slave system among them. Before running the crash software, the instigators may well have set up a feedback loop, via the rogue communication they were deploying, to validate that everything had been loaded successfully ready to commit the deliberate ditching of the planes into the sea. This would also explain the strange data found in the black box flight recorders.

If Mark was correct in these theories then the loss of the four aircraft signalled a completely different level of complexity and capability of the people responsible. The attacks in Paris, although they had been lethal to thousands of innocent people, had been crude in comparison with these aircraft attacks that must have involved an intricate, and so far unknown, set of software and other communication technology. However, Mark continued to explain, from some of the other investigative work he had carried out, Milshner had extensive commercial interests in aerospace, communications and the development of computer software.

Most people just do not know the scale of technology today or ever ask how it all works or is regulated. Satellite television and the navigational system that Louise had used to find her way to Himbledon from Oxford were examples that Mark used to show that much of what we all take for granted today, would have been regarded as fantasy and science fiction just a few short years ago. He asked Joseph how many of us had any idea of the range of technology involved in beaming instant television pictures of events from the other side of the world into our living rooms, how satellite navigation for our motorcars could be so precise yet our cell phones so pervasive. Just these few examples made Joseph realise how beholden the modern rich world is to technology, and those who develop and control it.

Furthermore, Mark continued, in the last twenty years the speed of software development alone had been without precedent. India had become a vast low-cost software factory for the world, producing highly complex programmes using large teams of programmers very quickly. Milshner had invested heavily in some of these outsourced overseas software companies and, via his aerospace and communications commercial interests, probably also had access to communication satellites.

Mark had received a call from his father just before breakfast, and he said he would be bringing home some vital information that he had learnt at the meeting with the prime minister the evening before, and wished to have a one-hour discussion with the two of them late afternoon before dinner.

"What time are you picking up Father from the station?" Joseph enquired, thinking about the run he had arranged with Louise earlier.

"Not sure, I am waiting for a call from Father," Mark answered. "If we meet with Father at five-thirty, that will give us an hour together until we need to get ready for dinner."

With his jog with Louise safe, Joseph asked Mark whether he had any theories about the rail crashes and Mark had continued with his presentation.

High-speed trains, as with commercial aircraft, are under the control of a human being, either a pilot or train driver. High-speed rail lines are also regularly maintained and they are fenced off, so such attacks had probably required a multiple *modus operandi*. Mark said his best guess was that there had been some interference with the signalling system and the speed of the trains. Most conventional rail derailments occur because of human error, badly maintained equipment and rail lines, or obstructions on the track. Something as obvious as an obstruction on the tracks he thought to be unlikely. Most high-speed trains rely on what is called cab signalling that is communicated to the moving train through digital signals communicated from the rails to antennas positioned under the train. Mark said without, going into the detail of how these juggernauts travelling at high speeds are managed, according to a line length block system and sophisticated traffic control centres, the point was that the driver, like a pilot, has to rely on different forms of computer intelligence to drive the train.

The speed of these trains is high enough that the driver or engineer cannot reliably read signals along the trackside or handle the welter of data about the train's movement fast enough. Human reactions are simply too slow and unreliable for long periods.

These systems manage gradients, bends, and external ambient temperature, closing ventilation vents and retracting overhead pantographs when entering tunnels. They also compute and report the speed of the train and all this information is displayed on various computer screens in the engineer's cab.

"So where does all this leave us, Markie, as to how these trains were derailed all at the same time in three different continents?" asked Joseph with a glint in his eye at the affectionate name used by Charlotte the evening before.

Mark smiled and, looking at Joseph, said, "I will appreciate if it you will not call me that again, even when Charlotte uses that name, she does it to embarrass me. Now can we get back to more pressing matters?" and he continued to describe his theory about the train derailments.

Mark believed that these attacks involved a number of elements which, when combined, proved lethal to the progress of the trains. Rogue data transmitters could have been installed at the precise locations where the trains were to be derailed to transmit incorrect data via the rail track signal that usually consists of a thirty-two bit digital unit with each bit related to a specific frequency that is encoded on the transporter frequency on the various rail circuits.

"All right Mark, I am sorry about getting personal earlier, but please spare me all these technicalities," and the two men smiled at each other.

Putting it more simply, Mark explained that either a sudden acceleration or a sudden violent breaking, probably the latter, was what he thought had induced these trains to climb the tracks and derail in the way reported. Somehow, and this Mark had little idea about, they had again interfered with the computer intelligence to make the train do something that derailed it, and it all happened so fast that the driver could do absolutely nothing to avert the disaster. The rogue transmitters could have been planted weeks or even years before, and just left awaiting the moment they were required, to deliver their deadly signals and being very small would have been almost impossible to find on thousands of miles of rail network. The final thoughts that Mark shared with Joseph again raised this whole nightmare to another unimaginable level of reality.

One of Milshner's business interests was rail car manufacture and high-speed rail line maintenance, particularly the various telemetry and monitoring circuits. They could well have contracts all over the world and could easily have placed these sensors and transmitters. Just a few global conglomerates that work across the world now perform many of these highly specialised infrastructure construction and maintenance activities. As part of the day-to-day outsourced maintenance contracts that keep the modern high technology world spinning, Milshner could have laid destructive devices and systems almost anywhere, inside Nuclear Power Stations, within the turbine blades of huge hydroelectric schemes, in shipping navigational systems, in hospitals, indeed anywhere.

"This has been going on for years, Joseph. This loony and his mistress have probably laid secret preparations for a final firework display that will make the atomic bomb destruction of Hiroshima appear modest, despite its horrendous death toll," Mark said grimly, continuing. "I also think this whole thing has probably been programmed. You remember the mathematical series I mentioned yesterday, and my suspicion that we are now following some deadly timetable? Well, perhaps this whole nightmare is being triggered not by Milshner or his nutty lady friend, but by some elaborate computer programme working through the Internet or cellular phones, which is executing some evil timetable of horrendous events leading up to a final end state, probably intended to be the end of the world."

Mark continued to tell Joseph of some disturbing material he had analysed on Tim's laptop computer that their father had brought back from Paris in January. Among a range of weird material in various secure files, there had been a Doomsday computer simulation game that had, as part of its plot and interactive theme, the destruction of Paris and the downing of aircraft. Mark suggested that perhaps Tim was onto something much bigger than just the Paris attack, and this was why he was murdered, to silence him and avoid the perpetrators being uncovered and stopped.

Joseph remembered Francesca's remarks about the Trimbledon family being infiltrated and the need to be very careful, and he asked, "If they knew Tim was onto something, then they will also suspect that we are involved in some way in trying to stop them?"

"Yes, of course, they have been trying to closely monitor us and our activities for months. I thought you knew this, and that Father had warned you. This is why Freddie had accompanied you and Louise to Croatia, for this very reason," Mark replied, with an element of incredulity in his voice at Joseph's apparent naivety.

"I thought that was simply because we are always vulnerable from a number of evil groups who suspect the existence of a fraternity for good, and will wish to destroy us if they can."

"Yes, correct Joseph, but the Milshner cult have two very important reasons to have us gone, the obvious one being that we are Roman Catholic and they hate the church for a whole range of misguided and paranoid reasons. But the second reason of special importance, is that they fear us and regard us now as their greatest enemy with the potential to stop them," Mark replied and then he continued to explain this last statement.

According to Mark, the whole doomsday nightmare unleashed by Milshner and his collaborators was to destroy the modern rich world first, using the very technology that had made it rich and powerful. They were skilfully playing on the arrogance and greed of the modern world and its carelessness regarding the regulation and control of this ever-growing level of technical complexity and reliance that rich people had on such information technology, machines and remote systems. The cult with the Japanese influence in recent years had also taken on a range of strange beliefs and activities whereby they appeared to believe themselves to be some form of new world technological order with the power to end the world. Having crippled the rich world they would rely on the inherent systemic problems of the developing world, without the rich world, to fall into rapid chaos, internal strife and disease. The cult may even be wishing to enact some final destructive act by unleashing a plague to mop up any remaining survivors. This was probably why John Holmes' mission with Francesca was important to them, to be able to steal drug resistant strains of unstoppable viruses and bacteria. Joseph, reminded of Francesca and the danger she was in, was cast further into a feeling of hopelessness.

Mark continued. "The worship of technology, common today, will, however, probably provide a weakness in these people's armoury that will enable us to help defeat them, just providing we can find it in time. Milshner will also have intelligence about the Trimbeldons and the other great families of the fraternity and how, over the centuries, this group has helped to preserve freedom and morality. Unlike modern technology, global enterprise and the other tools deployed by Milshner and his cult, much of the fraternity's value system and *modus operandi* is unintelligible to Milshner and his associates."

It was an ageless reality that Milshner was simply unable to comprehend; it operated according to values of justice, service, sacrifice and love that were completely foreign to them. Not understanding how it all worked with this silent enemy, just increased Milshner's paranoia and fear of them.

Mark ended his explanation by simply saying, "He will be anxious to stop us before we are able to stop him, Joseph."

There was a brief period of silence before Mark closed the presentation on his computer. Just then, Mark surprised Joseph when he said, "You know Joseph, despite the power they have and the awfulness of recent events, we are going to defeat these people. Never under estimate the power of prayer and the fact that it will only ever be God who decides the end of the world, certainly no mere earthling."

Mark suggested they get some coffee from the kitchen above and have a break, before wrapping up their discussions before Mary and Louise return.

Standing together in the kitchen drinking coffee Mark looked at Joseph, smiled and said, “There is no need to look so gloomy Joseph, despite their sinister intentions and undoubted resources to inflict massive destruction, through prayer and other things we have helped defeat terror and misguided people over the centuries, and I am sure this will be no exception.”

Joseph looked at Mark and replied, “I wish I could share your optimism Mark, it all looks terribly bleak to me right now, I know we must have faith and ultimately trust God to bring this to an end, but I just wonder if it isn’t different this time. There is just so much we do not know, time is ticking and these fanatics appear so well organised and indestructible.”

Mark smiled and said, “Not so, Joseph. What you have to remember is that human beings create computer intelligence and systems; therefore somewhere within them they have frailties. Just look at some of the commercial software we use every day. Furthermore, we know that Milshner and Adler are vain, narcissistic and disturbed people who, despite having this awful ability to destroy, also have frailties that may yet prove to be the key to their capture and downfall. You Joseph, as a historian, will know that on countless occasions in history, tyranny and despotic people have been brought down through their own weaknesses or obsessions.”

Mark continued and said, “Just take Hitler as an example. Had he not been a Nazi who actually implemented his lunacy, the Germans may well have won the war. The persecution of the Jews denied them access to top brains who came over to the allies, and when Hitler ordered the invasion of Russia and opened another major front, this was a huge mistake for them. It was Hitler’s arrogance and his obsession with Arian dominance that led him into Russia and this folly cost them thousands of soldiers and equipment in the harsh winter conditions. This, and other incredulous acts by Hitler, driven by his obsession about the indestructibility of his armies, probably turned the war with the Allied troops fighting in various other theatres of war, led to the weakening of Germany and a major turning point that led ultimately to their defeat.”

Mark argued that Hitler, as powerful and ruthless as he and the SS may have been, committing all manner of atrocities, were driven by a wholly corrupt and psychotic set of values. Madness has incompetence that will destroy itself in the end. In his arrogance Hitler also completely underestimated America when he declared war on them after Pearl Harbour, leading to further catastrophic consequences for his ambitions. So it will be again, with this wholly unsustainable campaign of terror to destroy civilisation.

Just then the phone rang in the kitchen and Joseph answered, “Hello, Father. How was the meeting last night?”

“Revealing. Listen, I will be arriving later on the five-thirty train if one of you can pick me up and Ruth will be with me. I want the four of us to have a meeting first thing tomorrow since we will not have time this evening after we arrive and then dinner. Will you please tell your mother that Ruth will be staying over and that we will be arriving later, please?”

“Yes of course, and Mark will be meeting you at the station.”

“Many thanks, see you later, goodbye,” John replied and Joseph replaced the telephone receiver.

“That’s better, we can now have a decent break before dinner and we will be fresh for the meeting tomorrow. But I wonder why Ruth is coming up?” asked Mark.

They looked at the television for a few minutes back in the downstairs meeting room before Mark said that there was one other matter that he wished to debate with Joseph. They would then need to break again for when their mother and Louise returned and Mark reminded Joseph that their father was waiting for comments on his draft economics address to be given at Oxford in November.

Mark mentioned that he was pleased Ruth was arriving since she could possibly throw some further light on the behavioural characteristics of Milshner and cult members to refine Mark’s current ideas on the matter. He had a half developed theory for this possible timeline. He had studied various prophecies, checked the international calendar of world events and two in particular had correlated closely with the multiple evaluative criteria he had used.

"Time is getting on Mark," Joseph interjected, seeing that it was now after two-thirty. He was also feeling hungry, despite Mark always being able to ignore such things as food when he became engrossed in work.

"Ok yes, Joseph, let me quickly summarise then, before we go upstairs," Mark answered before he continued to explain the possible consequences of his theoretical timeline.

He believed there would be another major attack in January next year, and then other smaller attacks, each of which would essentially be testing attacks. There would then be something really major, possibly to coincide with the World Cup Soccer Tournament scheduled to be held in South Africa in 2010, and it would probably be at this time that they would announce themselves to the world with bizarre messages and other extreme activities.

There will certainly be something about the end of the world at their hands, he thought.

Strangely, according to the time series calculations, things then would go fairly quiet for a number of months, before reaching the zero point and the possible final apocalyptic event would be triggered. The zero point coincided precisely with the date of the opening ceremony of the next Olympic Games in London in 2012.

Mark explained that he had run some correlation validations and that his predictions all looked to be highly probable. He ended his remarks by mentioning that it was no coincidence that the ancient Mayan calendar predicted that 2012 will be the end of an age and the beginning of a new one. While this ancient information and its validity today are debatable, it could, nonetheless, have had a major impact on cult members' beliefs and those of Milshner and Adler.

"Something to think about; what do you say, Joe?" Mark asked as he piled up the papers on the table before him and closed his laptop.

"I feel a little brain dead, Mark, and need some time to digest all of this, but I am very impressed at the speed with which you can analyse all this information and come up with quite robust explanations," Joseph replied.

“Thanks Joe, now let’s go and get some fresh air,” Mark replied, and they both walked upstairs, talking to each other.

When they arrived upstairs Mary and Louise were already there before them with shopping bags littering some of the chairs in the kitchen.

“Have you eaten?” Mary asked and Joseph replied that they hadn’t, so Louise offered to make them both a sandwich. Mary said that Louise had bought a beautiful dress in town and was sure if Joseph asked her nicely she would wear it for dinner. The two ladies had enjoyed lunch together at one of Mary’s favourite small restaurants in the local market town and they had chatted together almost non-stop since leaving Himbeldon some hours earlier.

As Louise handed Joseph a sandwich she gave him a kiss and said, “Hello darling, have you been working hard?”

“Yes we have, at least I have,” said Mark now sitting at the table enjoying his sandwich.

Joseph smiled as he ate his sandwich, still contemplating all the information he and Mark had discussed earlier. Yet again he felt a strange sense of detachment and security sitting in these mundane surroundings while he also turned over in his mind the greater knowledge he now had about the extreme peril the world faced.

Jogging slower than he usually did, Joseph guided Louise along the different paths, over fields and through woods, over stiles and through gates that he opened and then closed behind them. It was glorious to be out in the countryside again. Louise was a regular jogger, was fit and strong, so Joseph had also enjoyed some good jogging as he mounted the top of the hill behind the Grange where he stopped and turned, waiting for her to join him. As she came over the brow of the field Joseph could see her breathing deeply and he reached out for her as she came to a standstill with her arms at her side. He hugged her and then turned her around slowly as she caught her breath, to look out on the Grange and the green scenery beneath them.

They stood for some minutes without talking as their breathing returned to normal, and then Louise turned around to face Joseph and said, “I feel so at peace and at home here,

Joseph, and your mother is so kind. We had a really good time together this morning and I even asked Mary for some advice about my big decision for next year and her comments were so helpful, really made me think. Did you know that Mary knows a lot about the law, Joseph?"

Joseph smiled. "Did she tell you that she was a local magistrate for a while, but then fell out with some civil servants about some matters that I now forget?"

"No," replied Louise. "But that would explain her legal knowledge."

"Come on Louise," Joseph said, "We had better be on our way back and get ourselves cleaned up for dinner and this new dress of yours. I have also got to quickly look at a draft for Father. He is bound to ask me about it later."

V

The World Out of Control and Personal Courage

24

Next Steps

DINNER AT HIMBLEDON WITH THE FAMILY WAS ALWAYS a rather special occasion, especially with everyone there, apart from Paul who was still in America. The troubles elsewhere felt far away and this was precisely what Mary had intended when arranging the meal with their cook and generally presiding over affairs. Mary knew John would be tired, that her sons needed a break from their grisly work earlier, and with Louise and Charlotte there as guests meant that tonight was to be a relaxing and enjoyable evening together for everyone. That was exactly how it happened, and Louise and Charlotte talked and laughed at the humour, Ruth told various stories about Joseph and Mark when younger which, while embarrassing them, provided further enjoyment. Louise looked radiant in her new dress and Charlotte had a beauty and practical country charm that everyone enjoyed.

It was after they had finished dessert and were enjoying some cheese and port that Mary asked Louise if she would mind her raising the question they had discussed earlier. It regarded an important decision that Louise had to make shortly about whether to accept a teaching post in the U.S.A., to go into chambers in London or to take a junior prosecuting council position that may be available at the International Court of Justice in The Hague the following year when she finished at Oxford.

"Not at all, of course," Louise replied to Mary's question, and everyone at the table discussed the merits and negative aspects of all three positions. Everyone had their own preferences, but, after a lengthy and, at times, hilarious discussion, it was Charlotte who suggested they all vote on each of the options. A simple voting system was proposed by Mark that involved writing a number for each option on a piece of paper and placing it in an empty wine cooler. Mark counted up the votes and, by quite a large margin, the position in The Hague was voted the favourite. This ended a delightful evening where both Charlotte and Louise had been made to feel so welcome and a part of the family.

It was late when Joseph retired to his bedroom and remembered his father's draft address for Oxford and, looking through his papers he extracted it, sat on the edge of his bed and read it through. There were just two minor items that he wrote a brief comment about in the margin for his father's attention. It was an impressive, compact and highly relevant address with numerous insights of importance to the current economic crisis that was spreading around the world. Joseph smiled to himself when he re-read the opening quotation that his father had chosen to set the tone of the address.

It read: 'The budget should be balanced, the Treasury should be refilled, public debt should be reduced, the arrogance of officialdom should be tempered and controlled, and the assistance to foreign lands should be curtailed lest Rome become bankrupt. People must again learn to work, instead of living on public assistance'.

Cicero 55 BC.

The next morning, everyone gathered for breakfast around the large table in the kitchen as Mary produced a stream of fried bacon, tomatoes, sausages, mushrooms and eggs. It was decided that John, Mark and Ruth start work together immediately after breakfast and that Joseph would join them at around ten after Louise had left to drive back to Oxford. Joseph and Louise decided to take a walk, since it was a bright mild morning, and then she would need to leave just before ten to get back to Oxford in time for an early afternoon faculty meeting.

As they walked hand in hand down to the lake they talked easily and Joseph said he hoped to be back in Oxford within about three days and would stay for two days before then going to Paris. He said that Louise should visit him in Paris as soon as he had settled in and he asked her whether the voting the previous evening at dinner had influenced her thinking at all about what to do next year. Louise said that The Hague had certainly risen up her list of choices, but that she needed a little longer to think about it. She also said a big factor in her decision would be Joseph's own movements the following year, since she did not want to be working miles away from where he may be. Louise stopped every so often and turned and stood in front of Joseph and kissed him. She felt more in control of herself now than their last terrible parting in Croatia, and despite Joseph not being able to love her in return, coming to Himbledon like this and being with the family had somehow further cemented the deep friendship between them. Louise felt more secure and had a deep sense that, whatever happened in the future, she and Joseph would always be close, very special friends.

"Please text message or phone me once you are back, Louise," Joseph said as Louise waved through the open car window and moved off slowly down the drive. Joseph watched her move all the way down the drive, watched the large gates open and Louise disappear in to the country lanes.

When Joseph arrived in the meeting room, his father said that he had arrived at an opportune moment since they were about to break and get some coffee. It was Ruth who first said what a lovely girl Louise was, so bright and beautiful, and then John said that he liked her more and more every time he met her and that Mary had enjoyed her company the previous day. Such unanimous warmth toward his lady friend touched Joseph, and again made him a little sad, since he was unable to love her, and he passed off these kinds remarks with a joke, asking if they had the solutions to the world's problems.

The four of them reconvened at just before ten-thirty, John quickly summarised the latest position and the information the three of them had discussed in Joseph's absence. He summarized the information about the Japanese secretive and pioneering Judaire, the computer game that the PM had asked him to comment on, and Ruth had provided information about brainwashing, or re-education as it is sometimes referred to, how this may be part of the cult's *modus operandi* and how both John and Ruth agreed with Mark's theories about a timeline, Milshner needing at some stage to make himself known and to be acknowledged as the power behind all the destruction. Ruth also spoke about Anna, saying that she had displayed symptoms of some sort of mind control, and was in a highly traumatised state, but in treatment and was gradually responding. John described the computer game and other information that Mark had discovered on Tim's computer and that there appeared to be a connection with the material the PM raised. It was clear that Anna had spent time at some stage before meeting Tim with the cult, that she had been planted in Tim's life to monitor him and that when Tim had discovered information that could seriously damage the cult, they had him murdered. Ruth was quick to point out that they did not believe Anna had murdered Tim, but that probably some intelligence she had fed back to the cult had led to him being killed without her knowledge.

Ruth then spoke about Anna and what had possibly happened in Paris. It was clear from various incoherent conversations that Ruth had had with Anna in recent weeks, particularly just before her mental health began to rapidly deteriorate, that she was suffering dreadful guilt and psychological dissonance. She had never intended to hurt Timothy and Ruth believed that she loved him. However, Anna also started to talk about a past under some hypnosis that Ruth had suggested she undergo, and, when she agreed, Ruth confidentially arranged for a professional psychiatrist to see her. From various remarks that she made under hypnosis, it appeared she was a lowly member of some religious extreme group in the U.S.A. when she was completing her studies and that she had taken on some of the beliefs and that there was work to be done to save the world, certainly never to destroy it. What had probably started as a well-meaning, although arguably misguided mission to get to know Timothy, and to keep an eye on his activities, feeding snippets of information back to a contact in the U.S.A., then turned into a nightmare for her. Those who persuaded her to befriend Tim, once she had agreed to do so, soon started to blackmail her and she could find no way out. Ruth believed that all Anna did was to keep her cult contact briefed about the confidential files on his computer and probably when she discovered certain files, the cult decided Tim was getting too close and that he should be silenced. Anna believed that she was responsible for his death and the trauma of what happened in January and her involvement was what had caused her mental illness.

John, Mark and Joseph sat in silence listening to these torrid revelations that had led to Timothy's death. Each had different emotions and it was John who spoke first when he enquired whether Anna would recover and what further could be done to help her. He appeared to ascribe no direct responsibility to Anna, and his further remarks about her being a mere pawn and being duped into this extraordinary situation received Ruth's support and agreement. Like Timothy, Anna was a victim and needed the fullest support of the family. Ruth indicated that a recovery was possible, although it was going to be a slow and painful process.

Joseph asked about the computer files and the video games and Ruth went on to explain her views about them. She thought they could be simple reinforcement tools to keep those cult followers who lived remotely from other members constantly refreshed in the culture of the cult. To the non-indoctrinated, these games would appear as all other computer simulation games do; a form of entertainment, while perhaps often being violent and unpleasant, acceptable in the world today. However, on another level, the game on Tim's computer, and the one advised by the PM, carried other messages that were instantly received and understood by the receptive cult indoctrinated mind.

The whole matter of mind control was extremely controversial, she explained, and the notion of triggering human beings who have been conditioned to behave like automatons, was still highly suspect. That was not to say that the cult did not use a whole range of indoctrination techniques to compel certain behaviours and to keep followers in line.

Ruth looked at her father and smiled and said, "It was the

Catholic church and the many inquisitions, particularly those in Spain and Portugal, where brutal persuasion was inflicted on thousands of people to make them adhere to what the church believed was right at that time. Quite apart from what went on in the Korean War in the early nineteen fifties and in China many years before, the Catholic church committed dreadful crimes against people when trying to deal with what they regarded as heresy."

John looked across at Ruth, raised his eyebrows and added, "Yes, you are quite correct Ruth, the great inquisitions that were ruthless and bloody were also intended to frighten the mass of the population to adhere to the rules of the church, through fear. Hardly what Our Lord had intended."

"But be that as it may," replied Ruth, and she continued to say that she did not believe there was any triggering mechanism in the video games and the notion of mind control in the execution of these dreadful atrocities should not be the first line of investigation. In her view, probably only a small handful of senior cult figures had any idea of any grand plan of destruction, and if there were such a thing they would certainly not have it known throughout all the autonomous cells. No, rather she thought, these cells and their local leaders received some direct instruction to act and carry out attacks that would have been well rehearsed and prepared beforehand.

John turned to Mark and asked him to please summarise all this latest intelligence since it would be necessary to give it to the prime minister, as he had promised at his last meeting with him at Downing Street.

Mark said, "Of course, Father, I will have it later for you today. So we are still left with not knowing how these attacks are ordered or who orders them, apart from Milshner and Adler being prime suspects and this Judaire character being involved with all this computer wizardry?"

Everyone agreed, and the debate then turned to the next possible steps they should be taking.

It was also agreed not to mention the connection between Anna and Tim's death to Mary, since it would only cause her unnecessary worry. Ruth would continue to look after Anna and assist with her recovery and Joseph said that Mary had asked him to visit Ruth and Anna in London, and while this would no longer be necessary, it would be necessary to say something to her. Ruth agreed to do this before returning to London the following morning. The conversation turned to two other important matters.

How could they obtain intelligence about the cult to confirm that they are responsible? Furthermore, if they were responsible, how would they order the attacks, and who did so? Joseph spoke about Francesca and the impostor John Holmes and the two detainees in Dubai being possible sources. While John Homes may be a good line of enquiry they all agreed that the two Americans in the Dubai jail were unlikely to have such knowledge unless they could lead the local special police to the leader of the cell that had carried out the Paris attack, and that was unlikely. Ruth said that Francesca was taking a huge risk in attempting to get information from this John Holmes, and Joseph immediately agreed, asking whether there was not some other way to obtain this information. No one could suggest anything, and this particular matter was left in the air.

John said that the official authorities appeared to be getting themselves well organised, and through these channels perhaps further useful intelligence would be forthcoming. He remembered the phone conversation with Thomas and his impending visit to Boston and asked Mark to please advise him of the Jesuit Friar and his contact details for him to make contact.

"Is that wise, Father?" Mark immediately asked.

There was a pause and John looked at Mark and answered, "Thomas wanted to help. And anyway, I would very much like a member of the family to personally thank this man, because without him passing the various video footage and the Oscarbo information to us, Milshner and Adler would not even be under suspicion. I am sure it will be all right and I will speak to Thomas again about being careful."

The second matter that was discussed was the infiltration of their family by people associated with the cult. Anna being one, there could be others, and the danger they all faced in the days ahead. Mark reiterated what he had spoken to Joseph about the previous day, and that they, together with some of the other fraternal families, would surely be known about by Milshner and his people. John replied that he certainly believed they knew about the Trimbeldons and would have been watching them; so they must all exercise extreme care in the days ahead. He also said he would speak to Mary and ensure that she was protected in the customary manner, and that Ruth should consider returning to Himbeldon and bringing Anna there for safety, but Ruth said she felt safer in London. A compromise was struck whereby Ruth finally agreed that her father would arrange for someone to move into her Kensington home, as some added protection. Then there was Paul, still in the U.S.A. and only expected back in a few days time. It was agreed that John would speak to him, brief him on the situation and he need not to linger in America. The three children looked at their father and asked about his safety since he must be the number one target as head of the family. John replied that he would not take any unnecessary risks and anyway, life had to continue and they must not permit themselves to be intimidated by these people. It was hardly a satisfactory answer to his children, but they knew there was no useful purpose to be served by continuing this line of conversation.

The matter of the other families was then considered, and Mark reminded them that the encrypted CD, provided at the board meeting in London, had given specific warnings and that sensible precautions needed to be taken. After some further discussion it was agreed that a revised brief with the latest available intelligence and further notice that fraternal families may be under direct surveillance by cult members be prepared and issued through the customary channels.

With the meeting drawing to a close, Joseph passed a copy of the draft address to his father and drew his attention to the two comments. John said he would like a little time with Joseph later in the day to discuss Paris and Dandler. It was now well passed two o'clock and they all agreed it was time to try to resume their normal lives and have some lunch.

It was later the same day that Mark received a brief, confidential email from Francesca saying that she was well and working on their joint project, and hoped to have something of value in the next few weeks. She also asked to be remembered to Joseph. Mark instantly understood what she was wishing to communicate, that she was continuing to try to obtain further intelligence about the cult from the impostor John Holmes. As the family met for supper later in the day, Mark took his father to one side and quietly told him of the email and he nodded. After they had eaten John asked if Joseph would join him in his study for a discussion about Paris and Dandler.

Away from the rest of the family, they were free to speak freely about the various matters that needed attention in Paris and for Joseph to be able to make the necessary arrangements to visit Oxford. John spoke about the meeting with the prime minister and the public announcement made earlier in the day on national television that they had all watched. In view of recent developments it was now not necessary for Joseph to be in Paris for long, he needed to wrap up Tim's affairs there, spend some time with the board of Dandler Aggregates as a representative of the family to settle everything down again after the horrors of the spring, and to bring home Timothy's personal possessions from his apartment in Montmartre.

"Four to six weeks should see this assignment completed," John told him.

John handed Joseph a computer memory stick with information about the family business and the people and operation of the London office and he asked that Joseph start to familiarise himself with these affairs. The first priority was to try to assist the public authorities to apprehend those responsible for the attacks, but, once this had been completed, Joseph would need to start getting fully involved as John's understudy in the business. John again asked Joseph to be vigilant and careful before telling him that Mark had received an email from Francesca who was well in Boston and that she sent her regards.

As they were coming to the end of their conversation, John asked Joseph about his feelings for Louise and it became a brief period of awkwardness between them both. Joseph was straightforward in his answer and did not attempt to conceal his deep dilemma about Louise, and John listened sympathetically to his son speak.

John then said, “Yes Joseph, these things are never easy. Louise is a fine woman and she loves you very much, that is plain to see. I am sorry to have to ask you about her, but Mary wanted me to say something and to remind you that you must look after her and fully understand the special responsibility you have toward her now that things have developed as they have. A woman’s love for a man and the converse is an arbitrary affair and although those involved rarely have any control of such matters, we all have the ability to act properly. I am sure you will understand and no doubt do not require me to be saying such things. So let us leave it there.”

* * *

JOSEPH LEFT HIMBLEDON THE NEXT MORNING AND DROVE to Oxford where he spent three nights wrapping up his affairs and saying goodbye to his professors, tutors and friends. The most unpleasant of this activity was packing up all his books and personal possessions from his rooms, and then stacking the boxes ready for collection and conveyance to Himbledon. The other thing he was not looking forward to was his farewell to Louise. When it came, Louise made it very easy on Joseph and there was not the intense sadness or anything to remind either of them of their parting in Croatia.

Louise had organised a small dinner party in a function room of a restaurant in Oxford and had invited various close friends of Joseph and some of the academic staff of his college. It was a delightful evening of good conversation, wonderful food and stories about the many happy times they had all shared together in the ancient university town. They had exchanged plans and hopes for the future and, apart from a brief conversation early in the evening about the atrocities elsewhere, it was an evening to toast Joseph, to indulge him a little and to wish him bon voyage in his future endeavours. As they walked back to Louise’s rooms, arm in arm, they were happy and relaxed and the parting of the following day was out of mind and far away.

The following morning after breakfast, Louise walked with Joseph to his college where he picked up his bags and loaded them into his car. As they stood together on the kerbside they both knew their lives were to change utterly from that moment forward. Louise had important work to finish and then to decide what was next for her legal career, and Joseph was rapidly entering a global business world far removed from the gentle spires of Oxford. Words could not convey what they were both feeling and it was Louise who took control of the situation as they stood together with their arms around each other, without a word.

"Joe, it is time for you to go my darling. Please phone me once you get to Paris. I know there is so much I do not understand about your life, but please be careful. I will see you in Paris in a few weeks and we have plenty to keep ourselves occupied in the meanwhile. But before you go, I have something for you," and she delved in her bag hanging over her shoulder. It was his old worn Bible. As she handed it to Joseph he looked and did not take it from her.

"No, Louise. You keep it for now, if you wish to. I have been using the one you gave me in Zagreb. Keep it and we can exchange them when we are next at Himbledon together," he said.

Louise was touched and pleased to keep this book, so near to his heart, and she smiled and said, "Now you must go, love you my darling," and she held his head in her hands and kissed him and then stepped back, releasing herself from his embrace.

Joseph smiled rather helplessly and reached for her hand and gave it a squeeze before walking to his car. He glanced at her as she stood on the pavement with her arms folded and she gave a smile as he drove away.

25

Paris and Boston in the Fall

PARIS WAS BLEAK AND IT WAS NOW OCTOBER as Joseph looked out across the city from Tim's apartment. Life in the city had resumed a modest air of normality, although evidence of the attack in the spring could be seen everywhere. There were still some recovery activities taking place on the metro and there were many emergency personnel to be seen around the city attending to the last of the clear-up operation. The road system was functioning again, although the scars could often be seen everywhere with new areas of tarmac and concrete having been laid to restore some of the road underpasses, and if one looked closely there was visible damage to the support pillars where vehicles had crashed into them on that dreadful morning. The emergency camps and mortuaries were also still there, although they were mainly empty now and were soon to be removed. There were military personnel to be seen walking, driving and still flying over the city in helicopters. Along the Seine, where emergency jetties had been erected, there were dozens of inflatable and other river craft moored. The metro was still not fully functional, with some lines still inoperable as the few remaining emergency teams worked deep below ground with breathing equipment clearing the grim crash sites. Bodies were still being found and sterile body bags were a frequent sight as they were respectfully carried to awaiting vehicles to be taken for identification, notification of relatives and burial. This process of recovering the remains of the dead and the agonising procedures for relatives marked the loss of a loved one, and traumatised the whole of Paris. Everyone, it appeared, had lost someone, some had lost their complete families and others had the burden now of caring for a disabled and deeply wounded family member or close friend.

As Joseph stood looking out over the grey city landscape before leaving to go to the Dandler office, he understood, after the last few weeks, that while buildings, roads and other material things can be repaired, in time, the human aftermath of such an atrocity will never be fully healed. There was a dread among Parisians now; there was no joy or laughter anymore, just anguish and pain in people's faces. People felt it now wrong to laugh, to exchange a joke, in case in some way it may be disrespectful to the hundreds of thousands who had lost their lives. Paris and its people were in a state of deep grief, even anger had subsided as they tried to come to terms with what had happened, and why they had survived yet others had not. Living and working in the city there was no escape from it all, it was everywhere on every street corner and in everyone's faces. There was a hush in the city; there was no shouting, no music to be heard from the many cafés, only a sombre movement of people having to attend to their daily lives with the sound of the traffic as a perpetual background.

Later at Dandler Aggregates, Joseph had systematically cleared Tim's office, which had remained locked since his arrival. He could not face it when he first arrived and had spent the first two weeks clearing the apartment, a room at a time. With that now done and having spent time with the Dandler management team and attended a funeral of one of the senior staff— whose body had been recovered from a metro crash site— he felt he could delay no longer. This was the final part of why his father had sent him to Paris and there was little more for him to do after this sad task had been completed. There were no other leads or lines of enquiry worthy of his time here, the focus now needed to be miles away.

Since he had managed to wrap things up faster than anticipated, he now wanted to leave Paris, to get away from this dreadful pall that hung over the city. However, he knew there were still some important matters to attend to, and he had not yet managed to meet with Archbishop Guggar, who was to arrange a confidential meeting with a senior figure in the local security police. The two captives in Dubai had shown that they knew little more than what had happened in Paris, and they had received no direct instructions from the cult, but said that it had come through a local contact in Dubai, who had subsequently disappeared, despite strenuous efforts by the local police to search and apprehend him. Joseph hoped to be away from Paris, all the work completed, by the end of October and to be back at Himbledon. The previous day Paul had phoned Joseph from America, explaining that he had been delayed by a few commitments there and would only be back in London toward the end of October, so Joseph had another reason to finish up in Paris and to be back in England for the autumn.

Thomas and Liska had a good flight on the British Airways Boeing 747 across the Atlantic from Heathrow to Logan Airport in Boston. The dance company had arrived two days previously and were busy rehearsing for the run of performances at the Wang Theatre in Tremont Street. This particular theatre must rank as one of the world's most beautiful theatres with seating for over three thousand that regularly hosts touring productions from Europe. Liska was to join the company the following day for three days of rehearsals before the opening night and then a run of eight days. This meant Thomas would have more than enough time on his own to visit his favourite places in and around Boston.

Martha and her daughter, Lucinda, were there at the airport to meet them and help load their luggage into the large utility vehicle before they were soon on the road leading to the tunnel under the Charles River into the city.

It was late afternoon and the sky was clear and it was still a beautiful fresh day as they all talked in the car.

"Let me show you where you will performing Liska, and then we can make our way to the house," said Martha as they passed under the river tunnel.

"How is Charles?" enquired Thomas.

Martha replied, “He is well thanks Thomas, due in from Florida later tonight and then he isn’t flying for a week while you are here.”

Thomas and Charlie were good friends, despite being complete opposites. Thomas a musician, romantic and buccaneering sort of character while Charlie, a commercial airline pilot, was a more considered, meticulous and reserved personality. This was probably one of the reasons they enjoyed each other’s company so much and Thomas had been thrilled at the thought of Charlie being around for his stay.

With Lucinda having an interest in ballet and theatre, Liska asked if she would like to accompany her to the rehearsals and she replied excitedly, “If that is okay aunt Liska, that would be great, eh Ma?” and Martha smiled at Liska and thought that perhaps her brother’s current visit may be less troublesome than his last visit to the city.

Boston is full of wonderful buildings and parks and has an adjoining coastline that witnessed much of the early history of the puritan settlers who in sixteen thirty under the leadership of John Winthrop occupied the Shawmut Peninsula and the new city of Boston was created. The name Boston was given in honour of the native English town of their leaders. In sixteen thirty-six the puritan leaders established a college at a place now named Cambridge to train future generations of clergy and this became Harvard University, named after John Harvard, a local minister who left his books and half his money to the college. Boston played a role with the American Revolution with characters like Paul Revere with famous battles between the militia and British troops and the Boston Tea Party, until 1783, with American independence, with the Treaty of Paris. Led by Samuel Adams, the Sons of Liberty protested against the king’s tax on tea by boarding three British East India Company ships and throwing their cargo in to Boston Harbour, this marked a turning point to local independence from the British.

In the mid eighteen hundreds, Irish escaping the potato famine arrived in Boston in tens of thousands looking for a new life. Many settled in the south of the city and by nineteen hundred the Irish were the dominant ethnic group in Boston.

This Irish and Catholic influence was to finally lead to the election of John F. Kennedy as president in 1960. Grandson of Irish American mayor John 'Honey Fitz' Fitzgerald and son of Ambassador Joseph Kennedy, John F. Kennedy, represented Boston in both houses of the U.S. Congress before he became the first Roman Catholic elected President of the United States. It had been in 1995 that John F. Kennedy's mother's funeral had taken place at St. Stephen's church, located in the north end of the city. This neo classical church has an interior that is open and relatively simple, with little ornamentation and whenever Thomas visited Boston he always made it his businesses to attend at least one Mass here during his stay.

Thomas hoped that he and Charlie might be able to escape Boston city for a couple of nights and go down to their summer house just outside Plymouth, a coastal town a few miles down the coast from Boston, and do some sailing together. At the harbour in Plymouth by the State Pier there is the Mayflower II, which is a major tourist attraction. Further south are Newport, a playground for the rich since the mid eighteen hundreds, and wonderful cliff walks overlooking Narragansett Bay. Yet further south is the island of Martha's Vineyard with regular ferries from the mainland and further history and the great homes of the nineteenth century rich whaling captains. Cape Cod lies to the east with some of the most spectacular beaches in the world with good surfing and boats sailing through the Cape Cod Canal. Then there is the Boston Red Sox, the local baseball team, who are leading in the league, so perhaps he and Charlie might get to see a game while he is here at Fenway Park. Boston at this time of the year is popular with tourists, and a blaze of different colours in the many parks and wooded areas as the leaves change colour during fall.

Across the river is the Massachusetts Institute of Technology – MIT– the scene of scientific and technical research since it was founded in the eighteen sixties. This leading technical university is still at the forefront of much contemporary computer, engineering and medical research. It was here that the Internet was born in the early nineteen seventies and where Francesca was working today with a team of scientists on measures to combat various bacterial and viral infections that continue to inflict suffering and death on millions of people, particularly the poor in developing regions of the world. It was here where Francesca, her mother Portia, and Achmed from Dubai came to collaborate with others at MIT in their strenuous efforts to develop holistic practical solutions. These pioneers were excited about the possibility of having found a simple solution to ensuring that tuberculosis—TB— patients continue to take their medication for the required six months by combining medication treatments with a mobile phone incentive scheme.

For TB patients to be effectively treated, they had to take antibiotics for half a year in order to eliminate the bacteria that caused the infection and remove the risk of antibiotic resistant strains developing. However, for the patients, often poor and with limited education, the symptoms of TB disappeared after about two months of being on the treatment, so they often simply abandon the medication. This tendency was further compounded since the side effects of the drugs were unpleasant, creating headaches, diarrhoea, insomnia, and nausea. However, the research team also knew that certain TB drugs also turned patients' urine, tears and sweat a shade of reddish orange, so they had come up with a small patch that, when exposed to the patients' urine, changed colour in such a way that it could generate a number that could be sent via a mobile phone. By linking this number to free airtime and other needs of the treatment programme, the researchers believe they have found a way to properly monitor patient's diligence in taking the drugs while also providing them with a practical incentive to do so.

Francesca had been working with medical engineers at MIT and it was time to run extensive field trials in selected developing regions of the world. She had good contacts with the South African Medical Research Council and the University of Cape Town medical research centre, and since TB is highly prevalent in South Africa, had recommended a series of trials in the poor townships in the Cape and Natal Provinces. Thomas was looking forward to contacting

Francesca and spending some time with her since he had not seen her for about three years, since his last visit to Rome.

Martha pulled the car up and reversed into a reserved parking bay outside a large terraced house in Beacon Hill. Although terraced, the five-floor property that dated back decades was grand, with large rooms with high ceilings, an elegant staircase and even a lift at the rear. Many of these homes that are two hundred years old have become almost priceless and command prices and rents among the highest in the world. This is where much of the old money still resides in Boston, and through his family heritage, Charlie had come to own the house, inherited from his parents. Beacon Hill is a delightful part of Boston with antique and bookshops, old-fashioned grocery stores and ivy clad façades. There are lovely gardens, the Massachusetts State House with a stained glass image of a Native American in a grass skirt and the cobblestone streets of Louisburg Square, modelled on the traditional residential squares of London in the early eighteen hundreds.

As they alighted from the car, Martha grumbled at Lucinda and said that she must phone the Boston Gas Company again, get them to come and remove the compressor and other equipment near their parking bay. The local natural gas company had repaired a gas leak in the road a day before and although they had resurfaced the road and finished the job they had left behind some rubble and plant with yellow warning fencing around it. While all these great old houses were heated with natural gas and most also used gas for cooking and the attractive fuel effect fires in their impressive fire grates, few of the residents were too concerned about how the fuel reached them. They certainly did not want the quaint appearance of their exclusive surroundings spoiled with ugly engineering equipment. Thomas smiled inwardly at his sister's remark, the attitude of slight intolerance and disdain at people having to dig up her road and then have the audacity to leave this thing parked near her home.

26

A Savage Rape

It was sudden and violent. She knew she had been playing with fire, and when the phials she had given him proved to contain nothing more than innocent serum, he knew he had been duped and his life was now expendable at the hands of other cult members. Driven by anger and lust, he did not have the courage to face her, but struck the first blow while standing behind her after they had arrived back at her apartment. She took the first blow to the side of her head and fell forward across the sofa, and then his body was on hers. Although he was the same height as her, his greater body weight enabled him to hold her down while he unleashed himself on her stunned body. She had fought feverishly to defend herself, but the second blow to her face ensured that she lost consciousness for a few moments. He raped her, repeatedly hitting her to keep her submissive and terrified, as he plundered her body.

When he had finished, as he looked down at her bruised body lying unconscious on the sofa, he could not bring himself to commit the final act of murder. He had suddenly become scared, gathered up his clothes quickly, and fled the apartment. It was some hours later that she had regained consciousness and felt the pain throughout her body, then staggered to the bathroom to see her bruised and bloody face in the mirror. She had managed to stagger to the phone, and had called a close female friend before collapsing with the phone still in her hand.

It was only the afternoon, when Thomas had been notified with a frantic call from Joseph after hearing the news from Achmed, that he and Martha were able to visit Francesca, who was in a private recovery room at the Brigham and Woman's Hospital, in Francis Street. Portia, her mother, was flying from Rome and arriving early the next morning and Joseph had wanted to catch a flight from Paris immediately when he had received the news, although after speaking with his father, had listened to his calming words and the logic of leaving Thomas to represent them, since he was already in Boston. When Thomas and Martha eventually found the room where Francesca was recovering, they spoke with the nursing sister on duty, who warned them not to be too alarmed at Francesca's injuries. The nurse explained that Francesca was out of medical danger, and the bruising would heal, although it did look alarming, but they should not stay long, since above everything else just now, Francesca needed rest.

They quietly entered her room and saw her lying on her back, her upper body lifted with the bed raised slightly, and she was sleeping with her head on one side. There were drips into both of her arms, one a saline solution to avoid dehydration and the other an antibiotic to counter any infections. As Thomas looked at her from the end of the bed, he noticed a large bruise on the side of her face, her eye was swollen and blackened and one side of her lip was swollen and red. She was wearing a hospital smock and her upper chest and arms were uncovered and there was very nasty bruising on her neck with some abrasions on her chest. On both of her upper arms there were more bruises consistent with finger grab marks from her being forcibly restrained.

Without any comment, Thomas and Martha looked at each other and registered in their faces the awfulness of what lay before them— a beautiful young woman, who had been savagely attacked and almost left for dead.

"Thank God she is all right, Thomas. He could have killed her," whispered Martha to Thomas, who then whispered that they should pray for a moment, leave the flowers and a message that they had visited, for when Francesca awoke.

After a few moments, while they both stood in silent prayer, they looked at each other and Thomas held the door for Martha to leave the room. Thomas sought the day sister again, since he wanted to know of her other injuries and what the prognosis might be. He also wanted to enquire about her security because he was concerned that since this wicked person had done this, her life could still be in danger.

The nursing sister said that the genital injuries were extensive, although nothing that would not recover. She explained that since female genitalia are highly vascular, with many small blood vessels, injuries tended to start healing quickly and even within forty-eight hours significant natural repair would have taken place. They had thoroughly examined Francesca and whilst it had been a brutal attack and rape, she had no broken bones, head injuries or internal lesions. The nurse concluded her remarks by saying that the major area of concern would be Francesca's emotional recovery, and that while the physical injuries would heal, such attacks do terrible potential damage to victims in invisible ways. It was still too early to know how serious these aspects would be to treat, and everyone had to be patient.

Thomas asked about security, and the nurse said that there was already someone there handling the matter, and that it was outside her jurisdiction, but she introduced Thomas to a gentleman who he had noticed when he and Martha had first arrived at the recovery rooms. The gentleman suggested that Thomas and Martha accompany him to a small lounge at the end of the corridor, and after they were alone he said he was a plainclothes police officer from the Boston police department. They had been requested by a senior member of the local FBI to provide security for the young lady and that he was due to go off shift in a couple of hours and another officer would take over since it was twenty-four-hour security that was being provided.

It was the following day, after Portia had arrived and Martha had collected her from the airport and deposited her bags at the house, that Thomas and Portia caught a yellow cab to the hospital. It was midday when they arrived at Francesca's room and she was awake, although a little drowsy since she was still being lightly sedated. Portia, being a medical doctor, knew what to expect and she entered the room first and walked to stand beside the bed with a gentle smile on her face. Francesca turned and looked at her mother and she stretched out her arms and Portia bent forward and gently embraced her daughter. They did not say a word at first, and they both had tears on their cheeks when Francesca released her arms from around her mother and looked across at Thomas, who was standing now at the foot of the bed, and smiled at him. The bruising on her face looked worse than it had the day before and there was antiseptic cream on the various lesions above her eye, on her chest and her badly swollen lips. Francesca looked as though she had done twelve rounds in a boxing ring with a bare-knuckled opponent, but, despite this, one of her deeply set, beautiful dark eyes still shone out through the horror of her injuries.

Portia sat beside the bed, holding one of Francesca's hands and comforted her daughter in a way that only a mother can. She told Francesca that she was staying with Martha and would remain in Boston until Francesca was well again and Francesca nodded.

Then, Francesca leant her aching body up on one arm and, looking at her mother, said, "Thank you, Mother. I will be all right in a few days. I was not conscious for much of the attack, which was a blessing, so do not worry, I will be all right. They are taking good care of me here."

It was clearly painful for Francesca to talk and her jaw was still painful after the beating she had endured. Thomas stood up and, looking down at Francesca, asked if there was anything that she needed and he wrote down his mobile phone number on a piece of paper that he left on her bedside table. Francesca smiled at Thomas and thanked him and then asked if she could have a few moments with her mother.

"Of course, Francesca. You are in our prayers and just call me if there is anything you need," replied Thomas, and he left the room and waited outside.

Francesca looked at her mother and said that she had discovered some important information from the impostor John Holmes just before he attacked her and that Portia must convey it as soon as possible to Mark and Joseph Trimbledon. Portia instantly knew the importance of what Francesca was about to tell her and she moved closer, leaning on the edge of the bed, and listened carefully as her daughter spoke slowly, laying on her side facing her mother. Francesca said there was information related to the attacks and the cult that she had obtained from John Holmes who had come to believe that she was helping him. It had been a tortuous few weeks after returning from Dubai and Rome, when she had agreed to smuggle out some bacteria from the MIT secure laboratory, he had lowered his defences and had begun to trust her. Francesca had taken a secure phial from the laboratory, had put some harmless laboratory liquid in it, and had passed this to Holmes, knowing that she only had a few days before the cult would discover her deception. It had been an elaborate deception to try to obtain further crucial information about the cult and its leaders and it had paid off, despite the huge risk that she had been taking.

Francesca said the orders to the remote cells to carry out the attacks were given by Adler, and not Milshner, via some sort of computer system. They sometimes continued to link them to apparent prophetic dreams that she was supposed to have a few days or even hours before the command was given. Adler had also fallen in love with Judaire after he started working with the cult several years ago and this had caused all manner of deceptions and conflict within the top echelons of the cult. Then, four years ago, when Milshner had his suspicions confirmed, he almost killed Adler in a jealous rage, but Judaire had come to her rescue. However, in this deathly struggle, Milshner had a serious heart attack and stroke, and was now confined to a wheelchair. It was Adler and Judaire, between them, who controlled the cult and the Milshner global business empire, and it was they who were directly behind the attacks.

Milshner, like his father before him, had become a recluse, and survived on a cocktail of various drugs prescribed and administered by his personal doctor. He had a small team of bodyguards, cooks, a nurse, and his own pilot, but these appeared to be under the control of Adler. Milshner spent regular periods in a luxury cabin in the mountains on the family estate in Montana, just looking out across the countryside to where his mother had had her riding accident.

Judaire, who was younger than Adler, also had a small group of personal bodyguards who were all Japanese, and the cult had morphed into continuing to be a fanatical cult operating superficially as a radical religious group, but had also now taken on many Eastern values, including concepts of honour and avenging ancestors. Francesca mentioned repeatedly that no one should underestimate the hold that the cult had over its followers and that Holmes was terrified at the mere thought of any hint of failure on his part and what they would do to him.

There were two final pieces of information that might also prove crucial in bringing these attacks to an end. Judaire had embraced the personal sacrifice of oneself for the honour of one's family and emperor that had been a feature of the Pacific battles of World War II. Many of his personal followers and certainly his bodyguards would behave as the kamikaze pilots had during the war, readily sacrificing themselves to honour their families and Judaire. Something else that might very well be relevant was that Judaire's Japanese mother's family were wiped out when the Americans dropped the atomic bomb on Hiroshima.

Francesca lay on her back, exhausted and relieved to have been able to communicate this vital information. Portia sat quietly looking at Francesca for a moment, arranging the information in her mind, and told her daughter to rest and that she would convey the information to the Trimbledons immediately.

Portia put her arms around the broken and sore body of her daughter again and gently hugged and kissed her. She whispered in Francesca's ear how much she loved her, how brave she had been and that she must try to forget about the cult and the attacks and leave matters to others. She had played her part and her work for the fraternity was finished, for now, and that she must rest and get strong again. Just then, the nursing sister came into the room and introduced herself to Portia and in a kindly manner suggested that she should leave and let Francesca rest.

It was less than two hours later that Mark received at Himbeldon a secure email from Portia providing a summary of the information that he then provided to his father. Mark called Joseph in Paris and told him Francesca was in recovery, that she was recovering well and that Portia was there with her. John Trimbledon spoke to the prime minister just four hours after the conversation between Francesca and her mother and updated him on the latest intelligence.

27

Wales Revisited

IT WAS A GREY AUTUMN DAY IN OCTOBER WHEN LOUISE drove over to Wales on the Friday afternoon for a long weekend with her family. It had been a long time since she had been home and felt a break from Oxford, without Joseph being there, would lift her spirits. She had also arranged to have lunch on the Saturday with an old school friend and was looking forward to catching up with the local news.

When she arrived home her father was not there since he was taking a late tutorial at the local university, but her mother greeted her warmly and they sat for a while in the kitchen talking before Louise brought her bag in from the car and deposited it in her old bedroom. Then later her parents, her brother and Louise had a meal together at the house and caught up on all the family news. To her surprise Louise found that little appeared to have changed much since she had left several years earlier to go up to Oxford. As it was getting late and she was tired, Louise had excused herself and gone to bed.

Next day she awoke to an overcast sky with a low-pressure system over the Irish Sea. She took one look through the curtains and decided to go back to bed and sleep some more. It was only after eleven when she finally rose, showered and dressed and descended the stairs for some coffee. There was no one else in the house and seeing that it was midday she put her raincoat on and set off for the town. She wandered around the town a little before meeting her old friend, Hilda Morgan, for lunch at the Ambleside Hotel on the seafront.

Hilda had been the vice captain of the tennis team when they were in sixth form together, and she had given up the idea of going to university although she was a clever girl and had remained in the town and attended the local teacher training college, and considered herself fortunate to have landed a job as a teacher in one of the local primary schools. She had recently married the son of the owner of the second largest grocery shop in the town. They were regular Chapel goers, well respected in the town and were happy together and hoped to have a family once they had saved up the deposit for a small house, they had to be patient because Edwin, her husband, did not earn much since he would inherit the business from his father one day.

What Louise had hoped would be a happy reunion between old friends became a relentless chatter about Hilda and Edwin, their affairs, what they thought important, the type of house they hoped to buy, how they got groceries at a big discount so ate well, how many parents did not appreciate their children's teachers who were lucky they didn't have to put up with foreign teachers like they do in Cardiff. It just flowed out of Hilda's mouth and Louise scarcely said a word apart from ordering and then later paying for their lunch. Never once did Hilda enquire about Louise, how she enjoyed Oxford, there was simply no interest. When Hilda started to move onto local gossip about many people that Louise still remembered, Louise decided enough was enough. She made a gracious comment about it being later than she thought, wished Hilda well and bade her farewell.

As Louise walked along the promenade and back up through the town she felt a stranger in her hometown. Places that had always been remembered as large were now seen as being smaller, coffee bars where she had flirted as a teenager with local boys, as tatty and run down cafes; and, the Chilwick Arms on the corner of Chiltern Street and Coldway Lane, where she had excitedly started her first experiments with alcohol, to be a grubby and smelly place with a broken pane in the mock stainless glass door. As she eventually neared the large detached house where she had been brought up with her brother, she thought it would be good to spend some time with him when he comes in from rugby training. Although the sky was full of grey clouds and it was still dry there was a chill wind from the sea and she was pleased to walk through the side kitchen door next to the detached garage to the warmth of the gas heating.

Her father was there and he offered her some tea, fresh in the pot, just made. She poured herself a cup and asked where her mother was, and learnt she had popped out to get some last-minute groceries for a dinner party she had organised, in Louise's honour, at the house the same evening. This was a surprise to Louise and she enquired who was coming. Her mother had invited a number of people, since her father rarely concerned himself with such matters. The guests were mainly academics from the university, mostly friends of her mother, her father did not know precisely, and suggested Louise ask her when she got home. As he excused himself to go back to the lounge to watch the second half of Wales playing Scotland in Cardiff, he suddenly recalled something and turned and looking over the top of his glasses, told Louise that he thought that Eric Fish had also been invited. Louise's heart sank as her father closed the door behind him.

Louise went to her bedroom and checked her mobile phone to see if there was any message from Joseph, but it was blank. As she lay on her bed reading she could not concentrate, lay back and began to think about the time when she had left Aberystwyth, her time at Oxford, and that she had only managed to get home three times in the eight years since she had been gone. Her parents had come to Oxford for the various graduation ceremonies, and they had kept in touch, but such contact had declined considerably in recent times. There had always been overseas trips during the summer months, varsity tours with this or that society going off to some interesting location. Before meeting Joseph she had also enjoyed some romantic interludes with various people so time had just flown by in the intervening years. Looking around her bedroom at some of her old possessions still there, she wondered whether she was at fault or she had neglected her parents in some way, and this thought lingered with her until she heard the back door open below.

She came down to find her brother had just got home, not from practice, but from an inter-club rugby match that they had won. Louise again felt out of touch with everyone's lives here, even her brother. She was further saddened and rather hurt when she learnt that he would not be home for dinner and had only popped home to pick up some more money for an evening with his rugby friends. Just then, her mother arrived with three big bags of shopping and some wine bottles.

Standing in the kitchen Louise helped unpack the shopping and put some of the wine to chill in the fridge alongside several existing unopened bottles.

"Goodness mum, why so much wine?" she enquired.

"Some of our guests tonight enjoy a drink and we would hate to run out, wouldn't we?" she answered and Louise was reminded how irritating some of her mother's affectations could be and thought why use the word 'we' when she actually meant 'I'.

"Dad tells me you have invited Eric; why did you have to do that?" enquired Louise.

Her mother looked at her, raised her eyebrows, and replied, "He still loves you, you know, and he has done so well at the university, he is such an asset to the Sociology Faculty, and anyway I thought that both of you would have so much to talk about and catch up on. He has never married."

Louise could not resist a mild display of extreme irritation as she banged the fridge door shut.

"You should be pleased Louise and he is looking forward to seeing you, so why are you being so funny about it?" her mother continued, oblivious of the embarrassing situation she was putting her daughter in.

"Have you said anything to Eric about me mum?" Louise enquired suspecting something more convoluted in her mother's usual motives.

"No nothing, only that you are still single and never talk about anyone serious in your life."

As though I would, and especially about Joseph, a devout Roman Catholic who is a history scholar, she thought, as her memory started to inflicted thoughts on her about Eric, a highly sexed teenager who had tried to grope her on the way home from school so many times, and who would talk dirty to her, thinking this the way to impress young ladies. They had only been sixteen at the time, and she hoped that he had attained some maturity since then.

Later, the dinner party that had started cordially enough grew into something that Louise found increasingly unpleasant. The conversation was often pompous and self-opinionated, with little sensitivity to the opinions of others. Although Louise tried, on several occasions, to converse, she was often not allowed to even finish a sentence or fully explain herself before one of them, particularly her parents, would interrupt on the pretext of understanding what she was about to say, and then dominate the conversation for several minutes. Quite apart from being boring, much of the behaviour around the dinner table was rude and frequently obnoxious. Certain guests openly competed with one another over some academic or other issue with many personal derogatory remarks beginning. As the wine flowed so the conversation became more tedious to Louise, it was full of personal vanities and arrogance yet being empty of any real substance. When Louise went to help her mother with the coffee they had a brief conversation in the kitchen. Her mother asked her if she was enjoying the evening and how was she getting on with Eric, without the merest understanding of how Louise was actually feeling. When Louise asked her mother to sit down for a moment and she did, she tried to talk to her about Joseph and their trip to Croatia, her mother showed complete disinterest and said they must get back to their guests.

It was not much later that Louise excused herself and said goodbye to everyone, while her mother glared at her, and she went to her bedroom and went to bed. The last episode in the kitchen with her mother had been a sad experience for Louise, up until that moment she had tried to dismiss the feelings of tension in the household and her parent's continual dismissal of her, and their closed minds to anything she wished to share with them of importance. As she lay in bed, listening to the fatuous drunken banter below, she wondered if it had been a mistake coming home like this.

What she had regarded as a liberal atmosphere she now saw as a grey bleak place, without love or empathy. She now saw her mother suddenly as a lonely, sad ageing woman who had wasted her talents on the relentless pursuit of vanity and her own pleasure. All attempts to talk of her own experiences, trying desperately to bring a different perspective to them, but they were intent only in believing their own rhetoric. She felt a gulf between herself and her parents. They were not listening or understanding her entreaties to them, as caring and insistent as they were. Louise so wanted them to experience some of the joy in her heart. She was filled with compassion for them and she felt deeply saddened and frustrated by the bigotry she experienced at their hands. They continued to think they know best, they appeared to mock her sincerity in front of the dinner guests, said she needed to get a grip on herself and get back to reality and stop living in a child's fantasy world. The two realities appeared irreconcilable to her, and her parents were now strangers, the mere shadows of how she had previously remembered them.

Sunday morning Louise rose just after seven, a little earlier than she was accustomed to in Oxford, pulled back the curtains and it was raining and it was that type of rain that only Wales can produce, a drizzle from grey low clouds that penetrates everything. She walked to the bathroom, showered and dressed and came down stairs to find the debris of the night before, wine glasses, cashew nuts ground into the lounge carpet, crumpled napkins dropped beside the fireplace and empty wine bottles everywhere. Her parents were still in bed and she could hear her father gently snoring and her brother who had probably arrived home late breathing heavily in his bedroom opposite hers. There was a smell of stale beer as she looked around his half-open door, and closed it. Just then, her mobile phone buzzed, and it was Joseph in Paris.

Am going to Mass; if you are up, phone me after 11 ur time; take care, Joe.

She made herself breakfast and put on a raincoat and walked out through the kitchen door onto the rear patio and looked over the large bedraggled back garden that led up to a wood and hills beyond. She breathed in the fresh damp air and she felt better, she just wanted to be away from the house for a while, to walk alone and to be with her thoughts.

As she descended the wet pavements through the streets of the outer town she did not feel cold and the gentle rain, without any wind, felt kind on her face. Then she heard a bell ringing and she knew it was from the Chapel she had passed so often in her youth, appealing for the faithful to arrive for the Sunday morning service on time. A curiosity rose in her mind, and looking at her watch she checked that it was just before eight, and the Chapel was close enough for her to attend the service.

To be able to tell Joseph she had been to church was alone sufficient reason to go, she thought, smiling to herself. *He will never believe it.* She quickened her stride and was soon approaching the Chapel with its black Welsh slate roof, dark stonewalls and rusting railings by the pavement. There was a step, a small path and then the entrance and she was soon walking toward the door where an elderly gentleman stood with a Bible in his hand in an overcoat. He smiled at her, said welcome, and she nodded and smiled in return as she walked out of the drizzle.

As she adjusted her eyes to the interior of the church an old lady standing at the back of the church handed her a hymnbook and Louise looked around for a place to sit. There was organ music playing and there were many empty places as she walked up the isle on red and white tiles between the dark wooden pews. She sat down half way along next to the isle and various people sitting in the church looked across at her as she removed her rain hat and shook her blonde hair to fall across her shoulders.

Looking ahead she could then see the organist, a few people nearby who were the choir and a pulpit, that was high to one side at the back of the church and there on one side was a cross, but she noticed it was empty, unlike the crosses she had seen in Croatia, Christ was not hanging there. As she looked forward she noticed most of the congregation were old and she could find no young faces or children, and then the organ music fell silent.

The gentleman who had been standing at the doorway walked up the isle briskly and stepped up onto what was rather like a stage by the choir and pulpit and disappeared through a door at the side. In a moment, he had returned without his overcoat and he stood at the front of the stage, welcomed everyone and then announced a hymn number. The few elderly members of the choir stood up, the organ started playing and they started to sing, everyone in the church apart from Louise, who just stood there enveloped by energetic wonderful voices. As she listened to the hymn it was vaguely familiar from a few academic occasions she had had to attend at Oxford, when there had been an Anglican vicar in attendance to say a few words and for everyone to sing something. She thought for a moment that, whatever they may say about the Welsh, they could certainly sing, however old they might be. Then someone came to the front and read a passage from a large Bible that lay on a wooden lectern after which everyone sat down and there was silence for a moment. It had been about people many years ago living in the desert and killing animals to sacrifice to an angry God. Then the organist started to play again and everyone rose to their feet and started to sing again. Just then Louise noticed beside the pulpit some numbers in a wooden frame and opened her hymnbook and found the appropriate number and she followed the words in the hymnbook.

Then the man who had been wearing the heavy overcoat walked up into the pulpit and she looked up at him. He asked them all to bow their heads and they prayed. Then he read from the Bible before him, and again asked everyone to bow their heads and they prayed. He then spoke about broken people, that we are all broken and lost without the help of Jesus who died for our sins and that we cannot save ourselves without his help. He said that we must repent and ask for mercy and thank God for his son Jesus. Again they bowed their heads in prayer and the man up in the pulpit announced another hymn, and Louise turned to the number in her hymnbook, it was Amazing Grace. As they got into the first few lines and the organ led them in the haunting melody and

Louise read the words in her hymn book she started to cry, she just could not help it, not loud sobbing or anything, just tears gently running down her cheeks and she started to join in, singing with everyone else, carried along with this enchanting sound filling the old rafters of the roof above. Then it ended almost as abruptly as it had started, the man with the overcoat stepped forward again to the edge of the stage and invited everyone for tea in the hall next door, and walked to the front of the church again.

Louise sat down picked up her rain hat and wiped the remaining tears from her cheek. She waited a moment as various people moved out of the pews, walking and talking slowly out of the church. She rose slowly, stepped down out of the pew, and walked to the back of the church intent on walking home to see if the rest of the family were yet awake. As she stepped out of the church doorway the man in the overcoat was there waiting, inviting everyone to have tea. He had a wonderful speaking voice that reminded her of Richard Burton, and he turned to her with a warm smile.

He was an elderly man with grey hair and he said, "Thank you for coming to our humble service this morning, are you new in the area?"

He extended his hand. Louise shook his hand and replied, "No, I grew up here and have been away and am just back for the weekend visiting my parents."

"Come," he said. "Let's get out of this drizzle and have a nice hot cup of tea."

The next thing Louise was standing in the small hall next to the Chapel with a hot cup of tea in her hand eating the most delicious warm scones with fresh jam and butter. A large lady behind a trestle table kept refilling her cup, adding milk and holding out a sugar bowl to her. The old man who had led the service introduced himself and then proceeded to introduce Louise to everyone individually in the hall with a brief resume on each person. There were about fifteen people having tea and they were all quite old, at least to Louise, but they were so warm and friendly she found the whole experience very touching. They all asked her about Oxford, what she was studying, what she planned to do and they appeared really interested in her.

Then she met the organist, a tall man who was probably very handsome when a young man and Louise said what a lovely hymn Amazing Grace is.

"Yes," he said, "and do you know the origins of it and who wrote it?"

"No," answered Louise, so he told her the true story of John Newton the sea captain of slave ships who prayed one night in a terrible sea storm, was saved, and dedicated his life to Jesus and the abolition of slavery. It had been William Wilberforce who had led an evangelical pressure group known as the Clapham Sect who had campaigned for social reform and Christianity in the work place, and the abolition of child labour and the slave trade. It was in 1833 on his deathbed that Wilberforce finally saw the slave trade abolished throughout the British Empire.

"So the words of the hymn are real then, about a real person?"

"Yes my dear, and they are as true today as they were then when he wrote them," the tall man said.

As Louise walked back to the house in the continuing drizzle, she contemplated the fact that she had just experienced the first real conversations with other human beings since back in Aberystwyth. It was a poor and humble little church with not many worshipers, but they had made her so welcome and feel so special.

Then she looked at her watch and it was just after ten so she stood in under a doorway of a public house to get out of the drizzle and phoned Joseph.

He answered almost immediately. "Hi Louise, so how is sunny Aberystwyth?" he teased.

"Don't be cruel Joe, its raining here, as usual."

"How are your parents and brother?"

"Oh fine, just the same, rather wrapped up in themselves, I will be rather pleased to get back to Oxford."

"Now, now Louise, I know that tone, stop being hard on them and so critical, oh to see ourselves as others do eh, I wonder what they are making of you after not seeing you for so long; be gentle with them; they are your own flesh and blood after all, so stop being so intolerant."

"Yes all right Joe, stop lecturing me. How is everything there with you in Paris?"

"Fine, it is a dry day here although the atmosphere is still dreadful. Listen I reckon I can probably finish everything here in the next couple of weeks and we should then meet at Himbledon. Why don't you come to the Grange for the weekend when I get back? Louise, I do not think you should visit me here in Paris, it is not a good place to be right now, what do you think?"

There was a brief pause before Louise answered, "Yes, of course I would love to, but when do you think you will be back?"

Joseph replied, "I think it should certainly be by the end of October. I must speak with Father, but, with just a few more meetings to finish up, a couple of weeks from now at the most."

"Please be careful there, Joe, and I will plan then to see you at Himbledon at the end of October," replied Louise.

"Okay then, I will be in touch again nearer the time. Remember now be kind to your father and mother, and be careful driving back to Oxford and text me once you get home."

"Thanks, Joe; of course I will; be careful over there, darling."

"Don't worry, I will; bye."

The call ended.

Louise's spirits had been raised to the wet rooftops as she walked quickly back to the house with thoughts of being with Joseph again at Himbeldon and the family that had become very special to her. When she arrived her father was pottering around clearing the debris and Louise helped. At half-past twelve, her mother emerged, looking the worse for wear after what had been a heavy night. She immediately snapped at Louise that she thought she was very rude going off to bed so early, and that Eric had clearly been very disappointed. Remembering Joseph's words on the phone, Louise was conciliatory and offered to prepare lunch. Her brother meanwhile was still in bed. After Louise set the lunch table, served lunch for her parents she mentioned that she had visited the Chapel earlier and how nice the people were. Her mother was the first to start with dismissive comments and how silly Louise had become, filling her head with such fairy tales and getting involved with such rubbish. Then her father joined in, saying how surprised he was at Louise and had she lost her mind. She tried again to get them to see her point of view, as confused as it still was, she just knew there was something there she had to be certain about, and to dismiss it all in this cynical way hurt her.

She then packed her things, put them in the car before going upstairs to say goodbye to her brother, who raised one eyelid and groggily said "cheers" and went back to sleep. It was an uncomfortable few moments as she said goodbye to her parents and then she was away, with Aberystwyth disappearing behind her. Once she got into England, away from Wales, and headed east she began to cry and sob in the car, travelling on her own. Her mind was full of thoughts about the weekend and her parents, who she now found to be sad people. She also felt they did not care about her, and wondered if her parents ever actually had, they were wrapped up in their own lives, selfishly excluding any of her ideas or dreams. As she wiped the tears from her eyes and switched off the windscreen wipers, she felt that her tears were not for herself, but more for them and the distance that had grown between them.

28

Flying to Montana

THE OPENING NIGHT AT THE WANG THEATRE was a great success, there were several encores and the congratulations flowed at the party held afterwards at the theatre with the cast and friends. It was sure to receive good revues the following day in the Boston newspapers and media programmes, ensuring full houses for the remaining performances. Thomas had enjoyed meeting up with many old acquaintances and was delighted at Liska's happiness at performing so well for her audience. It was only in the late hours when they had all returned to the house that Charlie had passed a small piece of paper to Thomas with a Friar's name on it and a phone number that he had taken off the answering machine. It also read "Congratulations on a wonderful performance— it was spellbinding." Thomas thanked Charlie and, looking down to read the note, realised that the Jesuit Friar who he had been asked to contact by John must have also been at the performance earlier in the evening.

Before going to bed, Thomas switched on the large television in the first floor lounge, and flicked between those news channels still broadcasting at such a late hour. The news was still dominated by the high-speed rail attacks, the international efforts to apprehend the perpetrators and continuing investigations. There was also news of infestations of insects and rodents that were appearing in parts of Paris and concerns about the spread of infections from some of the worst of the disaster sites. On one of the channels there was a report on the global impacts of the attacks and the international economic chaos that was accelerating across the world. It did not make for happy viewing. The financial sector was in turmoil, with further bank failures, stock markets had wiped off trillions, and consumer confidence was at its lowest level on record, there was a flight to gold and unemployment was beginning to soar. There had also been all manner of increased security measures introduced around the world, with severe flight restrictions now in place in the U.S.A. and Europe. Civil disorder was also continuing to increase, particularly in Europe and in Brussels where there were various measures being hurriedly finalised to attempt to manage the deteriorating situation. Many European police forces had been bolstered with military personnel to try to control outbreaks of violence and to show a strong presence at flash points and where racial minorities lived.

It was a report by the United Nations and several international aid groups that Thomas also found particularly depressing. The U.N. was reporting that the economic crisis had pushed up to three hundred and fifty million more people into extreme poverty, and that the reduction of foreign aid could cause more hunger and disease. The U.N. was urging the rich nations not to reduce their financial assistance budgets. Several aid groups had also reported that the souring economy had made more people dangerously sick and U.N. Aids had said that a cut in foreign aid is likely to lead to millions of preventable deaths. The risk of new infections had also risen dramatically and the International Red Cross had warned of growing epidemics of dengue fever, meningitis and other diseases that poor countries would need help in fighting. One of these reputable aid bodies reported that fourteen million people were dying already every year from avoidable infectious diseases and that this figure was rising alarmingly. Thomas switched off the television and any thoughts of perhaps being able to get away for a few days to sail and relax with Charlie were fading fast; there were more pressing matters that needed his attention.

Throughout the United States, Jesuit brothers and priests serve in more than seventy parishes located in business districts, suburbs, Native American reservations, inner city areas, rural areas and academic centres. There are also more than twenty retreat centres across America where Ignatian spirituality is shared. There are also twenty-eight colleges and universities affiliated with the Society of Jesus in the United States and these academic institutions enrol more that one hundred and eight thousand students and offer more than two hundred and sixty undergraduate, graduate and professional programs of study. St. Ignatius Loyola had said many centuries earlier that since young people turn into adults, their good formation in life and learning will benefit many others, with the fruit expanding more widely every day. It was at Boston College in Chestnut Hill, one of the oldest Jesuit Catholic colleges in Massachusetts and the United States that Thomas was to find Patrick Flynn, a Jesuit Brother, the next day.

They had spoken briefly on the phone the following morning and Brother Patrick had suggested that Thomas come to the university in Chestnut Hill, where he would meet him outside the library building on the campus and they could then talk in his study, which was located in an adjoining building. When he had asked Charlie if it was far from Beacon Hill, he had said no, and that he would drive Thomas over if he wished, but Thomas had declined, preferring to go alone and take a taxi. Charlie agreed with Portia that he would take her to visit Francesca before mentioning to Thomas that the Boston College was quite close to where he sometimes played golf at the Newton Commonwealth Golf Course.

Thomas and Patrick had somehow instantly recognised each other, and after the customary greetings the tall Jesuit led the way briskly across the campus to his rooms. Patrick Flynn was in his seventies, Irish by birth from Dublin, where he had joined the Jesuits in his early twenties and some years later had come to Boston to take up an academic post at the university. He had been there ever since and was now a distinguished member of the history faculty as well as his other service as a Jesuit Friar. Thomas asked if he managed to get back to Ireland, and Patrick said that he did, but on an irregular basis, and asked Thomas to call him Pat and to forget all the other nonsense.

After making a cup of tea for himself and a cup of coffee for Thomas, they sat together in the untidy study and talked easily, and Brother Pat said how much he enjoyed the performance at the Wang the previous evening. Thomas soon thanked him on behalf of the family for his help.

"Yes, a dreadful situation we all face again, Thomas, and we must do whatever we can to bring it to a satisfactory end. My part was minor, but I will help in any way I can," Pat said before continuing. "Your nephew Mark Trimbeldon is a very clever young man and he handled the information I sent with great discretion, unusual in a young man these days." They both smiled at each other and then the Friar said to Thomas, "I think it would be helpful you know, if you met my brother Brendan, he is some years older than me and is a parish priest in a small town in Montana. He has been there for years and although rather decrepit now, his mind is still sharp. He knew the Milshner family years back, particularly Hank Milshner's mother, who had been very kind to the poor of the parish, with various donations before her death.

"Brendan spoke to me on the phone just yesterday and when I mentioned you were here in Boston, he said he would like to meet you."

Thomas was taken aback by this suggestion, and thoughts of Francesca in hospital, Liska performing at the Wang and Portia being in town, all flooded through his brain.

"How long might the journey be from here to where your brother lives?" Thomas enquired.

Patrick answered, "Well…" He paused. "… By road, it will take you a long time— it must be around three thousand kilometres from Boston— but you will need to fly; it is a good day's journey if you leave early from Boston."

Thomas thought for a moment, and then, remembering that Charlie had his own small aeroplane, asked, "Is there an airfield in this small town where your brother is; do you know?"

"There certainly is; I once flew in there with a friend from the college who was visiting the area a few years ago." He replied before rising from his seat and removing from the bookcase a large map book, and then showing Thomas on the map the name and location of the small town.

Pat Flynn wrote on a piece of paper the name and contact details of his brother Brendan, said he would walk out with Thomas and take him to where he would get a taxi back to Beacon Hill. It was a beautiful university campus, with many fine buildings, and as they approached the taxi rank Thomas turned to Pat and invited him to join him and the family for dinner before he left America. Patrick smiled and said that he would like that very much and would await a call from Thomas to confirm the date; in the meanwhile he would let his brother know to expect a visit from Thomas. They shook hands, and, as the yellow cab made its way back to Beacon Hill, Thomas thought, *what an interesting man; few would have taken him to be in his seventies, since he appeared to be much younger*.

It was later in the day when Thomas was able to speak with Charlie discreetly over a drink before dinner. When Thomas mentioned his impending expedition to Montana, Charlie jumped at the opportunity and said that with a fuel stop they could make the outward trip in a day in his Cessna, and that he would relish getting away together and doing some real flying for a change. They would need to leave early, Charlie had said, and he would check the weather conditions for the following morning.

"Have you ever been to Montana, Thomas?" Charlie enquired.

"No, never," replied Thomas.

"Well, you are in for a treat. It is our fourth largest State and the natural beauty there is staggering. I think you will like it, especially where we are going, and there is supposed to be great climbing there. It must be one of the largest natural areas left in the world that has not been spoilt by people, you could disappear there and never be found," said Charlie and Thomas quickly replied with a chuckle.

"Well let's hope we don't disappear there Charlie, I trust your flying skills will get us there and back safely."

"Sure will," replied Charlie, as he walked to the phone and was soon talking to the service company at Logan Airport, where he kept his plane, to have it ready and fuelled first thing in the morning. Charlie phoned a buddy in the local air traffic control centre and advised of his flight the next day and that he would phone later with his flight plan.

"Yes, if you will, please. I will be flying through their air space, I will be in touch again later," and he hung up. Thomas looked at Charlie, who explained that since they would need to fly over Lake Michigan and through Canadian air space, the flight had to be registered with them beforehand. Charlie had flown for the US Military, jet fighters and helicopters, some years before he took up civilian flying and had the reputation of being an ace pilot when younger.

It was just a few moments later that they were joined by Martha and Portia. Liska and Lucinda had left earlier for the theatre and would only be back at the house after midnight after the performance, so Thomas and Charlie had plenty of free time after dinner to plan their trip.

"So what is going on Charlie, you both look like Cheshire Cats?" enquired Martha noticing the excitement between the two men.

It was Thomas who answered, "We are going to take a trip tomorrow and will be gone for three days and Charlie has kindly agreed to fly me there…"

"Flying where?" enquired Martha, with a rather stony look in her eye.

"Er, just over to Great Falls…" Charlie said.

Again, Martha interjected with a glare, "Which Great Falls?"

Sensing that matters were rapidly getting a little tense, Thomas took control and said, "Martha, I must go and visit someone rather urgently near Great Falls in Montana and we will be back in three days. It is perfectly safe, so there is no need to worry. I will tell Liska tonight when she is back and there is nothing here for Charlie and me to do for the next couple of days, so we will get away from being under your ladies feet." He smiled warmly, trying to exercise maximum charm.

Martha was silent for a moment and then said, "Well, I just hope it is safe Thomas, and not like your last escapade, when you were in Boston."

"No, no, nothing like that Martha, I assure you," and turning to Portia, quickly wishing to change the subject, Thomas continued. "How is Francesca today, Portia?"

She replied, "A little stronger, thank you Thomas. She is fit and strong and she is healing well and there do not appear to be any complications." Portia looked at Thomas sadly and raised her eyebrows in a look of continuing concern for her daughter.

Thomas and Portia had always been close friends, and he stepped forward and in a natural movement put his arm around her shoulder to comfort her. Martha invited them to move to the dinning room for dinner.

There was a frost on the ground when Charlie and Thomas arrived at Logan Airport and parked on the other side of the airfield, away from the commercial air terminal and big jets. It was also dark, and Charlie had been up early to give his flight plan to the air traffic controllers, ready for their take-off slot at seven fifteen. They hurried through the cold morning air, carrying their bags slung over their shoulders, and entered through a side door of a large hangar where several small aircraft were parked, with some undergoing refits and maintenance. Just then, an elderly gentleman wearing a grey jacket with Personal Air Services printed across his shoulders appeared with a clipboard.

"Hi there, Charlie. She is already for you," the man said in greeting and shook Charlie's hand, who then introduced the man to Thomas. "Let me just run through this checklist Charlie and then she is all yours. Tom, you will find some hot coffee in the small lounge," the man said, pointing to a room at the side of the hangar, strongly implying that he wanted Thomas otherwise engaged while he ran through the final checks with Charlie. Thomas was only too pleased to oblige, having been woken far too early and feeling cold.

It was about forty minutes later when Charlie appeared and smiled and said, "Okay Thomas, we are ready to go. Jump aboard and they will pull us out. If you take the right seat, I will try to fly us from the one on the left." Charlie chuckled as they entered up some small steps on the side of the aircraft and stepped through to the cockpit.

Once aboard, while they were waiting for the hangar doors to be opened and they hitched a small tractor to the front of the plane, Charlie said, while they fastened their seat harnesses, “Isn’t she a beaut, Thomas?”

Thomas stared at all the dials and instruments before him and, not having the faintest idea about such matters, replied, “Yes, she certainly is. What type of plane is this Charlie?” Trying to show enthusiasm far beyond what his mind would have preferred at such an early hour.

Charlie was in his element and relishing the trip ahead since he had not flown his baby for about six weeks owing to other commitments. His plane and his sailing boat were his toys, as he called them, and he jumped at any opportunity to spend time with them. Charlie answered Thomas’ question, “It is a Cessna C 421 Golden Eagle and it is certified to fly in icy conditions, ideal for flying out of Boston. It is also a pilot’s plane with a top speed of four hundred and forty kilometres per hour, but we will be cruising at around three sixty today and being pressurised we can fly at up to twenty-seven thousand feet, although I will try to maintain about ten thousand, depending on the winds and weather. We also have enough fuel on board to do two thousand seven hundred miles, so if everything goes to plan we only need to make one refuelling stop. With these turbo engines, the fuel consumption isn’t that great, but then you get what you pay for.”

Just then, the man in the fur-lined jacket unhitched them and Charlie became preoccupied with all manner of technical matters, and Thomas looked over the broad, cold expanse of Logan Airfield, feeling warmer after the coffee earlier and snug next to Charlie at the controls.

After starting her up, checking several technical matters, including the icing equipment, engine revs and going through a detailed checklist, Charlie waited a moment for the altitude indicator to stabilise and for the gyro to be aligned properly. They then taxied out to the run-up pad, and Charlie tried the brakes, ran the throttles up to fifteen hundred revs per minute to check all the engine gauges and the propellers, and then brought it back to nine hundred. Just then, he realised that

Thomas did not have a headset on so he reached over and dangled it in front of Thomas, who placed it over his head and ears. He was instantly listening in on Charlie, who was in periodic conversation with a male voice with a heavy Bostonian accent talking to him from the control tower. It was all technical talk, although occasionally the guy in the tower said the odd brief phrase that indicated he knew Charlie, and then they were ready to go. Thomas looked at his watch and it was seven fifteen. Everything appeared to move forward after Charlie released the brakes and he pushed the throttles open and suddenly they were airborne with crackling messages in numbers coming in over the headphones. Once they were clear of the airfield and Charlie had confirmed his heading with the control tower, things became more relaxed as they climbed into the blue morning sky out beyond Boston below.

After levelling off and settling the engines at eighteen hundred and fifty revs per minute and the autopilot, they were on their way. They flew west out across Lake Ontario, near Toronto, and then the Lakes of Huron and Michigan and on over Wisconsin, Minnesota, North Dakota and onto Montana. They refuelled and stretched their legs in Fargo on the border between Minnesota and Dakota before coming into the air space of Great Falls which is the country seat of Cascade County in Montana, about a hundred miles south of the Canadian border. It lies near the centre of Montana on the northern Great Plains and it has an altitude of around three thousand feet. Great Falls with a population of around sixty thousand people is also known as 'Electric City' because of the five hydroelectric dams that operate nearby along the Missouri River. The city has a university, a minor league baseball team and it also has the Malmstrom air force base, one of the Intercontinental Ballistic Missile Wings of the U.S. air defence system. The local missile operations group provided the personnel to launch, monitor, and secure the missile alert facilities. Great Falls International Airport is also the base of the Montana Air National Guard's Fighter Wing that fly F-15 Eagles fighter aircraft and Charlie has an old friend at the base. They had spoken the previous evening when Charlie had enquired about the landing field at White Sulphur Springs, a small town about two miles from Great Falls, their final destination. He had been assured that the airfield was long enough for him to land his Golden Eagle safely, and his buddy who he had flown with when in the military, gave Charlie some suggestions on his approach.

They were about thirty minutes out from Great Plains when the radio traffic between Charlie and the local control tower increased. They were exchanging various technical information, local weather conditions and approach flight path headings and data to bring the Golden Eagle safely to land at White Sulphur Springs' modest airstrip. Apart from the last few hundred yards being a little bumpy, it was a perfect landing and Charlie taxied the Eagle to some hangars on one side of the airfield. After doing some more checks and talking to a guy on the ground through hand signals, he turned off the engine and everything fell silent. Thomas could not believe that they had almost crossed America and had chatted most of the way, apart from the periods when Charlie was preoccupied with either landing or taking off. The weather had been good and they had only once needed to alter course to avoid some storm clouds and turbulence. As they had circled the airfield Thomas had looked down on White Sulphur Springs and seen it to be a small town with streets like a checker board. The small airfield had two runways, some hangars, and there almost in the middle of this small town, Thomas could see a large stone church with various buildings in the grounds and he wondered if this was St. Bartholomew's Catholic church where they were to meet Brendan Flynn, the elderly parish priest and brother of Patrick Flynn in Boston.

After Charlie had arranged for his cherished plane to be parked in an old hangar and Thomas had picked up some dog-eared old flyers about the town from inside the small waiting area in a single storey building near the main runway, they enquired about a lift into town. A mechanic who had been working on an old crop dusting plane offered to run them to St. Bartholomew's, if they would wait for a few minutes for him to close up, since it was near his knocking off time anyway. As they sat in the late afternoon sun it was getting cold and Charlie looked across the airfield to another well-maintained hanger with two helicopters inside with bright markings. He could just make out the word Rescue on the side of one of them. As the mechanic drove them the short distance into town, Charlie enquired about the helicopters and the local man explained that they were the mountain and medical rescue unit that was financed by the county with local volunteers and that every year they brought down several bodies, mainly of tourists, off the nearby mountains. Then they were there, outside this impressive stone church with a large rectory in the same stonework next to it. They clambered from the pick up and grabbed their bags off the back and thanked the man for his kindness.

"That's okay, pleased to oblige. Say hi to Father Brendan for me."

There was a separate gate to the rectory that was set in a neat garden next to the church and it was Thomas who reached the large solid door first and rang the bell. After several moments, the door opened and there was a large, tall lady who smiled at them and enquired whether they were Thomas and Charles from Boston.

"We sure are," replied Charlie, who was standing behind Thomas and the upright lady extended a hand and introduced herself as Ingrid Bosch, the housekeeper, and she showed them into a large comfortable lounge with rather well worn furniture.

"Father Brendan will be with you shortly. Would you like some tea or coffee?" Both Thomas and Charlie settled on coffee and they thanked her.

She said, "I will show you to your rooms once you have said hello to Father Brendan." She left the room.

Thomas and Charlie looked at each other, thinking they would have been booking into a local roadhouse, but after a long trip were pleased to have arrived at their final destination.

It was not long before a tall, rather sprightly man came bustling into the room and walked straight up to Thomas and said that he must be Thomas from England shaking him by the hand, before turning to Charlie and congratulating him on making such good time flying them here all the way from Boston. For a man they took to be well into his seventies, Brendan Flynn could have passed for a man in his late fifties. He spoke slowly, still with his Dublin accent, but with many American words and turn of speech. After the usual pleasantries, Father Brendan then said that they must stay at the Rectory while in Sulphur Springs, as he referred to the town, and that apart from a brief meeting he had after dinner with the local Catholic Women's League and Mass the following morning at nine, he had cleared his diary so he could give them his undivided time during their short visit. He then went on to say that dinner would be at seven thirty, breakfast at eight for them the following morning, and that they would probably like to see their rooms and freshen up before dinner. Thomas and Charlie were already impressed by this man's hospitality and no nonsense approach to the arrangements, they also suspected that any attempt to dissuade Brendan from these matters, would bring the wrath of his large housekeeper down upon them both.

Their bedrooms were large and comfortable and the one Thomas had been allocated even had its own en suite bathroom with a shower. After investigating the upper floor of the Rectory, rather like two naughty schoolboys, Thomas offered Charlie the use of his shower since the bathroom down the corridor only had a bath. As Thomas unpacked his bag he took out a large bottle of Jameson Irish Whiskey he had bought at the airport Duty Free that he had packed in Boston, thinking that it may be an appropriate token of their appreciation for Father Brendan's kind assistance. There had been few priests in his experience, particularly Irish priests, who did not enjoy the odd glass of good whiskey. At seven fifteen, both Thomas and Charlie arrived again in the lounge below to find the curtains drawn and a log fire burning in the large fire grate. Shortly they were joined by Ingrid the housekeeper, who offered them each a glass of sherry before disappearing again, leaving the sherry bottle on the sideboard.

It was just a few minutes later when Father Brendan came in, poured himself a glass of sherry and joined them in one of the armchairs in front of the fire.

“The fire is nice, isn’t it?” he said in a matter-of-fact way before continuing. “Although it is pleasant enough during the day, when the Chinook wind doesn’t blow, our temperatures at night drop and it gets very cold. Tonight will probably go down to minus six or seven degrees, and in December it is not unusual for us to have minus forty degrees and that is cold, especially for me, coming from moderate rain soaked Ireland. Do you feel the cold, Charles?”

They continued to chat away and later as dinner progressed Thomas had the increasing feeling he could be in a bar in Dublin talking to Brendan, certainly not a hundred miles from the Canadian border.

The Irish have an ability to make wherever they may be feel like home and to have a friendly familiarity. As they were finishing their dessert, having enjoyed the excellent wholesome cooking of Ingrid, Thomas suddenly remembered the bottle of Jameson he had left on the side table in the lounge, so he excused himself momentarily and quickly reappeared to present the bottle to the elderly priest who was clearly touched by Thomas’s kindness. Charlie was feeling tired now and Thomas’s eyelids were also getting heavy and the perceptive Brendan, seeing this, said he would see them both at breakfast the following morning and wished them a good night’s rest. He then went off to meet the local ladies of the Catholic Women’s Guild.

At breakfast the following morning Thomas and Charlie were on their second helping of scrambled eggs, fried bacon, tomato and locally baked bread when Father Brendan came in through the back door. Ingrid poured him a large mug of coffee and he pulled a chair out from the large kitchen table and sat down.

It was Charlie who noticed that he had old fashioned metal black bicycle clips around the bottom of his dark trousers, and asked, “Do you still ride a bicycle, Father?”

Brendan replied with a slight smile on his face, “Yes, of course, why shouldn’t I?” He turned to Ingrid. “Ingrid, Mrs. Blather is not well this morning; you had better tell nurse, and I see that Tom Belt’s middle daughter is sporting something of a tummy; I suspect she may well be pregnant.”

After a brief conversation, it transpired that Father Brendan had been up since five o'clock already, had taken Holy Communion to several sick and elderly in the small parish, had collected and scanned the Great Falls Tribune, and chatted to several local residents on their way to work on his bike ride back to the Presbytery. As Ingrid busied herself with more toast, fresh coffee and the dishes for their two guests, Father Brendan, in the next twenty minutes or so, spoke gently and often with humour to provide his guests with a swift rundown on Sulphur Springs, himself and then ending with some tantalising information about the Milshner family, as a prelude to their more serious discussions scheduled after Mass.

He had joined the Franciscan Order in Dublin a few years before his younger brother had joined the Jesuits, probably largely influenced by his devout Roman Catholic mother who had reared her two sons on the poor side of Dublin with an abusive and heavy drinking father who was forever in and out of casual work. Brendan had come to America to continue his studies sponsored by a Franciscan Community and large Catholic parish in Bavaria in Germany. Once he arrived in his mid twenties, he never really left again and had served in this area of America ever since. He had served in the tough slums of Phoenix, in Great Falls and for a brief period in East Seattle, but had always returned to Sulphur Springs, the parish where he had started his pastoral calling.

By this stage something was bothering the mathematical brain of Charlie, who interjected, "If you don't mind me asking, Father, how old are you?"

Father Brendan looked down at his hands and paused for a moment and looking at Ingrid with a slight glint in his eye replied, "I will be eighty-two next March, won't I Ingrid?"

"Yes, you will, Father, if God continues to spare you."

There was a moment's silence, and Charlie and Thomas were even more surprised by his youthfulness, while Brendan wanted to get on with more important matters.

He then spoke about Sulphur Springs, about the area and that farming, logging and hunting were the main activities; that the scenery, mountains, climbing and skiing brought many tourists to the area. The local hot springs were also a major attraction and prove to be very popular with visitors after a day's climbing, riding or hiking. The town had a population of around twelve hundred people, the average age was forty-four, there were five percent more women than men in the town, and that over ninety percent of the local people were white with about five percent being Native Americans and with a few Hispanic people. The church had been built at the turn of the century, funded largely by the Bavarian parish he had mentioned earlier. Interestingly, he explained that the ancestry of today's population of Sulphur Springs was roughly speaking, thirty percent German, fifteen percent each being Norwegian, Irish and English with the small balance made up of Scottish and Americans – hence part of the explanation for such a substantial Catholic church in such a small community. He also hastened to add that he was a great friend of the local Lutheran minister and the pastors of the other churches in the town. Thomas looked at Charlie, and thought about how Father Brendan, with his Irish charm, could be on friendly terms with everyone, whoever they may be.

With time getting on, the priest then said, "But that is not why you have travelled all this way, to listen to me chatter on about Sulphur Springs. We will meet again if it suits you, in my study after Mass, and I will tell you about Hank Milshner, his father and his wonderful mother, God rest her, and the estate way off over there and into the mountains. If you will excuse me then, I must go and say Mass." With that, Father Brendan got up from the table, took a bunch of keys off a hook by the kitchen door, slipped his coat on and left.

Both Charlie and Thomas thanked Ingrid for the splendid breakfast and walked across to the church for Mass. There was only Father Brendan on the altar and, after reading the Old and New Testament readings, he gave a ten minute homily related to the Bible readings that made them both reflect on various spiritual aspects of their lives. There were only about twenty of the faithful at the service, with it being mid-week, with most people now being at their place of work.

It was just before ten when the three men sat together in

Father Brendan's study and he asked Thomas, "Where would you like me to start? These attacks are so bad aren't they, who would ever want to do such things?" he asked rhetorically, before pausing and looking through the study window to the mountains beyond. "I have not seen Hank Milshner for many years, but I did meet him many times when he was a boy and his mother was alive. Hilary Milshner was a wonderful person, God rest her soul, not a Catholic, but she did more than most of our own parishioners ever did for the parish and the needy. It was really through her that I met Hank, and I also met her husband a few times. They were lovely people. But that was many years ago and a lot has happened since then."

"Perhaps I should go back to the beginning, just stop me if you have any questions," the priest continued. For the next two hours Brendan Flynn spoke gently about the Milshners, as he had known them, how Edward Milshner had been a generous benefactor to many local charities and the needy. How Hilary Milshner, an attractive and charming blonde, used to come into Sulphur Springs with little Hank, from their spread out on the prairie. She loved horses, was an excellent horsewoman and she even used to help the farmhands break in wild horses. Hank was a fine, chubby little fella always smiling and happy and Hilary had no airs and graces despite their fabulous wealth. Her life was the ranch, her son, husband and piano music, particularly Sergey Rachmaninoff, Claude Debussy and Aaron Copeland, the American composer.

Hilary had once acted as a local patron for a fund raising event that involved entertaining small groups of people in the homes in Sulphur Springs and she had entertained people together with some other local musician's right there in the Presbytery, on the old upright piano in the lounge, still there to this day. Brendan recalled she had played "Rodeo" by Copeland and Hank had been with her, being cared for by a local lady attending the concert.

Edward Milshner was a quiet sort of chap, really humble for a man in his position, ideally complemented by his slightly younger, outgoing and friendly wife. He was clearly devoted to her and the few times Brendan had met them together, one could tell he loved her very much. It was at that time; in those happy early days that Edward began buying up many of the local spreads and several that led up into the mountains. He even built a small lodge up in the mountains where he, Hilary and Hank used to spend vacations in the summer to enjoy the cool clean air up there and look out across their farms on the prairies below. Hilary had tried to interest Hank in the piano, but he had never shown any aptitude for music, although she used to play to him, and they even had a piano up in the mountain lodge. One of Brendan's parishioners at the time, a lady of Norwegian descent, now dead, used to be Hank's nanny. There were a few in the town who used to work for the Milshners and they were always regarded as good and kind employers.

The main farmstead was a large place with several houses, barns, sheds, paddocks and a large dam adjacent to the main farmhouse. There is also a small airstrip out there that Edward's pilot used and the whole spread is enormous covering hundreds and hundreds of miles. It is at least an hour's drive just from the farmhouse to the main gate of the property, which is another hour's drive from Sulphur Springs.

Then there was the dreadful accident and everything changed. Hilary was thrown from a horse and broke her neck on impact, died instantly and mercifully did not know anything about it, since it had happened so quickly. They flew her body to the hospital in Great Falls, but she was already dead. Word at the time was that Hank had somehow been involved in the accident, had run out as kids do to see his mother atop the horse, and the animal took fright, reared up, and poor Hilary fell backwards and onto some fencing poles, and broke her neck. It was an innocent act by the young boy, although his father had become ever more resentful of the boy, according to some folk, who worked out there in the months after her death. Hank must have only been eight or nine, at the time of the accident, and it was a year or so later when Edward his father began to become more withdrawn and depressed, leaving the boy to be reared by a succession of nannies, most of them hired from out of this State. Edward gradually stopped employing local people and the farm and activities of the Milshners then became a mystery to local folk. Brendan reckoned that Hank must have been about fifteen or so when his father died of a heart attack. There would be the occasional story or other, about things happening over there, from the odd local who had heard something from others. The farm is now managed in a family trust that Edward set up before his death, and he and Hilary are buried out there. We heard about Hank getting into trouble down in Colorado and taking up with some beautiful young lady and then any news of him just stopped for many years.

It was then quite a few years back that Hank suddenly reappeared, not that Brendan saw him at all at this time, and people from various Milshner companies tore down the old modest mountain lodge and they built a much larger luxurious lodge on the same site. They took about three years to build the place and although no one ever saw them, it was rumoured that Hank and his lady friend used to spend time there. Brendan had never seen this new lodge close up, but, according to what he had been told, it was quite a construction, built into the side of the mountain, somewhat higher than the original lodge.

Just then Thomas asked, "Is there anyone in town who might know about this place since it will be useful for us to know what it contains and if Hank Milshner ever goes there these days?" He was unaware of the information that Francesca had shared with her mother earlier, and, after a pause, Brendan Flynn answered and explained that quite a few locals had worked on the construction of the place, but that had been many years ago. About fourteen years or so ago, Milshner had made some alterations after he had visited Germany, and a local guy, Rob Yeates, who was a structural engineer, had been involved, if Brendan had remembered correctly. Rob still lived in Sulphur Springs; he was retired now, but perhaps he could help, and Brendan said he would look up his phone number in the local directory and give him a call at lunchtime.

"How about I ask him to join us for dinner tonight, how would that do?" enquired Brendan.

"That would be great," responded Charlie, who was

enjoying his new role as a sleuth.

The conversation then moved onto when the first rumours had started circulating in the town about some or other secret religious sect that Hank led. They had started many years back and at first they were treated as a joke, no one took them seriously. However, as certain things started to change out at the Milshner spread, local folk began to get more suspicious. By now, almost no one from the town worked or had anything to do with the place and on the perimeter fence of the estate, sophisticated security equipment started to appear and there were armed patrols of guys in a uniform. A local hunter had been forcibly thrown off Milshner land, and this story had spread quickly, so many locals started to avoid the farm. A couple of local young people were also reputed to have joined this sect, although this was never proved, apart from the young man who had provided the video and other material.

It transpired that the young man who had been found murdered by the Inter State Highway had known Brendan Flynn when he was growing up in Sulphur Springs and had brought the information to him a few days before he was murdered. He came from a local family and his mother had been a Catholic in the parish, and not knowing whom to turn to, he had passed the information to Brendan.

As he shook his head slightly, the priest said, "I did not know myself what to do with that weird material, so that's why I passed it to Patrick, being the clever one of us, he seemed to know what to do with it, and here we are today. So he was right, I suppose?"

Thomas and Charlie smiled at the elderly priest, who continued to share all he knew about the Milshners and Hank. There had been visits to the town by Federal agents a few times, Brendan recalled, asking about Milshner and just recently, they are back again, arrived a couple of months back asking questions. He remarked that they seemed reluctant to go to the farm itself although since the rail accident in Washington there have been more of them in the town.

Since it was now well past midday Father Brendan suggested that his guests might wish to have some refreshment and take a walk through the town after lunch. Charlie said he wanted to go out to the air field to make arrangements for refuelling his aircraft and preparing for their departure the next morning and Brendan reminded himself to call Rob Yeates. Later after lunch Thomas had sat in his bedroom making some brief notes from the discussion earlier with Father Brendan and then he had dozed for a while. When he awoke the light was beginning to fade and as he looked through the bedroom window everything was still outside.

For dinner Ingrid had prepared a delicious goulash with plenty of fresh vegetables and Brendan had produced some excellent bottles of red wine. It was a cold night and the fire in the lounge was warming the adjacent dining room. Rob Yeates was American, medium height and friendly. The conversation soon got onto the Milshner Mountain Lodge and yes, Rob had worked with several out of town engineers more than ten years earlier on some changes to the place. He had visited the Lodge many times, had pored over the original design drawings, done calculations and provided specialist advice regarding the load bearing capacity of certain parts of the original structure, so he knew the lodge very well. He was thrilled to talk about the place and share his knowledge with these two charming 'out of towners', and so he did.

The Lodge was a modern reinforced concrete structure built into the side of the mountain and it had a helipad on the roof since that was how Milshner and his people always travelled to the place. It was a Frank Lloyd Wright-looking building, with large cantilever load bearing reinforced steel beams supported and anchored by solid legs sunk deep into the face of the mountain. It had four floors, a swimming pool, gymnasium, electric lifts, its own power plant and water supply. It was a veritable fortress built by Milshner and Adler, with no expense spared and several of Hank's out of town construction and engineering companies had been involved in the design and construction. They had even used heavy military type helicopters to fly in the heavy equipment needed to build the place and other supplies. There were services on the ground floor, staff quarters and kitchens on the second floor, guest accommodation, the swimming pool, conference rooms and a medium-sized auditorium on the third floor, and on the top floor were the lavish private rooms of Milshner. The top floor had the most spectacular views with large, reinforced glass windows and doors that led out onto a balcony. Milshner even had a grand piano airlifted in there that was in the huge lounge on the top floor. Rob then did some rough sketches of the layout of the place on some paper that Brendan brought from his study.

"Now that you come to mention the piano, do you know, Rob, whether Joe Wiese still gets picked up and goes up there to keep the piano tuned?" asked Brendan, quite suddenly.

"He certainly still tunes pianos, but whether or not he still goes out to the Milshner place, I don't know," replied Rob.

Johan Wiese, an elderly Jewish gentleman, who had come to Sulphur Springs during the last war, had a small musical instrument and music shop in the town.

"Would it be too late to call him, do you think Rob?" asked Brendan.

Rob, looking at his watch, replied, "In half an hour it may be, but for now, it is early enough."

Brendan excused himself and went to the phone. While he was gone, Thomas asked how supplies were delivered and handled and Rob explained that there was a lift and a small service building below the mountain, although most things were brought in by helicopter and that the helipad on the roof had been built to take heavy payloads.

"Is this place one of the cult compounds I've heard about?" asked Charlie.

Rob replied, "No, I don't think so. Hank Milshner built it as a private place for himself. He is supposed to have homes all over the world, and from what I gather he never spends much time up there. There is a small permanent staff that always keep it ready for his visits."

Just then, Brendan quietly bustled back into the room and immediately there was a gap in the conversation he said, "He certainly does, you know, he was up there two weeks ago and although he did not speak to him, he got a glimpse of who he thought might be Hank, in a wheelchair. Joe also mentioned that there is no one up there who plays the piano so he cannot understand why he is still needed."

They then talked about these extraordinary matters, how real life is always stranger than fiction and if you read this type of thing in a novel, you would take it with a pinch of salt. Brendan had given his theory about the strange piano tuning to Joe, over the phone, as a way Hank possibly honoured his dead mother or felt in some way still connected to her, and Joe had agreed. On two other visits that Joe had made to the Lodge over the years, when Milshner had happened to be there, he had asked Joe to play a few pieces of music for him. Brendan suspected that Hank had never properly accepted his mother's death, still felt some deep guilt and shame about it and had never forgiven himself for what had happened, despite it being just a tragic accident.

Little did they know that Hank Milshner had been staying at the Mountain Lodge for some weeks, alone, apart from his few staff, confined to his electric wheelchair and the spectacular views of his farms and where his happy childhood had come to a troubled end. He was lonely, depressed and only a shadow of the former person he had once been. He felt betrayed, particularly by Adler who he had trusted before her new Japanese lover had appeared. He spent many hours just sitting, staring out across the vast prairies and looking through an array of telescopes and binoculars on tripods that his staff had carefully set up for him in front of the balcony. He could move his wheelchair and select the particular view he wished to look at through one of the different telescopes and one of these was trained on the gravestones of his mother and father far below. He may even have witnessed Charlie landing his Golden Eagle and the arrival of them both in Sulphur Springs.

Charlie then asked a question that had also been on Rob Yeate's mind, "Why don't the Feds just go up there and arrest this guy, if he is there, and put an end to all this trouble?"

No one knew the answer, but Brendan suggested that, with the number of agents around, they were preparing for something, but appeared to be holding off for some reason. Thomas asked Charlic, since he had been in the military, that with there being a major U.S. air base in Great Falls, presumably the FBI or CIA were able to liaise with the military to keep an eye on matters at the Lodge? Charlie replied that there was probably all manner of aerial surveillance and that the authorities were keeping a close eye on what was going on up there and that if Milshner posed a threat, they would probably have moved on him already.

The murder of Timothy, just nine months earlier, came into Thomas's mind and he had a sudden and rather fanciful idea.

"I wonder if Milshner ever has any guests or people who might play his grand piano for him."

The other three men looked at Thomas, and then each other in bewilderment at what he was meaning.

"I would rather like to meet Hank Milshner, assuming he is up there."

"What on earth for?" enquired Brendan and Charlie and Rob nodded their support for the question.

"Well for one thing, I would like to know, first hand, whether he was the person who ordered the murder of my nephew in Paris earlier this year," and before Thomas could continue, it was Charlie who interrupted.

"I don't think that a good idea Thomas, best to leave him to the Feds, anyway how are you going to get near him with the security he has got?"

By now Brendan and Rob had become a little intrigued by where Thomas was leading the conversation particularly when he answered, "I will write him a letter and say I would like to meet him and I will play for him on his grand piano. With me being a Trimbledon and a pianist he may well find it irresistible."

Charlie thought for a moment, his mind racing, firstly with what he imagined Martha's reaction might be if she ever found out about this bizarre idea, and he then thought this type of behaviour just proves that the English are all mad.

Charlie then asked, trying to deflect Thomas from such dangerous thoughts, "Oh yes, Thomas, and how do you propose to deliver this letter?"

"Simple," Thomas replied. "Via Joe Wiese, the piano tuner."

They all laughed, and then went on to talk about other

matters and finishing the bottle of Jameson.

After breakfast the following morning, they thanked Brendan Flynn and Ingrid for their generous hospitality and Brendan called them a cab to take them the short distance out to the airstrip. After saying their farewells and getting into the cab, it was a few moments later that Thomas asked the cab driver to please take them passed Joe Wiese's music shop on the way to the airstrip, and he happily obliged. Charlie was speechless and just said nothing looking out of the cab window until they pulled up outside this modest shop with two windows either side of a glass door. Thomas jumped out, stepped quickly through the door and was gone, for no more than five minutes, before returning smiling and saying what a pleasant man Mr. Wiese had turned out to be. It was an hour later as Thomas looked back over his shoulder to see Sulphur Springs below them that he looked in the direction of the Mountain Lodge and there he could see something, white and flat against the upper face of the dark mountain, and he said to Charlie, "I wonder if Hank Milshner is actually living there or not?"

29

Back at the Grange

IT WAS NOW NOVEMBER AND JOSEPH WAS PLEASED TO BE BACK at Himbledon, away from the grief and sadness of Paris and to have dealt with Tim's affairs and possessions. There had been some items that Joseph had found among Tim's things and brought back to the Grange that Mark had found particularly intriguing, particularly how they had come into Tim's possession and whether they had any connection with the attacks. Mark and Joseph had sat with their father in the meeting room by the underground canal as Mark had explained the possible significance of these items. There were two in particular that he had focussed his attention on.

There was a mobile phone or radio device, larger than a normal mobile phone with some highly innovative battery technology that he had never seen before. The batteries were not lithium batteries, but used some other chemical compounds and tiny solid-state electronics that were highly sophisticated. He explained to his father and Joseph that these were a new generation of batteries, very much more powerful and long lasting than anything he had seen previously. The other interesting thing about this device is that it is a new breed of extraterrestrial radio transmitter and receiver. Existing communication devices are available that use satellites for sending and receiving data, including speech and they are normally larger than conventional cell phones that rely on local cellular radio masts and networks. This communication device enables people to communicate from anywhere, in the middle of the ocean, deserts, the icecaps or the Amazon jungle where there are no ground based radio networks. These devices are already in use by the military, but the older heavier versions no doubt.

The other device was a small touchpad with screen that fitted in the palm of the hand. Its function was to produce numbers; not random numbers, but numbers that would enable the owner to gain access to computer or other systems. It was a smaller version of what some banks already use to handle Internet banking security, at least a broadly similar idea. This device, however, appeared to generate a range of numbers, either in sets of six, eight, ten, or twelve characters long. The number of mathematical permutations with these types of number sets was almost limitless, and, as a security access device, it was extremely robust and clever. To operate it one needed certain identification codes that it would be virtually impossible for Mark to ever discover. Mark continued to explain that these two items of technology might well provide clues as to how the cult communicates with the independent and imbedded cells located around the world. He was convinced such communication was not via terrestrial mobile phone networks since these were open to surveillance and could be unreliable. To operate more secure communications a dedicated series of radio frequencies, transmitters and receivers would be necessary. However, to identify these special frequencies and radio transmissions required highly sophisticated equipment and facilities that only the military would have. Mark also believed that if his suspicions were right, that these special frequencies would continually change and have many different source locations. Mark concluded by saying it was rather like looking for a needle in a haystack, but during an earthquake.

John suggested he speak with the prime minister the following morning about this radio tracking and to find out whether there was anything more the security agencies had managed to find out. Joseph then raised the matter of the independent cells and whether there might be some other way of identifying and neutralising them. After a further discussion it was agreed that since no one knew how many cells there were or where they are located, they had to be stopped somehow from the centre and this is why they were continuing to focus on the triggering mechanism. John then suggested another paradigm; following a conversation he and Mark had the previous day. Although current thinking was around trying to stop the cult from triggering attacks, perhaps they actually do not trigger them at all, since they are already scheduled in some way and happen by default. This was a notion that Mark had been working on for some days now and John asked him to explain it to Joseph.

It related to the idea of a doomsday scenario or timetable of horrendous events leading up to a final apocalyptic event and the mathematical series he had been working on and already discussed with Joseph. Mark had made a series of tentative predictions that there was to be another major atrocity involving the number three early in the next year, certainly before the end of the first month, January. This would then be followed by some further events, the next in the middle of 2010 at around the time of the World Soccer Cup in South Africa, and then things would remain relatively calm until the final apocalyptic event in the middle of 2012, probably to coincide with the Olympics, scheduled to be held in London. What this might be and where, he had no idea and he hoped he was wrong. However, if correct, then Mark believed this whole nightmare had been pre-planned or pre-ordained with no detail left unattended. Mark had spent much time trying to almost get inside the head of Judaire, to try to understand his thinking and the way he might have set this whole thing up.

“He may well have already programmed this whole thing and it is being managed by computer intelligence in some way, and that unless there is some human intervention, nothing will stop his whole programme of destruction just rolling on to the ultimate final act.”

John looked across the table at Mark and said, “Let us hope you are wrong on this one Mark, but why would he program it in this way?” he asked.

Mark then continued to provide a lucid justification for his assumptions and theories. Firstly, a machine properly engineered and programmed is more reliable than a human. It also has no emotion, no second thoughts and no sudden weakness or compassion. Another reason is that apart from Paris, when thirty-five plus a few other cult members were involved, the other attacks with the aircraft and the high-speed trains were instigated via technology. Yes it is true, humans had probably laid the rogue transmitters by the rail tracks and set up all the rogue technology necessary for these attacks, but it was most likely to have been a computer code, an electronic signal or some other technical phenomena that actually triggered the other local technology to malfunction and crash the aircraft and derail the trains. These attacks were also highly sophisticated, precisely timed, taking place all across the world at the same time. The amount of data involved is huge and would have to have extensive computer processing capacity and some very sophisticated programmes to be able to handle it fast and accurately enough to be able to execute these atrocities. The final piece of logic, at least to Mark who appreciated such niceties, is that a scenario as described would completely enthral and captivate a mad computer genius, this is likely to be his precise *modus operandi*, his opportunity to be able to turn his wildest fantasies into reality.

"So what you are saying, Mark, is that there is some death machine somewhere doing all this?" enquired Joseph.

"In a manner of speaking yes, but it is more complicated than that, in my view," replied Mark.

He went on to explain that there would not be a single computer, but, rather, distributed intelligence, possibly all over the world. There would be multiple systems, so that, if one went down, another would take over. It would have built into it everything man knew today about technology, the very technology that normally flies aeroplanes safely, manages high-speed trains travelling at two hundred miles an hour at just four minute intervals between them, and all the many other technological wonders we all take for granted. However, he explained, these people have managed through the Milshner trillions to go way beyond the level of known technology, they have in a sense, accelerated existing technical development trends and put it all together systematically to destroy life rather than protect it. Mark then used the simple analogy of global warming, that due to man's excessive addiction to carbon the world was possibly set on a different type of doomsday path and there appeared little that man, either individually or collectively, was going to be able to do to stop it. Imagine now if you can, Mark asked, if some mad delusional genius was able to get his hands on limitless technology and harness it for destructive purposes. There was a sudden pause in the conversation and John looked over to Joseph and raised his eyebrows gently.

"This doomsday machine or death machine as you call it, Joe, is immensely powerful and deadly. It not only executes these attacks and follows a carefully laid down timetable, but it also has highly complex feedback and other intelligence gathering and management capability," Mark said before continuing to explain that in order to crash the planes and trains they had to be able to monitor the movement of these vehicles, know where they were located despite them travelling at high-speeds, indeed they almost had to be in the cockpits and train drivers cab, or at least the computers that committed the attacks had to be. This type of technical capability is a huge step forward in terms of the technology we know about. But for the last fifteen years or so this loony technical genius plus his band of whiz kids with the unwitting support of software and other commercial companies within the Milshner empire have been busy putting this whole thing together. Through Milshner's engineering, utility and aerospace companies they have also been poisoning all manner of chalices around the world probably nuclear power stations, utilities, hydroelectric schemes, rapid transit systems and air traffic control systems. Something that Mark had only recently found out about from his forensic auditor is that some of Milshner controlled companies are also into anti virus software development.

"I dare say, between ourselves, that if these people have the type of technology I suspect they have, then they could probably crash two thirds, if not more, of all the aircraft currently flying in the air. The attacks to date are mere demonstrations of their deadly power and a series of warnings leading up to the final global attack."

John then said to Joseph, "The other thing that we must remember is that even where human beings are involved in these attacks or future ones, they may have either already completed their deadly tasks in laying in the rogue technology that is just waiting to be triggered, or where people are still necessary, how on Earth do you identify them?" He continued to summarise a brief report Mark and Ruth had put together for a member of the prime minister's national security team, while Joseph was away in Paris, about the possible nature of the independent terrorist cells. They are independent in the sense that there is no conventional command structure or contact. They are also made up of apparently ordinary people just going about their daily work – aeroplane maintenance mechanics, high-speed rail line construction and maintenance tradesmen, computer personnel in utility companies, outsourced technical specialists maintaining nuclear power stations and so forth. Through the Milshner global business empire these fanatics had been professionally placed within all these vulnerable occupations. It was the man next to you in the coffee shop or the lady in front of you in the grocery shop queue. These people were colleagues, friends, supervisors and individuals that ordinary people work and live with each day. They dress the same, talk the same and have no distinguishing features.

Mark said to both his father and Joseph, "We must not underestimate these people. They are very smart and may well have pulled off the most momentous of all crimes against humanity. The only possible chance we have of defeating them in time is to try to somehow get inside their reality, however shocking or preposterous it may be."

Joseph felt it was all like some science fiction dream he was experiencing again, listening to his father and especially Mark. Yet he could not find a shred of evidence or logic to be able to dispute anything he had been told in the last couple of hours. Something, however, did continue to concern him and, in contrast to all this technical and other complexity, was a rather simple matter. How do we catch these villains and stop the killing. The three of them had already digested the intelligence that Portia had sent from Francesca, and had already moved their thinking to focus on Judaire rather than Milshner.

Mark then said, “I need a cup of coffee. How about you two?” They both nodded, rose from their seats and the three of them made their way upstairs to the kitchen. As they walked together beside the underground canal Joseph asked Mark whether he had any ideas on how to stop them and whether the security people around the world still needed to wait before moving in on the compounds.

When they reached the kitchen, Mark said briefly, and rather uncharacteristically, “Two things, Joseph: intercepting the radio signal, if it can be found and neutralised, and, as far as holding off from Judaire and Adler, just one more major attack, and they need to be taken out, but kept alive to reveal how this computer system operates. If we can neutralise these radio signals then we have a chance of stopping the clock ticking toward Armageddon.”

As they drank their coffee, John reminded Joseph that they would need to leave early the following morning for London, where various business briefing and review meetings had been arranged at the office. Joseph was beginning to get his legs under his commercial desk at the office as his new role in life rapidly broadened, and John passed more business matters of importance to him. They were planning to be back Friday afternoon at the Grange and Louise was arriving from Oxford for the weekend. While in London Joseph and his father had also planned to have dinner with Paul who was back from the US and back in London for a period. They still had not managed to have a game of golf together, but life had been rather chaotic in recent weeks, and other pressing matters had occupied Joseph’s time. He had spoken to Portia and Martha on the phone to enquire about Francesca and had also spoken to Thomas in Boston when he got back from Montana. He had also asked Thomas if the local police or FBI had apprehended the impostor John Holmes and Thomas had explained that although they were pursuing him, he had disappeared. Thomas had spoken with John his brother on the phone and told him about his meeting with Patrick Flynn and his brother Brendan in Montana and that immediately he and Liska got back to Cheltenham, John and Mary must come over for dinner so they could talk about the recent developments in the US.

A few days earlier John, Mary and Freddie had visited Thomas and Liska in Cheltenham and Mary was shocked to hear further details about the violent rape of Francesca, and was pleased that Portia was there with her and that Martha and Charlie were close at hand. Although Mary was not directly involved with the service that her husband, two surviving sons and daughter were involved with, she intuitively knew much more than they ever realised. Her role was to support and be there for them, and as hard as it so often was, to stand aside and let them do as they had to. It was when danger to her family was involved that she found it almost unbearable and would pray with great intensity for their protection. Mary knew the sacrifices that were involved because John had even discussed it with her long before they were married. It was at moments like this, when those she cared for such as Francesca and the death of her eldest son, that she had to reach elsewhere for courage, love and fortitude and then try to hand on these very qualities to those around her.

Thomas always had the sensitivity to know of Mary's trials and tribulations in these matters, and could quickly identify in her when these worries and concerns pervaded her mind. Often with charm, wit and even outrageousness, he would distract her, make her laugh or simply put an arm around her until Mary regained her inner composure and her innate courage reasserted itself. It was the same when they had visited Thomas's large old house in Cheltenham. Thomas also described his visit to Montana and how good it had been to be with Charlie again and he gave some of the details about Hank Milshner and Mary had commented that he sounded a very sad, lonely and tortured soul. Thomas had provided a highly sanitised version of events and he had made no mention of Joe Wiese the piano tuner.

The weekend at Himbeldon was delightful; the weather was

bright and fresh during the day and the open fires in the Grange in the evenings provided a warm comfortable atmosphere on the cold autumn nights. Joseph and Louise had jogged and taken long walks over the estate and had enjoyed the companionship of the family in the evenings at the house. Mark and Charlotte had joined the family for dinner on the Saturday evening and everyone, apart from Louise, had gone to Mass on the Sunday morning. Joseph had taken Louise to meet Freddie and Ann at their house and at mid day on the Sunday, Charlotte had invited Louise to accompany her on a call to the horse stud.

It had been a relaxing and happy weekend for the whole family and Louise had spent some time talking with John and Mary, without Joseph who had gone to attend to something in the nearby village. She felt ever more a part of the family and at ease in the house and John and Mary made her feel so welcome that she realised she had not only fallen in love with Joseph, but was also falling in love with the Grange and its occupants. Mary and Louise were forming a particularly close friendship and a bond was gradually developing between them, no doubt partly because they shared a similar relationship to two Trimbeldon men and Mary could empathise with Louise and the truth that lay behind her friendship with her son. Louise with her highly attuned perception and quick mind could also relate easily with Mary who also had a legal background and Mary was beginning to become a surrogate mother to Louise. Rarely did Louise now think of Aberystwyth or the uncomfortable weekend she had recently spent with her parents.

There had been the inevitable conversations about Thomas' visit to Boston and Montana and the rape of Francesca. Whenever there was talk about Francesca and Joseph was present, Louise intuitively recognised in him a special interest in her, a greater concern than exists in just ordinary friendship, and it made her feel jealous and suspicious. Not to leave matters unresolved, it had been on the Sunday afternoon when they were both out walking that Louise broached the matter of Francesca again with Joseph and asked him how he felt about her. He was surprised and uncomfortable at the question, and had given an evasive answer, but one that indicated to Louise that Joseph did have feelings for this lady that perhaps even he did not fully understand right now. Louise could see that he had been deeply affected by her rape and the thought of her lying injured in a hospital, and that this incident had touched deep emotions within him. Louise quickly noticed his discomfort and tactfully changed the subject, but it had been in those few moments, as they walked under the oaks shedding their leaves, that she had felt that Francesca meant a great deal more to Joseph than ordinary friendship.

At every mealtime together at the Grange, a member of the family would always say grace before the meal. It had been something Joseph had done when they were on holiday in Croatia and Louise and Joseph had joked about it. Louise particularly noticed it this weekend and was intrigued by it, particularly the way all the Trimbledons appeared to speak so naturally to some distant person, thanking him for the food and the companionship. It was something strange to her and it had been on the Sunday morning after everyone had returned from church, when Louise was alone in the kitchen with Mary that she asked her about praying. Mary had found Louise's question surprising at first, but then quickly saw it as a genuine and straightforward inquiry about something that Louise had no experience of. They discussed prayer, the different types of prayer and Louise took some minutes to grasp the notions of faith and talking to this person Jesus who was not physically there, but according to Mary was there with the Holy Spirit. Louise found it all rather confusing although she was surprised how easy the actual act of prayer appeared to be from Mary's gentle answers. It was also the way Mary spoke with Louise, none of Louise's questions were ignored or misunderstood and she had felt safe and not at all silly discussing these things with her. Mary clearly respected Louise and understood her upbringing; there was no judgement in Mary's remarks as she spoke calmly and warmly with deep conviction and belief in what she was saying.

Mary had been very touched that Louise was able to talk to her in such a personal and intimate way, and had mentioned eternity and that our human life on Earth was so short, but a prelude to other things.

Louise had asked, "If there is a God, why does he allow such awful things to happen?"

Mary had talked about the freedom of choice that he had given everyone and that it was the consequences of silly, misguided human decisions, and not God, that caused the problems. God did not force these matters on us, Mary had explained, since he had given everyone the right to choose for him or herself.

There were many elements to this conversation that confused Louise, but she had come to understand a little more about these fairy tales, as her parents had so often described them, and her curiosity and intellect were stimulated by these ideas. It was Mary's final few comments that particularly struck Louise before John came into the kitchen looking for his mobile phone. Mary had said the whole thing is actually about love and that without love, life is meaningless, and that if we want to really understand and experience love then we just have to read the Bible, particularly the New Testament.

"We just have to open ourselves to God, he will do the rest," Mary had said, before Louise spotted the mobile phone and picked it up off the dresser and handed it to John.

Louise had left the Grange on the Monday morning early to drive back to Oxford, and as she drove away from the house she felt refreshed and invigorated and ready for her work back in Oxford. The idea of the International Court of Justice was also becoming more appealing and she thought that this week she must make her decision and notify all the different parties. The uncertainty of what she would be doing next year unsettled her, and feeling ever more confident that this decision to be the right one, it was now decision time. The Hague was also only an hour's flight from London and she would be relatively close to Himbeldon and Joseph, which were now becoming the cornerstones of her private life.

VI

Murder Up Close and Unexpected Repercussions

30

Professor John's Address at Oxford

JOHN WAS DUE TO GIVE HIS ECONOMICS ADDRESS at Oxford at the end of November and he had invited Louise to attend together with Joseph. Mark had declined the invitation joking that he regarded economics as a load of mumbo jumbo, and adding that it had already got the world into a mess. Mary never enjoyed these academic occasions so had decided to remain at the Grange and prepare a late supper for them all on their return. With it being a Thursday afternoon, Louise had arranged to return with Joseph and John to Himbeldon for the weekend and after the reception after the address, they had all hoped to be able to leave Oxford at least by seven in the evening. Freddie would drive them and they would pick Louise up from her college before driving the short distance to John's old college for the address.

When the phone rang in the kitchen at four o'clock in the afternoon it was Mary who answered. It was Portia calling from Boston and Mary instantly asked how Francesca was, to be told that she was well over the worst of her injuries, had spent the last few days staying with her and Martha at Beacon Hill and they were making plans to return to Rome together.

"I think Francesca will be fine to travel towards the end of the month and she is going to come home for a few weeks before deciding what to do next. The FBI has said that she can leave and they will be in touch if she is needed here for any legal matters," Portia said, before continuing. "We would like to visit you all, Mary, there at Himbeldon on our way back to Rome, if it is not too much?"

Mary immediately interrupted, "Yes of course, it will be lovely to see you both, and John and the boys will be delighted." A tentative date was agreed and Mary asked that their love be conveyed to Francesca, Martha and the family, and they said goodbye.

John and Joseph were away in London on business and it was the same evening when talking to John that Mary told him of the impending visit. He was thrilled at the prospect and said he would let Joseph know the following morning when he was due to see him again at the office. Joseph was with Ruth that same evening and Anna, although she had stabilised, was still very sick. Ruth had asked Joseph over supper in Kensington how he was enjoying getting to grips with the business world and Joseph had replied that he was actually finding it all more interesting than he had ever imagined. They had discussed the future treatment of Anna, her parents and how Ruth had kept in regular contact with them and the possible need for Anna to be admitted to a secure clinic for further observation and care. Joseph had said to Ruth if that was what was necessary, just to let him know and he would arrange for all the costs to be met without any fuss.

The next morning at the office when John told him about the likely visit of Portia and Francesca, Joseph felt an uncontrollable sense of excitement, so much so that he had to consciously suppress it in front of his father.

The global investigations were continuing with ever-greater intensity to track down the perpetrators of the attacks. Little new evidence from the rail crash sites had emerged and the rail companies were now busy repairing the lines, having removed the debris and bodies of the dead. The global economy was beginning to stabilise and, since there had been no further attacks, life everywhere was returning to some fragile state of normality. The social disorder had also declined significantly and the activities of the police and enlarged local home security forces were yielding results. Despite these more positive developments, there was a mood of trepidation across the world. Everyone knew this horrendous affair was not yet over, and that further attacks were a possibility. Much of the intelligence that had been reviewed at the Grange, and then swiftly passed to the government, was still highly secret. The government had set up a media liaison office to manage the media, and it was doing a remarkable job under the circumstances. Little of the true horror and what lay behind the attacks was ever made public to avoid panic and the inevitable social chaos that would follow. It was also vital to keep much of the intelligence secret in order to properly pursue and apprehend the people responsible for the attacks. There was also a global team working together to sift information, follow up leads and do the hundreds of surveillance and other activities necessary to try to bring this thing to an end. The threat of global annihilation had suddenly galvanised the international political community to temporarily put their differences to one side, in a common effort to track, arrest, and bring these people to justice. The tracking of radio transmissions and satellites orbiting the Earth had also now been started in earnest and the American, Russian, Chinese and European space agencies were all cooperating to try to isolate those satellites that may be involved in the attacks.

John sent a car for them to the British Airways Terminal Five at Heathrow and they had landed on time in the morning after an uneventful flight from Boston. Joseph had re-arranged his schedule to be at Himbledon when they arrived, and it was late morning when they arrived at the Grange. Mary greeted and welcomed them both and buzzed downstairs to Mark and Joseph to tell them they had arrived.

Mark was working on his computer and Joseph was next door in another smaller meeting room looking through some business presentations when Mark put his head around the door and said, “Portia and Francesca are here, Joseph.”

Joseph looked up and Mark could see the excitement in his face and he clicked the presentation closed and walked across the room to walk upstairs with Mark.

They heard voices in the kitchen as they entered the passage at the top of the stars and Mark walked first into the kitchen. The three ladies were standing talking and Mary was offering to take their coats and Francesca had her back to the door and Joseph's eyes immediately fell on her tall gracious body and black hair over her shoulders. Portia was the first to turn and smile at Mark, and they greeted each other as Francesca turned. Mark extended his hand to her, but Francesca simply stepped forward and gently kissed Mark on the cheek. Joseph was then suddenly standing in front of Francesca, he looked closely at her face and could see where she had been injured and one of her eyes was still slightly swollen. She was exquisite, he thought, and Joseph was suddenly oblivious to the others in the room, and it was as though time was standing still as Francesca stepped forward and leant up to kiss Joseph on the cheek. They exchanged no words; they just looked at each other as though wishing to drink each other into themselves.

Everyone in the room noticed this invisible magnetism that there was between the two of them, the lingering nature of their greeting and the way they could not take their eyes off each other.

It was Portia who first sensed the slight air of awkwardness that existed in the room and said, "Hello Joseph, it is good to see you again," reaching forward to greet him with a kiss. Then the tension quickly subsided and Mary offered them some refreshment and asked Mark and Joseph to take their bags up to their rooms. They were to stay in the large suite that Thomas usually used when at Himbledon, and Portia had discreetly asked Mary on the phone from Boston a few days earlier if she and Francesca could possibly share a bedroom because her daughter was still very restless at night. Mark and Joseph had been told by Mary that Portia planned to be at Himbledon for four nights before continuing their onward journey to Rome although no reason for their detour via the Grange was ever mentioned apart from Portia wishing to discuss some matters with John.

It was raining outside with low grey clouds yet Joseph felt a sense of happiness that he had rarely experienced before. After taking their coats Mary served lemon tea, ordinary tea and coffee and produced some snacks as they all sat around the kitchen table talking. They discussed Thomas and Liska, how wonderful Liska's performance had been at the Wang, the excellent medical care in Boston and Mark and Francesca had chatted about the medical mobile phone trials, MIT and how medicine and technology were moving closer every day. Joseph felt rather like a little schoolboy and he noticed how Francesca continued to glance his way and look at him. Portia was just as Joseph had remembered her from the board meeting in London earlier in the year, very beautiful, poised and fashionably attired. After a while Mary suggested that Portia and Francesca have a rest and that some afternoon tea would be brought up to their room a little later. Mary confirmed that John would be home later in the afternoon and they would all have dinner together at seven. It was Mark who said, as they all began to get up from the table, that they should relax at Himbledon and rest, and that if there was anything they needed just to ask. Mary looked across at Mark and then smiled at Joseph as Mark assumed the role of butler and courteously showed them both to their room.

Once back in the kitchen, Mark sat down at the table and, glancing at Joseph and his mother, said, "What a pair of beautiful ladies. Francesca is even more beautiful now than when I first met her a while ago, and she seems to be coping with this whole rape thing very well."

Mary looked at her sons and immediately replied, "Do not be so sure of that Mark, rape is a terrible act of violence against a woman and I think Francesca is putting a very brave face on things. So you two, just be gentle and sensitive, please, to them both while they are here."

Both young men nodded and were silent before Mary asked whether they did not have more important business to attend to rather than moping in the kitchen. Then, rather like putting on a light switch, Joseph and Mark stopped daydreaming, stood up, thought for a moment, then strode off toward the stairs down to the meeting rooms.

As they disappeared, Mary smiled to herself, and thought, *some things never change*.

As hard as he tried, the rest of the business presentation did not enjoy Joseph's full attention. His mind kept darting off to Francesca, now probably lying down two storeys above him right now. The person who had preoccupied many of his idle moments of thought for the last several weeks was actually here, in person, so nearby. What's more, the actual person was more beautiful and attractive to him than his mind had ever been able to imagine. Francesca was also responding to Joseph in an entirely different way to when they had met in Dubai. In the kitchen earlier he had sensed in her, a need she felt for him. As he sat back in his chair by the small conference table trying to digest business statistics, critical performance indictors and trends, his mind was simply becoming unavailable to all this boring material. But then, he thought, he had to be sensible and careful with Francesca, since she had been through so much recently; her needs had to come first. As he gave up on doing any more useful work and closed the computer, he also felt somewhat bewildered about Francesca, his feelings for her and the affect she is having on him; and, his special relationship with Louise.

He leant around the door and said to Mark, "If it has stopped raining, I am going for a run; see you later, Mark."

Mark replied, "Okay, Joe, see you at supper."

It was the next day after breakfast that Joseph and Francesca had the first opportunity to be on their own. It was a dry day, and Joseph had suggested a short walk together and, despite a concerned look from Portia, Francesca readily agreed. Mary had quickly gone to get an extra coat to put around her shoulders before Francesca and Joseph walked from the Grange down through the garden to the lake. Although it was dry and bright, there was a chill in the air, but they both felt relaxed at being on their own away from the scrutiny of family. At first, they just walked together, saying little; Joseph just wanted to be close and to know that she was warm and comfortable, and Francesca just wanted to be with Joseph on his own for a while.

When they reached the boathouse and a nearby seat, Joseph asked her if she would like to sit for a little while, and she smiled and said yes.

After a few moments Joseph looked at her and said, "I am so pleased you are okay Francesca, I have been desperately worried about you." Francesca looked into his face and there were tears in her eyes.

She had less make up than the previous day and the healing injuries on her face were still evident as she wiped the tears away. She looked at Joseph and smiled a little before saying, "I was wrong to have done what I did, to mislead him, and I do not blame him for what happened. He will be murdered you know, it is only a matter of time." She turned and looked out over the lake.

Joseph did not respond immediately, but just leant slowly toward her and reached for one of her hands that were together in her lap.

As he held her hand he turned to her and said, "What you did was very brave and necessary. The information you obtained from him has focussed the world's security agencies to now start looking in the right place to try to stop all this madness. It was the only lead there was and you managed to obtain critically important information that may very well save millions of lives. You must not blame yourself at all for what happened... you must stop thinking this way," and there was a pause.

She replied, "If only it were that simple Joseph, I keep seeing his face and the rage that I caused in him because of my deception. He had come to trust me and I betrayed him. It all seemed so logical and the right thing to do when I started after returning from Rome. But you know Joseph, to deceive someone in the way I did, is a terrible thing to do."

Joseph noticed, now that they were together without any pretensions in front of others, that Francesca was different from when he met her in Dubai, the sparkle had somehow gone. Apart from the terrible trauma she had experienced and the injuries, there was something else; something was missing. She appeared bruised deep inside; something had been taken from her and had been replaced with a dreadful guilt and self-doubt. As he held her hand Joseph noticed that Francesca did not respond, her hand was lifeless in his. Again, he appealed to her not to blame herself, but to see her behaviour as an act of heroism, and said that she must just rest and get strong again.

Francesca moved on the seat and turned her whole body

toward Joseph and said, "I persuaded my mother that we should come here for a few days before returning directly to Rome because I wanted to see you again Joseph, to see if my experience of you in Dubai was real or whether I had imagined it."

Joseph was confused by her remark and just looked at her as she continued. "Thoughts of you, Joseph, have never been far from my mind since Dubai, and my memories of Tim, you and our service, were what gave me the strength to do what I did after getting back to Boston. After I was raped my whole world became confused and I just had to see you again, I cannot really explain it." Francesca looked into Joseph's eyes, watching him intently, studying his reaction.

He did not know what to say, apart from how happy he was to be with her again and that she too had been constantly in his thoughts and that he was never comfortable with the risk that she had taken with the impostor John Holmes. It was after he had said this, that Francesca gripped his hand and then moved her other hand to place both her hands in his.

Francesca gave a little shiver and Joseph suggested that they make their way back to the warmth of the Grange. As they stood up Francesca straightened her back, raised her head and stood for a moment, with her hands together in front of her below her waist looking out over the lake.

Her black hair glistened and her beautiful facial profile and upright body almost took Joseph's breath away and he said without thinking, "Francesca, you are so beautiful."

She turned suddenly toward him and blushed slightly and reached for his hand and replied, "And you Joseph, are so handsome."

They burst out laughing. They continued to hold hands and talked about how glorious the countryside looked as they began to walk back to the house.

They were halfway up through the garden when Francesca stopped and pulled Joseph to a halt with his arm and, turning to him, said, "I am pleased we have come here Joseph, you know that was the first time I have laughed for weeks." They both smiled at each other.

Francesca then moved away from Joseph, and gently

removed her hand from his and, although they were standing near each other, Joseph suddenly felt that Francesca had put a barrier between them, as though she did not want to continue their closeness, but rather withdraw into herself. Joseph put his hands together behind his back and measured his step to walk next to her, so near yet so far he thought as they neared the house.

It was late in the afternoon when they were together again in the lounge at the house after Francesca had rested and Joseph had completed more business papers and briefing documents. They were having tea with Mary and Portia with a warm fire burning in the large grate and Francesca was smiling at her mother and Mary, sharing memories of when they were first married and the children were small. The visit to Himbledon was also proving to be good for Portia, a place where she could relax and feel secure with old friends who had been close to her for so many years. Just then John came in and poured himself a cup of tea and sat next to Portia on the long settee and reminded Mary that he would be going to Oxford the following day and suggested they all have a late supper together once he, Louise and Joseph had returned. Portia and Francesca nodded and smiled and Mary said that she would prepare some pasta dishes and that perhaps Portia could add some authentic flair to the meal. Francesca and Joseph glanced at each other and Joseph noticed a sudden change in Francesca, she had looked away slightly, withdrawn into her thoughts, and something appeared to be troubling her.

Joseph had a brainwave and asked, "How would you like to see our underground canals, Francesca?"

Portia said, "You must go and see them Fran, they are fascinating." She had attended meetings at the Grange and knew the rooms below quite well.

Mark was away in Cambridge and everything was in darkness as Joseph switched the various lights on and they descended the stairs. Francesca was amazed at what lay beneath the Grange and Joseph reached out for her hand several times to help her along the walkways beside the canal.

"It is so beautiful and unexpected," Francesca said as Joseph showed her into the large meeting room with the screens, computers and other equipment.

They then sat by the large table and Joseph looked at Francesca and asked, "You don't think, Francesca, that the awful rape you suffered would make me feel any differently about you, do you?"

Francesca looked away from him and was silent for a moment before answering, "It would not surprise me if it had Joseph, many men find such things off putting. It has even made me doubt myself, doubt my feelings and whether I am worthy of another's love."

He immediately felt her vulnerability and sensed a mood of shame at what had happened and he wanted to reach out to her, to make it all better and to hold her. However, she was resisting what she knew instinctively he was trying to give her, because she could not forgive herself; she could not escape this terrible feeling of darkness that had enveloped her since that dreadful night in Boston.

Francesca straightened her back and, looking directly at Joseph, said, "I also do not want to cause you any difficulty with Louise, Joseph. I know what you are struggling with in your relationship with her, and it is not fair of me to add to these problems."

Again, Joseph was surprised by Francesca's forthright and perceptive statement and he replied, "I want you to meet Louise and for her to meet you, I have been praying about my relationship with Louise and that we can remain very special friends, that she will continue to come to Himbledon and be close with the family despite me not loving her the way she loves me. I wish it was different, but it simply is not, and there is absolutely nothing I can do about it. It is such a difficult situation yet, through nothing I have done, it seems to be gradually resolving itself. But you know Francesca, I will always care for Louise, probably more like a sister than a lover, and I believe Louise is gradually coming to accept this."

There was a pause as Francesca looked at Joseph and he looked at his hands on the table.

She smiled a little and said, "I hope you are right Joseph and it is good that you have put it in His hands. But for the moment Joseph you need to be thinking about Louise, not me and my needs. I would never wish to come between you both in any way."

"I do not agree, Francesca. You are also very special to me, and you have not come between Louise and me; if you had never existed, there would still be this situation between Louise and myself. But I must avoid hurting Louise any more than I already have. But if you can both meet and get to know each other a little, that can only surely help the situation, can't it?" Joseph asked in an almost imploring manner.

"Perhaps, Joseph, Let us see and I am looking forward very much to meeting her when you all return from Oxford tomorrow," she replied.

Francesca stood up and walked to the large window overlooking the canal and watched the water gently flowing by and her face was reflected in the glass, as Joseph remained seated. She had placed her long arms on either side of her body resting her hands on the window sill, and Joseph was struck again by her grace and overwhelming beauty.

He sat up in his chair and leant on the table and asked, "When did you last have the Eucharist, Francesca?"

Francesca turned to face him with a startled look in her eyes. "Why do you ask, Joseph?" she asked.

"How long, Francesca?"

There was a pause and she turned away and looked through the window again. After a few moments Joseph could see she was crying and he walked over to comfort her and put his arms around her and she stood gently sobbing.

"I did not mean to upset you," he said gently.

She looked up at him and said, "No, that is all right Joseph, it has been many weeks since I had communion. Not since I returned from Rome to Boston and at the moment I cannot even bring myself to think about Confession. I feel this terrible barrier between me and God at the moment and it frightens me."

At that moment Joseph's empathy with Francesca gave him a sudden insight into her awful state of mind, she felt she was to blame for the rape, that she had betrayed her rapist and was to blame for his possible murder and she felt deep shame.

Not being in a state of grace she could not have communion, yet her intense feeling of personal guilt was blocking her from her deeply held belief system and trust in God. She had condemned herself and was allowing herself to be enslaved by these feelings and thoughts, and was trapped in this horrendously dark place.

Joseph released her from his embrace and holding her gently by the shoulders he looked into her face and said, "Francesca you must stop this, you must go to confession and to the Eucharist, God has already forgiven you but you must now go and experience his forgiveness in the only way we know how. Please Francesca, stop torturing yourself like this. This is madness; please listen to me, you more than most people will know what I am telling you is the truth, and that unless you can forgive yourself through the mercy of God, this could destroy you emotionally. Stop trying to deal with this thing yourself, you are not able to, none of us would be able to. Promise me you will go to confession and the Eucharist soon."

Francesca stopped crying and wiped the tears from her face and looked calm as she smiled at Joseph. "Yes you are right Joseph, I know what I must do. Please do not worry, I will attend to it when I return to Rome."

* * *

THE NEXT DAY, IT WAS RAINING AGAIN, AND MARY took Portia and Francesca shopping after breakfast. She had laid the table with a light early lunch for John and Joseph, who were leaving at one o'clock when Freddie was due to pick them up in the large Range Rover and drive them to Oxford. They had departed from the Grange in good time and had picked up Louise, as arranged and had arrived at John's college. It was almost four o'clock when Mary, Portia and Francesca arrived back at the Grange having enjoyed lunch in the local village after completing their shopping earlier. Mark was still busy downstairs with some of his academic work and the ladies had retired to their rooms for a rest as the afternoon light gradually faded to dusk. It was now almost dark as Mark emerged into the kitchen to get some tea before going for a shower since he was meeting Charlotte in the village for a drink a little later.

The phone rang and Mark lifted the receiver and said, "Hello Himbledon Grange." He instantly recognised Charlie's voice on the other end.

"Is that Mark?" Charlie enquired.

Mark replied, "Yes, how are you, Chief Superintendent?"

Charlie continued, "Listen Mark, there has been a bad incident in Oxford, happened a little while ago... your father and Joseph have been shot. I am so pleased you answered rather than Mary. I think you must come immediately and I am sending a car to the Grange, it will be there in about twenty minutes. I just got this terrible news from our operations room. Sorry to have to ask you this, but will you please tell Mary? I will see you shortly, goodbye."

Mark slowly put the receiver down and stood frozen for a few moments before the adrenalin started to work through his body.

In just a few short minutes he had told Mary, phoned Charlotte and told her and asked her to come immediately to the house. Portia and Francesca insisted that they wished to go to Oxford as well and within half an hour two cars were travelling quickly away from the Grange toward Oxford. In the lead was Charlie in his large, official police car with his driver, himself in the front and Mary, Portia and Francesca in the back. They were followed by Charlotte driving her Land Rover with Mark beside her and Ann Hardwick in the backseat with Paul her son. Charlie was taking them to the medical trauma unit of the Oxford Infirmary where he had been advised over the radio that the victims had been taken for emergency surgery. As the police information was coming over the radio, they learnt that John, Joseph, Louise and Freddie had all been shot and were being treated at the hospital. Mary, who was listening intently to the radio messages, knew instinctively that the situation was very grave, and then she thought about Louise being injured, and asked Charlie if he could possibly get a message to her parents in Aberystwyth and, after some exchange of some details,

Charlie asked someone in the police control centre to deal with it. It was nine o'clock when they arrived at the trauma unit. No one could tell them anything except that there were emergency operations under way and could they please wait and would be advised immediately there was something to report. There were armed police at the medical centre and Charlie went and spoke to them.

Bystanders had thought that they were making a film when the shooting and mayhem had started. As Freddie pulled up outside the entrance to the college and John had got out of the rear near side seat of the Range Rover and waited momentarily on the pavement for Joseph and Louise to join him, he noticed John stumble and fall forward. He then felt an intense pain in his right shoulder, and heard a bang as something had smashed the side window of the vehicle. Joseph with Louise immediately behind him were now clear of the Land Rover, and as Joseph rushed forward to help his father he was hit in the left shoulder and Louise saw the bullet explode in his back and without thinking, had thrown herself forward to protect Joseph. Another bullet tore into her body just below her waist and another ripped through her upper body to the left of her neck and exited and continued into Joseph who now lay beneath her. It was all happening so fast yet to Freddie it was all happening so slowly.

The single thought in Freddie's mind was to stop the enemy fire as he grabbed the shotgun from under his seat. As he ducked down, opened his door, and swiftly swung out of the Range Rover, he was hit again in the upper back, but his bulletproof vest had protected him, although he was momentarily winded by the impact of the bullet. By now, he knew where the fire was coming from and he ran across the road, weaving from side to side and crashed against the door of the tea room, that burst open, and he rolled onto the floor and instantly spotted a smallish man with a handgun. Freddie fired the shotgun and he saw the man lurch back and down onto the floor. Then crouching low Freddie moved swiftly through between the tables and saw three young ladies bound and gagged lying behind the counter and one of them signalled with her eyes upstairs. Freddie's right shoulder was bleeding badly although he still had feeling in his right arm and with his left hand he removed the handgun from his body holster.

He walked up the narrow old stairs to the room above and the door at the head of the stairs was slightly ajar. As he neared the top step crouching low there were shots and he felt a pain in the side of his neck where another bullet had entered his body just above the top of his protective vest. He raised the shotgun again and slowly nudged the door open and could see a man at the far end of the room and a rifle on a small tripod standing on the ledge of the bay window. Then he could see the legs of another man closer to him. Without hesitating he leant upwards a little, pointed the shotgun and fired sending the farthest man sprawling against the far wall. With the handgun in his left hand, he pointed at the other man, who had now turned with a rifle in his hands, and, as he was almost facing Freddie, a shot rang out from Freddie's handgun, and he hit the man in the stomach. The wounded man reeled on the floor and reached out for the rifle as Freddie, who was now bleeding profusely and beginning to feel faint, dropped his handgun and managed to cock the shotgun once more. They both got to their respective triggers almost instantaneously and there were more shots, Freddie discharged his shotgun into the man at short range and a shot from the rifle hit Freddie in the head. They both lay dead, Freddie sprawled across the top step of the stairs with his blood dripping down the steps and the man with the rifle lying like a rag doll, jack knifed into one of the Tudor bay windows of the quaint tea shop. The whole blood bath had taken just a few short minutes, but it was now over; the three assassins lay dead.

The three Japanese men had taken over the teashop just a little while before Freddie had pulled up outside the college. They had subdued the three lady waitresses, tied them up and gagged them and, turning the little wooden sign hanging on the leaded glass door to 'closed', had pushed the single old bolt on the door shut. The two snipers had gone upstairs, set up their deadly equipment and the old Tudor bay windows with curtains had been ideal resting places for their weapons. They had then waited calmly to commit cold-blooded murder from a distance. The passage of the large black Range Rover had been skilfully tracked after it left the Grange and the assassins had been notified just a few minutes before the unsuspecting victims had arrived, to get ready. In the mayhem a stray bullet from the assassins had wounded a young woman on a bus, but it was a superficial wound. The police and paramedics had arrived on the scene quickly once the college gatekeeper had notified them. The whole area was quickly secured and sealed off as a murder incident area and the road closed. Just a few minutes later the forensic team arrived to start their painstaking work, marking the sites of bullet cartridges, taking measurements and photographs. The current number of firearm incidents in England has increased in recent years with over five thousand injuries and five hundreds deaths each year.

Many paramedics have received specialist training to deal with such cases and when they advise the trauma unit that they have an estimated time – ETA– of arrival of around ten minutes it means they have the life of the victim more or less under control. However, when they report an ETA of two minutes it means things are desperate with the patient and pandemonium breaks out in the awaiting hospital trauma unit as a trauma team of about fifteen medics assemble and prepare to work on the victim. The problem with bullet wounds is that a single victim may need head, heart, bowel and orthopaedic surgery because bullets cause multiple internal injuries. The first hour after admission is always the most critical in saving victims lives – when typically all the life saving measures are carried out to stabilise the person before more lengthy surgical procedures that often take several hours. The paramedics had declared John and Freddie dead at the scene, and had worked feverishly to save the lives of Joseph and Louise, who were bleeding profusely and had sustained several life-threatening wounds. They had both been rushed to the trauma unit, where two large teams of medical staff, many of whom had been called in especially, were operating on them. The three assassins were also declared dead at the scene, and it was just as Charlie, Mary and the others were arriving at the trauma unit that the bodies of the dead were carefully removed from the death scene.

It was just before ten when Charlie Harris came to Mark

and Mary and asked them to accompany him to a small lounge in the hospital. Mary knew in Charlie's manner that he had some dreadful news for them and when he told them that John was dead; Mary just sat silent with her hands in her lap. Mark went and sat next to his mother and put his arm around her and they just sat silently and the tears were running down Mary's cheeks. Mark asked Charlie about Freddie, Joseph and Louise and Charlie said Freddie had also died defending them and that Joseph and Louise who had also been hit, were still in surgery and the situation was very grave. A few minutes later Ann Hardwick, Freddie's wife joined them with Paul her son and Mary rose to her feet and put her arms around Ann and they both sobbed quietly and Mark put his arm around Paul's shoulder. Just then a nursing sister came in with a small tray and offered Mary and Ann a light sedative that they both took with a sip of water from the small glasses on the tray. The nurse then looked at Mark and Paul and they shook their heads.

In the main lounge area Portia was sitting at the end of a long seat silently praying and Francesca was dozing fitfully with her head on her mother's lap. Charlotte was sitting and then standing up and walking around and in all the fuss Mark had forgotten that she had not been told of the death of her father. He walked quickly to the lounge and asked Charlotte, Portia and Francesca to join them in the quieter smaller lounge. When Mark told Charlotte of the death of John and her father she walked to her mother and Mary who were still in each other's arms and put her arms around them both. She did not cry, she felt she had to help others, and held her tears back while she comforted the two older women. Francesca asked Mark quietly how Joseph and Louise were and after he told her; she walked to a chair and sat down with her head in her hands. Portia just sat on her own praying and looking at Mary.

It was a little while later that Thomas and Liska arrived, and Mark shared with them the details of what had happened earlier. It was nearly mid night when a doctor came into the room and said that they had finished operating on Joseph, they had removed a bullet and that he was now in intensive care and that the other team were still working on Louise. He suggested that there was nothing they could do now at the hospital and should perhaps book into the hotel opposite the hospital and try to get some sleep. Mark and Thomas went across the road and organised several rooms to cater for everyone and they all moved to the hotel. No one slept much that night, and before it was light the next morning Mary was the first to be up and dressed, and she walked across to the hospital to get news of Joseph and Louise. To her relief, although they were both still dangerously wounded with damage to various internal organs and bones, they were still alive. Mary was told that it was now just a matter of waiting and that the hospital would have further news about them by midday.

The next two days proved to be an agonising wait and there were several times when hospital doctors almost lost them both. Mary had asked to see John, and Charlie suggested there was no need, conscious of the appalling head wounds he had suffered. Mark also persuaded her not to go to the mortuary and that he would attend to the identification and Charlotte had volunteered to identify her father. There had been a rather frosty meeting between Mark and Louise's parents, particularly her mother who implied that she had wished her daughter had never got involved with Joseph, and this would never have happened. Louise father was more sympathetic and had been very gracious when he met Mary and Ann and had thanked Ann for her husband's bravery in defending Louise and Joseph in the way he had. Mary had felt deeply for them with Louise lying near death across the road in the ICU, and he had been moved by her compassion toward them both and her deep concern for Louise who she spoke about almost as a mother would do about her own daughter.

31

Life and Death in Oxford

THIS ATTACK AND THE NATURE OF THE THREE PEOPLE who had carried it out now confirmed in Mark's mind precisely who it was behind these cold-blooded murders and the other mayhem around the world. It must have been Judaire and Adler and the three assassins could well have been members of his private bodyguard. It was later the following day after the shooting that the prime minister's secretary phoned Mark on his mobile phone and a few moments later he was speaking directly with the PM, who conveyed his deepest condolences on the death of his father and asked that the family request any assistance that they may require. He did not speak for long, but said that he would be in touch again with Mark regarding the security situation.

The arrival of Thomas the previous evening had been a tremendous support to Mary and he had remained near her since arriving apart from when she went to the hospital at daybreak. It was late morning when Ruth and Paul arrived from London and there were several huddled meetings in the hotel and the waiting room of the hospital. It was just after mid day that Mary spoke to the same doctor she had seen just after daybreak. He said that Joseph was stable although the young lady was continuing to give them concern and they were both in ICU and that if Mary wished to see Joseph she could do so, but only immediate family members were allowed to see them and she should not stay long.

Mary went with Mark immediately to see Joseph and he

was lying on his back with tubes protruding from all over his body, machines surrounding his bed and a heart monitor that blipped quietly nearby. Mary felt her legs weaken when she first saw her son and Mark had steadied her for a moment before she just stood at the foot of Joseph's bed looking at him and silently praying. Mark walked over to the side of Joseph and calmly spoke to him even though he was unconscious and carefully held his hand for a moment without disturbing the tubes in his arm. Looking across to the heart monitor Mark watched for a moment the consistent pulsing on the electronic display monitor and the low bleeping sound and took some comfort in the regularity of Joseph's heart beat. As they stood there a nurse came and smiled at them and changed one of the plastic bags hanging on a tripod next to the bed and reinserted the small pipe connected to Joseph's arm and adjusted a small valve, smiled again and moved away.

As they turned to leave ICU, Mary looked over to see where Louise was and could only see two other patients on the far side of the unit. Mary walked to the control centre of the unit where there were a number of nurses and a doctor was standing looking at various charts. Mary enquired about Louise, and the doctor came around the desk and said that she had been taken back to theatre because there had been internal bleeding, but he could tell her no more for the moment. Mary's heart sank; it was hot in the ICU, and she felt faint and exhausted after not sleeping the night before. She looked around quickly for a chair and one of the nurses seeing her condition immediately came and helped her to a chair by the desk, and then fetched a glass of water. Mark then came and suggested they go back to the hotel and that he would stay in touch with the ward and inform his mother immediately if there was any change. Mary knew there was nothing more she could do at the hospital and agreed and returned to her room at the hotel with Mark who had been given a sedative by one of the ICU nurses that he gave to his mother before she laid down to try to get some sleep.

After breakfast the following day, Thomas had spoken with Charlie Harris who came to the hotel after talking with the local police. Charlie emphasised to Thomas that the whole family are now at great risk and that he had instituted armed protection for them at Himbledon and both Joseph and Louise would be under police armed protection at the hospital. He also said that to have the whole of the Trimbledon family here in Oxford together in one place was also a major security risk and he suggested that only the immediate family remain in the town until Joseph and Louise are out of danger. He also said that Joseph was very fortunate to be alive; had Louise not thrown herself over him, and had Freddie not shot the three assailants when he had, then Joseph would also be dead today. They had clearly been after John and Joseph and they were professional killers judging from their *modus operandi*. They probably know Joseph is still alive and they are likely to send further assassins to finish the job. Charlie suggested to Thomas that he and Mark have a discussion with everyone and suggest that apart from Mark, his mother and Louise's parents that everyone else should go back to the Grange and that he would ensure the immediate family also have police protection while they remain in Oxford.

It was an hour later after a discussion with everyone in a small lounge next to the hotel lobby that these arrangements were agreed. Charlotte offered to take Portia, Francesca, and Ann and Paul Hardwick back to Himbledon, and Thomas said he would take Liska, Paul and Ruth. Thomas and Ruth also spoke with Mark and offered to start attending to things back at the Grange since there will be inevitable media attention and they needed to have a member of the family there to handle telephone calls and other matters. As everyone was getting ready to go to their rooms to get the few possessions they had brought with them in the rush on the day of the shooting, Francesca spoke to her mother quietly.

Mark looked across at them both and could see that Portia was not happy with what was being discussed before Francesca walked over to him and said, "Mark, I am staying here in Oxford, I will not get in the way or be a nuisance, but I want to stay please."

Mark looked at Portia, who shrugged and indicated that Francesca had made her mind up and there was little she could do about it.

"All right, Francesca. But you must also rest here at the hotel and I will let you know immediately there is any change. Why don't you go up and join Mother? I am sure she could do with the company, if she is not sleeping," Mark said to her.

Francesca smiled, thanked him and said she would go to Mary's room once everyone had left.

Mark spoke to Louise's parents and asked if there was anything they needed and they agreed to keep exchanging information as they received it in the hours ahead.

It was only the next day when Mary and Mark went to visit Joseph that he had regained some consciousness, although he was still very weak and had been sedated to reduce his restlessness. Mary had sat with him on one side of the bed and Mark on the other, and for a brief moment Joseph had opened his eyes and looked at his mother before dozing again. Louise was also stable now, although the internal haemorrhaging continued to give the doctors concern for her survival. Mary and Mark had prayed by her bed and Mark had been shocked by her appearance and had spoken to the doctor about her. He had been told that she had lost a lot of blood and that they had given her large blood transfusions and if they could be sure that the internal bleeding had stopped she had a good chance of pulling through, but the next few days were still critical. Louise had not regained consciousness since being brought to the hospital, but her heart and vital organs were functioning, which was encouraging. They were both receiving large doses of antibiotics via the intravenous drips to try to manage infections, since gun shot wounds also invade the body with germs from the bullets and the lead. The doctor had also told Mark that they had removed a bullet from Louise's lower body where there had been major damage, ruptures and bleeding. Thankfully, the bullet had missed her lower vertebrae although it had damaged her pelvis and certain organs in her pelvic area.

As Mary and Mark left the ward they passed an armed policeman sitting outside and then across the road in the hotel as they made their way to Mary's bedroom, there in the corridor was another armed policeman. Francesca was sitting in the bedroom reading when they both entered and she was eager to know the latest news. She was relieved to learn that Joseph had regained consciousness and from Mark's answers, with her medical training, was able to quickly make her own assessment of his condition. Francesca then asked about Louise and was alarmed at what Mark told her although she concealed her thoughts not to further upset Mary. Mark phoned the Grange and updated Ruth with the latest news. She told him not to be surprised when he gets back to the Grange, with the armed police and media at the main gate. Mark asked Ruth to please phone Charlie to see if anything could be done to get the media to respect the family's privacy at this time and Ruth told him that Thomas was already dealing with this matter.

Then Ruth asked, "Mark will you find out when they will release Father's and Freddie's bodies? We need to get them back to Himbledon and start making arrangements for the funeral. Things are like a madhouse here; the phone never stops ringing, and these reporters at the gate are a nuisance. Thomas found a man with a camera by the kitchen door yesterday and I think had I not intervened just in time, the poor man would have been hospitalised. Thomas was furious."

It had been good for Mary that Francesca had remained behind in Oxford and she had slept in Mary's room, and apart from when Mary went to the hospital, had been her constant companion. The days just passed and there was little relevance of what day or month it might be. Their minds were constantly preoccupied with the two gravely injured loved ones across the road. Mary prayed and the local priest had popped in regularly to see and sit with her during this anguished time. Luke who had now arrived at the Grange from Rome also had spoken with Mary and asked if he should come to Oxford and she had suggested that it would be better if he remained at the house and helped Thomas and Ruth. Mark had enquired with Charlie about the return of the bodies of his father and Freddie and it had been confirmed that the authorities would be able to release them shortly, once they had completed the necessary procedures.

Outside the hotel and hospital the life of Oxford continued with the bustle of shoppers, traffic in the streets and undergraduates cycling around the town. The street where the attack took place was now open although some of the police markings on the tar were still visible and the attack that had been the talk of town was now gradually abating as other matters took peoples attention and interest. Little did local people know the life and death struggle that was continuing in the hospital with Louise's life still hanging by a thread.

There had been several occasions when Louise's parents had visited her when Mary and Mark were also at the ward. They had interchanged with Louise's mother and father sitting by Joseph's bed for several minutes just staring at this unknown young man who meant so much to their daughter. Mark had comforted her father and had chatted to him in the hospital waiting area about varsity life, law and mathematics. Mary and Louise's mother had also talked and any barriers between them had quickly fallen away as they tried to help each other to deal with this agonising motherly anxiety they both felt. They had all had breakfast together, and one morning Louise's mother wondered who the beautiful young Italian lady sitting next to Mary was. Mary quickly realised that they had never met and promptly introduced them. Louise's father had talked with Francesca about her work at MIT and Rome and she had gently enquired about his daughter and their life together in Wales before she went up to Oxford. Everyone was desperately trying to retain some degree or normality whilst battling with their own personal fears and anxieties about Joseph and Louise.

It was the next day after returning from the hospital that Mary said that it would be all right for Francesca to visit Joseph and she had visibly brightened at the suggestion. The ICU staff did not like more than two visitors being with any patient at a time and actually preferred no visitors since they often got in the way of their vital nursing duties. Mark had visited earlier with Mary, and Louise's parents had also spent some time next to the bed of their daughter, who was still unconscious but stable, at least again today. When Mary and Francesca arrived at the unit, Joseph was sleeping, and Mary took Francesca to where he was lying, and then excused herself to go to the hospital shop, but also to leave them alone.

Francesca just stood at the foot of the bed feeling a physical numbness yet her mind was in two places. Her medical brain was looking at the equipment, the various monitors and the inert body of Joseph in the bed. She was able to quickly assess the medical and physical things that lay before her and she could quickly see that he had been very seriously injured and was not yet out of danger. However, it was the other thoughts and feelings that began to flow through her that were more troubling; she just wanted to hold him, to lift him up out of the bed to full life again, to heal him and let him fly off like a dove released from the hand to live and be happy again. Francesca straightened her back and placed her hands together in front of her and closed her eyes and prayed and asked God to spare him. As she stood there a nearby nurse saw her, such an elegant and beautiful woman standing calmly amidst all this hurt, machines and medical urgency and she wondered if Francesca was all right. "Are you all right Miss?" the nurse enquired gently touching the woollen sleeve of her long dark coat. Francesca opened her eyes and looked at the nurse and smiled and said, "Yes, thank you," and the nurse could see tears in her eyes.

Francesca then walked to the side of the bed and removed her coat and placed it on a nearby chair.

She pulled up another chair and sat next to Joseph and gently took his hand in hers and spoke softly to him. "Hello Joseph, what is happening to the two of us?"

Joseph could smell her perfume and, although drowsy, opened his eyes and smiled slightly at her.

"Don't talk Joseph, just rest and get strong again. Let me just sit with you for a little while," Francesca said, looking into his face.

Joseph squeezed her hand.

"What happened? Why am I like this in hospital?" He focussed his eyes on her.

Francesca thought for a moment, and then, leaning toward him, replied, "You have been shot, Joseph, and the doctors say you are going to be all right, but must rest. I am going to stay in Oxford until we can walk out of this hospital together, arm in arm." She smiled at him.

Joseph asked about his father, Louise and Freddie and Francesca forced a smile again and after a brief pause answered, "Louise was also injured, but is getting better, and they are very pleased with your recovery." She could not bring herself to tell Joseph in his condition that his father and Freddie were dead, and she was relieved as she noticed him lapsing back to sleep.

Whatever they are giving him to keep him calm, it must be strong medication being regularly administered, she thought, as she released his hand. She sat for a moment, and then got up and walked over to the area where Louise was being treated. She was inside a small inner room with large glass windows and there was a nurse sitting beside her. Francesca could see her golden blonde hair on the pillow, and her long body lying semi covered just with a light sheet. Even in these dreadful circumstances Francesca could see what a beautiful looking woman Louise is, with her strong face and Scandinavian features. Again Francesca stood erect with her hands in front of her and prayed for Louise that she too will be spared and she asked that God please intervene to help the doctors and nurses make her well again.

Francesca turned and walked to the central ICU station and a young doctor seeing her approach immediately put down the clipboard in his hand and smiled at her. Within seconds of starting to talk together the junior house doctor immediately sensed he was talking to another doctor from the unexpected questions this lady was asking him. Francesca was interested in two things, when did they anticipate rousing Joseph to full consciousness, withdrawing the sedative and getting him onto his feet; and, had they isolated and secured the internal bleeding with Louise. Without ever thinking to ask who this attractive lady was, the doctor provided Francesca with the information she had requested. They would probably rouse Joseph early the next day, and they were satisfied that they had isolated all the internal bleeds with Louise, but were still concerned about the head injury she had sustained when she was thrown onto the pavement over Joseph after being hit in the back. Francesca then asked a series of further questions about Louise's head injuries and when she had the necessary answers, smiled at the young doctor, thanked him and started to walk to the door, pausing a moment by Joseph's bed to see him sleeping.

Ruth had insisted that Ann Hardwick move into the Grange to be with the rest of the family. Once his mother had been settled Paul Hardwick went home and explained to his wife that he had to go away for a few days, that she must not worry and that he would be in touch with her every day until his return. He had said goodbye to his young daughter and hugged his wife before walking to his father's small barn at the back of the cottages. He had taken various items from the large safe at the back of the store area and had driven back to Oxford. With the death of his father his job was now automatically to ensure the safety of Joseph and Louise who he knew were still in great danger, despite the armed police guard at the hospital. Paul was taller than Freddie and very strong and had all the skills that his father had plus his recent training and experience on the front line in Iraq and Afghanistan before he had finished his army commission the previous year. He had booked into a small hotel near the hospital, but away from the large hotel where Mary and Mark were staying, and he had thoroughly inspected the hospital, all the entrances, emergency exits and fire escapes. He had spotted a particularly vulnerable part of the hospital near the laundry and he believed if there were to be a further attack this was the most probable route they would take.

It was not the next day, but the following day, when Mary, Mark and Francesca visited the ICU after breakfast that they found Joseph and his bed had gone. The ladies were initially alarmed, until Mark found out that Joseph had been moved from ICU to another area of the hospital, since he was now out of danger and required less intensive care. He had been moved up two floors to a two-bedded room with a young gentleman who had multiple fractures after a motorcycle accident.

They quickly found the room on the third floor to discover Joseph awake and sitting up in bed with just two drips and all the other machines absent. Mary's face lighted up, and she walked quickly to stand beside the bed, and asked how he was feeling. Joseph smiled and said he felt various aches and was sore in his back, but was all right. Mary stepped forward and leant over the bed, silently and gently hugging her youngest son. They then sat around his bed and talked and Joseph just kept gazing at Francesca. It was not long before he asked about Louise, his father and Freddie and Mary, Mark and Francesca just glanced at each other knowing he still did not know about the death of his father and his beloved friend Freddie.

It was Mary who, now sitting beside the bed, reached for his hand and said, "We have some bad news, Joe. I am afraid your father and Freddie are both dead, they were shot when you and Louise were shot."

Francesca flinched inwardly at Mary's composure and honesty and stared at Joseph for his reaction.

He simply looked ahead with a dazed look on his face and looking at his mother said, "Thank you for telling me, Mother." There was then silence as Mary looked at her son who was visibly shocked by the dreadful news and smiled sadly. Mark had gone to the window and was looking out across Oxford trying to control his emotions and Francesca just stood nearby with her hands in front of her desperately trying not to burst into tears.

Joseph just blinked repeatedly as the shocking news began to penetrate his brain. He had already been through so much in recent days and since he remained lightly sedated, was unable to fully grasp at that moment the enormity of it all. Mark continued to stand with his back to Joseph knowing that if he faced him, he would lose control to the sorrow and grief he felt deep within himself. Mary, just looked at Joseph and the perplexed look on his face, and she could not stop the tears from gently running down her cheeks as she sat silently near him.

The silence hung in the air for some moments before Mary rose to her feet, quickly wiped the the tears from her eyes and said gently to Joseph, "I know your father is with Our Lord, Joseph. We must now take his body back to

Himbledon where it belongs and lay him to rest. We must also now get you and Louise well again, and get you both home to Himbledon". In just these few comforting words, Mary had helped them all to retain their self-composure and to be brave again.

They had started to get Joseph up at regular intervals and were helping him to walk a little, a little further every time. For the first day, the nurse had wheeled the tripod along beside Joseph, but then, on the second day, they simply detached the pipes from the catheters in his arm so he could move more freely. It was the second day after he had started to walk around that Francesca arrived unexpectedly and she was shocked to see the medical dressing covering the wound in his left shoulder and another lower down his back on the left hand side. He was only wearing a hospital gown that was open at the back.

After he had got back into bed Joseph said, "I would like you to meet Marvin, Francesca. He is a great card player and also rides a mean motorbike."

Francesca walked over to the young man who had a leg in plaster up to his hip and his opposite arm also in plaster. The young lad smiled, offered his left hand to Francesca and they shook hands a little awkwardly and he blushed. Francesca then walked over to Joseph as the young lad stared at her shapely lower back and she leant forward and kissed Joseph tenderly on the forehead. As she pulled a chair up to the bed she looked across and smiled again at the young man opposite and noticed his face had turned a deep crimson colour, for some reason.

Properly alone together for the first time since the shooting, Joseph and Francesca just looked at each other for a few moments and she could see tears glistening in his strong eyes. Joe reached out for her hand and Francesca now sitting close to the bed clasped his hand firmly between both her hands and looked at Joseph reassuringly and with deep sympathy in her eyes.

When he spoke, the first thing Joseph asked Francesca was how Louise was and if she would help him get down to ICU to see her. It was only after promising to go down to ICU after her visit to him, and saying she would find out about him visiting her, did Joseph resume a normal conversation with her. He told her that Louise's parents had visited him the previous evening and they were obviously concerned about Louise; that he had felt very sorry for them and he had apologised for what had happened. They spoke about when he might be discharged and he said the doctor had said not yet for a few days because they wanted him to be a lot stronger yet and also wished to keep him under observation.

Francesca had forgotten about her own injuries and mental turmoil following the rape, and this had been largely displaced with worry about Joseph. She said she had visited Louise, and that she was very beautiful, but was having a battle with her injuries since she was more badly injured than Joseph.

"I know Francesca, and do you also know that Louise saved my life by throwing herself over me? Mark told me," he said.

Francesca replied, "Yes I know. She is a very brave and courageous lady, we must do everything we can for her."

Just then the nurse came with some tea and biscuits for Joseph and his roommate and suggested to Francesca that Joseph had probably had enough excitement for one day and she stood up, kissed Joseph on the cheek and left.

As soon as they were alone Marvin called over to Joseph and asked, "Is that your girlfriend, Joe? Cor, she is a looker, eh?"

Joseph smiled, put down his cup and replied, "Not actually my girlfriend Marvin, just a very good friend. My girlfriend is down stairs in ICU very sick, I am afraid."

Marvin stared across at Joseph and replied, "Oh, I am sorry about that mate, I hope she will be okay. It's a good hospital this yer know, they will know what to do." Joseph smiled and hoped he was right.

On her way out, Francesca called into ICU and by chance met the same young house doctor she had spoken to previously and she asked about Louise. He had looked concerned after she asked him, and he told her things were not looking good; they had done all they could for her, but she was still unconscious and, although they had seen some cerebral bruising on the scan, there was nothing they could detect that required further surgery or treatment. Francesca asked about her blood pressure and a few other medical details and, from what the doctor told her, she knew that Louise was now beyond medical help, and that she appeared to be getting gradually weaker. Francesca thanked the doctor and walked back to the hotel and decided she would return to ICU after supper to check on Louise.

It was around eight o'clock when Francesca returned to ICU only to find that in the few hours she had been gone that Louise's condition had deteriorated. Being a regular visitor and herself a doctor the staff on the unit had started to treat Francesca almost as one of their own. Francesca stood outside the cubicle looking through the glass screen.

Seeing her, the young doctor came out and had a grave look on his face and was taken aback by Francesca's direct question, "Is she dying doctor?"

The doctor drew in a deep breath and raised his eyebrows in a look of consternation and said, "Tonight will be the turning point and unless things change with her condition, it does not look good I am afraid."

Francesca, looking serious, looked at the doctor and thanked him and then asked if Joseph could visit Louise and the young doctor replied, "Well yes, I do not see why not."

"Thank you, doctor. Where will we find clean masks and gowns?" she continued in a matter of fact way.

"At the desk there, doctor," the young man said using the term "doctor" without thinking.

Francesca faced with a dire situation had suddenly become her old self again, confident and professional. She quickly left the ICU and walked to the lift with her long coat swirling around her body and her high heels clicking on the hard surface of the corridor. She entered Joseph's room and he was out of bed sitting by Marvin's bed playing cards with him.

"Hello Francesca, what a lovely surprise, how good are you at gin rummy?" He asked her.

Francesca said hello to them both and then walked to the hand basin removing her coat and throwing it over the back of a chair as she did so.

She washed her hands thoroughly with the disinfectant soap from the dispenser and said to Joseph, “Get up and put my coat on, we are going to visit Louise, she needs you right now.”

Joseph was startled and Marvin just sat transfixed by this shapely woman ordering this bloke about in his hospital room. Within seconds, she had deftly removed the pipes from his arms and had the coat around him, and they were walking slowly down the corridor to the lift.

As they descended to the first floor, Francesca said to Joseph, “Louise is dying. I am afraid there is nothing else they can do for her medically; you and God are probably the only one’s now who can save her.”

Joseph was dumbfounded; firstly by what Francesca had said, but also by the way Francesca was behaving; she had fire in her eyes, and was in control, almost willing Louise to live.

On entering the ICU, the young doctor came over immediately to them with caps, gowns and masks in his hand, and Francesca helped to put them on Joseph, who was standing with bare feet on the soft sound-absorbent flooring. Francesca had her gown, cap and mask on in seconds and had wound her hair up onto her head. The doctor then led the way and quietly asked the nurse to leave for a moment and he and Francesca stood back as Joseph walked forward to see Louise for the first time since they had been shot. The doctor pushed a chair forward and Joseph grimaced with pain as he gently sat down next to the bed and Louise who had a pipe down her throat helping her to breath. Francesca could do no more for the moment and she looked over the bed to the heart monitor that had become slower and irregular.

Joseph just stared at Louise, and then leant forward, although it caused him pain in his lower back, and he spoke into Louise’s ear. The doctor could not hear what he was saying, but Francesca could.

He said, “I am here Louise, it is Joseph. I am all right and so are you.” Joseph reached for her hand that lay beside her still body and he lifted her arm and took her hand between both of his hands and again he spoke to her gently and insistently. “Don’t give up darling, you can beat this thing and we have so much to live for, please my darling we are waiting to take you back to Himbledon, all the family are rooting for you."

Francesca could not stop the tears flooding her eyes and down her cheeks and she had to make a conscious effort to get a grip on herself before she moved forward and kneeled down beside Joseph with her elbows on the bed and she prayed silently again to the Almighty to spare this young innocent women. The young doctor was visibly moved by Francesca and offered her a small piece of paper towel to wipe her tears after she had stood up. Joseph then prayed in a low voice and in a way that perhaps Louise could hear and when he raised his head Francesca stepped forward and took his arm and helped him to his feet. Joseph looked terrible, his face was white and he looked beside himself at the state of Louise and Francesca knew she had to retain control of the situation. She put an arm around Joseph and guided him toward the door of the cubicle and a nurse who had been watching what had been going on had got a wheelchair and she waited outside until Francesca and Joseph were near and Francesca leant forward and pulled the wheelchair behind Joseph so he could slowly sit down and she lifted his limp feet onto the foot rests. Francesca thanked the nurse and smiled and then turned and smiled at the doctor and mouthed the words 'thank you' to him.

They were soon back to the third floor and Joseph's room and as they walked near the door, Francesca leant forward and kissed Joseph on the side of his face and then said in a low voice by his ear, "We must now leave it the hands of God Joseph, and pray, he will know what to do. It is all beyond us now and we have done all we can for the moment. I am sorry to have bustled you about the way I did, but it was necessary."

Joseph reached up and Francesca put her hand into his and they squeezed each other's hands before entering the room where Marvin was now watching television completely unaware of the drama that had unfolded a few floors below. After spending a few minutes with Joseph, Francesca then left and went back to the hotel where she picked up her small Missal and her Rosary. She had a cup of strong coffee checked on Mary and told her that she had just seen Joseph and he is getting stronger and doing well, and that she was going to sit with Louise for a while. Without saying any more Francesca then went to Mark's room and pinned a note on his door saying where she was if he needed her.

Francesca then walked back to the ICU unit and went to the small waiting room next door where she could look through various glass windows to where Louise was lying. Francesca took her Rosary and started to pray silently that Louise would be all right, that she had heard Joseph, that she would rally and fight back and that Our Lord would help her in her hour of desperate need. The night shift ward sister on duty in the ICU happened to also be a Roman Catholic and had met Francesca earlier in the week. This Irish nurse came to Francesca with a cup of coffee and sat with her for a little while and they talked. She knew precisely what Francesca was doing, that novena's had brought miracles before in this very room and she looked at Francesca and said in a kindly way, it will be between three and four thirty this morning that we will probably know, my dear. Francesca knew what this nurse was saying, that many people who are critically ill frequently die at this hour in the day.

Francesca prayed all night and the night nurse brought her cups of coffee at various intervals and would look across through the windows and give Francesca a thumbs-up sign that Louise was holding her own. When three o'clock came and everything was very quiet, Francesca stood up and put her Rosary down and walked gently backwards and forwards in the small room and she raged at God silently in her prayers knowing this to be the make or break time for Louise's life. She prayed to the Virgin mother, woman to woman, and felt her presence supporting and strengthening her. It felt like an eternity when Francesca looked at her watch again and it was now almost five o'clock and she looked over to the night sister who had just come from checking on Louise. She was still holding her own and the heart monitor was less irregular. Francesca pulled a chair in front of her and put her feet across and rested her head on the glass window behind her head. She felt exhausted, but she knew that God had not forsaken

Louise, that her prayers had been answered, and that Louise would live.

As dawn broke Francesca shivered as she walked back to the hotel and she decided that this act of mercy by God would remain their secret. Things were complicated enough with the situation with Joseph, she thought; this would only complicate matters even more. Francesca went to her bedroom where Mary was sleeping and quietly went to bed, quickly fell asleep and slept better than she had done for days. It was mid day when she awoke with Mary standing next to her bed with a cup of tea. Mary sat on the side of her bed and asked about Louise, said how grateful she felt that their prayers had been answered, that Joseph and Louise had been spared and that she was sure John and Freddie were now in Heaven, waiting for the rest of them to arrive one day.

32

Recuperating at Himbledon

OVER THE NEXT FEW DAYS JOSEPH RAPIDLY REGAINED his strength, and his wounds and shoulder bones were healing in a satisfactory manner according to the doctors. He had been given a number of simple exercises to do by the physiotherapist at the hospital and had been advised that it would be some weeks before his injured shoulder would be completely free of pain again. The funeral of John Trimbledon and Freddie had taken place at Himbledon. Mary had wanted John and Freddie to have a shared funeral and Requiem Mass together and Ann had readily agreed. Joseph and Francesca had gone to Himbledon for the funeral and had stayed away from Oxford for two nights at the Grange. Joseph had spoken with his uncle Luke and asked if he would hear Francesca's confession and when they arrived from Oxford the day before the funeral Francesca and Luke talked together quietly in the library. Luke, Portia and Francesca had a close friendship going back many years and Luke was the natural person to act as her spiritual confessor and mentor at this difficult time.

It had been hard for her, and Francesca had taken a long time in personal reflection walking down to the lake and back on her own before meeting Luke and going into the library together before saying the words, "Bless me, Father, for I have sinned…"

She had faltered several times as she talked about what had happened, what she firmly believed she had done wrong, her betrayal and deception of the impostor John Holmes and her inability to feel any forgiveness. Father Luke just sat patiently in front of her gently encouraging and helping her through this anguished catharsis and she talked about her inner feelings of darkness, loneliness and despair. He did not give her any act of contrition, but spoke to her quietly, and said that, just by what she had done in deliberately bringing all these things before God and Jesus in the way she had, she was forgiven. He said that Jesus knows more than any of us, the anguish of human pain, personal sacrifice and suffering, and that he knew precisely what had happened, why it had happened and Francesca's suffering as a result.

There had been moments when Francesca had spoken in Italian to be able to continue sharing her inner most thoughts and to be able to communicate her troubled feelings, and Luke had instantly understood, and had found this particular confession deeply humbling. The strength of her faith blazed through the whole confession and the possibility of being estranged from Jesus, even for a moment, had caused her such sadness and grief.

As he spoke about God's absolution for her, Francesca started to sob uncontrollably for a few moments as she felt this huge weight and darkness lifting from her whole being, and Luke said soothingly, "Yes I know my child, and so does He."

As Francesca lifted her head, wiped away her tears and smiled awkwardly, Luke ended the confession by asking Francesca to do two things in the days ahead. He asked her to keep focussed on the cross and whenever she looks at Christ hanging there, to know how much he loves her and that he always will. The second thing he asked her to do was to remember the impostor John Holmes in her daily prayers, to ask Our Lord to forgive him too and never to forget how much this poor disturbed young man needs her prayers for him.

"Come now Fran, we must join everyone else, tomorrow is a sad day for everyone here at Himbledon and we must help Mary and the family. You made a good confession, please also pray for me, Francesca, and God bless you," Luke said as they both slowly rose to their feet.

Joseph had been reading in the lounge opposite, and trying to keep himself free from anything, with so many people at the Grange, until Francesca was finished with Father Luke. As he had waited he wondered again about *Opus Dei* and whether Francesca was a Supernumerary member and if this had contributed to her eagerness to have her confession heard by Luke. When he saw her come out of the library in front of Luke and after he heard her thank Luke, Joseph called to her and she walked across the passage and forward toward him. Francesca was smiling and looked happier than he had seen her since Dubai, and as she approached he reached out his hand and she took it and sat down next to him.

"That must have been some confession Francesca, we all felt the Grange rumble on its foundations a few times while you were both in the library," Joseph chuckled and Francesca laughed and then looked at Joseph.

"I am so pleased that Louise is getting well and will be all right. It has been a terrible time for so many in recent days and I am so sorry about your father and Freddie, Joseph. I am so very sorry."

Joseph just looked at her, feeling anguish in the pit of his stomach as thoughts of the funeral the next day suddenly filled his mind.

He then looked away, composed himself, and said, "As soon as matters have been attended to here I will go back to Oxford to be with her until she is discharged and then I want her to come to the Grange to fully recover. She will be safe here," and he then hesitated before continuing, "When will I see you again? After you and your mother return to Rome after the funeral?"

Francesca touched their clasped hands with her other hand, and moving herself to the edge of the settee to be able to look into his face replied, "Very soon I hope Joseph. I would rather not have to leave, but there are now pressing matters I need to be getting on with, having been away for so long. Mother also needs to get back and Achmed told me earlier that some of their trials are now at a critical stage needing their attention. Why don't you come and visit us after Christmas in Rome for a few days with Louise? I am sure she will enjoy some time at the villa."

If only things were that simple, Joseph quickly thought. His first priority right now was Louise and her full recovery. "Yes, perhaps, we will see. But you must keep your promise and not return to Boston; should you have to go back for the police enquiries, I insist on coming with you."

Francesca agreed, and had something else she wanted to share with Joseph when she said, "You know, Joseph, you are not the only one who has been praying about your relationship with Louise. I have been praying, too. I have also been praying about our relationship, and that God will guide us for the best."

Before Joseph could respond, Thomas came into the lounge and said, with a broad smile, "Come along, you two conspirators; we need you in the chapel about tomorrow's arrangements."

Francesca and Louise had spent a considerable amount of time together in the hospital after Louise had regained consciousness. They had talked about so many things and had grown close in a surprising way and Louise had looked forward to her visits and calm presence by her bed. Louise had been touched several times by Francesca's help with the junior nursing staff in changing drips and even dressings. The staff all liked her and she had a natural way of talking with them even about quite complicated medical matters that she did not understand. Louise had come to feel in some way she could not fully understand that Francesca was a crucial part of her medical treatment and recovery. When Joseph was also present there was a happy ease between the three of them and she felt safe and secure with them both. Louise had come to trust Francesca and this trust was reciprocated and a firm and deep friendship had developed between the two women almost irrespective of Joseph. They were both very intelligent and perceptive women and could easily share ideas and subjects of mutual interest and Louise had explained certain legal issues easily to Francesca related to international law, jurisdictions and the problems of interfering in the affairs of poor countries. Francesca had explained her work that fascinated

Louise.

It had been a few days after Louise had regained consciousness that Francesca had been talking to one of the doctors about the precise nature of the injuries that Louise had sustained in her pelvic region, and that she became very concerned. Although it had not been the time to raise such matters and Louise would need to be much stronger before dealing with such longer term consequences, Francesca had a deep worry that Louise would never be able to have children and that her womb and other reproductive organs had been irreparably damaged and would probably require further surgery in the future. When she had prayed in her all night vigil, she had also had this overwhelming and recurring thought that from that night forward she would have a special relationship with Louise for the rest of her life if God spared her, and that she would also have a duty to care for Louise and to always safeguard her interests. It was a strange affair, and in further prayer, Francesca had become convinced that she had a special duty toward Louise and that this matter must always remain between herself and God and something never to be divulged to Joseph or Louise herself. At the hospital the doctors were naturally preoccupied with the immediate life saving care of Louise and had not yet broadened their prognosis beyond short-term imperatives. Francesca, however, with her medical knowledge, had already started to see the future for Louise, and it had been one of the reasons she had asked Joseph to visit her in Rome with Louise once she had recuperated and was fit to travel.

The day of the funeral had dawned very cold, dry and bright, one of those heavy frosty December days in England that makes the countryside look vivid and sharp once the early morning mist has lifted. There would certainly be heavy snow again within a few days. It was a traditional dignified Trimbledon occasion and the home secretary had represented the prime minister who had a previous unavoidable commitment in Washington. There had been many tributes to the two men, whose bodies lay in the simple wooden caskets in the Chapel. Father Luke had presided as the main member of the religious at the Mass and Mark and Mary had given touching tributes to John and Freddie. Brian Hardwick had also paid tribute to his father, and Ann his mother had been proud of her tall son in his naval officer's uniform giving such a dignified and touching tribute to his father and the man she had loved so dearly. Joseph also spoke about his dear friend Freddie, and Ann, Paul and Brian Hardwick had been consoled by his sensitive words and tributes to their husband and father. He had to control his own tears on a few occasions and he also managed to raise some smiles in the congregation when he said that Freddie was certainly right about most things, particularly the weather, and just a few weeks earlier had predicted the harsh winter, they were all now experiencing.

When Joseph returned to his place next to his mother and Francesca, both women gently touched him and Francesca removed her black leather glove and slid her warm hand across her lap to discreetly hold Joseph's hand. These gestures were a silent acknowledgement of a very difficult job that had been completed properly with dignity and love. Mary knew how difficult Joseph had found this public appearance especially when he too was in grief at the loss of his father and Freddie. Francesca had a black lace mantilla on her head, customary for Italian women at solemn occasions and funerals, and as he turned slightly toward her he could see her deep eyes turned his way in sympathy. Mary also turned slightly to look at them both sitting together next to her and in that instant, in this time of grief and sorrow for departed loved ones, she could see the love they had for one another and the strength pouring from Francesca to Joseph at this anguished time for him, and that in death there is also life.

It was when Joseph walked behind Francesca, who followed Mary to the Altar to receive Holy Communion with their heads bowed, that Joseph's mind was momentarily distracted by the presence of her before him. When they had returned to their seats having taken the body and blood of Christ and kneeled beside each other to pray and then sat down after the Tabernacle had been closed, Joseph felt this calm pass over him and an affirmation that he need pretend no longer about his love for her. Francesca now felt the full forgiveness of Jesus over whelming her as she gently lowered her head and she too also knew she no longer had to conceal her feelings; that she was whole again and destined to give herself completely to the young man next to her. There were no words that could come near to capturing what they both felt as they sat quietly with their hands before them in their laps, the joyous conviction and sudden freedom toward each other. Whether sooner or later, they both knew within their hearts that God had answered their prayers, had spoken into their hearts and had blessed the love they had for each other.

The next day Portia and Francesca were to depart for Heathrow and Rome mid-morning after breakfast and Francesca and Joseph were eager to spend a few moments alone to say their farewell. Despite the sorrow and laughter at the customary Trimbledon dinner the evening before, to pay tribute and say farewell to his father and Freddie, Joseph had felt a mixture of grieving loss for them both, concern and compassion for his mother and Ann, but also a nerve tingling anticipation every time his eyes had met those of Francesca. Despite Francesca's dignified and gracious outward appearance she had also felt a constant yearning to be close to him, to be able to be her full self with him.

When they reached the seat behind the boathouse the following morning, away from the gaze of the Grange, they just looked at each other momentarily before almost lurching forward and embracing. Joseph lowered his head and she raised her face to his and they kissed each other on the lips. He held her head gently between his hands as Francesca placed her hands gently on this shoulders and he kissed her again, and then again on each cheek and then tenderly on her forehead. Francesca reached up and again kissed him on the lips with her eyes closed, a long lingering soft kiss as she put her hands behind his neck and held the back of his head. They were gentle with each other, conscious of their recent injuries and then Francesca lowered her head and turned her face to the side to place her head lovingly on his chest. They both stood there with their arms around their bodies, there was no need for words. The days of constraint, uncertainty, embarrassment and not knowing the full truth about each other's feelings were over. There was no longer the need to protect their feelings in case the other was unable to reciprocate. In the ghastly circumstances of recent days, they had found themselves in each other, their confusion had been clarified and love had suddenly brought them together as a single entity. They now knew this reality, they felt it in every fibre, and they knew they were destined to be together for the rest of their lives.

As Joseph waved goodbye to Portia and Francesca as their car disappeared down the drive from the Grange, his mind began to return to more pressing matters. Since his father's murder, Joseph had become greatly more involved in family business matters. There had been discussions with Ruth, Paul and Mark and there had been a welter of legal and other business affairs to deal with. There had been visits by senior staff from the London office requiring Joseph's authorisation for a range of ongoing business decisions and he was rapidly coming to appreciate the huge workload his father had sustained for years as well as his fraternal service and responsibilities at the Himbledon Estate. However, the major priority that remained on his mind was Louise still recovering in the hospital in Oxford. It was just an hour later that Joseph and Paul Hardwick were driving together, back to Oxford.

Paul Hardwick had moved to the same hotel where Joseph was staying and after dropping of his bag in his room Joseph immediately went across to the hospital. When he entered the single room she was now in, she was standing by the washbasin and she turned with a broad smile and hugged him saying how good that he was back in Oxford. Some of her university friends and colleagues had been in to see her earlier and this had also cheered her up and Joseph noticed she looked stronger since he had last seen her and she had some colour in her cheeks. Her friends had brought a few of her books and papers from her apartment so she could start doing a little work to pass the tedious hours in the hospital. She sat on top of her bed with her legs stretched out and her back resting upright on the pillows and they talked about the funeral, her father who had now returned to Wales and her mother who was due to visit again a little later. Louise said that the last three days had dragged terribly and she was now looking forward to being discharged and getting to Himbledon to recuperate.

Joseph then noticed his old Bible among the books and papers on the bedside table, brought earlier by her college friends. He did not say anything, but wondered why it was there.

Louise then said something that rather startled Joseph.

She reached for his hand as he sat beside the bed and said, "Francesca is a wonderful person and I have never met anyone quite like her ever before. She helped me in so many ways since the shooting and I have really missed her since you both had to leave. I know getting shot and the trauma does funny things and makes us have strange ideas, but I keep looking for her to be here with me, and I have missed her terribly. We have become very close, Joseph. I cannot explain it all, and even some of the staff have said how special she was and so kind. Yesterday evening the Irish night sister from ICU popped up to see me for a little while, and said that I must mean an awful lot to that lovely Italian doctor because when I was very sick, Francesca sat near me all night. The nurse said that in her experience of this place not many people have such special friends and that I am blessed to have her as a friend and that God works in mysterious ways."

Louise stopped talking and just looked at Joseph with a perplexed look on her face. Joseph was lost for words and then remembered the evening when Francesca had jostled him down to Louise's bedside and all he could say in reply was, "Yes Louise, she is a special person and we are privileged to have her as our friend, she helped us both through this ordeal in ways, that even she herself, will probably never fully know."

But then Louise had more to say and she continued, "I know that Francesca and I will always be very close, you know Joseph, one just knows these things. We talked about so many things and some of my legal work may be able to help her work and she also felt I was doing the right thing going to the International Court of Justice next year. We also spoke about you a lot, but not in any competitive way, but in a way again I cannot explain. As though the three of us now all shared something very special together," again Louise paused, looking at Joseph and she then looked away for a moment appearing to collect her thoughts.

She then looked back at Joseph, smiling slightly and said, "Francesca loves you Joseph, I can tell, and I know that you love her."

Joseph started to interrupt her, but Louise squeezed his hand and said, "No Joseph, it is all right, let me finish. Since Dubrovnik I have known you are unable to love me as I love you and I have come to terms with it. It is not your fault or mine that these things happen. Now that I have got to know Francesca, as I have, I also know that you will both always be a part of my life. I know she will cherish you Joseph and will make you happy and this makes me happy too. You do not have to say anything Joseph, but we are supposed to be mature adults and we must be honest with each other. You must not distress yourself about all this Joseph, now with your father gone you will have quite enough on your mind. I am coming to terms with it all, trust me Joseph, and I am so happy now to have Francesca as a close friend as well as you my darling." When she finished she leant forward slowly and kissed Joseph on the cheek.

Again he was lost for words and his mind raced to digest what Louise had just said, this beautiful woman who had saved his life just a few days earlier. If only life were not so complicated, if only the three of us could live together happily ever after, but life is never so simple.

Joseph then remembered Francesca's invitation and said to Louise, "Francesca has invited us both to visit them in Rome early in the new year once you are stronger and able to travel, so we must arrange it once you have rested at the Grange." Louise face brightened and she smiled at Joseph.

Louise still had some difficulty walking and she needed to rest her left arm while the muscular tissue at the top of her back continued to heal. Her pelvis had also been injured and the reconstructive bone surgery also had to have time to heal together with various tissues in her pelvic region. Her head injury had healed and from a further scan she had just before leaving ICU all the internal haemorrhaging had also stopped.

The medical consultants and doctors had been surprised at her remarkable recovery in recent days and there were certain aspects of the healing process that they knew, they could not fully explain. Louise was also in good spirits and being a strong fit young lady with a determination now to get strong again she was co operating fully with all the recuperative routines she had been asked to follow.

It was just before Christmas on a very cold day with heavy snow all over the country when Mark and Charlotte arrived in Oxford to bring Joseph and Louise back to Himbledon. Mary had spoken to Louise's mother, and asked if they would also like to join the family for Christmas, but she had declined the invitation, but said they may try to get to Himbledon on Boxing Day. When Louise arrived at Himbledon after a challenging drive by Charlotte with the appalling weather conditions and with Paul Hardwick following in Freddie's old Land Rover, Mary, Thomas, and Paul were there to greet them. Paul and Thomas had never met Louise and they instantly fussed around this beautiful tall blonde, a little bird with a broken wing.

In the days that followed, life was very gradually getting back to normal at the estate and Mary was distracted from her loss somewhat by Louise at the house, someone she was very fond of and in need of her care and attention. Joseph was now busy dealing with the interests of the family business and Paul and Mark were only too pleased to leave him to it. Martha, Charlie and Lucinda had decided to take some extended leave and had stayed on after John and Freddie's funeral. The only people missing now were Luke who had to remain in Rome after he returned from the funeral and Liska who had been assisting some rehearsals in London. Liska joined them two days before Christmas from the West End and her arrival marked "house full" for the family Christmas together.

Almost every day Francesca and Joseph communicated and every time Francesca asked about Louise. They too spoke several times on the phone and Francesca asked Louise to make sure Joseph does not overdo things. They also talked about their visit in January and Francesca said how much she and her mother were looking forward to seeing them both again. There was no pressure on Francesca to return to Boston and she was continuing to work from Rome and was planning to go to South Africa sometime in February to follow up arrangements for field trials.

It was early on Boxing Day as Louise was phoning her mother on her mobile phone to find out whether they were coming or not, to be told that her father had a rather bad cold so they must send their apologies, that Thomas walked briskly into the lounge where a fire was burning and seeing Louise talking on the phone waved at her and promptly disappeared. He was all fidgety and walked to John's study and sat by the window looking down across the garden. He had just received a text message on his phone, evidently from Hank Milshner accepting his offer to play the piano for him at his mountain lodge in Montana. At first, he thought it was some sort of weird joke that perhaps Charlie had sent as a humorous stunt, since Thomas had not been completely open with him when they were in Sulphur Springs together. He needed to think this thing through very carefully before talking secretly to Charlie.

The message read, "You are welcome to play here. I would like to meet you. I am not responsible for your brother's murder. You will be safe here. Hank Milshner."

Thomas knew his bluff had been called and for one of those rare moments in his life, he wondered if he was not about to get into something above his head, something way beyond him. *It is no good*, he thought. *I must get out of the house and go for a walk, clear my head, and think this thing through very carefully*. As he crunched his way through the frozen snow across to the drive, that had been cleared, he thought that he couldn't tell anyone, apart from Charlie, whose help he needed. If this was going to work, it had to remain confidential, and he had to go alone to Milshner. Perhaps Milshner had something to tell him, perhaps he was not as psychotic as he had been told and the questions just kept tumbling through his mind. He had now reached the main gate and he nodded at the young man in the gatekeeper's cottage who kindly activated the gates so he could walk through. There outside was a police car and standing opposite was an armed police officer. It was approaching lunchtime so he decided to walk over to the local village pub for a pint. It was well after three when he returned through the main gates, but everything was now clear in his mind; he knew exactly what he had to do.

33
Freezing to Death

IT WAS AN EXCEPTIONALLY COLD WINTER in the northern hemisphere that year with heavy snowfalls on a regular basis. Northern Europe had been badly affected and there was daily travel chaos. America was suffering the coldest winter on record in many areas and special provisions had been called on for vulnerable people due to the consistent sub zero temperatures and heavy snow making many roads impassable. Yet in the southern hemisphere, countries like Australia were experiencing exceptionally high temperatures, heat waves and numerous forest and shrub fires. South Africa was suffering a bad drought with water usage restrictions across the country.

Joseph and Louise were planning to go to Rome toward the end of January and they had spoken to the doctors in Oxford who had said that providing Louise continues to progress well, that this would be in order. Louise recuperation at the Grange had gone better than anyone could have expected, and she had started to attend to some of her academic work again and had referred to some books in the library and was to be seen often working with her laptop computer in the warmth and comfort of the lounge. As with more than ninety percent of the homes in Britain, the Grange was no exception in using large quantities of natural gas for heating, providing hot water and for cooking. John had natural gas supplies laid in to the estate many years earlier and all the cottages and buildings on the estate relied on natural gas for their heating, hot water supplies and cooking. It had been costly, at the time, but had proved a wonderful investment, since natural gas is clean and inconspicuous once the pipes are installed underground, and it is one of the least invasive of all the energy sources from an environmental viewpoint.

At the back of the kitchen there were two large gas fired boilers with one of them dedicated to providing the heat for the whole house through the hot water radiators. The other boiler, slightly smaller provided all the hot water for the many bathrooms and the main kitchen. There was also gas pipe work to certain rooms where there were fuel effect gas fires and it was only in the lounge and the great hall where logs were ever burnt these days mainly for the visual warming effect. These rooms were actually heated with fan assisted large steel radiators that were concealed behind the oak panelling by all the main window recesses. Even the Chapel and the rooms below by the canal are heated with natural gas via the air conditioning system. The cutting of wood was a minor activity these days on the estate and the Grange only ever burned a few baskets of logs every year.

They are called intelligent pigs allegedly for two reasons. Firstly because many years ago large pipelines were cleaned with straw wrapped in a ball that was dragged through the large pipes and as these bundles were pulled through they made a similar sound to that emitted by pigs. The other reason may be that the terminology Pipeline Inspection Gauge also spells pig. Whatever the reason for the name, it was the Shell oil company back in the nineteen seventies who first started to use smart pigs, contraptions that moved through pipelines inspecting the welds, the condition of the pipe and looking for obstructions. Smart pigs enable pipelines to be maintained from within without having to close them down thereby avoiding any dislocations of supply and providing huge cost savings and efficiency improvements.

There are today many different types of smart pigs and pipeline construction and maintenance companies who work for the oil majors, gas transmission authorities and energy distribution companies. Modern intelligent underground inspection equipment has become highly complex and sophisticated, and they are essentially a computer that gathers different types of data as they travel along the pipeline. In most cases these smart pigs are launched through special chambers built into the length of a pipeline and they are removed after their battery driven journey underground, and the data is then recovered from instruments within the pig. In a few situations, permanent pigs are deployed that remain underground in the pipeline. Communications with underground intelligent pigs is a problem since up to now it is difficult to transmit signals from within large diameter steel pipes deep underground to the surface. However, the world was about to witness yet again the advanced technology that had been developed by Judaire, with devastating results.

It was in Australia in the third week of January that the first news came through of a series of explosions on bulk natural gas pipelines serving the city of Sydney. At first this was not regarded as that serious since Australia still uses large amounts of electricity generated from coal for many of its air conditioning and cooling facilities. There had been extensive local disruption of residential and commercial natural gas supplies and many people were buying up liquid petroleum gas cooking stoves and bottles to get by without natural gas. It had only been a few hours after the bulk gas lines had been disabled, before the local distribution company had to close down all natural gas supply to Sydney, particularly to the commercial air conditioning plants in several office complexes, hospitals, colleges and shopping precincts. Temporary mobile air conditioning plant was being rushed to Sydney from other parts of Australia and although a major disruption, the local authorities appeared to have the situation well under control.

It was the next morning after an early breakfast that Joseph and Mark listened to the news on the television in trepidation. Then it started to be reported, the second and then the third attacks, just as Mark had forecast some weeks before. Huge areas in the United States were without bulk gas supplies following a whole series of carefully orchestrated explosions that had virtually paralyzed the natural gas supply network all across the mid and northern states of America. With the freezing conditions there, this was a catastrophe in the making. The initial news reports were piecemeal and the extent of the crisis was getting bigger every few minutes as fresh reports poured into American newsrooms across the country. Every day the U.S.A. oil and gas industry supplies enough energy to heat more than eighty million homes and provides almost four hundred million gallons of petrol and diesel to enable around two hundred million motorists to get to work, go shopping and to take children to school.

It is a similar picture in Western Europe where gaseous and liquid fuels keep people warm in winter and provide the energy to transport people and goods. Most of the heating in homes, offices and factories in the urban areas is provided by millions of cubic feet of natural gas that is conveyed every day in a labyrinth of pipes under the ground. These lifelines, providing warmth and other critical services in the middle of the worst winter on record, were now rapidly emptying. For a variety of technical reasons when the pressure begins to drop in underground natural gas distribution systems or the combustion properties of the gas become disrupted, the supply lines must be shut down.

Many household gas-burning appliances from boilers to cookers are designed to operate safely at a relatively low inlet gas pressure at point of delivery, and appliances have pressure control valves. When the pressure becomes unstable and starts to vary wildly, then many appliances simply close themselves down with shut off valves. In other cases if a gas stream suddenly stops and pilot lights and burners go out there is nothing to safely ignite the gas once it starts flowing again. When gas supply starts again, large volumes of combustible gas can fill enclosed spaces just waiting for the odd spark, even from a faulty electrical light switch, to cause powerful explosions. Many older gas appliances such as water heating boilers also have few safety features and are susceptible to blow up under such extreme operating conditions. It was for these safety reasons that gas supply companies had started to activate the remote computer operated control valves to shut down the intricate supply networks, long before they had been completely starved of natural gas supplies from the bulk supply grid.

The balancing of demand and supply for natural gas is a highly sophisticated technical operation involving a vast network of pipes, storage and telemetry across whole continents. When severe weather conditions prevail, the margin of error and reserve storage margins narrow, and computer systems become ever more important in helping to manage these delicate operations. Unlike electricity, natural gas can be stored either in large pressurized vessels as compressed natural gas— CNG— underground in empty gas fields which have the right geological structure to enable the gas to be stored safely, or by increasing pressure in the large diameter bulk pipelines that weave their invisible path for thousands of miles underground. With the sub-zero temperatures many of these reserve storage margins were already being stretched to the limit. With additional volumes of natural gas being transported at maximum permitted pressures through many of these pipelines, when they had been ruptured due to the attacks, many had also exploded and the gas ignited sending huge plumes of flame into the countryside. In a few cases, these had occurred in semi urban areas destroying adjacent properties. Immediately the gas transmission authorities had picked up the attacks, they had no other option, but to start closing down the supply lines.

Liquefied natural gas – LNG– that, in simple terms, is frozen natural gas until it becomes a liquid, is also used to supplement gas supplies and many countries deploy the necessary sophisticated infrastructure to store LNG and then convert it from being a liquid back to being a gaseous fuel. The ratio of liquid natural gas to ordinary natural gas is around six hundred, so a unit of LNG produces six hundred times this volume when converted back to natural gas, so this technology, although expensive, is ideally suited to assist with managing the careful balance between demand and supply. As the world was suddenly discovering, one of Milshner's companies was a global leader in this cryogenic technology and the construction of LNG reformation plants and the special vessels required for the storage and transportation of

LNG.

Then the third attack was reported; a series of explosions in Eastern Europe, some undersea feeder gas pipelines under the North Sea from offshore gas rigs, and the connector line to Ireland had suddenly lost pressure. Other strategic gas lines across Europe had been attacked together with some liquid natural gas import and storage facilities in Wales and near London. As Mark and Joseph sat watching the TV downstairs by the canal, Mark just stood up next to the flip chart, and wrote the number 'three' in the first month on the board. Again, as before with the train attacks, they scribbled details down as the news reports came in from around the world. Various governments around the world had issued special secret security briefing bulletins to the energy industries warning them of possible attacks following the information provided by the fraternity. Larger natural gas reserves were being held, in many bulk user pipelines pressures had been raised with line packing to be able to provide a greater margin of reserve. Many of these precautions had been little more than fruitless in view of the harsh weather conditions and huge demand for thermal energy. Certain storage facilities such as the undersea caverns in the bay off Morecambe in the west of England were quickly pressed into service to try to maintain the pressure in the nearby labyrinth of underground pipelines and pressure stations, but had only provided a temporary respite.

There had also been attacks to the Ras Laffan LNG infrastructure in Qatar that supplies around a quarter of the world's LNG and a bulk gas carrier had been disabled in the middle of the Persian Gulf. As well as pipeline gas, LNG now supplies an ever increasing portion of the world's hunger for thermal fuels, and huge ships with large ball like containers, deliver the liquid gas at temperatures of minus a hundred and sixty degrees Celsius to gas reformation plants around the globe for treatment before being despatched into national gas supply networks. There is now a billion dollar global LNG market and the Milshner business empire had interests in this specialist form of shipping, and they had also been involved in some of the specialised construction at the Ras Laffan plant.

Mark and Joseph looked at each other with concern and they both felt the absence of their father and the added burden that now lay on their shoulders. Joseph had assumed some of his father's fraternal responsibilities and was acting increasingly as their family's representative, a role that Mark always declined and Ruth, although older, did not regard herself as being competent for this role. It was Joseph who said that they would soon be without natural gas themselves and needed to make contingency plans for the estate and the Grange. Mark mentioned what it must be like in the gas distribution control centres across the world, pandemonium and confusion.

"You will probably need to go to London tomorrow Joseph in view of this and liaise with various people. I will also quickly think about the necessary measures we will need to arrange here," Mark said and Joseph nodded.

The next few hours were frantically busy for them both. Then as they worked together trying to piece the situation together there was an interruption to all the UK television broadcasts and a special bulletin started to be televised. It was an instruction to all users of natural gas to immediately go and turn off their gas supply at the meter, and there were simple descriptions about how to do this. All gas appliances also had to be turned off immediately and as Mark and Joseph were watching these broadcasts, Mary came into the room and asked the boys what they needed to do at Himbledon. They then briefly discussed the contingency measures they needed to institute as a matter of urgency.

Mark said, "Let me go and turn off the gas and I will meet you both shortly in the kitchen." A few minutes later the three of them sat together and Mark said, "At least we still have electricity, but do not be surprised if that does not go down, because the gas powered electricity generation stations will now cease production. I have checked on the standby generator and the tank is full. But we must now conserve and look after everyone on the estate."

Within just a few minutes they had agreed an immediate plan of action and a list of priorities. They included shutting down all unused rooms at the Grange, calling Amos and getting gardening staff to immediately to start felling some trees and preparing logs, getting the old wood burning hot water boiler from the back of the storehouse and getting it reconnected temporarily to the hot water supply system, an urgent meeting with people from the estate later the same afternoon, an instruction to all staff to fill their vehicles up with fuel and to keep them as full as possible, to get out the mobile liquid petroleum gas cooking ranges used at the annual fete for the preparation of bulk hot food for the elderly in the church hall, temporary heating for the elderly home in the village, and the list went on. Within an hour via mobile phones the three of them had set the emergency wheels in motion to ensure no one on the estate either got cold or were without hot meals and drinks. Mary finally suggested that they set up a large bedroom in the lounge since the open fire there will keep the room warm at night for any elderly or any sick person on the estate, and her suggestion was immediately agreed.

With the air conditioning now switched off it was too cold to work downstairs by the canal, so Mark and Joseph agreed to set up their activities in what had been John's study. They both went to their rooms and put on additional clothing and Joseph spoke to Louise in the library about the various contingency plans that were being hurriedly made. Louise then insisted on helping so Joseph rattled off a list of queries that needed clarification such as whether the village shop had plenty of food in stock, how much liquid petroleum gas had the village petrol station in stock and other enquiries.

Joseph also said to Louise, "You must immediately go and put on warm clothing, it is going to get cold quickly in these low temperatures outside."

By later in the afternoon things were quickly being put into place throughout the Himbledon Estate, to safeguard people and animals, from the freezing conditions and sudden cessation of the natural gas supplies. While it had been relatively straightforward to put practical contingency measures quickly into place at Himbledon, this was not the situation elsewhere in Britain, especially in the cities where the absence of natural gas to heat homes, hospitals and offices was already being felt.

In many critical installations such as hospitals and frail care centres, many of the boilers were sensibly dual-fuel, and could be switched to burn the fuel oil or other liquid fuels contained in the adjacent storage tanks. However, homes, schools, shopping centres, and many other buildings were without these back-up facilities, and ambient temperatures had already dropped to dangerous levels. No one, either in government, local authorities or the gas supply companies had ever contemplated such a total loss of natural gas supplies, so there were no national contingency plans. Local authorities across the country were working closely with the police and other agencies to do what they could to set up temporary emergency shelters and facilities to provide hot food. At five o'clock with darkness outside and with a scarf around his neck, Mark watched the weather forecast on the television and was dismayed to see that temperatures were due to drop alarmingly again tonight to sub zero levels right across the British Isles, and that more heavy snow was due in several counties by day break. Not only would these weather conditions hamper the efforts of repair crews being rapidly assembled by National Grid to be flown to the attack sites in British territory, but also it would make the delivery of liquid fuels from refineries by rail and road difficult. In London the Ministry of Energy had started to assemble an emergency team, and the emergency services had all been put on high alert with the police to assist with the worsening situation.

The main concern in the minds of engineers in the energy supply companies was the severity of the damage both to the bulk supply lines across Europe and the LNG supply infrastructure. Once the system could be repaired and the gas could start flowing again, at least there was some hope of overcoming the prospect of millions of people freezing to death in Britain and Europe. In the meanwhile, the gas supply utilities were appealing for additional manpower to assist with house-to-house calls to ensure that all gas meters and appliances had been turned off to reduce the risk of gas explosions. Hospitals had been put on high alert for an increased number of hyperthermia cases and various welfare groups such as the Red Cross and Help the Aged, were busy getting themselves organised ready to assist. The minister of energy was calling for an urgent assessment of the extent of the damage and how long it would be before gas could start flowing again. The early reports were not heartening, especially those related to the undersea lines feeding Britain, and the extent of the damage in Eastern Europe was still unknown, despite repeated calls to the authorities in the Ukraine and Gasprom in Moscow.

The whole of Northern Europe, Scandinavia and the northern Mediterranean countries had been impacted. France, which uses extensive quantities of gas for residential and commercial purposes, had been impacted, but was better off than many other European countries. They have extensive nuclear electricity generating capacity. Germany, Italy and Spain all rely on natural gas and had been badly affected, although the weather conditions along the Mediterranean were somewhat more moderate than further north. Scandinavia was also impacted although with extensive hydro electricity generating capacity, the use of traditional high efficiency woods stoves and their experience with dealing with low temperatures in the winter, they were better equipped to deal with the crisis. Holland and Belgium were particularly vulnerable since they use large quantities of natural gas and the various European Union and Parliamentary buildings in Brussels were without gas supplies. In Britain, National Grid, responsible for the bulk transmission of electricity and natural gas to local distributors was in a stronger position to try to get hold of the situation than many of the transmission authorities elsewhere, which were fragmented.

The next great threat in all those countries that were suffering badly was that there had been a massive switch by consumers to electric space heating, electric kettles and microwave cookers. This had already pushed up the electricity demand load on the national grid to unsustainable levels, and National Grid had to impose grey outs involving cutting off electricity supplies for periods of between four and six hours to maintain the stability of the national electricity supply network. All across Britain, users were experiencing periods of up two hours when they were without electricity. The conventional coal and oil-fired power stations were running at maximum output, as too were the few remaining nuclear stations. The natural gas-fired combined cycle power stations had all been shut down and national grid were trying to squeeze every available kilowatt hour from industrial co-generators, the many small combined heat and power plants in hotels and other commercial premises and the renewable energy wind farms scattered around the country. Many of the smaller commercial generators were unable to supply anything since they too relied on natural gas. Many of the wind farms had also become useless in providing a little more electricity since the extreme weather conditions had led to excessive icing of the huge exposed blades, and they could not turn to generate electricity, despite frequent blizzard conditions in Cornwall and other coastal regions of the country.

Conditions at many of the airports around the country were also becoming bad. Heathrow airport had started to impose restrictions on departing aircraft particularly to the U.S.A. and other parts of Northern Europe. The cavernous interior of Terminal Five was now cold since the natural gas air conditioning plant had ceased functioning. The various support and service areas of the airport were also now cold. Staff and technicians were finding it increasingly difficult to do their work. Even refuelling aircraft from the bulk storage tanks was slowing as fuel began to become denser without supplementary heating in the handling systems. As temperatures were due to drop again that night and with further snow on the runways, the airport was gradually seizing up. This picture was being repeated across Northern Europe and the U.S.A. Many unimaginable aspects of life were now being imperilled by the extreme cold.

All across America emergency teams were out busy trying to repair the badly damaged bulk gas mains, there were teams of State Troopers and others going house to house checking on people, emergency shelters were being set up and people were being evacuated from their freezing homes. Many areas were also without electricity since the harsh winter had brought down power lines and now with the unprecedented demand for electricity, where it was available, the transmission authorities were imposing supply restrictions to safeguard the electricity supply grid. If things were bad in the countryside and rural communities, the situation in the cities was grave. Joseph phoned Martha now back in Boston who said they were managing, but it was not easy. Charlie had managed to get some paraffin, some logs and bags of smokeless fuel and they had pulled out the fuel effect gas fires and were having fires again in some of their open grates. Logan Airport had been closed as had all the cities schools and there were emergency provisions in force at Harvard and MIT.

The rail network in Britain was already operating on a reduced schedule of trains owing to the severe weather conditions. However, the next day, Joseph still managed to get into central London, despite a long and difficult journey from the Grange. He met with the senior managers at the office and they reviewed the situation in terms of the impacts on certain companies. He was pleasantly surprised to find that many contingency plans had already been prepared and in most cases were being smoothly implemented with the health and welfare of employees and customers always at the forefront of the various plans. He phoned Louise at the Grange who told him that Mark and a local plumber had managed to reconnect the old wood burning stove that was now smoking away and heating some hot water for the house. Louise had spoken to her parents in Wales, and they, too, were without gas, but were managing, although the university had decided to close until the crisis was over. Francesca had also called Louise from Rome and things were bad their as well, largely because of the abnormal weather conditions and Francesca had joked that rather than coming to Rome that she and Joseph should perhaps meet her in Dubai where they would at least be warm.

When Joseph got back to the Grange late the same night there was an eerie calm about the place, it was extremely cold with snow everywhere and there were paraffin lamps burning in the windows of those rooms being used. The lounge was full with various elderly people from the estate and Mary, Mark and Louise had rigged up some liquid petroleum gas hot plates in the kitchen where there were several pots of steaming food. There were old-fashioned large kettles that he remembered from when he was very young and a general air of busyness, everyone helping one another and frequent outbursts of laughter. Outside it was cold and still, inside it was like a bustling village market day. After he put down his bag Louise greeted him with a kiss and asked if he could take two cups of hot tea through to the elderly couple that had arrived just before him. Mark then appeared with a basket of logs he was about to carry through to the lounge and he rested them on the edge of the kitchen table and said, "Hi Joe, good journey? Get yourself some supper and then we need to talk," and he then heaved the basket up off the table and disappeared toward the lounge.

It was a little later when they sat huddled in the study with a fire burning in the old grate.

Mark was the first to speak. "I don't suppose you have been able to check the news out much today? The FBI has moved on the cult compounds in the U.S.A. and the whole assault is going on as we speak. They managed to get intelligence in recent days where these places are and after their first gas lines went down, Washington gave the order. This is the right thing to do Joseph, and this whole thing has gone on long enough now. Trouble is, this round up and assault on the compounds will not stop anything; it had to be done, but it will just tie up hundreds of American Federal agents sorting out who all these people are and what role they may have played in this nightmare. I suspect they will also not find any new intelligence of any value."

Joseph looked at Mark's face flickering slightly with the light from the flames in the fireplace and replied, "What about Milshner, have they arrested him, do you know?"

Mark smiled and answered, "Now that is an interesting one Joseph, just before you got home I had a call, on the secure line, from one of the security advisors to the PM wishing to query some of the details about our report on the time series that included our prediction of these recent attacks, and I asked her about Milshner. Evidently from what she had heard from her U.S. counterparts, the FBI know that he is at his mountain lodge, they have the place under surveillance and believe he cannot help them so are content to leave him there for the moment while they concentrate on trying to find Judaire and Adler. It is quite extraordinary, Joseph, because the Americans are actually listening, and are putting a lot of investigative effort in to the radio transmissions, rogue-satellites and where these signals might be coming from. They must originate somewhere from the Earth, and are simply bounced via the satellites. Unless this technology can be disarmed, they can do what they like with Milshner, Adler and Judaire, but it won't stop anything. These terrible gas-line attacks appear now to have finally convinced them, at last, of the reality we are trying to deal with."

They then just glanced at each other and looked into the flames before Joseph turned to Mark and said, "Thanks for looking after everything here today. It looks as though everything is under control."

Mark just nodded and replied, "Thankfully, yes Joseph, for the moment at least." He then looked at Joseph and said, "It is their new battery technology that is one of the possible keys to these gas supply attacks. These blasts were unlikely to have been set off by radio signals, but probably by devices left in the pipelines with highly sophisticated timers. Probably atomic clocks, or something as accurate, left inside some intelligent permanent pigs."

Joseph looked at him, puzzled and asked, "Intelligent what?"

Mark replied, "No time to explain now, I need to do some work with my computer. I just hope the radio network does not go down with all this chaos."

Joseph smiled and then decided to go and check on Louise.

34
Postponements

THERE HAD BEEN APPEALS BY THE GOVERNMENT FOR PEOPLE not to travel unless absolutely essential, due to the chaos rapidly spreading across Europe and the northern part of America. Joseph and Louise spoke with Francesca in Rome and agreed that it would not be wise to travel and they postponed their visit. There was still much to be done at Himbledon to assist in managing the emergency situation, and the latest reports from the natural gas authorities indicated that it would still be several days before there was any possibility of restoring any gas supplies. They had also warned that even when the bulk supply pipelines had been repaired and gas began flowing again, it would probably take weeks to bring the whole system back up to full operation again. It would have to be done systematically in phases across the whole national gas transmission and distribution network, area by area. Some towns were likely to be without gas for weeks and it would also be necessary to call again on every property before pressurising the supply pipes again, to ensure there were no uncontrolled leakages. There had already been a number of devastating gas explosions in some locations across Britain killing a number of people.

The gas transmission teams had now located all the attack sites and were busy, despite the appalling weather conditions, repairing the huge underground and undersea pipelines. In most cases, the damage to the undersea pipelines was proving to be a major technical and engineering challenge to repair.

The bad weather conditions with gale force storms in the North and Irish Seas, was also stopping the huge specialised steel pipe laying ships from operating, on several days they had to seek in shore shelter from severe storms. On land it was also proving to be an arduous task involving excavating the attack sites, stripping out whole sections of damaged pipeline and then relaying and welding new sections into place. In Eastern Europe where the winter weather conditions were particularly bad, getting the heavy equipment operating at the sites of the damaged pipelines had been a tortuous affair and some of the specialist workers had been killed in the attempt. Word had spread quickly throughout the gas-supply engineering sector to strictly enforce safely regulations for all manpower involved with these heavy engineering activities and this was now also slowing down the whole repair process. The specialised welders who connect up these mighty pipes were also suddenly in short supply with there being such a demand for their services, and they were able to make the same money in a week as they would have normally have made in many months. It was a desperate situation and desperate measures were required to rectify matters.

The impact on people's lives had been profound. Fresh food supply to shops had been disrupted, there was rarely any fresh bread since the big commercial bakeries were unable to operate without natural gas, trading on the London and New York Stock Exchanges had been suspended, there had been mass evacuations of children away from the cities to smaller towns and rural communities where they could be taken in. There were now a large number of children being cared for at Himbledon from two of the large midland cities in England. Rural boarding schools had become large dormitories for city youngsters, and anyone with wood lots available to them, were suddenly those managing to stave off the freezing conditions. It was almost war like conditions again all across the country with people eking out each day with limited food and heating. The large national supermarkets had been asked by the government to preserve non-perishable food and ration sales to avoid panic buying and hoarding. They had been quick to act and it had contributed to getting the civil population through these dire times. There had been several deaths mainly through hyperthermia and among the elderly and very young. Many people were staying at home and many public libraries book stocks had been depleted. Toy and game shops had reported a sudden demand for board games such as Scrabble and Monopoly and electric blankets could be found nowhere.

The impact on the global economy had been catastrophic, coming as it did after the earlier attacks. Vast amounts of value in shares and other financial instruments had simply disappeared, gone forever with the premium currencies now being hot food, fuel and warmth. There had been cases of looting, but these had been quickly dealt with by local police, and, with many breweries unable to operate, beer and other alcoholic beverages were also in short supply, leading to a welcome sobriety, particularly among young people. Various oil refineries around the country were operating at maximum output trying to provide additional heating fuels and liquid petroleum gas that were being delivered and stockpiled in strategic sites around the country under military guard. The volume of traffic on the motorways had dropped drastically as people stopped travelling, since in many instances they had no reason to travel, many places of work had closed and the whole country had taken on the appearance of an eerie deserted landscape. It was a similar situation across Northern Europe and large swathes of America. Politicians and business people had been forced to use video conferencing to communicate and manage only those affairs now considered essential. The countries affected had stepped back to a slower and moderated life style focussed on a single imperative: survival.

It was some days later that Joseph and Mark, working in the study, managed to continue to piece further information together. From a conversation Mark had with one the prime minister's security people, some debris from one of the gas pipeline attacks had been retrieved and analysed by gas engineers, explosive experts and other specialists. They had discovered pieces of an intelligent pig and in reassembling it had found remnants of material similar to that in the advanced batteries in the Earth to satellite communication device found in Tim's apartment. Mark had put together his analysis of the situation that he shared with Joseph before sending it to London. It appeared that the perpetrators were using a mixture of technology to commit these crimes. The Paris attack had been the most unsophisticated and the aeroplanes had been brought down with rogue communications from a satellite. The trains had been derailed with rogue transmitters positioned under the high-speed rail tracks that had been triggered with some radio message probably from a satellite. These gas pipe explosions had been detonated by rogue equipment left behind probably during maintenance or even construction and they had been precisely timed to explode when they did, with long life battery technology and highly sophisticated clock technology. The thing that perplexed Mark was that Judaire and Adler had not used cyber attack technology to carry out some of these attacks and that they were probably keeping this in reserve for future attacks.

What they did now know was that advanced technology was being used as deadly weapons of destruction and that Judaire and Adler had ordered the systematic placing of numerous rogue devices within non-military infrastructure, under cover of routine maintenance and construction activities, by Milshner companies around the world. Mark's worst fears about their being a timeline also appeared to be correct. However, in order to stop the clock ticking toward Armageddon, it would be necessary to disable all these various destructive approaches that were being used. This presented a major challenge, since they had built in a very high level of obsolescence, unless they could locate the computer and software programmes that were orchestrating some of these attacks. They still desperately needed to track down and capture the highly elusive Judaire and Adler alive, and get them to talk, if that was possible. The security authorities also needed to try to identify the satellites involved with sending the killer radio signals, and either jam the signals or destroy the satellite.

"Surely that should be straightforward enough," asked Joseph.

"Well," replied Mark. "The American Space Surveillance

Network – US.SSN – established in 1957 after the Russians put up the first Sputnik, have tracked thousands of man made space objects put into orbit since then. Over twenty thousand have decayed since and there are at least thirteen thousand still in orbit with probably twenty percent of these still in operation. It is like a junkyard up there and they are having difficulties tracking any rogue radio transmissions. While it is possible to take satellites out either with guided missiles or other techniques, you have to be sure what you are aiming at."

Mark then went on to explain that there were many countries now with the capability of putting satellites into space and that it had become a relatively inexpensive and a frequent event that these countries lifted their clients hardware aloft for military, communications, research and other activities. The Tridium satellite phone system have about sixty low orbit satellites to provide good reception anywhere on Earth. These users, mainly military, connect directly to the satellites. There are also about thirty Global Positioning System – GPS– satellites orbiting the Earth and dozens of secret military surveillance satellites with unknown capabilities that their owners are not happy to talk about.

Mark suggested that Judaire and Adler could well even be deploying what the SSN think is space debris to bounce radio signals to their rogue weapons. If these transmissions could be identified then they could be jammed or the satellite disabled, and it was for this reason that the authorities were busy scanning the airwaves trying to locate these signals. Even this was being extremely challenging for two simple reasons. The transmissions are brief and they are probably being sent from mobile transmitters. If they were using a permanent transmitter located in one place then it would be a great deal easier to spot than a moving transmitter. Mark also had a hunch that the computer systems, probably multiplexed, would also be close to these transmitters.

"What about the raids on the cult compounds by the US authorities, have they turned up anything of value?" asked Joseph, and Mark described what he had learnt from his security contact in Downing Street. They had stormed a few dozen of the compounds in the US and were now holding hundreds of cult members in detention centres and interviewing them. In most instances these people do not know anything and have been released. From a careful scrutiny of the actual compounds, apart from some rather weird artefacts, again they have not yet found anything to help with tracking Judaire, Adler or the senior inner circle responsible for these attacks. One good thing is that the FBI and CIA are collaborating closely and they have put a team together to analyse various computer files and other computer technology found at some of the compounds. It appears that Judaire and Adler and any trace of them at any of these compounds are absent. They did, however, discover a list of other cult compounds around the world and, as we suspected, they are extensive, and the various authorities in the relevant countries have been notified.

"The thing is Joseph, the cult, these compounds, the people who placed the rogue technology and even Milshner, are now probably all irrelevant as far as the continuing attacks are concerned they have served their purpose, so are now expendable."

"So it is all down to still trying to catch Judaire and Adler, and stopping these radio transmissions," Joseph said.

Mark smiled and replied, "In a nutshell, yes."

It was now approaching the end of February and Louise had been back to Oxford a few times to liaise with her academic colleagues, as best she could, and continue to progress her work. The doctors at the hospital were also pleased with her progress and she continued to get stronger and was now able to almost walk normally again. Joseph was also stronger and his regular exercise routines had greatly strengthened his left shoulder and arm muscles. Francesca had continued to work in Rome and Achmed had travelled to them on two occasions from Dubai to progress various projects. Francesca had also delayed her trip to South Africa until later to wait for the spring in the northern hemisphere when it was hoped life might return to some state of fragile normality. Life at Himbledon had continued, despite the very difficult circumstances everyone had been living under.

The Ministry of Energy working with National Grid and

the natural gas and oil supply sector had devised a detailed recovery plan for when the natural gas would start flowing again. They had devised a detailed listing of cities, suburbs, towns and villages in conjunction with National Grid that prioritised which areas would get gas first. In many instances this was dictated by the configuration of the national gas network, although where ever possible places like central London, airports and other sites of strategic importance were to be re-supplied first. Many parts of Scotland and Ireland, once the feeder gas supply lines had been connected, would be receiving gas long before some small villages just outside London. The Himbledon Estate would not be getting gas again until probably mid April since it was regarded as low priority and able to look after itself in the meanwhile. All these plans were ready and it just now needed the undersea, East European and LNG engineering teams to complete their repairs.

Then in the first week of March the weather suddenly changed across Northern Europe, temperatures began to rise and the big freeze started to rapidly abate. This gave the gas line repair crews a window of opportunity to accelerate their repairs and it lifted everyone's spirits in Britain and Europe as spring finally started to make an appearance. People started to be seen in larger numbers walking around the estate; the roads across Britain became busier and it was as though the whole country was gradually awakening from a long period of hibernation.

It was also early in March when Thomas phoned Mark from Cheltenham and said he had some urgent information for him and he would be driving to Himbledon later the same day and could he ask Mary to arrange for him to have his usual room. He said he would be coming alone.

VII

A Rash Meeting, Truth, and Forgiveness

35

Face to Face

LOUISE HAD RECEIVED A POSITIVE RESPONSE from the International Criminal Court of Justice in the Hague and they had written requesting her to an interview with some of the senior prosecuting advocates. They had studied her credentials, taken up extensive references, spoken with her law professor at Oxford who had recommended her for the vacancy, and this meeting was viewed largely as a formality before they made her a formal offer of employment. They had advised that they needed to see her before the end of April in order to finalise all the necessary appointment arrangements for her to start a few days after she finished in Oxford in June. After she had got the call from her professor telling her about their request, she was delighted and instantly went to look for Joseph to tell him. Louise found him in his bedroom busy with a pile of business papers and his laptop computer.

"They want to see me in The Hague before the end of April and it all looks very promising Joseph," she said after entering his room.

"That's marvellous news, well done, they obviously like you. Why don't we travel to The Hague and then go down to Rome to see Francesca and Portia for a few days? Make it one trip together?" Joseph suggested, and Louise's smiled broadly and agreed.

Thomas had not mentioned it to the rest of the family and had sworn Liska to absolute secrecy, just telling her that he had to go to America for a few days. It had been mid

February when he eventually managed to get a flight out of Gatwick to Boston and Charlie picked him up at Logan Airport. He had stayed just one night in Boston before he and Charlie had left the next day for Montana. They had a difficult flight and landed in Great Falls late in the evening and Charlie had made prior arrangements with a military buddy at the base to hire a helicopter the next day, subject to weather conditions. Thomas had sent a message to Hank Milshner telling him he was coming and that he would contact him again a day before arrival. Fortunately there had been a break in the weather and on a freezing cold yet sunny day, Charlie had skilfully put the helicopter down on the roof of the mountain lodge at about midday. Just after the rotor blades stopped turning a man appeared in a heavy overcoat and waved to them and they both walked quickly across the exposed roof to some railings and stairs that led below.

The man, probably in his early fifties was a member of Hank Milshner's staff and said "Welcome gentlemen, Mr. Milshner is waiting for you Mr. Trimbledon." Then turning to Charlie he said, "May I assist you sir in securing the chopper in case the wind comes up?"

Charlie replied, "Good idea, I was about to ask you."

The three of them then fixed some securing wires to the skids of the helicopter and Charlie thought that this must be a regular routine up here for these guys.

The wind was quite strong as they walked across the rooftop and Charlie said to Thomas, "Two to three hours Tom, and we need to leave, before the weather conditions close in again," and Thomas looked at him and smiled.

Within moments they had descended down the stairs and the gentleman in the heavy overcoat had closed the heavy steel door and they descended down a long flight of concrete stairs and through more double doors into a carpeted corridor. Thomas and Charlie could hear music playing in the distance and then the gentleman asked for their coats and ushered Charlie into a small room with shelving, books, a television set and several large armchairs and suggested he would be comfortable there and he then led Thomas down the long well appointed corridor.

There were large paintings hanging on the walls and beautiful ornaments, pots and various plants adorning the long richly decorated corridor.

As they walked the gentleman suddenly turned and said, "Forgive me, let me introduce myself, I am Stanley, Mr. Milshner's personal butler, and I will serve lunch at one o'clock. I will also provide refreshments for your pilot while you are with Mr. Milshner. Before we enter sir, may I suggest you try not to excite Mr. Milshner, he has not been well again recently, and his heart concerns the doctor. He also sleeps from three thirty to five before he has a light supper."

"Thank you Stanley, we will need to be gone before Mr. Milshner has his nap anyway, to avoid the bad weather forecast for later," Thomas replied, while feeling surprised by this professional and civilised reception.

Stanley then coughed slightly and, putting his hand to his mouth, asked Thomas, "I am sorry sir, but may I see what you have in the leather satchel please?"

"Certainly, it is sheet music," replied Thomas.

"Thank you," and Stanley looked inside the case. "Thank you very much sir," he said again and smiled.

Thomas then looked at Stanley and asked impishly, "Shouldn't you also body search me Stanley?"

The polite gentleman then looked serious for a moment and replied, "There is no need for that Mr. Trimbledon; the electronic sensors in the walls of the stairwell would have detected if you had been carrying any weapons on your way in." Suddenly Thomas was brought up with a jolt as to where he was now standing, and whom he was about to meet.

"This way please sir," Stanley said, and he walked in front of Thomas down the corridor that led to a pair of large solid doors.

Thomas could hear the music as Stanley pushed open both doors ceremoniously, and held them for Thomas to enter. It was a huge room, wide and very deep with huge plate glass windows on the opposite side from where he was standing.

Stanley led Thomas to a large leather armchair and offered him the seat with a flourish of his arm, and then whispered to Thomas, "Lunch will be at one, sir," and then promptly departed.

The music that filled this vast room was by Aaron Copeland and Thomas recognised it immediately. As he looked around he could smell fresh flowers and then as he looked closer he could see large photographs and paintings of a man and woman all around the room and there were large displays of fresh flowers under all the pictures. The whole room, although very expansive, was elegantly furnished with many beautiful pieces of period furniture. There was also a long and impressive dining table to one side of the room and Thomas could see it had been laid for two people with wine glasses and silver cutlery. As Thomas adjusted his eyes to the bright light streaming in through the large windows, he then noticed the telescopes that he had been told about when with Father Brendan, and an eerie feeling, began to engulf him. *Keep focussed*, he thought. *And where is the piano*, he wondered. Turning his head to the right to inspect another part of this room, he spotted it, a full grand piano with the lid down.

The orchestral music continued to fill every corner of the room and then he noticed him, sitting with his back to the door Thomas had entered. From where Thomas was sitting, some distance away, Hank Milshner appeared to be looking out through the huge windows while he listened to Copeland. Thomas could just see the top of his head above the back of a chair. Then looking closer, Thomas noticed this was no ordinary chair, it appeared to be closed in all around with a flat back, and he could see the edge of an arm resting on one of the armrests, moving slightly in time with the music. Thomas just sat patiently waiting for the music to come to an end, and ordinarily would have relaxed and entered into Copeland's wonderful rich world of music that depicts the open prairies and majesty of American scenery, had he not started to feel a heavy sense of apprehension.

The music then stopped and Thomas heard an almost inaudible humming sound as the chair and Hank Milshner suddenly spun around, and there he sat, a small, rather rotund man, balding with wispy grey hair.

"I am pleased to meet you Mr. Trimbledon, and thank

you for coming all this way to see me. You will recognise the music, I am sure," Milshner said in a harsh, heavy American accent.

Thomas rose to his feet and walked forward to greet Milshner, and they momentarily looked into each other's faces. "There is no need for English manners here Thomas," Milshner continued and moved his electric wheelchair slightly to one side so Thomas could no longer look into his face.

They did not shake hands and Thomas moved awkwardly and sat in a large upright chair, just to the side of Milshner, that also faced the window, and said, "Yes, Simple Gifts from Appalachian Spring by Aaron Copeland, and a particularly good rendition, if I may say so."

"Yeah," replied Milshner, "The Boston Symphony Orchestra, I am a patron of theirs."

"May I offer you a drink, Thomas? I believe you are partial to one at this time of the day. What would you like? A beer, gin and tonic, scotch?"

Thomas replied, "A small gin and tonic will be fine." Thomas then noticed Milshner do something with some buttons on the right arm of the wheelchair contraption, and then a small table on wheels arrived next to him with a gin and tonic.

"I will have some wine with lunch so will not be joining you Thomas." Milshner said, continuing to dominate proceedings.

When Thomas had briefly looked into Milshner's face he had captured a mind's eye picture of the man. His face appeared distorted down one side and he had deep lines on his forehead and cheeks, and one eyelid appeared to be drooping. He was dressed in a simple woollen jumper and blue jeans and had tartan slippers on, and his feet were resting on a broad footrest at the front of the electric wheel chair.

Then suddenly Milshner spoke again as Thomas sipped his gin and tonic, "I admire your bravery Thomas, in coming here in the way you have. I am mad you know, and could have you murdered at any second. But I promised you safety, and that is what you will have. You were curious to meet me and that is why you sent me the letter. I was also curious to meet you, a

Trimbledon, a member of a very special family." There was a brief pause and then Milshner asked, "What are you going to play for us today? I think you will enjoy the piano, although it has not been played for years."

Thomas looked at the side profile of Milshner and said that he had brought various pieces of music, and thought that anything from Rachmaninov, Bach, Debussy or Copeland, whatever he would like him to play.

"No, you choose, Thomas; surprise me. But would you like to eat first?" Milshner asked, and looking at his watch.

Thomas noticed that it was still not twelve-thirty.

"I can play before lunch – there is still time – and then perhaps something after we have eaten."

There was a long silence, and Thomas just sat for a few moments before he asked, "Would you like that, Mr. Milshner?"

Milshner seemed to stir in his wheelchair, and said, "No need for such English formality, Thomas; my name is Hank. Yes, let's do that, but I want to talk to you first."

Thomas rose to his feet and walked across to the grand piano and lifted the lid and took some of the music out of his leather satchel and placed it on the stool in front of the keyboard. As Thomas stood by the piano he glanced around again and was struck be the whole room appearing to be a large shrine to Milshner's parents, full of these pictures and flowers.

Thomas then asked, "Are these pictures of your parents Hank?"

Again there was a pause before Milshner replied, "Yes they are, my mother and father. They are buried below on the farm. You will also know grief and loneliness Thomas, particularly recently, with the death of your nephew and brother John. I had nothing to do with their deaths and I wanted to tell you this, face to face. I also have some other things to tell you before you play."

The mention of John's murder made Thomas feel angry and reminded him again of the real purpose of this extraordinary meeting. "So who did order their murder, Hank?" Thomas asked.

There was no pause now and Milshner answered immediately, "A man called Judaire and a woman I once loved, Michelle Adler, they were the ones who ordered the murder of John Trimbledon and your nephew Joseph. They failed to kill Joseph and they must fail to fulfil their dream of dominating the world."

Thomas was surprised by what Milshner had just said, and how lucid this apparent psychotic invalid was behaving.

"Why did they have my brother murdered?" Thomas continued.

"To stop him, he was getting too close to stopping them, that is why." Milshner replied before continuing, "Have you ever been betrayed Thomas, used and then discarded like a piece of useless flotsam, by people you trusted, people you loved and people who you thought loved you?"

Thomas could detect that Milshner was becoming a little agitated as he spoke and replied, "No, not betrayal in that way, but I can imagine how hurtful it must be."

"Can you, Thomas, can you?" Hank continued. "To have your whole life stolen by two self-serving, evil people who think nothing of murdering millions of innocent people, in your name. No, I do not think you can imagine Thomas." There was a brief pause in the conversation before Milshner continued, "You see Thomas, we are both Christians, admittedly on different sides of a high fence, but it was never my intention to murder people in the way they have done. They used my business interests and myself for many years without my knowledge, a cynical deception, and they fooled me at first. I have now given instructions, months ago, that all my companies be removed from Michelle's grasp, but I am afraid I was rather too late, the terrible damage has already been done."

Thomas was taken back again by the man's directness and honesty and he realised there was much here that he did not understand as he said, "Would you like me to play now Hank?"

Milshner replied, "In a moment Thomas, in a moment, but first I want you to listen to me," and he continued talking. He told Thomas how for many years he had been confined to a wheelchair, paralysed down one side of his body, how he could not eat normal food and how he was always in physical pain. After his heart attack, he had learnt how Adler had tried to keep him a prisoner with staff under her control, but he had changed all that some years earlier, and that everyone here at the lodge were now totally dedicated to him and this is why he could ensure Thomas's safety. Milshner knew that the FBI agents were nearby, monitoring his every move, and that it was just a matter of a short time before they would come and arrest him and take him into custody. The thought of a public trial, all the media attention and public humiliation he would suffer, having already suffered for several years, was clearly almost unbearable for him to contemplate.

After such a candid series of revelations Thomas felt sufficiently emboldened to ask, "So why did you plan the end of the world, and enslave hundreds of young people in your religious cult?"

Milshner suddenly interrupted and said with a raised voice, "Yeah, yeah, Thomas, I know that is the distorted view that the world has of me, but it is wrong. I never intended the end of the world, all we wanted to do was to make the rich world stop and take a hard look at itself, the excesses, the greed and all the rest, before it destroys itself. The end of the world was a mere euphemism Thomas. you will know more than most, that man himself must never be allowed to destroy what God has created."

Thomas increasingly felt out of his depth with this type of conversation, and not being familiar with much of the secret fraternal intelligence, had little to guide him now, as he felt himself entering stormy uncharted waters. He was also concerned about Hank's increasing state of agitation, so he suggested he play something and Milshner said, "Okay, we can then continue to talk over lunch," and he moved his chair to face the piano.

Thomas walked to the piano, lifted the top and secured it, and positioned himself on the stool with his feet above the pedals. He rummaged through his music and pulled out some sheets of Debussy and Copeland piano music and spotted the brief piece, Down a Country Lane by Copeland and placed it on the stand before him. In seconds the grand piano came to life gently filling the large room with its glorious sound and Hank Milshner raised his emaciated body and positioned his head so he could experience the full joy, of the sound that Thomas was creating. Thomas then moved on quickly to two brief haunting pieces by Debussy, and as he was coming to the end of the second piece he could see Stanley, in the corner of his eye coming into the room with a tray.

After finishing the piece, Thomas just sat for a moment on the piano stool and Hank Milshner said, "Bravo Thomas, that was great, you are a very fine pianist. Come let us eat."

They sat opposite one another, and Stanley provided soup and offered Thomas wine before Hank Milshner said grace before they started to eat. At first, Thomas thought this a bizarre act for such a man, but, as the conversation continued, he learnt that Milshner still held strong Christian convictions. He noticed Hank Milshner being served a different soup from himself that he took through a long straw device, and his wine glass also had a special attachment so he could drink. Milshner was paralysed down the left side of his body and his left arm remained in his lap and when he spoke the left side of his face drooled uncontrollably. Thomas even wondered if it caused the man discomfort even when he spoke. The relationship between Stanley and Hank was almost like a mother and her child, with Stanley being extremely patient and with an obvious affection for the man in the wheelchair.

Behind Milshner's head Thomas could see a large oil painting of an attractive blonde lady with a nineteen sixties hairstyle.

Hank, noticing Thomas looking at it said, "That is my mother, Thomas, she broke her neck after I made her horse buck when I was nearly nine on the farm there," and Milshner pointed with a finger on his right hand toward the window.

Thomas sensed, that even after all these years, it was still a source of great unhappiness to him, something that remained unresolved and deeply painful, and he felt a fleeting touch of sympathy for the man and said, "But it was not your fault Hank, sadly these things happen, how were you to know the horse would do that?"

Milshner looked across the table into Thomas's eyes and said, "Wrong again Thomas, it was my fault and it has haunted me ever since. But let us continue our earlier conversation," and he continued to talk slowly.

Milshner explained that his father had also never forgiven him for his mother's death, and that her death had led to him dieing earlier than he should have done. Year's later Hank had found some respite from these obvious feelings of guilt by immersing himself in what he regarded as good works, and the early years of the religious movement he had started. He spoke about Judaire, his genius and how they had appeared to share similar Christian beliefs after they first met and started to collaborate. He never mentioned Adler and the betrayal again, but he then started to say some things that Thomas found very unsettling. In a brief cameo with Stanley during lunch, Thomas thought he heard Milshner say something about with this being his last meal he could have more wine.

At first Thomas dismissed this, thinking he had misheard, but then Milshner started to talk in an altogether different and troubled way, when he started to explain why he had invited Thomas to the lodge. He spoke about longing to be with his parents again, below on the farm, about returning to happier times. Milshner said emphatically that he had suffered enough and that be believed God had cleansed him through this suffering, and that he simply now wanted to die, to join his parents, particularly his mother. Thomas now knew he was in over his head and he started to have serious regrets about having ever embarked on this escapade.

Then Hank Milshner said something that suddenly touched something in Thomas when he said, "Our families, the Milshners and the Trimbledons, share much in common Thomas. They are both wealthy, Christian and honourable. My mother and father were good people, they were faithful to the teachings in the Bible and I let them down. I lost my way somewhere, as did your great Catholic church, so many times, and what makes it all the more indefensible, we have all made these errors in the name of Jesus. I have had more than enough time Thomas to think about what He must have felt, also betrayed and forsaken, even to this day, by so many of us."

Although not a religious man, Thomas was immediately able to connect with what Milshner was saying as Milshner continued, "But thankfully, I will die soon, and then I will be before my maker, and He will judge me in a way that no man can." Just then Stanley reappeared and started to clear the diner plates, and he poured both Thomas and Hank a further glass of red wine.

In this brief pause in Milshner's diatribe, Thomas's mind was racing. He was quickly forming this view of Milshner as a deeply anguished man, in great physical suffering, with a possible terminal illness, desperately seeking some form of peace and contrition before meeting his final judgement. Thomas also had this uneasy feeling that there was something rather sinister going on between Milshner and Stanley, even perhaps an assisted suicide.

Thomas was shaken from his thoughts after Stanley had left the room and Milshner spoke again, "But before I die Thomas, there are just two things that must be done."

Thomas felt numb and just stared at Milshner, as he continued, "First I must help put an end to the evil of Judaire and Michelle, they must be stopped, and I must do everything with my remaining strength to help you and the fraternity do so. I don't know everything, but what I do know may help."

"Yes," Thomas replied, rather sheepishly waiting to hear what the second matter involved.

Milshner continued, "You are also an honourable man Thomas, trustworthy and a man of your word, like all your family, I know this and have known it for many years. When they murdered your brother I knew I had to act, and when your letter was delivered to me late in December, I knew we had to meet."

Things were now rapidly falling into place in Thomas's brain as he sat with his wine glass in his hand and listened intently to the words slowly coming from Milshner and he instinctively knew Milshner wanted something from him, quite apart from just playing the piano.

Thomas then asked, "What do you want me to do Hank?" and there was another brief pause before Hank Milshner spoke again.

"The first thing I want you to do Thomas, is to give me your word that you will personally see to it that my mortal remains are laid to rest properly, next to my parents, on the farm that lies below this lodge. I also want the various authorities to recognise the help I am about to give you to bring Judaire and Adler to justice, and that the family name of Milshner is publicly disassociated from all these evil attacks and loss of life. Can you do that for me Thomas, will you give me your word?"

Thomas was silent for a moment and then said simply, "Yes, you have my word Hank."

For the next thirty minutes or more Hank Milshner then spoke at length about what he believed Judaire and Adler were planning. He believed the attacks had been warnings to show the world the great power they both had, and that there would be more attacks linked to notions of a doomsday scenario, but that this was just a smokescreen, and they did not intend trying to end the world, but rather wanted to intimidate everyone and to obtain power and domination. He spoke about some of the technology that he knew about, and that they had a number of satellites that his companies had put up into space for communication and other commercial purposes and they had probably moved the ground base control activities to containers that were continually moving around the world, to avoid easy identification by the authorities. He believed they would announce themselves after seizing control, via rogue computer software, of one of the global television networks, probably CNN and that this would happen before the end of the year.

Milshner also believed that they had developed a dreadful computer system and it this thing that emits the radio signal that triggers the rogue devices they have planted and that it will go on destroying unless it is stopped. It has no choice, no notion of right and wrong, it has no conscience, no criteria with which to judge what is good or bad, it simply does one thing, it destroys, this is what it has been programmed to do. Judaire had described these ideas eighteen years earlier when they had met, and Michelle had been fascinated by the idea.

At the time, Milshner had disagreed and opposed any such notions, and he thought it had ended there, mere lunatic ideas. However, they had obviously worked on these ideas, with his fortune, without his knowledge, and this had all been part of their deception.

Thomas then noticed Milshner reach into a side pocket on the right side of his electric wheelchair and he pulled out a large beige envelope and after some awkward movements he managed to put them on the table.

Looking across to Thomas he said, "Please take these papers and give them to your nephew Mark, I think they will help him with the important work he is doing to assist the authorities."

Apart from anything else Thomas was amazed at just how much Milshner knew about himself, his family and even the talents and activities of individual relatives. Thomas leant across the large table and picked up the envelope and walked across to the piano and put the envelope securely into his leather satchel before returning to sit again at the dining table.

He then went on to tell Thomas that both Judaire and Adler had undergone extensive plastic surgery, had changed their identities and would prove very hard to find and take into custody. Hank suggested that Judaire would probably commit suicide before allowing himself to be captured.

"Where would you suggest we look for them?" Thomas inquired, trying to gain as much information as possible.

"Difficult to say," Milshner replied and there was a pause and then he continued. "They will probably rarely ever travel together and I would think they now lead rather separate lives. Judaire was always obsessed with his technology, always looking for ways to improve it and find refinements. He sometimes worked for days on end in front of his computer terminal without even eating. I don't know where you will find him, but it is likely to be near his computer, from where he feels in control of things. As you will see from the papers I have given you, one of his ideas all those years ago, had been to keep moving around to avoid detection, possibly even at sea somewhere. Michelle hates sailing and anything to do with water, so she would spend her time on land, somewhere comfortable."

Thomas was trying to commit all this information to memory as he listened to Milshner be as helpful as possible in answering his questions.

Milshner then continued, "Michelle is smart and she will never wish to be apprehended here in America, we still have the death penalty in certain States. No, I suspect she will go to somewhere like Europe, perhaps to Bavaria, where we bought a castle some years ago together. It was where she and Judaire apparently fell in love," and Milshner suddenly fell silent.

"Oh, just one other thing that may help while I think of it, Michelle also likes wigs and has wardrobes of them. She used to like to dress up a lot and in one evening appear with different wigs, but that was a long time ago," and again Milshner appeared to drift off in silence to some other time and place.

Both men just sat in silence for a few moments and then Milshner looked at Thomas and asked him to play again.

"Yes of course, what would you like me to play?" Thomas asked.

Milshner replied, "Rachmaninov's Number Two Piano Concerto please Thomas, it was one of my mother's favourites."

Thomas rose from the table and walked to the piano and took the music from his satchel, placed it on the stand, looked at Milshner who had moved to position his wheelchair again by the large window, and he started to play. Again the music filled the great room high in the mountains and the acoustics were perfect. During the Moderato he looked up occasionally to see the side of Milshner and his right arm moving to the music.

After this first piece, Thomas paused for a few moments, and he heard Milshner say, "Thank you Thomas, that was beautiful." Thomas then played again for some ten minutes, Adagio Sostenuto, and Milshner listened intently and was carried away to distant places and memories.

When Thomas again finished and paused before moving to the final Allegro Scherzando, with a notoriously difficult left hand passage, he noticed that Hank Milshner had turned his wheelchair around to face Thomas again, and, before Thomas started to play, Milshner looked over to him and said, "Thank you, Thomas, for playing so wonderfully for me, despite your climbing injury; you still have a great gift, and you use it well. When you have finished, you may leave; it has been good to meet you." He turned his wheelchair again to face the window.

For the third time, the great piano burst to life and Thomas played with panache and exhilaration with a fast tempo, concluding with a virtuoso climax. At the end, Thomas just sat with his head bowed; satisfied that he had given his best, and tired after this technically demanding piece. He could feel his heart beating in his chest, and then, after a few moments, he spotted the time; it was just after three o'clock.

With ingrained English old fashioned courtesy, as he stood and put his music back into the satchel; he thought he could not just walk out, and at least had to go over and say goodbye properly. He pushed the piano stool back and stepped clear of the piano and walked over into the window area and toward Hank Milshner. At first, he thought he was sleeping, but, as he got nearer, he could see that Milshner was not breathing, and he felt sick and a feeling of panic ran through his body. Milshner's head was slumped forward and his right arm was hanging over the side of the wheelchair and unlike his agonised facial features earlier, his face looked relaxed and at peace. This had been an assisted suicide Thomas realised, and that probably in his food or wine, Stanley had administered some lethal drug or even some prescription drug, that in Milshner's feeble condition would end his life. *How many times*, Thomas wondered, *are patients put out of their agony with extra doses of morphine by doctors and caring nurses?* He wondered for a moment if this was any different, even though, as a Catholic, he was repelled by the mere thought of suicide.

As Thomas stood there with both his arms holding his music satchel to his chest, the door opened, and Stanley walked across the room and said, "Do not be alarmed, Mr. Trimbledon; yes, he is dead; he had wanted it this way, and he is now at peace. The world can hurt him no more. I look forward to seeing you again for his funeral below on the farm, and we will let you know when this will be. He specially requested that he only be buried with his beloved parents, after all these terrible atrocities have come to an end, and we will keep his remains safe until then. Now it is time for you to leave; your pilot is becoming a little agitated."

Thomas just stood, numbed by it all, and looked through the window to the vast territories lying below. He now knew that he had been involved in a carefully orchestrated scheme put together by Milshner and his trusted manservant, Stanley. As he stood there, he simply did not know what to think or how to feel.

Stanley, sensing the anguish in Thomas, said, "Would you like to see his parents' graves, sir?"

Thomas mumbled, "Yes, I would, very much please."

Stanley lead Thomas to one of the telescopes and, without touching it, put his eye to the eyepiece.

There he could see two modest grave stones standing above the snow, he could read their names inscribed on the stones and their dates of birth and death and then he could see a third gravestone that was blank next to his mother's grave. On both the grave of his father and mother there were fresh flowers.

Thomas felt deeply emotional and just then as he was bent forward looking at the scene below he felt a gentle touch on his arm and he looked around.

It was Stanley who said, "Thank you for coming, Mr. Trimbledon; it really is time for you now to leave, before the weather starts to close in again. I will attend to everything here; there is no need to concern yourself. But just one more thing, if I may. We will keep Mr. Milshner's death completely confidential, of course, until after they have apprehended Mr. Judaire and Miss Adler. It could complicate matters if word got out that he is dead, and Mr. Milshner asked me to mention this to you before you departed." He gently smiled.

Thomas stood up and said, "Yes of course, of course yes, I will keep it strictly confidential. Thank you, Stanley," and Thomas walked slowly to the door of the large room, in a dazed state of mind, to meet Charlie.

They were soon in the helicopter and back at Great Falls where they stayed the night before flying back to Boston the next day. Thomas did not eat anything more that day and took a bottle of Bourbon to his bedroom on the base, and went to bed early, leaving Charlie with his buddy and some other military guys in the bar. Thomas had sat late into the night writing down every detail he could remember from what Hank Milshner had told him earlier, ready to pass it on to Mark, who he knew would know what to do with it.

Throughout the bumpy flight from the Falls back to Boston, Thomas had been largely silent, and Charlie had noticed that as they had boarded the helicopter and waved goodbye to Stanley, that Thomas looked as though he had seen a ghost. It was only when they got back to Boston that Thomas began to start acting somewhat normally again although he said little about what had transpired in the three hours he had been with Milshner, in that great room overlooking Montana. After thanking Charlie and Martha for their hospitality and help, Thomas eventually departed Logan Airport after a lengthy delay due to the bad weather conditions. He was high above the Atlantic when he suddenly remembered the beige envelope that Hank Milshner had given to him and he took his leather music case from the baggage compartment and retrieved it.

For the next four hours, he was engrossed in the various papers. Some of the information was unintelligible, there were scraps of paper, and old stained sheets torn from a notebook with scribbles, diagrams and schematics. There were lists of companies and their activities, particularly related to infrastructure construction and maintenance and information about the Milshner shipping lines, with the names of the bulk carriers and container ships in the fleet. Information about liquid natural gas technical services, construction companies, aerospace engineering companies, telecommunications, computer software development companies in the U.S.A., Europe and India. There were Banks, rapid share trading services, insurance, global energy suppliers, medical and research bodies. The information also included mining and mineral processing activities, tea plantations, food processing, logistical companies and even some fast food global chains. The lists just went on and on; it was mind blowing for Thomas, and he recognised many of the company names, as global leaders, quoted on various stock exchanges. He had no idea of how all this was going to help Mark, but he just knew he had to get it all safely back to Himbledon as soon as he could.

As he was getting to the end of the pile of papers, some in folders, others lose with just paperclips keeping them together, he came across three sheets that had been folded in half, and it appeared as though they had accidentally got mixed up with the other papers. When Thomas folded them open and focussed his eyes with the aid of the mobile lamp beside his seat, he saw listed various charities, church organisations, educational, and cultural bodies. All six sides of these three sheets of paper were full. There was no heading and just a figure next to each organisation with a dollar sign next to it. As he cast his eyes down the column of figures his mind reeled at the huge amounts of money involved. He noticed a figure against the Great Falls Catholic Archdiocese, CAFOD the global Catholic aid organisation, the Red Cross, various Aids charities, child welfare and feeding schemes in various African countries, a whole range of Christian welfare groups from Anglicans to Baptists to several evangelical groups, cancer research donations, the American Association for the Blind, numerous educational bursary schemes, numerous cultural organisations, even the Boston Orchestra, housing schemes for the homeless and several charities that Thomas had never heard of before.

It was now late, and everyone else in his section of the business compartment were sleeping on their flat beds, and his area was the only one, still with a light on. He just sat there, with the low roar of the jet engines in his ears, staring ahead dazed and emotionally exhausted. Just then an attractive stewardess came and asked if he would like anything and she looked at him with slight concern in her eyes that Thomas immediately detected.

"No thank you, but I like your watch," Thomas said noticing that she was wearing a double-faced watch, no doubt with US and British time. As she smiled and then walked away Thomas put all the papers safely back into his satchel and put it beside him in the seat, and let the back down as he reached for a blanket.

36

An Urgent Meeting

IMMEDIATELY THOMAS HAD CLEARED FORMALITIES at Gatwick Airport he went straight to the parking garage and clambered into his old Aston Martin that, despite the freezing conditions, started on the third pull. Although he had only slept for a few hours towards the end of the flight from Boston, he felt alert and was quickly on the motorway driving toward Cheltenham. He wanted to go home and see Liska briefly, pick up some things from the house and then drive straight to Himbledon. It was late morning after talking with Liska and settling her mind that he phoned the Grange and it was later the same afternoon when he eventually parked near the kitchen door.

It was Mary who first saw him arrive and she greeted him in the kitchen and said, “Mark is in John’s study and has been expecting you. Your room is also ready and we will be eating at seven. Thomas, where have you been? I am afraid to say, you look awful,” and she gave him a hug and a kiss.

“Yes, yes my darling,” Thomas replied rather impatiently and continued, “I am just going to get my bag from the car, would you be a sweetie Mary, and please make me a strong cup of coffee?” and he leant forward again, lowering his towering body and planted another big kiss on Mary’s cheek.

Mary just laughed and said, “That’s not like you Tom, yes of course I will.” As Mary reached for the coffee percolator she felt happy to have Thomas back at the Grange again, despite what he might be up to.

Mark was busy on his computer and John's study had papers stuck up all over the bookcases and even over his grandfather's austere painting that hung over the fireplace.

"Hello Thomas, good to see you, where have you been? We had a mysterious phone call from Martha the other day saying you were in America." Mark said, and rose to shake Thomas by the hand.

"Yes, good to see you too, Mark. Hello. Bloody women, they can never keep their mouths shut about anything can they?"

Thomas bobbed around with his satchel under his arm and the coffee mug in his hand looking to see where he could put down his coffee safely without disturbing the chaos he was standing amidst. Noticing his air of agitation, Mark stepped forward and took the mug from Thomas and placed it on the desk and then threw some papers off a chair and pulled it toward Thomas to sit down.

"Thank you Mark, that is the second act of kindness I have received today, the first being your mother kindly making me coffee. It is so good to be back at the Grange, I don't think I will ever leave again," and they both burst out laughing.

Thomas relaxed for a moment, sipping his coffee, loosening his tie and telling Mark about Charlie's amazing flying skills. Mark could wait no longer.

"Come on Uncle Thomas, what have you been up to? Your story will be safe with me, come my child tell me everything," again they both laughed and then Thomas composed himself.

"Mark, I have just experienced the most extraordinary few days and everything I am going to tell you must remain completely confidential until we have sorted a few things out."

Mark readily agreed and then Thomas described his trip to Montana, meeting Milshner, playing the piano for him and some of the disclosures. Mark just sat listening, absorbing the information, almost in total incredulity but for the fact that it was Thomas who was telling him these things, and, with Tom, anything was possible.

Just then Mary knocked on the door and walked in saying supper will be served in five minutes.

Thomas immediately spun around with a furtive look in his face, and Mary walked across to him, put her hand on his shoulder, and asked, "What are you up to, Thomas? I hope you have not done anything silly."

Thomas turned and said, "No, of course not, and it is nothing you need to worry or concern yourself about, my dear."

Mary smiled and told them both not to be long and returned to the kitchen. Thomas turning back in his chair looked at Mark and asked, "How has your mother been since I have been gone Mark?"

Mark smiled warmly at Thomas and said, "Not too bad, Thomas; Mother has had much to distract her with this energy crisis ,and having Anna Hardwick also staying at the Grange appears to be helping them both. Louise has also stayed on, and you know what Mother is like with anyone who is sick. Not that Louise is sick anymore, but I think she has also been good for Mother at this time."

They both rose to their feet and made their way to the kitchen and Mark noticed Thomas clutching his music satchel.

After supper Thomas and Mark continued to talk and then Thomas asked where Joseph was, and Mark said he was down in London and would only be back the following day. The Grange still had various people staying over in the lounge and Thomas suggested that they keep John's study locked, and Mark smiled and said they were already doing that since moving from downstairs. It was quite late in the evening when Thomas finally handed to Mark the various papers that Hank Milshner had given to him, on the condition that Mark put them in the safe and that he did not discuss them with anyone until they had completed their own discussions the next day. Mark agreed and suggested that Thomas go to bed, and they agreed to meet again in the morning after an early breakfast.

When they met the next morning Mark was curious about the other matters that Thomas had suggested earlier, that needed to be agreed regarding all these Milshner revelations. Mark had also worked late again into the night going through all the papers that Thomas had given to him and he had drawn out a whole raft of vital information that dovetailed with his earlier fraternal work. Suddenly a clearer picture was emerging and this information from Milshner was invaluable, and may just enable the destructive and murderous attacks to be stopped.

"So what were those other things you wanted to discuss Thomas?" Mark asked curiously.

Thomas then went on to explain that the death of Milshner must remain a secret, for obvious reasons, that arrangements had to be made with the US authorities to keep the media away from Milshner's mountain lodge, and that the FBI must be pulled back and not authorised to go near the lodge until after Judaire and Adler had been apprehended.

"Okay, and what else Thomas?" Mark asked, intrigued while turning these emphatic requirements being stated by Thomas over in his mind.

Thomas then stood up, rather theatrically, and stood in front of the table where Mark was sitting. Thomas loved Mark and they were very close, as all the Trimbledon family are, but Thomas was always a little wary of Mark because of his icy objectivity, his considerable intellect and his apparent inability at times, to Thomas at least, to be able to empathise and to show his emotions. Thomas wanted to be sure that what he was about to tell Mark was not negotiable, that somehow it will happen, and that Mark, with other members of the fraternity were going to make it happen. Not being a member of the fraternity himself, he had always had some suspicions about them, and he was determined that what he had agreed with Hank Milshner was going to happen, just as agreed, with or without the bloody fraternity.

Thomas stood with his hands behind his back in front of Mark, his imposing tall body leaning slightly forward toward Mark with body language that Mark had never experienced before with his uncle, the odd man out in the Trimbledons. The brother who had scorned convention, the approval of others, preferring to be led by his heart, loving and living life to the full, generous and kind, always good for a joke, loveable and affable. Mark was suddenly to discover another Uncle

Thomas, a man of great conviction, true humility and real courage, a man without all the sanctimonious pride of other less honest men, despite his drinking and womanising. Mark actually felt for the first time in his whole life intimidated by Thomas, and he sat back and tried to relieve the tension by giving a nervous smile.

"There are three things Mark, that you, the fraternity, your brother, the prime minister and whoever else needs to be involved, are going to do before I pass to you some other material that Hank Milshner gave me, things I do not understand, but things that will enable bright young lads like you, to probably decipher and then have them applied, to bring an end to all this carnage."

Mark was taken aback, he felt personally confronted by the manner and attitude of his uncle, something he had never experienced before in his gentle academic life, and Thomas continued, "Unless I get a cast-iron agreement from everybody that will need to be involved, and I insist on it before handing over this important information, I will simply leave Himbledon, return to Cheltenham, pour myself a stiff gin and tonic, make love to Liska, get drunk and wait for the end of the world, at least as we know it. Do I make myself perfectly clear Mark?"

"Yes, absolutely, Uncle Thomas," Mark replied and Thomas noticed that Mark was holding the edge of the table and his knuckles were white.

Thomas continued, "Firstly, there will be a media blackout as far as Hank Milshner is concerned and all these imaginative reports on the television and newspapers about him will cease. He was, despite all the recent hype, an honourable man who had no responsibility whatsoever for these atrocities." Mark looked at Thomas and furrowed his brow slightly and noticing this Thomas said, "If you do not listen and trust me Mark, I will leave right now and you will not see me again."

Mark could feel his heart beating in his chest as he raised a hand toward Thomas in an act of submission and said, "Okay Thomas, I am sorry, please continue."

Thomas then said, "Once Judaire and Adler have been apprehended and the authorities have put an end to all this death and destruction, as a result of the information that Hank Milshner provided to me, I am going back to his mountain lodge and farm, and I am going to ensure he has a proper dignified Christian burial next to his mother's grave. It will also be a quiet service, without the prying eyes either of the media or security agents."

Mark then said, "Are you telling me Thomas, in all seriousness, that you are going to give this man your blessing at his graveside, a Trimbledon, the man who murdered your brother, my father..." and Thomas stepped forward and banged on the table with his fist.

"That is precisely what I am telling you Mark, because Hank Milshner did not murder John or Tim. I thought I had explained all this yesterday evening to you, but, as I suspected, you did not listen; your generation rarely does. You are blinded, Mark, by your hatred for this man and, underneath all your outward calm, there is nothing more you yearn for than revenge. Well if that is the way this thing is going to play out, without the real truth being told with proper justice to Hank Milshner, the man he really was, then the world can go to hell."

Thomas sat down again suddenly, glaring beyond Mark to the tall window beyond. There were some moments of silence as Mark reflected on what Thomas had said and then Mark began to cry, silently, the tears running uncontrollably from his eyes.

He felt embarrassed and stupid, but Thomas, noticing his situation, looked at him, his large strong face full of sadness for his nephew, and he said, "I am sorry, Mark. I am not angry with you, and I also miss John terribly. Yes you should let it out, the pain and sorrow you feel, you have been strong for others, and there is no need any longer to hold it back. Do not be embarrassed, what you are experiencing is entirely natural and right."

Thomas just sat there, all his frustration and anger now gone; he just wanted to quietly comfort his young nephew by just being there. After a few moments Mark gathered himself, dried his tears and looked at Thomas and apologised.

Thomas said, "There is no need to apologise Mark, I have

also cried since John's murder. I cry often, just thinking about Mary, now on her own without him by her side, so strong for the rest of us. But Mark, we must see justice done, bring the murderers before the courts, but we must never seek revenge because we too will remain damaged and deeply scarred."

Mark looked up at Thomas and smiled a little and replied, "Yes you are right Thomas and I am sorry for questioning you as I did, it is just that the last few weeks have been the worst in my life, I have felt so powerless and father and Freddie did not deserve to die, it is all such a waste."

For the first time since that dreadful sickening call from Charlie Harris, Mark had not permitted himself to confront his own grief, his own loss yet in the last few minutes it had all come tumbling down on him, when he least expected.

"But why were you so angry earlier Thomas?" Mark asked. There was a long pause as both men regained their personal composure.

Thomas then explained that Hank Milshner had already been tried and found guilty by the media, the government, the fraternity, and even himself. He had gone to Great Falls with the conviction he was about to meet the Devil himself. What he had actually found was a very different situation. A man in deep suffering, a man who had carried terrible personal guilt from the age of nine, a man who had never been able to forgive himself, a man who was fundamentally good and decent. That he had been betrayed and misunderstood and that the cult had been wrongly demonised by a world that itself is broken and sinful and has no right to judge. Thomas went on to say, there have been many terrible miscarriages of justice, when innocent men have gone to the gallows, when their reputations have been cast down and their families vilified. It would be easy and popular to condemn Milshner with the baying crowd, and leave his body and reputation for the media and political vultures to pick over and feast on, but this would be very wrong, it would damage justice itself. Thomas said that in the space of just three hours his whole attitude toward Milshner had been turned upside down and that the world, the self serving world would not honour the commitment that he had given to Milshner without force, without the use of similar tactics that the world used carelessly every moment of every day to pursue its own ambitions and greed. He felt he had to turn the tables to get Hank Milshner justice and he would stop at nothing to do so. The final reason that Thomas explained for his plan is that after listening to Milshner, he believed that Milshner, through his own personal and family sufferings, had come to recognise that the world cannot continue as it is. Milshner was trying to live a good life and that when he had found that Judaire and Adler had duped him, he acted with conscience to rectify matters.

Mark looked solemn, he had listened carefully to every word that Thomas had said and he knew his uncle was right.

"What is the third requirement Thomas?" Mark asked.

Thomas drew in his breath and replied, "After all this is over, once Judaire and Adler have been brought to trial, I want a memorial concert in Boston to pay tribute to Hank Milshner and his family and I want the President of the United States and our prime minister there. Then the media can have their day, and they can pay tribute to Hank Milshner for saving us all. Before you say anything, Mark, please look at this list of donations that Hank Milshner and his family made to various worthy needs."

Thomas stood up and took from his pocket the three sheets of paper and placed them before Mark on the table. He then smiled, and walked from the room into the kitchen to get some coffee.

It was then that Mark phoned Joseph in London and after a brief conversation it was agree he would return immediately to the Grange. It was early afternoon when Joseph arrived and he and Mark met immediately and discussed the recent developments with Milshner and the conditions that Thomas had described to Mark before he would hand over the further critical information. It was now late afternoon and Joseph asked Mark where Thomas is and he replied that just before Joseph had arrived Thomas had gone for a walk, probably to the pub for a drink. Joseph then went and put his coat and boots on and went for a walk toward to village pub in the hope of finding Thomas. It was a clear dry day, but still with a chilly breeze as he walked down through the gardens, past the lake toward the main gate.

It was some distance from the Grange when Joseph spotted Thomas walking back along the twisting lane toward the Grange. Thomas was wearing a deerstalker cap to protect his head from the chill and Joseph could see it bobbing up and down as Thomas strode along under the hedgerow.

As they both rounded the corner in the road, they smiled broadly at each other, and Thomas walked up to Joseph, put an arm around his shoulder, and said, "Good day to you, Joseph; good to see you; what are you doing out here?"

They shook hands, and Joseph replied, "Looking for you, actually, Thomas. Mark has explained your remarkable trip and news of Milshner, and I wanted to talk to you about what we must do next. It was rather foolhardy of you going off like that; we were worried about you. Thankfully, you are all right and back safely. Mother thinks you are up to something silly, but I told her you went to see an old friend in America, so it will rest there with her."

"Quite right, Joseph; it is very good to see you again, and yes, in hindsight, it was rather daft of me to have gone off like that, but I had no alternative under the circumstances. Anyway, as things worked out, it was for the best, don't you think?" Thomas replied.

After a pause as they walked beside each other toward the Grange, Joseph said, "We will have to speak to the prime minister personally as soon as possible and get him to talk directly with the U.S. president. I think there also needs to be an instruction to the media liaison group to sort out your media stipulations and I suggest you hang on to your bargaining chips until this is all sorted out first. I can quite see your viewpoint Uncle Thomas, and I will stand with you on this one."

Thomas suddenly stopped dead in his tracks, smiled broadly across at Joseph and said, "Bravo my boy, good that you understand my position, now we must get on with things."

They continued walking and talking together, and it was not long before Thomas had Joseph in fits of laughter. Thomas was also impressed by how quickly Joseph had assumed his more responsible role, since his father's death, and how promptly he had displayed a humble yet firm and sensitive leadership.

Within hours various wheels had been set in motion, contacts made, urgent meetings held and the prime minister had agreed to abide by the conditions that Thomas had stipulated to Mark. He actually had little alternative and when he phoned the US president, it was a difficult conversation, but, eventually, he obtained his word that the FBI would not go to the mountain lodge, they would keep a safe and discrete distance and that a media no-go zone would be set up. He also said that only he and his immediate security advisors would be notified that Milshner was dead and it would remain a secret. The prime minister also agreed that none of this information would leave Downing Street and that no one in the European Union would be told, with this last requirement being the one aspect of this whole thing that he was rather pleased about.

It was late the following afternoon that Joseph walked to Thomas's bedroom and called, "Are you there Thomas?" and Thomas opened the door and invited him in.

Joseph stood in the middle of the large bedroom and handed a piece of paper to Thomas and asked, "Is that good enough Thomas?"

After reading it Thomas sat on the edge of the bed looking up at Joseph and exclaimed, "How on earth did you get this so quickly?"

It was a brief handwritten letter, on the prime minister's official notepaper briefly listing the various matters that had been agreed with himself and the US president, and it was signed by the PM with strictly personal and confidential written in capital letters across the top of the page. It had just been faxed through from Downing Street.

"Don't even ask Thomas. Is it sufficient now for you to give the other information to Mark?"

Thomas smiled and said, "Well done, my boy. Yes, of course, it is." He walked over to his leather satchel, rummaged around, and pulled out several pieces of paper.

They were the handwritten notes torn from a writing pad and some other papers with the aerospace, software development and telecommunication company information that he handed to Joseph.

"Thank you, Uncle Thomas," Joseph said, and he smiled and turned to leave the room. "If you will excuse me, I will give these to Mark, who is waiting in the study."

He then left.

37

All at Sea

WITH THE VIRTUAL COLLAPSE OF THE GLOBAL ECONOMY, the world of shipping was in a dire state. Joseph had held an urgent business meeting in London with some of the senior management to review various vessels that they had ordered and it was decided that negotiations should proceed immediately to have these postponed. They also set up some temporary financing to support their cargo fleet until the global economy got back onto its feet again and they were better positioned than many other shipping lines, since they were involved in bulk ore carriers transporting iron ore and coal from Australia and South Africa to China. With the depletion of coal stocks at power stations throughout Europe due to the natural gas crisis, there was also a frantic effort to get large tonnages of steam coal shipped from South Africa and Australia to Europe and America. While the shipping rates were abysmally low, it at least helped with cash flow and would enable them to stave off bankruptcy. Dandler Aggregates also had a reasonable order book under the circumstances, largely due to large fiscal stimulus packages that governments around the world were pumping into infrastructure repair projects.

While they had a few container vessels, the main weight of their fleet, was in bulk materials, specialised refrigerated and other types of vessels for carrying perishable food cargoes. The bottom had dropped out of the container freight business and many ships had been laid up idle with their crews taking compulsory shore leave. In various parts of the world, from Falmouth to Subic Bay in the Philippines large swathes of cargo vessels were at anchor, silent and temporarily redundant. Maritime authorities such as Trinity House, who are responsible for lighthouses and the provision of sea pilots, had estimated that over fifty percent of the world shipping tonnage was lying idle. So too were many of the huge cruise ships, many moored idle off Florida, since no one wished to cruise during these uncertain and dangerous times. A number of banks, some heavily involved in shipping finance had gone bankrupt and the world's second largest shipping company was urgently seeking state financial aid to remain barely solvent. The oil super tanker trade had also been severely hit with the widespread contraction in demand for petrol and industrial heating oils. The International Energy Agency had already reported that oil demand had dropped by a staggering fifteen million barrels of oil a day. Shipbuilding yards around the world were also in a slump, and there was now a vast over supply of freight-carrying vessels. However, it was the box trade, as container shipping is called, that has been the worst hit, being largely decimated with the sudden collapse of the need for container services between Asia, Europe and America.

As well as the postponement of new ship orders and the temporary financing arrangements, the management of the shipping line also advised Joseph and other colleagues in their London offices, that they had implemented a whole range of cost saving measures. These included instructions to all their masters to avoid the Suez Canal to avoid the high canal fees, to reroute their vessels and to implement slow speed steaming to reduce fuel consumption. Joseph had also been assured that all the crew and their families from those vessels that they had had to lay up were properly provided for and would remain on the payroll of the company.

In the stringent economic conditions that prevailed even the British Admiralty was required to impose severe cost cutting, since all military budgets had been slashed. There are around eighty commissioned ships in the British navy with destroyers, frigates, aircraft carriers and nuclear submarines.

About half of the submarines are ballistic missile boats and the rest are attack submarines. Many of these vessels had been placed on standby with only essential craft in full service at sea. Brian Hardwick's destroyer, where he is a second officer, was still at sea and would remain so, patrolling various strategic waters far from Britain. He had been fortunate that his ship was in port in Simon's Town near Cape Town in South Africa when the news had come through about his father's murder and he had been able to get compassionate leave and fly home to attend the funeral.

The destroyer he sailed on was one of the newest in the British navy, the HMS Freedom, and it was powered by gas turbines with booster units that could propel the vessel at speeds of up to twenty-nine knots, just in excess of fifty kilometres per hour. It was a helicopter-carrying, guided missile and anti aircraft destroyer and it sailed with two smaller frigates. The HMS Freedom was also armed with a range of guns including one hundred and fourteen millimetre or four and a half inch mark eight guns, and some other close range weapons. It had been serving in the Middle East until a few weeks earlier when the captain had received secret instructions from the Admiralty to move to a station in the South Atlantic. Brian would have preferred it, had they been sent to the east coast of Africa to assist with the hijacking of merchant vessels by local pirates, but then who at sea ever understood the thinking of their bosses in Admiralty Arch?

When Brian Hardwick had been on compassionate shore leave for his father's funeral he had spoken at length with Mark before leaving to rejoin his ship in Simon's Town and had asked if there was anything he could do to assist. Mark had told him confidentially that he believed Judaire was probably operating a transmitter located on a ship at sea, and that there might be various computer systems close to the transmitter containing software programmes. If these could be retrieved safely, then it might enable experts to see what they are planning in terms of future attacks. Brian had noted these comments by Mark before he travelled back to his ship.

Mark had worked non-stop after receiving the papers from Joseph and Thomas and had put together a further detailed briefing package for Downing Street. He felt that in the recent circumstances that he and Joseph should now involve Thomas in their discussions and the three of them met in the study. Everything was becoming a little clearer and now with the names and contact information of the various companies who may have been involved with the attacks, the security agencies could now be directed to focus their efforts.

"A rifle rather than a shotgun approach is always more accurate," Mark said and then realised what he had said in light of recent tragedies, and the three of them looked at each other, momentarily distracted.

Thomas then asked, "What did all that writing on the old papers mean, Mark?"

Mark then went on to explain his interpretation of it all.

"They are probably using satellites to bounce radio signals to remote receivers on the ground that have been installed in some of this rogue technology that attacked the trains and aeroplanes. They must also have either one or more powerful ground-based transmitters." Mark felt strongly that they were concealed aboard a large vessel that was moving around the world to avoid detection.

With information technology getting smaller and ever more powerful, Mark also thought that the highly sophisticated computers and software were, in all likelihood, located near the transmitters. If the security agencies could instantaneously raid these various hi-tech companies, it may be possible to obtain further information, code, or something of value to help to disable this technology.

As Joseph and Thomas listened to Mark speak, their hopes were being raised, but then he said something that raised a feeling of marked despondency in them both.

"The trouble is, I just wish Judaire would transmit long enough for the radio-monitoring agencies to get a fix both on where the signal is coming from and which satellite they are using. We need Judaire to stay on air, for a few minutes, and then we could probably get him."

38

The Hague and Rome

WITH SPRING MAKING A GRADUAL APPEARANCE IN EUROPE and America, life was slowly returning to a state of partial normality and many of the large cities had regular natural gas supplies. All the airports were open and fully operational so Joseph and Louise arranged to visit Francesca after attending to Louise's interview in The Hague. Thomas had returned to Cheltenham, and Mark had fully briefed the prime minister's security people with everything Thomas had learnt from Hank Milshner. It had also become necessary for Joseph to visit Cape Town regarding some policy matters related to their shipping line, with vessels now routinely rounding the Cape rather than going through Suez.

Louise was charmed and impressed by her reception at the International Criminal Court— Cour Penale Internationale— and they had been equally impressed with her. The International Criminal Court— ICC— is the world's first permanent, treaty-based criminal court. It has been established to ensure that the gravest international crimes do not go unpunished, to deter the commission of crimes and to ensure respect for international law and justice. The court is an international organisation with a diverse staff drawn from around the world.

Louise had come to understand more fully the importance of the work performed by the court and the critically important role it plays in the system of international justice. Her discussions with senior members of the court had been largely a formality. Although various papers still had to be issued and signed by both parties, they offered her a position as a junior prosecuting council and she accepted, there and then. With Joseph on her arm, Louise then spent a day looking at a number of apartments in the city in readiness for her arrival in June to commence her duties, and they left her details with two local property agents in readiness for suitable accommodation to be rented later in the year.

Francesca was at Rome airport to greet them with her warm smile and they were then into the city traffic travelling out to the family villa. Rome international airport is eighteen miles west of the Eternal City with its rich history, art and other treasures. The family villa is located east of the city toward Tivoli, a hill town characterised by its beautiful gardens and historic villas built in the sixteenth century. Tivoli is also famous for its many enchanting fountains.

Within seconds of greeting each other, it was as though the three of them had never been apart. Joseph noticed that Francesca looked rested and happy with no visible reminders of the terrible attack she had suffered almost six months previously. Francesca also remarked on how well Louise was looking and they chatted away about their time in The Hague, and Francesca congratulated Louise on her appointment with the International Court. Everyone agreed that it had been the right choice. Joseph asked Francesca about her trip to South Africa and she said she was planning to go down there in April to follow up some field trials that had now commenced in the Western Cape and KwaZulu-Natal. It was then Louise, who suggested that with Joseph needing to go to Cape Town on business that perhaps they should meet up in South Africa, and they all thought this a sensible idea. There was a natural ease between the three of them and, although it was never mentioned directly, each of them knew the love that existed between them, and the special love between Francesca and Joseph.

There are different forms of love, each with its own defining characteristics, and Louise, Francesca and Joseph were gradually coming to appreciate and understand these differences. During their time together at the villa and in the hills near Rome they talked about so many things, but love, its nature and what they were each feeling, was something they also discussed and helped each other to better understand. It had been the Greeks who defined love with four distinct words, '*agape*', which means 'I love you', referring to a general affection rather than the attraction of *eros*, a sensual desire and longing. '*Eros*' means a romantic love, and would apply to a dating relationship and marriage. '*Philia*' means friendship in modern Greek, and is a dispassionate virtuous love, and includes loyalty to friends and family and requires virtue, equality and familiarity. '*Storge*' in Greek means affection like that felt by parents towards their children, and sometimes involved mere acceptance or putting up with situations and the behaviour of others.

The fullness of love was something that the three of them had come to understand and through the dreadful experiences of recent months, they had all emerged with a true love for each other. They all felt *agape* and *philial* love for each other, a deep bond that would never leave them. Joseph and Francesca also experienced *eros* and so had Louise felt a romantic and sensual love for Joseph although this was now changing, becoming less of a demon in her life, being replaced by an ever stronger *philial* love for him. Louise had also come to experience *philial* love for Francesca, based on mutual loyalty, common interests and their love of Joseph. The charitable— *agape*— love between these two beautiful women was now an unconditional love of each other, a love that brings forth caring, regardless of circumstances, and the greatest and most permanent of loves. Francesca and Louise loved each other in the sense of a deep affection, but without sensual desire.

Since that night in the ICU in the hospital in Oxford, Francesca had been joined with Louise forever with the greatest of loves, charitable *agape*; the love described in the Bible, a love that cannot help itself. God had intensified her own natural love for Louise, and it was a love that gave freely without the left hand knowing what the right hand is doing.

For their first evening together in Italy, before leaving to have dinner, Joseph and Francesca spent a little time together while Portia took Louise around the beautiful gardens of the villa. Joseph had described the trip by Thomas to Montana and some of the information that had been handed over by Hank Milshner. Francesca laughed as Joseph talked about Thomas and his noble insistence on the various conditions regarding Milshner's funeral and said that Thomas was right to have behaved as he had, because rarely can one trust the expediency of politicians. Joseph asked if there was any more information from the FBI in Boston about the rape and she said there was nothing, and they had still not apprehended the impostor Holmes. As Portia and Louise joined them in the large lounge, Joseph's mobile phone rang and it was Mark saying he had received a call from Neville van der Walt in South Africa, and would Joseph please call him when he had a moment. Joseph asked if it was urgent since they were going out for dinner and Mark said that tomorrow would be fine.

The four of them had dinner at La Sibilla a delightful restaurant in Tivoli that is in a spectacular location overlooking Villa Gregoriana. It was a happy relaxed evening and Portia asked Joseph how Mary is keeping after the funeral and after reflecting together on the recent tragedies it was Francesca who raised everyone's spirits by describing to Louise some of the places they would visit together in Rome. Francesca also suggested they go riding together and Louise admitted she had limited experience of horses although she liked the idea of a trip on horseback. Italian dinners are relaxed and drawn-out affairs, although this night, with Joseph and Louise tired after their journey from Himbledon, Portia suggested they retire early. Francesca also suggested, just a single espresso, if they wished to sleep easily.

The next few days near Tivoli were sublime, three dear friends free to be together, to talk, laugh, explore and relish the treasures of Rome. Francesca took Louise to the Vatican, the world's smallest nation covering just one hundred and twenty acres within Rome. The treasures it contains are almost beyond compare with St. Peter's Basilica, the amazing Sistine Chapel, many museums, lush gardens and beautiful apartments. They met Luke and had lunch with him while avoiding all the restaurants around the Vatican with their menus in many languages. No wise Italian ever eats in these establishments. With the knowledgeable explanations provided by Francesca, wherever they went, Louise was spellbound by it all.

Their lunch with Luke, in a quiet dining room within the Vatican was also a special experience for Louise. She found Luke a gentle, caring and extremely interesting man with a wonderful sense of humour. As a monsignor, Luke, in his official surroundings, was also quite different from what Louise had expected; not at all pompous or stuffy, but the very opposite, and she was pleasantly surprised by how easily he related to her conversation, her legal interests, and virtually any subject that she raised with him. It was also noticeable to Louise how close Francesca and Luke were as long established friends, and the fatherly manner he had toward her.

While the ladies were visiting Rome, Joseph remained at the villa and attended to various business matters via his laptop computer and spent some time on the phone talking to people at the London office, at Himbledon and the shipping line chandlers in Cape Town. Joseph was also reviewing some potential investments in South Africa and had been invited to meet one of the major cellular phone operators, a co-operative of some produce growers in the Northern Cape who had representatives in Cape Town and the local trustees of a charitable bursary fund his family provided extensive financial support to, for young disadvantaged black and coloured children. Much of this business was highly confidential and consisted of matters that only Joseph was ever to know about.

He had spoken to Neville van der Walt first and had caught him on the family farm on the Karoo; just before he was due to leave the farmstead to attend to matters on the huge farm. Mark had mentioned to Neville, that it was likely that Joseph would be visiting South Africa on business, when Neville had phoned the Grange. Neville and Joseph picked up over the phone where they had left off, some months earlier, in the London office. Joseph asked about his father and Neville confirmed that he was well and the bypass surgery had been successful, before going on to explain the reason for his call the previous day. Without wishing to divulge too much over the phone, Neville asked that Joseph spend some time with him while in South Africa, since there were some strange things going on in a remote part of the hill country in Lesotho that he would like Joseph's opinion about. Neville had suggested to Mark that he fly to South Africa, but Mark, knowing Joseph's impending business trip, suggested that perhaps Joseph could combine these activities. Joseph agreed to advise Neville immediately his travel plans were firm and that he would put time aside to visit Neville, and they hung up.

One of the highlights of their stay in Tivoli was a dinner that Francesca and Portia prepared for the four of them and another Italian couple who were close friends of the family. Francesca's brother was overseas, so it was to be a traditional Italian dinner party for six people. It all started early in the afternoon when the three ladies moved to the kitchen and Louise quickly found her niche in helping to prepare various ingredients, vegetables and all the other things that ladies manage to occupy themselves with, while also conducting absorbing conversations with one another. It was no place for Joseph so he went off for a stroll around the countryside, to be on his own for a while, to reflect and gather his thoughts. He was back by six and had showered and was ready to watch the beautiful late afternoon sunset with the ladies before the guests arrived. As he stood on the veranda of the beautiful villa looking out across the hills, he wondered where the ladies had disappeared to when they all suddenly appeared. They had retired to dress, leaving the large stove in the kitchen to finish cooking dinner, and there in front of Joseph they suddenly appeared, three most exquisite and elegant ladies, all smiling at Joseph with a touch of mischief in their eyes.

"Would you mind looking after the drinks for us, Joseph?" Francesca asked and Joseph did not answer immediately, overawed by such beauty.

Portia was wearing a satin trouser suit and looked radiant, Louise had a lightly embroidered blue strapless top and body hugging slacks and Francesca was also wearing a strapless dress that had a calypso style hemline that came just below her knees. All three ladies had put their hair up and had helped each other to arrange simple yet stunning hair arrangements.

Joseph just stood there looking between them and it was Louise who said, "Joseph, has the cat caught your tongue darling?"

The ladies laughed and Joseph, grabbing his self-composure, said, "Ladies, you all look so beautiful, I do not know what to say."

Joseph was blushing slightly and it was Francesca who stepped forward and gave Joseph a light kiss on the cheek and said, "You will find some Lacrima Christi white wine in the large cooler in the kitchen. Come, let me help you, and I will get our appetizer."

Francesca led the way and Joseph followed her into the kitchen where she opened the cooler door and looked down to some bottles of white wine before going to a side table and carrying some plates onto the terrace. The four of them then sat looking out over the hills watching the sunset and had bruschetta, toasted bread with a light garlic-olive oil dressing topped with tomatoes. It was Louise who remarked about how delicious the white wine was and Portia explained that Lacrima Christi means 'Tears of Christ' and that this particular wine comes from the slopes of Mount Vesuvius near Pompeii. It was a few minutes later that their guests arrived; a couple in their late forties, and Joseph quickly went and fetched more glasses and another bottle of wine. The gentleman, who was a distant relative of Portia, was a cancer specialist who had an extensive practice in Rome. It was not long before he was charming Louise and Francesca joked that she must be careful of his flirting, innocent as it was, and anyway he could also flirt with his wife, Portia and herself as well. It was one of those very special evenings that one never forgets, the food was delicious, the company sophisticated and charming and Louise had been transported to another world, another reality.

When they moved to the table in the dinning room they had minestrone soup and as the light faded Portia lighted candles around the room. Time just slipped by as they talked, teased and laughed, before Francesca rose from the table, removed the soup plates and reappeared from the kitchen with hot dinner plates. She looked across at Joseph and asked for his help in serving the main dish of the evening. The doctor's wife was busy teaching Louise some rudimentary Italian and warning her to always avoid the buses that connect the main termini to St. Peter's, known by locals as the 'Pickpocket Express' and a sure route where you might have your wallet or purse stolen. In the kitchen, Francesca had just wanted to get Joseph away on his own for a moment and their absence was not noticed by those busy in conversation around the large dinning table. As Joseph walked behind her into the kitchen, he could detect her perfume, the same flagrance he had experienced when he first met her in Dubai.

When they reached the kitchen, Francesca reached for an oven glove and tea towel and then turned to face Joseph. They stood for a moment just looking at each other smiling, like naughty children, before Joseph reached out for her, to kiss her. Francesca just stood there and as he approached she lowered her head and he kissed her on the forehead.

Francesca then looked up at Joseph and said, "Come Joseph, there will be time enough for us to be together, now we have dinner to serve."

As before, Francesca was in charge, graciously and gently she guided Joseph to serve everyone at the table before they too joined the dinner party. They served Abbacchio Scottadito, a traditional Roman dish of roasted spring lamb with local vegetables. After placing the various dishes on the table, Francesca then asked Joseph to bring through some bottles of Torre Ercolana and fresh glasses. This red wine, rosso was from Lazio and made from Cabernet and Cesanese grapes and was delicious and perfectly complemented the spring lamb. Everyone ate heartily and again time just slipped by with animated conversation and much laughter when Portia asked the doctor about the rooftop restaurant at the Hassler. Had he eaten there recently and was it still good? He advised that when he had eaten there a few weeks earlier, it was still good food, so Portia then announced, this would be the dining venue for the last night of Joseph's and Louise's stay in Rome, to see the sunset and some of Rome's most breathtaking views.

The moment had then arrived for dolce, dessert and the special cuisine that Louise had prepared under the close eye of Portia. Again, it was a traditional local dish to conclude a long, exuberant and delightful dinner. It was biscuits with desert wine, cantucci con vin santo that was delivered to the table by Portia and Louise with hoots of appreciation. Italians temper their wine with water, either gassato, which is fizzy, or non-gassato, still water. Louise had not tempered her wine, and was now feeling somewhat elated, so Francesca suggested some espresso as they all retired to the lounge and sunk into the large armchairs and sofas. It was now late and there was a slight chill in the air as Francesca went and closed the doors leading onto the terrace. It was well after midnight when the doctor and his wife said farewell with insistent invitations to Louise and Joseph to visit them when next in Rome. It was very late when Portia excused herself and went to bed leaving Joseph, Louise and Francesca still talking in the lounge. Joseph mentioned his phone conversation with Neville and asked when Francesca was planning to go to South Africa, tentative dates were discussed and it was agreed they would try to meet while there. Louise began to yawn and Francesca excused herself and the two ladies walked away from the lounge, arm in arm to their bedrooms, leaving Joseph sitting alone.

They all awoke the next morning later than normal with Portia up first, preparing coffee, and an assortment of fruit and breads for breakfast. Louise and Francesca were next into the kitchen, and after some minutes Portia suggested that one of them go and wake up Joseph.

Louise looked at Francesca and said, "Fran, you must go and wake up your future husband," and she giggled.

Portia and Francesca exchanged glances and then Francesca slipped off the kitchen stool and went to rouse Joseph. It was later, at the breakfast table, as they all sat around in their dressing gowns, that Portia mentioned she was going to Mass at ten thirty at a nearby chapel, if any one cared to join her. Joseph accepted her invitation while Louise did not respond. Sensing an opportunity to speak to Louise on her own, Francesca also declined to attend Mass.

After clearing the breakfast dishes, Louise and Francesca showered and Francesca offered to arrange Louise's hair. As Francesca stood behind Louise sitting on a chair in her bedroom, brushing her hair, they chatted like two affectionate sisters. Francesca started to ask Louise about how she was feeling, how her injuries were continuing to heal. Louise trusted Francesca implicitly and had forgotten for a moment that it was a medical doctor she was now talking to as well as a dear friend. They discussed all manner of things, personal issues concerning Louise's menstruation, some pains she was still experiencing in her pelvic region and other matters. It gradually became clear to Francesca that Louise had not been told anything about the possible problems regarding having children. Louise did have some follow up appointments with various consultants in Oxford, after her return to England, and this was probably when she would learn about these problems. Francesca wanted Louise to be forewarned, gently prepared and to have the comfort of friendship in coming to terms with the matter.

Louise highly attuned perception eventually made her curious about Francesca's line of questions, and she asked if there was anything she should know about her injuries that the doctors were not telling her.

Francesca then sat opposite Louise and looked into her eyes and said, "You almost died in that hospital in Oxford, Louise, but God intervened and gave you life again. He did the same for me, when I was raped and Holmes did not murder me. We are the same Louise; we have been spared and have a purpose in His plan."

Louise just looked into Francesca's face and blinked, before Francesca reached forward and put her arms around Louise and hugged her.

Louise then spoke, "Please continue Francesca, I know there is something else you want to tell me."

There was a brief period of silence as Francesca stood up and gently stepped back from Louise who remained seated on the chair next to the bed. They just looked at each other for a moment before Francesca continued, "I cannot be sure Louise, but from the injuries you sustained to your lower body, there may be a chance that you will be unable to have children… but there are…" and before she could continue Louise interrupted her.

"Yes, I have suspected this for a while now, but Fran it is all right, if I cannot have children it is not the end of the world. I have never been one much for babies, anyway."

There was another pause as Francesca looked at Louise with deep concern in her eyes before Louise got up from the chair and walked and sat on the edge of the bed and said, "Thank you Fran, for caring so much about me, and being so brave to talk to me about it."

They were both sitting on the bed beside each other and Francesca turned toward Louise and took her hand and looking into her face said, "Louise, I want you to see a leading gynaecologist here in Rome and you must let me advise you about these medical things."

Louise smiled slightly and said, "Yes, I would like you to help me Fran, but let me see the doctors in England first. But there is also something else I want just you to know, Francesca."

Louise looked at Francesca and said, "Having children doesn't matter to me anymore because Joseph is the only man whose children I would ever want. This was never to be, and I have come to accept it. You will bear his children Francesca, you will make him happy and you will both make wonderful parents. A year ago, I would have scratched your eyes out for Joseph, but my whole life has changed and for some reason I cannot explain, I love you both and want you, rather than me, to have many healthy children by him, that the three of us can be parents to." Louise smiled slightly and squeezed Francesca's hand. For a few moments Francesca just sat looking at Louise not knowing what to say, and thinking that Louise was far more worthy of Joseph's love, than herself.

Then Francesca said, "I did not want to fall in love with Joseph, it has just happened. Without your understanding and blessing Louise, as much as I love Joseph, I will walk away from our relationship. Having come to know you, the person you are, I cannot have Joseph at the expense of you Louise and our friendship. I am three years older than Joseph, my work has been my life and I never thought I would fall in love the way I have…"

Louise interrupted, "I know Fran, I know, but you are both made for each other, everyone can see that and Joseph cannot help himself, he loves you so much. Of course you both have my blessing, providing we can all always remain close. I could not bear to think of losing either of you." She smiled before adding, with a slight giggle, "I also want to help you choose your wedding gown and be your lady of honour at your wedding."

They smiled at each other, with all tension gone.

What had been viewed as an opportunity by Francesca to care for Louise had turned out to be very different. Louise had blessed the love between her and Joseph; she had been the strong one between them, and Francesca the recipient of her virtuous love for them both.

The final dinner party at the roof garden restaurant of the Hassler Hotel in Rome came all too soon for Joseph, Louise and Francesca. They enjoyed another wonderful evening together with Portia gently organising the waiters, food and beverages as they relished the wonderful views of Rome and the lovely sunset over the city. Francesca was a little sad that Joseph and Louise would be leaving the next day for Joseph to return to Himbledon and Louise to Oxford. For Joseph and Louise it was also coming to the end of such a special visit, and Louise just knew in her heart, that this was to be the first of many visits she would make in the years ahead to Rome, to the villa near Tivoli to see Portia. Portia had taken a deep liking to Louise, her practicality and intelligence, and insisted that she start planning her next visit to the villa. For Joseph, he knew that, within hours, he would have to be busy with other matters, the family business, but particularly his service and doing whatever he could to help stop the world sliding into further tyrannical chaos.

39

In the Karoo

IT WAS LATE IN APRIL IN THE EVENING WHEN JOSEPH boarded the British Airways jumbo jet at Heathrow bound for Cape Town. Francesca had flown to Cape Town three days earlier from Rome via Dubai and was already busy with field trips, visits to clinics in the large sprawling townships located on the Cape Flats a vast flat area near Cape Town. There were many meetings that she had to attend with various local bodies such as the South African Medical Research Council, people from Durban and the Natal Province, the local department of health, other research bodies and health administration people. The trials had been going well although there were certain detailed aspects of the local arrangements that Francesca felt should be improved and better monitored.

The local research staff working with Francesca and Achmed were local people specially selected and trained and they were all doing a wonderful job, albeit in trying conditions. They were either Xhosa ladies living in the townships of Khayelitsha and Mufeleni, large sprawling poor communities near the city of Cape Town, or coloured ladies who lived in the large housing estates on the Cape Flats. They were trained nurses and Francesca had a high regard for them all.

Joseph's flight to Cape Town was overnight and he landed at six thirty local time and took a shuttle bus to the Vineyard Hotel that is situated under Table Mountain with the most spectacular views of the mountain across lush green gardens. He had arranged to meet Francesca at the hotel late in the afternoon and they would have dinner together. Joseph had three or four day's business to attend to in Cape Town and he would then meet Neville and spend time with him on the farm in the Karoo. That was the general plan, although Joseph was flexible and he wanted to chat to Francesca about her movements before calling Neville. After confirming some business meetings for the following morning at the Cape Town harbour and at Century City, a huge new area of development a few minutes from the city centre, and clearing business and personal emails on his laptop, Joseph strolled around the gardens of this historical hotel.

He had never been to Cape Town before, although Francesca knew the city a little, having visited South Africa a few times. He enjoyed the gardens with a stream running nearby and he came across a very elderly tortoise on the lawn, which had been a patron of the hotel for decades. As he looked up at the mountain above him, he had this urge to climb it, so went off in search of information from hotel staff as to the best routes and the essential local information one must have before embarking on such an expedition.

As he was standing in the cool foyer of the hotel with his back to the glass entrance doors, talking to a black member of staff, he suddenly detected the flagrance of Francesca's perfume and he turned, and there she was, waiting for him to turn, standing in her usual pose with her hands together in front of her, smiling at him. She had a wide-brimmed hat that was hanging on her back, her hair was up, and she looked hot and in need of a drink. Without thinking, they stepped forward, without a word, and hugged each other.

As they walked through to the large bar and patio at the back of the hotel to get a cool drink, they held hands and just kept looking at each other. Before turning into the entrance of the bar area, there is a carpeted corridor off to the right, and Francesca pulled Joseph by the hand into this empty area, reached up, and kissed him.

As they held each other, she whispered, "I have missed you since Rome Joseph, it is so good to see you again."

Joseph just squeezed her tall body to his and said, "Me too, Fran, come let's have a drink, you feel very hot, have you been in the sun all day?"

They sat on the patio and Francesca had a tall glass of grape juice and Joseph sank his first local beer.

Seeing the large swimming pool to one side of the hotel grounds Francesca said, "Can I have a swim here Joe? I was in Crossroads for much of the day and it was very hot and dusty, the thought of a swim is so nice."

"Yes of course, I am sure it will be all right, but aren't you also staying here?" Joseph asked.

Francesca burst out laughing and replied, "I have an admission Joe, although I recommended this hotel to you, I am staying in town near the university and the hospital and sharing a room with one of our field staff. It is not far from here." Noticing Joseph's surprise and disappointment she continued. "Thing is Joe, I am not a high powered business person like you, and my purpose here is entirely different from yours. I must be close to the people we are working with and to go off and stay in some luxury hotel when I am working with poor people, well, it simply would not be right. But it will only be for another few days and then my work will be finished for this trip, it is going well and I may even be able to get finished sooner than planned."

Joseph smiled, instantly understanding what she was saying, and replied, "When can I come and meet these people and see what you are up to?"

Francesca looked into Joseph's face, smiled, and said, "That would be wonderful; sure you don't mind walking around dusty townships? It's a very different world, Joseph, to what you are accustomed to, but yes, I would like to show you the other face of Cape Town."

It was still warm, and remembering the idea of a swim Joseph asked, "Do you have a swimming costume or should we buy one for you?"

Francesca said she had swimming clothes in her bag in the car outside, so they agreed to meet in Joseph's room in five minutes to get into their swimsuits.

They were soon walking across the gardens to the pool wearing white hotel dressing gowns and Francesca had a large pair of sunglasses on as they selected two sun beds at the far end of the pool. As they put their things down, Francesca turned to Joseph and asked that he put sun lotion on her and then she would smother his body. Francesca then slipped off the dressing gown and stood for a moment, she was wearing a white bikini and she adjusted her hair before lying face down on the white cushion of the sun bed. Joseph's breath was almost taken away as he looked at her almost naked body for the first time, her gorgeous olive skin, long shapely legs and perfect female form. She could have been modelled on one of those beautiful female marble statues that adorn Rome. She was stunning and Joseph felt like a tall white blob beside her and decided to keep his dressing gown on.

As he applied the sun cream to her back and legs, Francesca said, "I am pleased to see you have kept your dressing gown on until I have covered you with cream Joseph. You obviously know how to respect the sun, especially in these parts."

Little did she know that it was his feeling of embarrassment rather than respect for the sun, as he sat on the next bed, applying the cream to her firm body. When his turn came, he blushed slightly as he lay down, but then quickly felt her firm hands on his back and legs, applying the sun cream.

Francesca was the first in the water after she walked gracefully to the poolside and dived in, hardly without a splash. Joseph, a strong swimmer was soon moving down the length of the pool as they both swam beside one another and they completed several lengths of the long pool before coming to rest in the deep end, holding on to the pool side.

"That was wonderful, Joe, so refreshing. Come on, I will race you to the other end."

They then both swam as fast as they could and Francesca arrived at the other end just a second behind him. Joseph was the first to leave the pool and he lay on his sun bed watching her swim, stopping periodically and looking to face him, just her head above the glistening water, smiling.

His body was dry with the sun by the time Francesca swam to the edge near him; she placed her arms along the pool edge and rested while chatting to him. She pulled off her swimming cap and her long black hair fell about her shoulders and Joseph walked over and extended his hand to lift her up from the pool. As he walked toward her, Francesca looked up at his tall athletic body and muscular shoulders as he bent forward and extended his right arm and holding each other around their wrists, he lifted her from the pool in a single, almost effortless movement.

Francesca then stepped beyond him and turned to talk, when she saw the scar tissue on his left shoulder and lower back. Francesca instantly, without thinking, turned and placed her hands on his shoulders standing behind him, and Joseph just stood for a moment, and she kissed his left shoulder and then his wound on his lower back and put her arms around him, pressing her wet body against his back, and whispered, "I love you Joe."

It was during dinner, later in the hotel, that they made plans for their stay in South Africa. The following evening Joseph was invited to join her at a dinner with her field workers in an African style restaurant in town, and then the following night Francesca wanted to take him to dinner at a place she knew in Camps Bay. Having her own hire car there was no need for Joseph to have a car and there were taxis that could take him to his various meetings. Before leaving Cape Town they also planned to walk and climb up Table Mountain and take the cable car down and also to drive out to Cape Point together in the hire car. They agreed that they would spend time visiting the clinics and talking to people involved with the field trials, on their last full day together in the city.

Joseph then asked if Francesca would accompany him to see Neville and travel with him up to the Karoo and, after a few moments' thought, Francesca looked at him and said that, providing she would not be in the way and that it was all right with Neville, she would like that very much. It was all settled then, and all Joe now had to do was to phone Neville and make the arrangements. It was a little after ten thirty when Joseph walked with Francesca to her car and they stood in the warm of the evening, holding each other and kissing.

"Will you be all right driving around here on your own Fran?" Joseph enquired, as she got into the car. She looked up and said, “Yes, I will be fine, I keep the doors locked and where I am staying is a gated secure area and I have an electronic key to get in, I will be fine Joe, and I will phone you on the mobile phone once I am there.”

“Okay, be sure you do, and I will see you tomorrow here at six thirty. By the way how should I dress for this African dinner tomorrow?” he asked and Fran laughed.

“Just casual Joe, and certainly no tie. Have a good day tomorrow my love, bye,” and he stood and watched as she drove away from the hotel.

Francesca and Louise had been in regular contact by phone and text message since they had been together a few weeks earlier at the villa near Tivoli. Louise had met the medical specialists in Oxford and she had been advised that due to her injuries, her ovaries had been irreparably damaged and that she would not be able to enjoy a natural fertilisation and pregnancy. Other options had been described to her, although she had shown little interest. The formal medical process whereby she had learnt of these realities had been made so much easier, following the discussions she and Francesca had had in Italy, unbeknown to Joseph or Portia. They had a number of long conversations over the phone, between Oxford and Rome about these matters, and Louise had also always asked if Francesca was sleeping better, since the evening at the villa, when she had been awoken by Francesca having a nightmare, and going to comfort her in the next bedroom. They had come to have so many shared secrets and those mutual concerns that only truly intimate and trusted female friends have together. Ironically, although it was Joseph who had brought these two exceptional women together, they now had a friendship uniquely their own, quite apart from him.

After saying goodnight to Francesca outside the hotel, Joseph had phoned Neville and as they spoke on the landline, he could hear classical music playing in the background from where Neville was speaking. They confirmed the arrangements for Joseph to visit the farm, and Neville was delighted at the thought of Francesca accompanying him.

“Is she anything like her mother, Joe?” asked Neville.

Joseph replied, "Yes, just as clever and fashionable."

"That's not what I meant, but never mind; I will make sure the place is clean and tidy, since we will have a lady here with us." He chuckled.

Before they ended their conversation, Joseph then rather awkwardly asked Neville, if he knew a good jeweller in Cape Town, where he could buy an engagement ring.

There was a momentary pause and Joseph could hear that the music had been turned off at the other end and then Neville answered his question, "Shame man, if I heard you correctly, yes I know a diamond guy there who will sort you out, his name is Stewart Steinbeck and he has a shop in Long Street in the city. You will find the shop number in the book under his name and just mention my name Joe, and he will give you a good discount and look after you. If I may ask, who is this ring for, is it for Portia's daughter?"

"Yes, it is Neville, and you must not say a word, please," Joseph replied.

Neville answered immediately like a salivating lion, "No, not a word Joe, trust me, it will remain our secret, eh."

They then summarised the travel arrangements and said goodbye. Neville went and poured himself another glass of wine, turned the music up loud, walked onto the *stoep*, and gazed out over the garden and beyond, thinking, *yees man*.

The next day had been busy for Francesca and Joseph and they had accomplished much of their respective work and reasons for coming to Cape Town. Francesca appeared in the hire car at the Vineyard at just before six thirty and Joseph stepped into the front passenger seat next to her dressed in jeans, boots and a short sleeved open neck shirt. It was a lovely warm evening and they kissed before Francesca drove them to the African restaurant. With his arm around the back of her seat they chatted about their respective days as she drove into the centre of the city along under the mountain, University of Cape Town, Rhodes Memorial and the Groote Schuur hospital, where the first heart transplant had been performed in the nineteen sixties. They were soon down into the city and parked near the restaurant under the supervision of a black gentleman who promised to look after the car for them.

It proved to be an interesting evening, particularly for Joseph, unaccustomed as he was to Africa. They sat at long wooden tables and most of the other guests were black people and there was a buzz of conversation and laughter. There was a band playing music with bongo drums, an elderly black gentleman on guitar, a young lithe black lady on saxophone and a very large swaying black lady who was singing with a very powerful and melodic voice. Francesca moved easily amongst everyone and was clearly known and popular with many of those present, and they all greeted her warmly with handshakes, hugs and laughter.

After a couple of beers and talking to a black gentleman seated next to him at the long table, Joseph began to relax and get into the spirit of the evening. Francesca then joined him and sat next to him, and the gentleman he had been talking to moved away to talk to other guests. Then it was time to eat and everyone sat down at the tables and a number of waitresses placed plates of food in front of the guests. Opposite Joseph there was a rather large and jolly black lady who Francesca introduced to Joseph and her name was Precious and one of the leading organisers for the TB trials in the local township. It was not long before Joseph was chatting to Precious who smiled regularly at him in a shy manner as she spoke slowly to him about her children and grandchildren. Every so often another black person would call over to her and she would glance at Joseph, as though to excuse herself politely from their conversation, before answering in Xhosa, their home tongue.

It was not long before Joseph found Precious to be a gentle, modest and fascinating lady, and as they talked about her life and his, he became ever more engrossed in what she was telling him. Precious did not drink any of the red wine on the table and she was born in the Eastern Cape where most of her extended family still lived. Precious was a grandmother, a trained nursing sister and lived without her husband who disappeared some years earlier, and she lived in a small house in Mufeleni, one of the black townships outside Cape Town. Precious would often use the word "Yees" while smiling at

Joseph and she appeared so accepting of the harsh circumstances that she clearly endured every day. Precious cared for several children, orphans of various family members who had died of Aids, and her day would start at five in the morning to be able to catch a taxi to visit the various clinics she had to attend. Tonight, one of her younger daughters was looking after the grandchildren back at their small house, and Precious did not get out very often in the evenings, and rarely came into central Cape Town, so tonight was a special treat for her.

Then another black lady, younger than Precious, who introduced herself to Joseph, joined them. Her name was Grace and it was her room that Francesca had been sharing in the apartments near the university. Francesca had since left the table and was talking to various people around the room. Joseph, Precious and Grace continued talking and they were asking him about his life in England and Grace said that she hoped to visit London some time, before looking around to see where Francesca was. Seeing her well away from where they were sitting, she said that Francesca was a good woman, had done so much for them all and that the drug programme could save many lives.

"We need more women like Francesca who understand Africa and our problems to come and work with us, to show us what to do and we will do the rest," Grace said, looking straight at Joseph and then she continued. "You must look after her Joseph."

Precious said, "Yes," again and looked serious.

Before Joseph could say anything, Grace continued, "Francesca has nightmares, bad dreams that visit her in the night when it is dark and she wakes very frightened, you must stay close to her, and look after her."

Joseph blinked and felt a deep concern for Francesca and looked at the two black women looking into his face for his response and said, "Yes, I will look after her, thank you for telling me and being concerned for her." They both smiled and as some people were beginning to dance, Grace asked Joseph if he danced and whether he liked the music. It was moments later when Grace and Joseph were dancing doing a mixture of ‘home counties’ and African free dance together.

As they drove back to the Vineyard, Joseph could not get out of his mind what Grace had told him about Francesca and the nightmares.

As they approached the hotel, Joseph turned to her and said, “I want you to stay with me at the Vineyard tonight Francesca, please.”

He asked it in such a calm and insistent manner that Francesca was momentarily confused by his request.

“Why?” she asked.

“Because I want to take care of you Fran, because of your nightmares, I do not want you to be away from me at night for the rest of our time here in Africa.”

There was a silence before Francesca looked across at him and said, “But it would not be right for us to be together like that…”

He interrupted and said, “I will not seduce you Fran, this is not an attempt to get you to sleep with me, I just think it will be better and safer for you. Don’t you trust me?”

They were now at the hotel and instead of pulling up at the front door, Francesca drove the car into the car park and parked.

She turned to Joseph and said, “It is not that I do not trust you Joseph, I do not think I can trust myself since I hunger for you so.”

Joseph reached over and kissed her and smiled and said, “Leave that to me Francesca, I give you my word that you will be safe with me, I will watch out for us both.”

After a long pause, Francesca got out of the car slowly and stood for a moment, as Joseph closed the car door and looked across at her.

She then walked around to him, took his hand, and said, “Yes I would like that Joe, but you are going to have to be strong for both of us.”

Then they walked into the hotel together as he carried her bag over his shoulder.

He insisted that Francesca sleep in the bed, and he slept on two armchairs pushed together with a stool in between to make a temporary bed that was long enough for him to sleep.

They talked late into the night as they lay in their separate beds and Francesca felt an ease for the first time in months at having him close by. They eventually fell asleep and awoke the next morning to the bright sunlight coming through the windows. They had forgotten to draw the drapes the night before being so preoccupied with moving around the room and en-suite in such a manner to protect each other's modesty.

These sleeping practices soon became the regular pattern for the remainder of their stay in Cape Town and when Francesca had explained to Grace her new sleeping arrangements, Grace had said, "That is good Francesca, Joseph is a good man and he will take care of you."

During the next four days they attended to their remaining work in Cape Town, visited Cape Point, watched spectacular waves at Dungeons off Hout Bay, walked up Table Mountain and had dinner together each evening in a different and ever more enchanting venue. Joseph had become fascinated by Cape Town and the surrounding area, the stark contrasts, the overwhelming beauty of the place, the warmth and friendliness of all the people and how the many diverse lifestyles appeared to co exist peacefully with one another. There was such vibrancy to everything and he felt so alive, whether standing in the market in Green Market Square or talking to a coloured fisherman hawking snoek, a local sea fish, on the roadside.

There was real opulence and wealth with five star hotels and luxury all over the city, the busy and cosmopolitan waterfront with shops, boutiques and first class restaurants. Yet a few miles away there was abject poverty, with a completely different culture and lifestyle, essentially African, where poor black families scratched an existence on the dusty and hot Cape flats. Joseph had spent several hours accompanying Francesca to clinics in Mufeleni, the large squalid new township outside Cape Town. He had spoken to many local people, visited them in their tiny houses, sat with people dying of Aids, helped Francesca with discussion groups in some of the local clinics and had left with a deep feeling of compassion for these people, and a desire to return. He sat in a local beer hall where the large black lady proprietor spoke no English and he communicated via one of the TB nursing team, and he sampled the sweet beer made in large plastic buckets with meat cooking nearby over glowing wood charcoals. It was also the smell of the place he would never forget; sheep's entrails being cooked on street corners, the black taxis hooting at the drop-off points and the inquisitive stares he elicited from everyone, wherever he walked. Never once did he feel in danger although he sensed that it could have lurked nearby.

Cape Town also has some other features apart from Table Mountain, one of the world's wonders. It also has the fifth highest numbers of murders per capita in the world with Baghdad, the capital of war torn Iraq, ranked at number ten. The most dangerous city in the world is Mexico's volatile border city of Ciudad Juarez, followed by Caracas, Venezuela and the U.S. city of New Orleans. Cape Town is fifth, with sixty-two murders per one thousand residents with Baltimore in the U.S. with forty-five. Cape Town also suffers a horrendous drug problem, particularly among many of the poor coloured population, who also live in large sprawling low-income housing estates. Francesca had taken Joseph to a clinic in Mannenberg, a poor coloured area, and they had talked openly to two local "drug gangsters" as they are known, both armed and both admitting they had been involved in acts of violence.

They had talked with a coloured parish priest at a nearby parish church, who had described hearing gunshots regularly at night and that some months earlier, the sports field next to his church, had been a popular killing ground for the gangs to dispose of their enemies or rival drug traders. Homemade narcotics and a range of other low cost lethal concoctions were destroying thousands of lives, wrenching families apart and inflaming the high levels of violence. There were welfare and state supported initiatives trying to combat drugs, particularly in schools, but it was an endless struggle to combat the pervasive culture of drug abuse that had existed for decades since the days under apartheid, when mandrax had been deliberately introduced to these poor communities, by organs of state, to subdue potentially troublesome constituencies.

Francesca had spared Joseph little of the other realities of Cape Town in their brief time in the city yet there were two further places she wanted him to see and experience. On their last evening, before having a late supper back at the hotel, Francesca had taken him to the Red Cross Children's Hospital in Rondebosch, where she had friends among some of the staff. This hospital is in the front line in providing care for the poor children of Cape Town and one of the medical areas that it has become renowned for, is the treatment of burns. Each year some fifteen thousand children suffer severe burns in South Africa and many die from these injuries. The World Health Organisation estimates that fire related burns are the eleventh leading cause of death for children between the ages of one and nine years old and globally more than three hundred and ten thousand children die every year as a result of avoidable fire injuries.

Open fires and the widespread use of paraffin in the shantytowns cause the majority of these fires with appliances that are virtual firebombs, if they are accidentally knocked over. Joseph was silent as he walked in a white sterile coat and hat with Francesca as she talked with the doctor and nursing staff. In some cases he could just see small pairs of eyes looking out at him from the special dressings and he was appalled at so much needless suffering when there were alternative safer fuels that could be made available to these poor people.

They then travelled in almost silence as Francesca drove them into the city bowl and along to Nazareth House, a Catholic establishment that as well as containing a retirement complex, wonderful stone church and other facilities, also has a large home run by nuns, for the very young orphans of Aids victims. Each year the Aids pandemic in South Africa is claiming thousands of lives, leaving whole villages half empty and killing off parents and the productive younger members of society. The many babies and young children in the orphanage in most cases had no one to care for them, many had been abandoned and even some had been found half starved, crying beside the corpses of their dead mothers.

Joseph was coming to understand the passion that

Francesca had for her work, the vital role that her family and his had to continue to provide essential funding for many of these caring activities, and the critical importance of 'on the ground', well-established and efficiently run charitable organisations. Despite the efforts of the United Nations, the World Health Organisation and many other global and local state welfare institutions, they are clearly failing the poor and disadvantaged. In just a few short days, in the company of this remarkable and beautiful woman he loved, he had come to see, feel, touch and deeply experience another reality, the needless suffering and deprivation of thousands of people. He became determined to work with Francesca, to try to change these unimaginable depravities, in a so-called enlightened and rich world.

When they arrived back at the hotel there was a message for Joseph from a Father Henry who was in the bar and was waiting to speak to him. Joe and Francesca walked through to the bar and were greeted by an elderly man who introduced himself. He was related to Joseph in some distant way through his father and was a Franciscan priest who had served in South Africa since his early twenties, after coming over from Ireland. Luke had phoned him after speaking to Portia and told him that Joseph, John's youngest son was visiting and they mentioned the Vineyard Hotel and he had phoned to be told he was staying and leaving the next morning. The discussion that was to follow in the bar and over dinner was to be a turning point in Joseph's life, although he had not realised it immediately at the time.

They spoke about many things, the family, the dreadful attacks, Francesca's work in Cape Town and a little of Joe's business activities. The priest had said how very sorry he had been to learn of John's death, so soon after Tim, and he expressed his condolences to Joseph, his mother and the family. After the earlier impressions and experiences of the day, it was not long, before Joseph began to ask the priest about the awful plight of so many in the city.

Henry talked about his poor parish in a large coloured community near the city and how he had served in such parishes all his life, even during the dark days of apartheid, and that even in these harsh places, God still existed, worked and was ever present to those who were open to him. He described the many good things happening, the way many of the poor also help each other in a way that rarely happened in the leafy suburbs of the rich South Africans. Joseph listened intently to the conversation of his two dinner guests, he quickly distilled the truths from the conversation and had thoughts and aspirations that he had never been exposed to before. He could now understand Francesca when she had said to him that it is places like this where she wanted to be, close to these needy people, helping them and empowering them to help themselves, particularly the women folk.

He had remembered her remarks to him when they were together at the villa in Italy, that, once you have spent time in Africa, it will intoxicate you; there was nowhere else like it on Earth, and, despite its brutishness, there was just something that would always draw you back. However many times you return, or for however long you may live there, you would never fully understand the place or the people. You would always experience the staggering beauty of its scenery, the plants, animals, and its people, who would enthral you, touch you inside, and make you happy and laugh. However, you would also experience horrors, unimaginable brutish violence and thugs, ignorance, indifference to the suffering of others, and tyranny. He had come to know and understand, suddenly, that Africa was one of the front lines in a different type of war, a different insidious tyranny of ignorance, corruption, and indifference to human rights and dignity. As he drank his coffee, he had this overwhelming feeling that there was just so much to do, but one must start somewhere.

As the evening was drawing to a close, Henry then said something that stuck with Joseph when he said, where else for the last fifty or so years, could he have served any better, than here in Cape Town. He said that he had felt closer to his vocation here among the poor than anywhere else he had visited in the world, and he felt privileged that this had been where he had been required to serve as a priest. He felt that he had experienced a richness of living that few others experience and he was very thankful for this and appreciated it as a special gift he had been given. Joseph was struck by Henry's acceptance of things, his intelligence and knowledge about many aspects of life here and by his inner peace and tranquillity. Joseph also felt that in this humble, quietly spoken man, one could detect deeper truths that in giving we actually receive riches of the human spirit beyond compare.

This man is living his life to the full, but in a very different place to most of us, Joseph thought. *He does not measure according to outward appearances, material success or status, but to timeless values of justice, endless generosity and forgiveness.*

It was for these reasons he had such an impact on Joseph, a young man starting his journey through life, and it had been little Henry had actually said directly, but his overwhelming presence and manner toward him and Francesca.

As they walked out to the car park to find Henry's old and rather battered little car, he turned to them both and Francesca stepped forward and kissed him on both cheeks, and Joseph noticed the elderly priest blush slightly.

Henry and Joseph then shook hands and the priest said, "Do not leave it too long now before you come back, and on your next visit you must come and celebrate Mass with me, I think you will enjoy our choir."

As Joe and Fran walked back to the hotel, Joseph turned to Francesca and said, "Surely these men must get lonely, he is probably going back to some dingy empty rectory, how do they do it?"

There was a pause and Francesca looked a little concerned, thinking about what he had said, and she looked up at Joseph and replied, "Yes, I know, Joe. I often have similar thoughts, but you know, there is just so much we do not understand about a priestly life; they do not belong to this world, really; they are a little part of something much greater."

It was later that night, their last night at the Vineyard before flying to Port Elizabeth the next day, that Joseph was awoken by Francesca tossing and turning and speaking in Italian in her sleep. He instantly moved across to her and kneeling by the bed held her hand and gently squeezed it and she suddenly awoke and started to cry. She sat up in the bed and Joseph put his arms around her body, that was hot, and he whispered to her that everything was all right, she had a bad dream and she is safe. He then switched on the bedside lamp and fetched her some water and after she had taken some sips, she put the glass down on the bedside table and reached out to him. Her silk nightdress had slipped off her shoulder as he leant forward and gently held her body and comforted her. She reached behind his head and kissed him and lay back pulling his body toward hers.

Joseph gathered himself just in time, his state of arousal almost consuming him as Francesca whispered in his ear, "Please Joe, make love to me."

He continued to hold her, straining his body over the bed from his kneeling position and his left shoulder came to his ultimate rescue with a sudden pain from the bullet wound. He slowly extricated himself from her embrace and then leant on the edge of the bed as he drew the bedclothes over her body.

She looked at him with a longing look in her eyes, smiled and said, "Thank you Joseph. I am sorry for what I just did, but I could not help myself."

He smiled and said, "No, nor nearly could I. Come, we must get some sleep."

When they landed the next morning at Port Elizabeth from Cape Town, there at the airport stood Neville in shorts, a loud check shirt and boots. He welcomed them both warmly and shook Joseph's hand for a long time while he tried to compose himself to greet this lady with Joseph, who he had watched walking alongside him from a distance, who looked as though she had just stepped off a Hollywood film set. When Francesca greeted him with the traditional kiss on both his cheeks, Joe noticed that this young man, who he had previously found to be the epitome of self-assuredness and 'cool', was looking decidedly flustered. Sensing his awkwardness, Francesca walked out of the airport with her arm through Neville's, leaving Joseph to trail behind with the baggage trolley. It had the desired affect, and her Italian charm had quickly put the outlander at complete ease with her.

After leaving Port Elizabeth they rode in the large

Toyota diesel pick-up, travelling north-west toward Uitenhage, where they make cars, and onto Kleinpoort, Jansenville and Graaff Reinet. It was mid day after they passed through the last small town before heading for Graaff Reinet and the sun was up and the air conditioning was blasting away in the cab keeping them all cool. Joseph sat up front with Neville, and Francesca sat in the back looking out of the window at the flat countryside as the vehicle sped along, never dropping below a hundred and twenty to a hundred and forty kilometres per hour, apart from a few spots on the road where Neville knew there were sometimes traffic cops with speed cameras. As they travelled, Neville started to explain to Joseph the strange things he wanted them to investigate together. A close friend of his, a pilot with South African Airways, had spotted a couple of times something that looked strange in Lesotho as he had flown between East London and Johannesburg. It appeared that there were some wooden structures in a canyon, various gantries, some sheds and unmarked helicopters. What had made his friend suspicious was that the wooden structures looked like electricity pylons with short lengths of cable on them, but they did not go anywhere.

When they arrived in Graaff Reinet, a beautiful historic Karoo town, Neville headed the Toyota straight for a small hotel on the main street with a lovely church nearby. As he pulled up he said they could stop here for some lunch, drinks and to freshen up. When they got out of the car both Francesca and Joseph could feel the heat and the glare of the sun and they walked into the shade of the old Cape Dutch style building and cool interior.

Neville and Joseph were soon drinking Castle beer and when Francesca went off to freshen up Neville turned to Joseph and said, “Hey man, Francesca is beautiful. Did you say she is Portia’s daughter?”

“Yes that’s right Neville, and not a word about what we spoke about on the phone,” Joe said.

“Did my friend in Long Street look after you okay, Joe?” asked Neville.

Joe replied, “Yes thanks, perfectly,” and just then they

could see Francesca walk across to them from the washrooms smiling. "Red grape juice, Fran?" asked Joseph.

"No, thanks. Can I have a Peroni, please?"

Francesca then asked Neville over lunch what his plans were regarding this sighting and she asked it in such a way that no eavesdropper would understand. The plan appeared to be they stay on the farm for a day or so, get themselves acclimatised, have a bit of a holiday and then Joe and Neville would go off to Lesotho for a couple of days to investigate.

"So am I not coming with you both to Lesotho?" Francesca asked.

There was a brief awkward pause and Neville said, "Well no, it will be too dangerous and anyway, we are going to have to do a lot of horseback riding to get to where we have to go." Neville had never quite met a woman like Francesca before and it took Joseph to intervene.

"You know, Neville, it might be useful to have a medical doctor along with us and someone who is also an accomplished horsewoman. I will take full responsibility for Fran, so what do you think?"

There was another brief pause and before he could reply Francesca gave him a certain little smile, pouted her lips and said, "I can also cook for you both Neville."

There was no hesitation in Neville's reply, "Oh okay then, but this is not easy territory where we are going, but yes it will be good to have you along Francesca," and he blushed.

Neville was three years older than Joseph and still a bachelor who had various lady friends in these parts, but no one he had yet given his heart to. His father lived between two large farms, one a wine farm in the Western Cape and a large sheep farm up in the Northern Cape near Calvinia. Where Neville was taking them to, was his own sheep farm, way north of Graaff Reinet, deep in the Karoo where he lived alone in a large sprawling farmhouse with a coloured family who cooked for him and looked after his gardens and then a small village of local Xhosa stockmen, farm hands and their families. When he was not travelling, attending to the family businesses on behalf of his father, this was where he always wanted to be, on his farm in the Karoo. Within hours, Joseph and Francesca were to come to fully understand why Neville loved the place so much.

The hot dry Karoo has a sparse barren landscape where the main economic activity is wool and meat from hardy Karoo sheep particularly the Dorper. It had been in 1947 when local farmers and various agricultural research institutes had managed to cross Dorset and Persian ewes to breed a sheep suited to the arid Karoo conditions and the White Dorper arrived on the scene. From these humble beginnings the breed proved itself as a hardy mutton sheep with a top quality carcass from a relatively early age. Neville had one of the largest flocks of Dorpers in South Africa, living on his vast farm covering hundreds of square kilometres.

It was late in the afternoon when they eventually turned off the tar road onto a dirt road and Francesca noticed that Neville hardly blinked or changed gear as he moved the big vehicle on to the dirt. Their high speed hardly altered and every so often she could feel the diesel pick-up glide slightly across the ridges in the road. She looked out over the open back of the double cab and there was a huge plume of dust behind them as they travelled quickly over the wide empty landscape.

It was at this point she heard Joseph say to Neville, "By the way Neville, something I have been meaning to ask you. Was Wimpie van der Walt, the ace pilot in the last war related to you?"

Neville looked across at Joseph and smiled and replied, "Yes he was, he was my old man's father, my grandfather. He was quite a guy, passed away now, but I still remember him well; he only died a few years ago."

Joseph and Neville then chatted about bedtime stories, how his mother had told him of Wimpie's exploits and a firm bond was already developing between these two young men. Francesca then offered them both some water and they both took a drink and she asked how much further before the farm and Neville looked at her in the rear view mirror and said about another ninety minutes. Both Joe and Fran were now coming to realise just how big South Africa is and how long it takes to travel anywhere by road.

Dusk was descending and it was getting cooler as Neville put on the powerful headlights. Francesca could taste the dust at the back of her throat and she felt an increasing sense of exhilaration, being with these two handsome strong young men in this huge landscape, miles from anywhere. It was so different from Cape Town and this was her first time in the Karoo. The scenery then started to become hilly and as they came over the brow of a hilltop, there beneath them they could see this vast expanse of landscape with hills beyond, miles away with the sun slowly going down. There in the far distance they could see some lights twinkling through the early evening heat haze with trees and other vegetation.

It was the only sign of life they could see before them for miles in any direction when Neville said, "That's it, the farm where we are headed, about another twenty minutes or so and we will be home."

It was dark when they arrived at the farm, but there was light from the sky above. It was as though everything was in a gentle shadow as they pulled off the dirt road and drove down a long narrower dirt road for about three kilometres and then turned into a another even smaller roadway that passed between tall trees either side with lush gardens, palms and the lights of the farmstead came fully into view. It was like a lush oasis amide all this desolation they had travelled through for the previous three or four hours. When Neville pulled the double cab to a halt in front of a large barn, some way from the house, three dogs came running over and jumped up at him.

He heaved their bags off the bag of the pickup and banged them together to get rid of some of the dust and said, "Follow me folks," and he led Joseph and Francesca across a large area of dry earth, in between some trailers, a tractor and along a brick path to a gate with a rich green hedge on each side.

Having passed through the gate they entered another world of deep green grass lawns, some fish ponds, fountains and flower beds along a path to some steps leading up onto a broad terrace and then in through a large wooden door with stained glass windows into a hallway. Francesca could smell wood smoke and smell cooking as she walked into the farm house and then a coloured lady appeared, probably in her mid thirties, very attractive with an apron, and she smiled at Francesca. Neville was behaving a little jittery as he walked around inspecting everywhere to make sure things were as they should be with a lady now in the house.

He suddenly emerged again into the broad hallway and said, "This is Wilma, and Wilma this is Francesca and Joseph who I told you about."

They shook hands and Wilma said to Francesca, "Would you like me to show you to your room?"

Francesca smiled and said, "Yes," as Wilma took her bag from her.

Wilma led Francesca through the great house to a large bedroom that looked out over the lawns and gardens at the front and then went and fetched a fresh jug of iced water with a small net with weights around on top and placed it on the bedside table. The bedroom was huge with a vast double bed and another single bed to one side of the room near the en suite bathroom. There were Persian carpets on the wooden floors and there were many framed drawings and oil paintings on the walls.

As Francesca stood looking around the room Wilma offered to show her how the shower worked in the bathroom and they stood chatting in the bathroom for a while and then she said, "Neville asked me to serve dinner in half an hour, if that is all right?"

Francesca was charmed by Wilma and her politeness and said, "Yes, of course Wilma, I will just have a quick shower."

Neville had invited Joseph into the bar at one end of the lounge with the dinning room next door with the kitchen beyond at the back of the house.

They were both enjoying a beer and with Francesca being absent, Neville turned to Joseph and asked a little awkwardly, "I was not sure about sleeping arrangements Joe, whether you and Fran are sharing a room or you want your own room. There is another double bedroom next to where Fran is, and there is also a single in her room, so you can decide."

Joseph smiled at Neville and said, "Thanks Neville, we are not sleeping together, but since her rape in Boston we have shared the same bedroom because she still has nightmares, so we will sort ourselves out, thanks."

Neville then took Joseph on a quick tour of the large sprawling farmhouse that had six bedrooms, two general bathrooms and some en-suites, a large lounge, a small library, an office and very large kitchen with a large dinning room nearby.

"Where do you sleep Neville?" asked Joseph and he pointed to the other large double bedroom on the opposite end of the veranda.

"Most nights in the summer, though I prefer to sleep on the stoep. You will enjoy the evenings out here Joe, there is nowhere like it."

After supper they sat on the stoep drinking wine and talking and the chirping sound of crickets could be heard. It was a lovely still warm evening and Joseph noticed that there were music speakers positioned in various spots in the lounge and under the roof of the stoep.

"What are those for Neville?" asked Joseph and Neville replied that one of his pleasures was listening to music and the following night they could have a bit of a concert.

"I will also show you around the place after breakfast tomorrow."

Just then, Wilma appeared, standing on the stoep, and asked what Francesca and Joseph would like for breakfast. Fresh fruit, oats and toast with some coffee were agreed to, and Neville said he would have his usual, thanked Wilma, and said goodnight to her.

After she had left, Francesca asked, "Does Wilma stay in the house here, Neville?"

"Oh no, Wilma stays with her parents in another house just over the back there, I will introduce you to her folks tomorrow. She is the eldest, and her younger sister and brother, bright kids, are away at varsity."

As the insects flew around the light fittings, there were periods when the crickets fell silent and there was almost absolute silence and stillness. Both Francesca and Joseph kept looking up at the sky, the millions of stars above them, like a massive clear ceiling above their heads without a cloud in sight.

Joseph looked across at Francesca and said, “What a beautiful spot you have here, Neville; it is so quiet and peaceful.”

Neville turned to face Francesca, with his wine glass in his hand, and replied, “Ya man, it certainly is, and I don’t want to be anywhere else. Some more wine, Fran?”

Neville was now relaxed, having got over those first few awkward moments when he had welcomed them both to his personal domain, and Francesca held out her glass for some more of the delicious Cape red merlot.

They continued to talk about their planned expedition to Lesotho and the mysterious things in the gorge between the hills there.

“Just explain a bit more to us Neville, about these things in Lesotho?” Francesca asked and Neville continued to explain matters a little more fully.

He asked if they knew anything about live line work, and when they said they didn’t, he went on to explain about the generation and transmission of electricity in South Africa. He talked about Eskom, the huge coal fired power stations up country near the coalfields and the transmission of electricity thousands of miles across this vast country. Durban, Port Elizabeth, Cape Town, Johannesburg, Pretoria, Bloemfontein and all the other cities in South Africa rely on Eskom power. Even here, miles from anywhere, the farm is supplied with an Eskom farm supply. There are large and very long transmission lines running across South Africa and Eskom use what are called live line crews to maintain these power lines without switching off the massive current. They do it by suspending highly trained technicians from helicopters and then carefully placing them on the lines where they can work safely providing they do not earth the current.

“What happens if they do earth themselves?” asked Joseph.

Neville replied, “Not a happy result Joe, with these massive voltages, they simply explode and die instantly. They get fried rather like those insects up there, getting too close to the light bulbs.”

Fran, who was now lounging on a long sofa on the stoep, lifted her head and said, “That’s awful Neville, what a terrible way to die.”

Neville replied, “Yeah, I suppose it is, but it rarely happens, these live line crews are very skilled, as are the chopper pilots. I know one of the pilots and they are the best in the game.”

Neville then continued to explain matters and that it had been Michael Faraday in the late eighteen hundreds who believed that if you put a man in a metal cage then half a million volts could pass over a man’s body without any harm. There would be no physical interference with the man from the electricity and this has become known as a Faraday Cage. Providing this metal suit is energised at the appropriate voltage, the man inside remains safe. Wearing these ‘hotsuits’, men travel on helicopters above the high-voltage electricity lines, and, providing they are insulated from earth, they can perform what is termed ‘live line maintenance’ and other duties. These highly skilled techniques enable electricity to keep flowing to towns and cities across the world. In South Africa, Eskom employ their own highly skilled staff to perform this work and their own helicopters and pilots.

What had concerned Neville and his South African Airways friend was that the Eskom choppers were marked Sapphire Air, yet those helicopters spotted in Lesotho were unmarked.

“Okay, but what is the relevance of all this to Adler and Judaire and the other attacks around the world, Neville?” Joseph asked.

Francesca sat up and swung her long legs over the edge of the sofa, reached for her wine glass and looked across at Neville and asked, “Do you have, by any chance, any small cigars, Neville?”

Neville looked startled and looked across at Francesca, who was smiling at him mischievously, and he said with a sense of relief, “I certainly do, just a moment.”

He rose from his seat and walked through to the bar and returned with a box of small cigars and a packet of cigarettes that he dropped on one of the small tables nearby and he opened the box of cigars and offered one to Francesca, who looked up at him, pouted her generous lips slightly and gazed into his eyes, flirted for a moment and then reached in and took one. Neville then stepped back, picked up his packet of cigarettes, took one and returned to Francesca, who was now turning the small cigar between her long fingers, and he leant forward and lighted her cigar with his flip-top lighter. They glanced at each other, as smokers do, and he returned to his chair as the thought flashed through his mind, *if only this beautiful lady was not already spoken for. Ach man.*

"What were you asking, Joe?" Neville asked, as he relaxed with his cigarette and another drop of wine.

Joe just laughed and said "About the relevance, Neville," having witnessed another side of Francesca and why perhaps other people were so much at ease in her company.

Drawing on his cigarette, Neville now became very focussed and replied abruptly, "Because Joe, one way to bring down the whole of the South African electricity network, just eight weeks before the opening ceremony of the World Soccer World Cup, would be to take out some of our major transmission lines."

Then everything fell into place for Joseph, the reason why Mark had wanted him to come to talk and be with Neville, could this be the time when Judaire and Adler would declare themselves to the world? His mind was racing; all feelings of admiration and romance toward his beautiful Italian girlfriend had suddenly departed him.

He rose from his chair and he walked to one of the posts supporting the roof of the veranda and leant on it, looked out over the silent peaceful garden and darkness beyond, and said with his back to Neville and Francesca.

"When do we leave and how far is this location with the mysterious helicopters?" Neville immediately tuned into Joseph's thinking while Francesca just looked across at his broad shoulders and wondered why she had insisted that he protect her in bed against his romantic advances.

It was a little later that Francesca said she would turn in and Joseph took his bag and dropped it by the single bed in her room. After getting into her sleeping clothes, they put their arms around each other and kissed goodnight and Joe then tucked her into the large double bed, kissed her on the forehead and said good night. She fell asleep almost immediately and Joseph returned to the stoep to continue his conversation with Neville and to make plans for their expedition across the border into Lesotho. It was agreed they would leave the day after tomorrow, drive to the border, get horses from some friends of Neville and then trek to the map co-ordinates provided by the airways pilot. They would take everything they needed with them including hand guns and necessary food and camping equipment. With that they said goodnight and Joseph walked off to sleep near to Francesca.

After breakfast early the following morning, it was the pizza oven in the corner of the large garden that attracted Francesca, as she strolled across the lush green lawns listening to the birds and the sounds of the farm as it gradually awoke to another hot day. There was a round concrete swimming pool, pots with glorious flowers, shrubs and many tall trees providing shady spots where there were iron chairs, sun beds and tables. It was a peaceful and beautiful garden and just then Francesca felt some water splash over her and she saw a garden sprinkler watering the lawns and borders. Just then Neville and Joseph joined her and Francesca said she would prepare some pizza for them later.

"Come on then," Neville said. "Let me show you around, but Francesca you must put some jeans and sturdy shoes on and get yourself a hat from the stand in the hallway, it is going to be hot again today."

Within a few moments both the men heard the fly door close as Francesca came down the veranda steps to join them again, dressed as Neville had suggested and wearing a wide brimmed hat and sunglasses. They then followed Neville as he led them out through the lush vegetation at the bottom of the garden out through a large orchard with fruit trees and across a field to another gate that led into a large cluster of farm buildings. As they walked they could see large stockyards with many stub nosed sheep with tiny tails standing. Then they were at the stables where there were several horses and in another field were a few cattle.

"How many sheep have you got, Neville?" enquired Joseph.

Neville replied, "A good few thousand, but most of them are out in the veld grazing, although we have to augment their feed at this time of the year."

They were soon walking along a dirt lane with dry grass banks, some old fashioned electric lights on poles and trees that lined the straight road. It led them into a large bricked area with white painted single story houses or cottages, each with a small garage and neat gardens. There was washing hanging behind some of the houses and then Neville led them to the door of one and knocked and an elderly black gentleman opened the door and smiled at Neville.

"Morning Mandla, let me introduce our guests," and Neville introduced Francesca and Joseph to the farm Induna.

They stood for some minutes talking and saying hello to various black ladies who had gathered around, and a number of small children. All the stockmen and workers were already away working, many having left before dawn to enjoy the coolest time of the day. There are ten Xhosa families living in this small village and after saying goodbye to Mandla, they walked back down the lane to some more houses where Wilma's parents stayed.

As they walked together Neville told them that there were fifteen Xhosa stockmen and farm hands and three coloured workers and that the whole place was rather like a large family. Most of those living on the farm had been here for many years and Mandla was the headman or induna for the Xhosa workers. Everyone here has a share in the place, Neville had said, and it was something his father and Wimpie before him, had always insisted on, that all those who contribute to the farm should have a proper share and be properly looked after and rewarded.

"We even have a small financial trust to pay for the further education of the children who want to go onto either technical or university learning and we have a medical scheme for everyone." Francesca listened with interest, fascinated by these arrangements that are uncommon in Africa.

They were soon at the other houses and met Wilma's

parents and her father was busy doing some paperwork for Neville, and they chatted briefly about some queries he had. Wilma's mother, a tall coloured lady, offered to make some tea or coffee, but Neville thanked her and declined the offer, saying they needed to get the horses saddled and be on their way before it got too hot. Francesca and Wilma's mother talked about some sewing and a large sewing machine on the dinning room table before they said goodbye and left. The mention of horses had taken both Francesca and Joseph by surprise, but Neville planned to take them out on the farm for a few hours just to see how competent they both were with horses. He needed to know before they departed for the hill country of Lesotho.

Joseph could already feel the heat by the time they had walked to the tack room where a number of saddles and bridles hung.

"You take this one, Francesca, and that one, Joe, and follow me." Neville thought again, *let us see just how good these folk are with horses.* He led them across the yard to some stables where four houses were standing in their own boxes. The tallest, a beautiful grey coloured horse was Neville's and he opened the half door and walked in beside her and patted her on the neck. The horse lowered her head and nuzzled and butted Neville affectionately. He wiped down her back with something that looked like a brush, threw a small blanket on her back and then heaved his leather saddle onto her before tying it under her belly. She already had a halter on and he then led her clopping out into the yard. There was a hitch rail and he loosely draped the reigns over it before giving the horse a bucket of water and some feed.

Neville then led Francesca to a smaller horse in a nearby box, opened the door and invited her to come and meet her companion for the next few hours, and then he stood back and waited. Francesca sensed this was some sort of test and she smiled at Neville and walked forward with her arms by her side and straight toward the dappled horse so it could see her approach. She moved naturally and calmly and talked to the horse before patting and stroking the neck of the horse. The horse turned its head and looked again at Francesca who was now standing beside the front legs and was smoothing the horses back. Just then Neville carried in the saddle from where Fran had placed it on the hitch rail and was about to throw it up onto the horses back when Francesca stepped forward without a word and took the saddle out of his hands. Within a few minutes she had saddled the horse, put a halter over the horse's head and settled the bit and she was leading her steed from the box to stand next to Neville's horse. She had adjusted the stirrups perfectly for her height and the erect ridding position she preferred, and Neville had watched her faultless display, greatly intrigued that such a glamorous sexy lady, could be so good with horses.

They were soon some miles away from the farmstead riding easily across the barren landscape with small pockets of sheep everywhere. It was after a couple hours they arrived by a large water tank with a windmill above it with some trees and shade. They rested the horses and they drank from a trough nearby as Neville reached into his saddlebag for a coffee flask and his cigarettes. They sat on an old fallen tree in the shade next to each other and drank coffee and talked. As they looked out across the barren countryside everything was shimmering in the heat and there was a low hissing sound. Apart from themselves and the horses nothing moved. It was a dry heat that, although very hot, was not unpleasant, but the two men had beads of sweat on their faces and arms.

Francesca then noticed, on Neville's right upper arm, an ugly scratch that was turning a nasty red colour.

She got up, pushed her hat off her head onto her back and went and crouched beside him and asked, "What's this Neville?" as she held his arm.

He looked down and said he had scratched himself a couple of days earlier, but it would be okay.

"Have you put anything on it?" she asked.

"No, there is no need, it will be all right," Neville replied.

She looked up at him and said, "You must let me put something on it immediately, there is some infection here Neville," and as she leant forward again he looked down at her exquisite face.

He blushed as Francesca stood up and fetched a small blue

bag from the saddlebag on her horse. She sat next to Neville, pulled up his sleeve to the top of his shoulder, deftly took out a small bottle of something, shook it and cleaned the wound and then put a small antiseptic patch over the wound.

"Thanks doctor," Neville said.

Francesca smiled and poked him in the side as she walked away to replace her little first aid kit in the saddlebag.

Joseph was lying, stretched out along the dead tree trunk with his hat over his eyes and as Francesca returned she nudged him with her legs trying to topple him off the old stump. In an instant he was standing beside her and she ran away laughing around to the other side of the corrugated iron water tank, and she then stopped. Joe came to a halt in front of her and put his arms out and they embraced, laughed and kissed each other and just stood together feeling the heat envelop every part of their bodies. The troubles elsewhere in the world felt far away and they felt so happy here, with each other and Neville.

Just then they heard Neville call out, "Come on you lovebirds, we need to move on."

As they walked back to the horses hand in hand, Joe thought about how good it was to have Francesca there, and that it could well be that she ended up looking after them, rather than they her.

For the next three hours, they roamed around valleys, passed old ruins of homesteads, watched birds in the sky, looked at strange plants and cactus growing in these arid conditions. Joseph came to know how important the various water wells and tanks were out here and they regularly stopped to water the horses and themselves with the clean cool water from far below the ground. They learnt that Neville played rugby for a local club team, never felt alone out here, had satellite TV and communications at the house, and every convenience. Rustlers were still a problem and like all farms in the area there were hunting guns and other weapons. Once a month a local priest Father Emmanuel would come out to the farm for mass in the barn and those who are Catholic on the farm would always attend.

"Are all your workers Catholic?" Fran asked.

Neville replied, "Oh no, some are not Christian, but follow traditional beliefs of ancestor worship. No one is forced to do anything around here apart from being honest, look after their families and co-workers and do their work properly."

"Do you have much stealing?" asked Joseph.

Neville replied, "Never among our own people, but stealing is a national pastime here in Africa. We get the odd dispute between some of the Xhosa families, but Mandla usually sorts out these things. If he is unable to, then I am the chief around here, and occasionally have to step in."

When they arrived back at the farm it was still hot and they wiped down the horses and put the saddles back in the tack room before leading the horses out into a paddock with shade, water and a long feeding trough.

"How about a swim?" Francesca asked, as they walked back across the garden and she said, "then let me check your pantry to see if you have the ingredients for me to make some pizzas for supper."

"Good idea," replied Neville.

Joe smiled.

It was late afternoon by the time they had enjoyed the cool refreshing water of the swimming pool, dressed and started to prepare supper. Neville arrived with a huge dish of meat, bread rolls, salads and started to light the fire for the braai before he cleaned out the pizza oven ready for Francesca. The sun had gone down and the stars blazed in the heavens as they enjoyed supper under the trees near the pool at the bottom of the garden. It was a truly enchanting setting and evening, warm and so quiet.

Joe and Neville had already sunk several beers between them and Francesca had had two Peroni to quench her thirst, before they started to drink red wine with their meal. Everyone was relaxed, contented and laughing at each other's jokes and intimacies. After they had eaten, Neville disappeared into the house and came out with the box of small cigars and some blankets that he laid out in the middle of the lawn. Seeing the box of cigars, Francesca giggled and walked toward Neville and reached over and gave him a kiss on the cheek before deftly taking the small box from his hand. Joe sat at the table facing the large lawn and house beyond, watching Francesca and Neville stand some distance away in the middle of the lawn talking and laughing. Apart from their voices it was silent, there was not a breath of wind and the sky above provided this vast canopy of stars glinting and looking down on them from millions of miles away. As he looked up, listened and looked around the large garden with the low lights in among the shrubs, he could see the shadows cast by the flames of the fire nearby. He felt this feeling of exhilaration through his whole body as he experienced the enchantment of this place and he reached for the small box in the pocket of his jeans.

Neville then came over while Francesca just stood on one of the blankets on the lawn with her wine glass in her hand looking up at the stars. As he approached, Joseph looked into Neville's face and winked, and flashed the small box at him and Neville grimaced with his back toward Francesca showing he understood the moment to be soon.

As Neville placed more wood on the fire he whispered to Joe to wait for a moment until he got his camera and some sparkling wine and said, "I also have some music that may embellish the moment Joe."

It was not long before the voice of Andrea Bocelli singing the duet "When Love Flows", with an enchanting female accompaniment, flooded the garden and the front of the house.

Neville stood behind the fly-door watching Joseph and Francesca with a bottle of chilled sparkling wine in his hand, a camera in the other and two cymbals pressed together under his arm. He watched Francesca walk slowly across the lawn to the table where Joe was sitting, and she sat next to him and took his hand and leant forward and kissed him. Joseph noticed, as the music of love poured from the speakers and enveloped them both, that Francesca had tears in her eyes and he looked at her with a concerned look. She smiled awkwardly and shook her head a little as he moved to comfort her.

Francesca just smiled and said, "No, Joe, they are not tears of sadness, but joy; what beautiful music in this heavenly place." She smiled.

Neville then went and turned the music down and returned quickly to stand watching them again.

Joseph got up and Francesca turned and wondered why he had moved away from her, and she moved her chair as he walked behind her.

Just then he stepped beside her and went down on one knee and reached for her hand, and looking into her beautiful eyes, as the flames of the fire flickered nearby, said, "I love you Fran, will you please marry me, and be with me for the rest of our lives?"

It was a simple and loving entreaty and Francesca looked into his handsome face with a feeling of sudden excitement and joy and replied, "I will be honoured to be your wife Joe, yes I want to marry you so much," and she bent forward and placed her lips on his for a lingering kiss.

He then produced the box from his pocket and, still kneeling, slowly opened it and lifted up the ring for Francesca to see.

"Oh Joe, my love, it is so beautiful, thank you, it is just perfect," and Francesca took the ring from the box, handed it to Joseph who placed it on her extended finger and she held it up to glint in the starlight.

They both stood up and hugged and kissed, and after a few moments were brought back to their surroundings by the clash of cymbals as Neville noisily came down the steps and across the lawn saying, "Bravo, congratulations. Well done, my man."

Francesca stepped aside and reached for Neville and gave him a hug and a kiss and then Neville shook Joe's hand, congratulating them both, before asking them to stand together for him to take some photographs of them.

Neville was a proficient photographer and took several pictures of them both, in various poses. Francesca held out her hand with the ring, looking impish, smiling into the lens. Joe then took some pictures of Fran and Neville together and Fran took some of the two men together. Then Neville excused himself and rushed back with a tripod and they continued to photograph themselves all standing together laughing and fooling around. The best picture turned out to be one of Neville lying at their feet with a flower in his mouth with both Joe and Francesca each having a foot resting on him as though he was a dead African animal, they had won in a hunting expedition.

Neville then disappeared again, put some more music to play in the background and stood with fresh glasses pouring the sparkling wine and he toasted them and then they toasted him and then the two men toasted Francesca before she toasted her two handsome male companions. They then all went and lay down on their backs on the blankets on the lawn looking up at the stars and laughed and giggled. Francesca got up and fetched Neville's camera and took pictures of them both lying on the ground.

Neville then surprised them both when he asked them to come and sit together on the blanket and he sat opposite them, and asked them to bow their heads, and he prayed for them, that God would walk with them for all of their days, bless them and their children and keep them safe. Yet again, another unexpected aspect of Neville had been modestly revealed, he was a Deacon in the local parish, the most unlikely of individuals yet someone who shared their creed and their service. It could not have been a more fitting end to such a wonderful day and no better place for Joe to have proposed to his love, Francesca.

VIII

Southern Africa, Soccer, and Justice

40

The Dark Continent

THEY LEFT EARLY THE FOLLOWING MORNING AS DAWN was breaking with the Toyota pick-up loaded with all the necessary equipment. They had eaten a good breakfast and had food, coffee, two large cooler boxes with cold beer and wine and other provisions to last them for the next three days. They had covered a long distance before the sun started to rise over the nearby horizon and were soon through Mount Fletcher heading toward Qacha's Neck on the border with Lesotho. Francesca sat between Joe and Neville on the front seat in the double cab as they discussed the best way to safely investigate the mysterious camp, without being detected. Neville had the map co-ordinates provided by the airline pilot and they planned to drive within about ten kilometres of the location and then liaise with someone Neville knew to provide them with horses for the final leg of the journey. They would then leave the horses a safe distance away from the camp, before completing their exploratory journey on foot.

They stopped every couple of hours for a leg stretch and some liquid refreshment, and Neville regularly enquired that if Fran needed the toilet, just to shout and he would stop at the next small town or petrol station. He soon learnt that there was no need to concern himself; Francesca was well able to look after herself, even in these barren surroundings. It was late in the day when they left the tar road and drove along a good dirt road to Maluti, a few miles from the border. They crossed the border easily and continued to drive into Lesotho before finding a safe site to camp the night and they set up a tent for Francesca, and Neville braaied supper, while Francesca prepared the vegetables and salad with a delicious dressing.

As they sat around the fire enjoying their wine before turning in, Joe looked at Neville and asked, “You know, Neville, with a name like van der Walt, how on earth did you ever become a Catholic?”

Neville was smoking, with a cigarette in one hand and a wine glass in the other, and Francesca sat beside him smoking a small cigar. Neville laughed briefly and replied, “Yea, a good question Joe, it is an interesting story.”

Neville then continued to explain that his grandmother, Wimpie’s wife, had been brought up a Catholic by her mother. His great grandparents were members of the Dutch Reformed church; and staunch Calvinists, when his great grandfather, who was a local lawyer, was killed on his way home from work one evening in a collision with some stray animal on the road. His great grandmother had fallen on hard times as a result, and for some reason was shunned by their fellow members who appeared to believe that the untimely death of her husband had been some act of retribution.

The only people who helped were the local Catholic community, who were kind and charitable and looked after her and the children. There was no duress or anything, but his great grandmother and the children, after a few years converted to become Catholic. When his grandmother married Wimpie, it was a few years after their marriage, that he too converted and so today his father, the whole family and himself are all ‘Roman Candles’, he laughed. He went on to say that many others in South Africa always regarded his whole family as rather strange, particularly the way they tried to manage their business arrangements with their black and coloured workers. There had been times when they were shunned as black lovers by many of the adjoining farming community, but this had all now long since ended, and his father and himself, had good relations with their fellow citizens, at least most of the time.

It was late morning the following day when Neville and Joseph lay low on a hilltop looking through binoculars at the camp below. Joe had a notepad and Neville whispered information to him, the number of helicopters, the camp layout, number of sheds and the number of personnel he could see moving around.

They all appeared to be oriental men and Joseph asked, "Are they Japanese, do you think Neville?"

"Yes, it looks so Joe," he answered.

Joseph felt a tingle of fear run down his spine with Neville's confirmation that these people were probably part of Judaire's personal guard. There were a number of steel structures, careful imitations of some of the designs of the transmission pylons currently used across South Africa. The choppers had skids on and small platforms that were clearly used for the impostor 'live line' crews to use. Scanning the surrounding hillsides, Neville checked out the general topography of the area, access roads and other important items of intelligence.

After half an hour, Neville had seen enough and he turned to Joe and said, "Come on let's get out of here, what do you think Joe, have we enough information now to report this camp to the authorities?"

Joe instantly agreed, so they then walked low and quickly across the hillside, out of view of the camp below, and reached Francesca who was looking after the horses. Within an hour's steady ride they were back at the small village and left the horses there with thanks to Neville's friend, before driving away, as fast as they could in the Toyota, towards South Africa.

They camped a few miles within South Africa after crossing the border that night, and Neville sat with a paraffin lamp above his head as Francesca and Joe prepared supper, writing up his notes with diagrams and other information about the camp with the helicopters.

"As soon as we get back, I will report this information to the South African Security authorities; they should know what to do next and will be able to liaise with the Lesotho authorities."

"Do you think they are planning something Neville?" Francesca asked as she served him some delicious stewed lamb with thick gravy and vegetables.

"Yes, I think they have been practising live-line activities and that could be only for one reason, to disrupt our electricity network. You would only have to foul up four or five major transmission lines, to probably bring the whole network down. Once it gets out of balance, the automatic protective equipment would probably do the rest."

Then Joseph asked, "When and where is the opening ceremony of the Soccer World Cup, Neville?"

Neville threw his cigarette into the fire and replied, "Middle of June, about seven weeks from now in Cape Town."

Francesca said, "Oh yes, Joe, at the new Green Point Stadium, do you remember, we drove past it the other day?"

They all looked at each other and realised there was no time to lose to at least ensure that the authorities were properly advised about this possible threat and went to the camp to investigate.

It was late in the afternoon when they arrived back at the farm and as Francesca began to prepare supper for them, Neville and Joe sat in the office and prepared a brief report that they sent to Mark at Himbledon, and Neville sent it to a reliable contact he had in the South African intelligence service. Neville even managed to get Mark on Skype, and they chatted about the camp, and Joseph mentioned he had become engaged to Francesca, and she was returning with him to Himbledon. Mark smiled and congratulated Joseph, and said that Mother would be delighted, and then agreed to do a brief report to the prime minister's office and also ensure that the FIFA soccer authorities were promptly advised. When they had finished, Neville said he would follow it up the next day to make sure the local authorities understood the urgency and the need to visit the camp.

They then had supper under the trees and sat out under the stars on the lawn on the blankets listening to Chopin.

Francesca turned to Neville and asked, "Is Nieu Bethesda far from here, Neville?"

He looked at her and said, "Yes, a fair way, why do you ask?"

Francesca replied, "I would like to visit the Owl House and

have read about Helen Martins and Koos Malgas, the itinerant sheep herder, who together built all those sculptures. You know Neville, she was a lonely and tragic figure and we Italians can empathise with such true life stories."

Neville looked across at her and said, "Yes I know what you mean, I can also understand a little of what she felt and all the ridicule she suffered. You know at the age of seventy-six, when her eyesight failed, on a winter's morning, she drank caustic soda and committed suicide. Her body was discovered in the veldt near her beloved Owl House."

Francesca sensed that Neville had a special interest in this eccentric lady who had lived as a recluse and had suffered an unhappy love affair some years earlier.

Neville sighed, and then he looked over to Joe and said, "You had better come back here for your honeymoon, and then you can visit the Owl House Fran, I will take you there personally," and they all smiled at each other.

Joseph and Francesca were due to leave the following day and Neville felt a little sad at the prospect, although there was plenty for him to do around the farm and he had a trip to Cape Town and New Zealand coming up in the next two weeks, so life would quickly move on again. However, he had really enjoyed these two people; Joe was now a close friend and, having shared their engagement with him, the last few days had cemented a special relationship between all three of them.

It was the following afternoon when they said goodbye to one another at the airport in Port Elizabeth. Francesca had held onto Neville for a long time giving him a deeply affectionate hug after which she kissed him on both cheeks. Even Joe stepped forward and gave Neville a hug and said he must come to England soon and spend some with them at Himbledon. As the plane lifted off the airfield and Francesca looked down on the countryside below, the last blissful few days all felt like a dream, suddenly gone, until she looked down and saw the ring on her finger, and she reached for the hand of Joe sitting next to her.

It was just a brief spell they had at Cape Town International before they boarded the British Airways flight together, and they looked forward to arriving back at Himbledon, to celebrate their engagement with the rest of the family and Louise. Francesca had quickly re-arranged her schedules following the engagement on the lawn, had spoken with Louise and Portia her mother. Her mother was so happy at her daughter's news and Louise had giggled and congratulated Fran on the phone and said she would be at Himbledon when they got back.

After spending two nights at Himbledon with Joe's family and taking long walks with Louise, deep in conversation, Francesca returned to Rome to continue her work. Joseph continued with business affairs and arranged a special meeting of the family charity trust board to review their donation policy in Africa, specifically Southern Africa. Life on the estate and at the Grange had largely resumed its customary routine and natural gas supplies had resumed. Louise went back to Oxford excited with the engagement of her dearest friends, and had signed the various papers for her official appointment at the International Criminal Court. The diaries of Francesca and Louise had many dates entered, when they planned to visit each other and Francesca had offered to help Louise find the perfect apartment in The Hague, before the beginning of June when they planned to meet again. Francesca was sleeping better now and had not had another nightmare since the one at the Vineyard in Cape Town, and the horror of the rape was rapidly disappearing from her mind.

The information conveyed to the authorities in South Africa had taken several days to receive proper attention. There had been confusion among high-ranking national security officials and ambiguity as to who should be responsible for following up the information. The FIFA football authorities had read the report and contacted local football officials yet there had been no suggestion to cancel or postpone the event. There was just too much money and prestige involved, although FIFA had asked that the camp be investigated as a matter of urgency, and they be kept informed of the result.

It was many days later when eventually a group of police and security officials managed to execute a dawn raid on the camp. Neville was dismayed when he received the report conveyed to him by a friend in the South African security service, and he immediately advised Mark at Himbledon. When the small task force had arrived they found just piles of steel, the various temporary sheds had been flattened, there were some fires still smouldering and their was the corpse of a dead local police constable lying near the camp next to the burnt out wreckage of a car. The Japanese members of Judaire's own personal guard, who had been rehearsing various 'live line' activities at the camp, had fled and were nowhere to be found. No one knew for certain what had actually happened, just twenty-four hours before the task team arrived.

The black policeman had visited the camp having been befriended by the friendly Japanese man who had bribed him to keep them advised of local police activities. He had spoken with his Japanese contact, the leader of the operation, and told him that there was to be a co-ordinated raid on the camp the following day at dawn. The friendly Japanese man had thanked the black policeman, passed over a bottle of brandy and some cigarettes in reward in the customary way, and they had walked to the policeman's car talking and laughing. As they stood briefly saying goodbye, the inscrutable Japanese man had suddenly produced a handgun, and while sharing a joke, shot the policeman at point-blank range between the eyes. The broken bottle of brandy was found near his corpse.

The camp had then been quickly broken down, the vehicles loaded, the helicopters refuelled and they had left late the previous day before the raid the following morning. Unbeknown to the official authorities, this group had dispersed and joined two other groups of Judaire's elite guard members, and gone into concealment at three sites strategically positioned around South Africa. They were not intending to bring the electricity network down in a single act since they were a small part of a carefully orchestrated plan that had been devised by Judaire, months before.

Members of the media were now beginning to arrive in South Africa to report on the World Cup, to be staged from the middle of June across this large country. This event is one of the largest single global sporting spectacles, held every four years in various countries around the world. Thousands of media, soccer officials, national teams, coaches and spectators were already beginning to arrive, many visiting Africa for the first time. This was to be the first World Soccer Cup ever staged in Africa. The frantic preparations for the event had been going for years before with the construction of new stadiums, training facilities for the soccer teams and state of the art media and communication centres. New airports and transport systems had been constructed, there were new and improved roads, hotels had been built and refurbished; and, there was great excitement locally that Bafana Bafana, the national South African soccer team would excel in the tournament. With billions of people around the world watching this prestigious spectacle, what better opportunity could there have ever been, for Judaire to personally announce his tyranny to the world.

Eskom, the huge South African electricity utility, had also received confidential notification of the strange activities in the hills of Lesotho, and the chief executive had called a special meeting of his security and protection services people. Ironically, during the years of rule by the Nationalist government and apartheid, Eskom had a small army of its own security personnel, and even an extensive armoury, all geared for the protection of the utilities' infrastructure from terrorist attacks. The vulnerability of South Africa to the loss of such essential services had always been widely recognised by the controlling authorities in the country. Today these security people no longer exist, and the armoury of weapons was sold off a decade earlier. Despite this, Eskom still had extensive contingency plans and these were discussed at the meeting. Acute power shortages in recent years had already given Eskom some insight as to the impacts of sudden loss of electricity supplies.

Additional police and security guards were to be immediately positioned at all the key transmission points around the country. The skilled staff managing the national electricity control centre, just outside Johannesburg, and the local control centres in Cape Town and Durban, were to be put on full alert with all leave cancelled. The power station managers were to receive a confidential briefing and a hurried meeting with all the major electricity re-distributors across the country was to be convened. Two days following this meeting, the Eskom chief executive provided a detailed briefing presentation to the cabinet of the South African government and the World Cup security task team.

During the earlier Eskom meeting someone had suggested calling back some of the people, now retired, who had managed Eskom security years earlier and they managed to contact Kobus Williamson, now in his late seventies, a white Afrikaans gentleman who in the following days provided invaluable advice. The helicopters owned and operated by Eskom were to instantly start national patrols along all the major electricity transmission routes and to report anything suspicious immediately to a special security control centre that Eskom set up in Bloemfontein. They in turn would liaise with the local police and the Distribution Depots that Eskom had scattered across the country. After a few days of frantic preparations and setting up various security measures, there was little more to be done but to patrol, be vigilant and wait.

It was a cold and wet winter in South Africa with regular cold fronts blowing in from the Atlantic across the Western Cape and then up through the hinterland across Johannesburg and the high-veld. There was snow on the mountains across the Western Cape and the Overberg, and in between the wet windy cold fronts, there were glorious cold days with blue skies. By the end of the first week in June, most hotels and guest houses were full with visiting football fans and the media centres had proved themselves to be well equipped and operating to the satisfaction of the international, hard nosed, news crews and reporters. There was growing excitement among the local population, and the politicians and football officials were pleased, with what they had achieved in recent months in pulling off this global commercial bonanza for the country.

Knowing the worrying significance of the opening ceremony, Mark, Joseph and the rest of the immediate Trimbledon family had gathered at the Grange for a few days, to coincide with the event. Louise had returned from The

Hague having completed an induction programme at the International Court for an extended weekend, and Francesca had accompanied her after they had been busy furnishing and fixing up Louise's new apartment. June at Himbledon is a glorious time of the year, generally warm with long evenings and Thomas and Liska had also come for the weekend.

Mark had set up a large flat screen TV in the lounge and arranged all the chairs so everyone would get a clear view of the screen. They were all milling around and Francesca was making sure everyone had something to drink while Louise chatted to Mary when Mark looked at his watch and called everyone to order. Joseph then sat down at the back of the room next to Francesca and she reached for his hand, and Mark and Charlotte sat near the screen, so Mark could adjust the electronics as necessary. They then looked at the TV and there was an introductory piece about previous world cups, the wonderful game of soccer, some information about the many national teams participating this year before the BBC announcer started to talk through the build up to the official opening ceremony and the various people involved.

The lounge was now silent apart from the TV and even here, at the Grange, thousands of miles from the impressive new stadium under Table Mountain in Cape Town, there was an air of excitement and expectation. Then the ceremony started with massive colourful scenes from the huge stadium of people dancing, African music, large visual displays and they could see large monitors all around the stadium showing what was going on below. It was a spectacular show with hundreds of performers, wild animals, black men and women in traditional dress participating in the initial phase of the ceremony. There were shots of Table Mountain and the spectacular Cape Point and Francesca nudged Joseph and squeezed his hand.

Then there appeared the flags of all the countries who were members of this truly global sporting tournament and a wide variety of music and some dance troops of young children wearing costumes depicting the 'big five': elephant, lion, hippopotamus, rhino and buffalo. It was a truly sumptuous, African and spectacular performance that thrilled the local audience and made all the South Africans present and watching on TV, experience shivers of national pride for their country. No country, no nationality could have provided such a show with such African flair and verve depicting the diversity of the country, now united as one by a soccer ball.

Neville was watching the opening with some friends at the rugby club located about twenty-five kilometres from the farm in the nearest small Karoo town. There was laughter and many humorous comments, and the beer flowed, but it was only Neville who watched the screen with apprehension. Charlie and Martha were also watching in Boston, at an unusual hour, and Portia was sitting in the lounge at the villa outside Tivoli with some friends enjoying the show. Few televisions anywhere in the world were tuned to anything other than this spectacle. In football clubs, houses, hospitals, colleges and transport termini across the world, it was just all about football and South Africa. Few people were thinking about the horrors of recent months, suddenly these dreadful events had been eclipsed in people's minds by this fest of celebration and sporting excitement. Even in Paris all the television sets were tuned into the event as local people eagerly waited for their national soccer team to walk around the stadium.

It was some minutes later when the whole stadium was full of flags that screens around the stadium and televisions around the world showed Nelson Mandela, Madiba, the true father of this reborn multi-cultural nation, give a pre-recorded welcome to all the visiting nations and he wished all the competitors a happy and successful tournament. There was thunderous applause to this remarkable man and his brief address, the one man who had done so much, almost single-handed, for so many years to bring South Africa to a peaceful reconciliation of its troubled past with his wonderful leadership. His face continued to appear on the screens as he waved and smiled, now an elderly frail gentleman, an icon of justice, forgiveness and love in the modern world. Nelson Mandela, incarcerated for twenty-seven years on Robben Island, just beneath Table Mountain, a distinguished legal advocate, a visionary and man of such compassion and forgiveness had been educated in the Eastern Cape, just a few miles away from Neville's farm in the

Karoo. He had received an English education and attended a Methodist Christian Missionary School near his homestead in the Transkei before he moved later to attend university and practice law under the repressive apartheid system in Sophia Town, near Johannesburg. Nelson Mandela, the first president of a democratic South Africa, remained a giant among men. It had been his charisma, charm and humility that had helped so much to win this huge soccer tournament for the benefit of his country, for the country he loved deeply, for the young children, for the hope of future generations who would learn and grow up in a non racial free society where every person, whether rich or poor, of whatever creed or culture, could realise their potential and dreams.

This was to become a moment in human history when good and bad, freedom and tyranny were to come starkly into contrast. Judaire, a man of intense evil had also been watching the opening ceremony, waiting for the precise moment when like some cancerous destructive organism, he was to put an end to all this happiness, to vent his anger and arrogance on the world that he believed lay before him. The television screens continued to beam out this glorious occasion of the official opening of the 2010 World Soccer Cup and various men in suits were then seen walking to a large podium in the centre of the soccer ground. As they stood smiling and waving a choir assembled at the foot of the podium and they all become serious, as the choir began to sing the South African National Anthem. They were half way through the anthem, with most in the stadium singing too, when the screens around the stadium flickered along with the flat screen at the Grange, the TV in Neville's Karoo rugby club, and in front of Martha and Charlie in Boston.

The singing continued for a few moments and then fell silent as everyone in the Green Point Stadium looked up to scenes of horror appearing before them on all the television screens. There were pictures of Paris, wreckage on the roads, derailed railway trains, bodies being carried from the Metro by rescue crews, the large temporary mortuaries that had been set up in Paris the previous year. After these scenes that were shown in silence, further pictures of death and brutal murder were being shown to an accompaniment of some strange oriental music. Every so often there would be images of the atomic bomb that had been dropped on Hiroshima with the U.S. air force Flying Fortress bombers, before more brutalising scenes retuned showing more of the recent carnage around the world. There were inserts from international news reports of the families and loved ones at airports waiting for their loved ones after the loss of the four commercial airliners at sea, then pictures from each of the rail attack sites that were particularly bloody and spared no one the appalling suffering that had been inflicted. Without any commentary, and just with this eerie oriental music in the background, made these visions all the more dreadful.

It was a professionally edited presentation geared to terrify a global audience and it was having this precise impact. Coming as it did, and when it did, it was having the maximum impact on the billions watching who had now fallen into silence, shock and disbelief.

There were then pictures of America and Northern Europe, of the gas explosions, deserted streets and highways, deep snow and victims of hyperthermia being carried in body bags from their homes. There was a shot of the disabled LNG carrier in the Persian Gulf and huge fires at the nearby LNG plant. Joseph was now standing looking over the heads of those assembled in the lounge at the Grange and Francesca had buried her head in her hands. Mary stood up and said she did not want to watch any more of this madness and had left to make some tea. There were interspersed during these frightening scenes, pieces of video footage showing well know TV news anchor personalities who had reported the attacks and brief clips of world politicians and leaders asking the world to remain calm. It had all been very skilfully edited to convey a single compelling message; the world is not in any of these peoples' control, but under the tyranny of one man.

A part of the American national anthem then played briefly and there were pictures of U.S. aircraft carriers being dive bombed by Japanese aircraft during the Pacific battle in World War II and shots of Pearl Harbour being destroyed. Missile silos in the U.S. Midwest were shown together with pictures of emaciated children dying of starvation in the Sudan and a flash of the pope waving from the balcony in the Vatican, Moslems at prayers, Jews at the prayer wall in Jerusalem and a large gathering of evangelical Christians in America waving their hands above their heads. It then cut back to the pictures of the rail wreckage of the high-speed trains and still everyone just watched in silence, mesmerised by these scenes before them.

Mark had quickly checked the disk recorder to ensure all this was being recorded and then he sat back in his chair dazed by it all. Charlotte laid her head on his shoulder and he could feel her shudder every so often. Thomas had been unusually silent during all this and Liska sat beside him with her arms folded around her knees that she had pulled up under her chin, and she was crying silently with the tears dripping onto her black slacks.

The screen then merged with some clever editing and then expanded again and the music stopped. There was a still picture of a Japanese garden with stones and plants in neat pots, and then a face began to appear on the screen, small, at first, but it gradually got bigger until it filled the whole TV screen.

It was Judaire who presented a strange apparition and he smiled and said, "Hello everyone, I would like you to listen to me very carefully. Despite what your political and other leaders may tell you, it is now I who controls this world. If you have any doubt just remember the pictures you have just witnessed. My name is Judaire and it is a name you will all come to respect and honour in time to come. I will be giving instructions shortly to all your leaders what I intend for you. Any attempt to stop me will be harshly dealt with and any disobedience to my wishes will result in death. Goodbye – and have a nice day." He smiled, and the screens went blank.

Judaire had a strange face, almost without description and he had spoken perfect English and had smiled throughout his brief diatribe. It had been a bizarre, almost comical, but chilling, experience for the billions who had watched his performance.

The media channels were in turmoil, they had all lost

signals for the previous five minutes and some had even not managed to record the Judaire broadcast. Mark instantly stood up, took the disk from the recorder and looked straight at Joseph and Thomas. The three of them then walked from the room together and Francesca got up dazed, and Liska and Charlotte walked through to the kitchen to join Mary.

Standing in the study with the recording in is hand Mark addressed Joseph and Thomas and said, "Exactly as Milshner had predicted, he took control of international TV broadcasts somehow, probably via satellite transmitters and other jamming systems. Give me a few minutes, I want to replay this and take a closer look at the part with Judaire speaking."

"Should I phone Downing Street, do you think Mark?" Joseph asked.

"A little later perhaps, but I think you should continue to watch the TV and see what happens in South Africa. Here, take this empty disk."

It was just a few minutes later as Joseph and Thomas watched the TV that a normal service was resumed from Cape Town, but then other news started to be reported alongside the World Cup Opening ceremony. Those at the Green Point Stadium tried desperately to resume the proceedings, but it would now never be the same, there was fear in the crowd and many had started to leave. Police and some soldiers began to appear at the corners of the football pitch, security measures were already beginning to be implemented. News reports started to appear on all news channels that Johannesburg and Pretoria were in darkness. At the Eskom national control centre there was pandemonium, transmission lines had suddenly been disabled near some of the giant power stations that had all been at maximum production, their giant turbines operating at full output when the messages came through to urgently shut down. Within minutes other lines went out of service in the Northern Cape, Free State and Natal. Koeberg, the nuclear power station near Cape Town was told to stand down and idle and just a few minutes later the whole national electricity network in the country systematically shut down.

The lights that had been illuminating Table Mountain fell dark as the emergency lighting in the Green Point stadium kicked in. Television broadcasts now became sporadic and Cape Town itself was in darkness as the thousands attending the opening ceremony were calmly evacuated and made their way home through dark streets to their homes and hotels.

41
The South Atlantic

THE TELEVISION BROADCAST HAD JUST BEEN LONG ENOUGH for NASA, with their space tracking resources, to get a fix on the ground source of the signal and three satellites that had relayed the five-minute diatribe of Judaire to the world. The powerful signal had come from a location in the South Atlantic nearly two thousand miles off the Namibian coast and a thousand miles south of the small island of St. Helena. The Brazilian and South African air forces had been advised and had sent aircraft to investigate and an orbiting U.S. spy satellite had relayed pictures back to Earth of a large liquid natural gas vessel with spherical shapes on the deck as the likely source of the radio signals. Following urgent enquiries with Lloyds in London and other maritime shipping authorities, the vessel was identified as the Methane Colossus that was carrying a cargo of more than two hundred thousand cubic metres of LNG from Nigeria to Japan. It was one of the new super LNG carriers and had been built in a massive shipyard in South Korea. It was also one of the vessels on the list that Hank Milshner had handed to Thomas.

Some countries had naval vessels in the South Atlantic, but the nearest was the HMS Freedom that had left St. Helena, a British Protectorate, two days earlier, steaming south. It was just before dawn when the officer on watch went to rouse the captain with an urgent order from the Admiralty that they should urgently locate the vessel, request permission to board and conduct a thorough search for a transmitter or other suspicious equipment. If there was resistance from the captain of the *Methane Colossus*, the crew of the HMS *Freedom* had to do what was necessary. It was some hours later when on the horizon they had visual contact with the stern of the massive ship, and the communications officer was instructed to radio the bridge of the LNG carrier with a request for a British naval boarding party. The HMS *Freedom* carried four helicopters, and a small group of naval marines prepared themselves to be airlifted onto the deck of the Colossus while the HMS Freedom kept station a safe distance away while maintaining the same speed as the vast bulk carrier. The destroyer looked small in comparison with the Colossus, which was powered by slow speed diesel engines, giving thirty percent greater fuel efficiency than steam turbines.

Despite repeated attempts to raise the bridge of the *Colossus* by radio, there had been no response. As the HMS *Freedom* came parallel with the Colossus the order was given to reduce speed and the naval captain and his first officer looked through binoculars to the other bridge where they could see various men looking back at them. It was clear they were being ignored, so again further radio messages were sent until finally the captain of the HMS *Freedom* gave the order for the boarding party to proceed. As the helicopter was hovering over the large landing pad positioned at the stern of the vessel behind the bridge and crew accommodation quarters, a group of men appeared, armed with machine guns and a ground-to-air missile launcher. By this time, the chopper had landed, and the crew of the *Colossus* took the small group of marines and pilots captive. The radio room on the HMS Freedom received a message that someone wanted to speak to the captain. It was the skipper of the *Colossus* who demanded the HMS *Freedom* move away, claiming they had no jurisdiction in international waters to board a maritime vessel, and that if this was agreed they would release the marines, the pilots and the helicopter to safely return to the HMS Freedom.

There was an intense period of negotiation between the two captains and no mutually acceptable solution was reached. The captain of the HMS *Freedom*, to safeguard his boarding party, agreed to move away if they released them. Although a very tense situation, the officers of the HMS *Freedom* watched through binoculars as the marines and pilots emerged onto the chopper pad and quickly climbed aboard the naval helicopter, and as they did so the HMD *Freedom* changed course to pull back from the *Colossus*. After the marines and helicopter were safely back on board the destroyer, the captain immediately called for a meeting with his officers in the mess.

One officer was left on the bridge and it happened to be Brian Hardwick, the first officer of the HMS *Freedom*, and he continued to watch the bridge area of the *Colossus* that was gradually moving away from them, through his binoculars. Earlier he had instructed one of the junior officers to get onto the ship's database and communication network and prepare a detailed report for the technical officer and captain of the *Freedom* of what precisely they were dealing with in terms of this huge LNG bulk carrier.

The technical officer of the HMS *Freedom* was briefing the captain and senior officers in the mess with this information.

They quickly went through all the nautical information that most of the senior officers already understood, and it was the captain who said to his technical officer, "Okay, Stuart, now explain to us the details of the cargo this thing is carrying and what we are dealing with here."

The technical officer went on to provide a precise description of LNG, the low temperatures involved, and the numerous rules and regulations regarding the safe transport of this material in bulk at sea.

"LNG has a remarkably good safety record, despite being a highly flammable substance that is transported in huge quantities routinely around the world. Since LNG is stored at very low temperatures, no pressure is required to maintain the gas in its liquid state. Special materials have been developed to ensure the safe storage and transport of LNG. As LNG is stored at atmospheric pressure, no puncture of the huge cylindrical containers will create an immediate explosion. However, the danger of LNG arises from three different features of this liquid. Firstly, the extremely low cryogenic temperatures at which it is liquefied and transported. As a liquid, LNG will crack steel plates and cause extensive damage to materials not protected from such extremely low temperatures."

The technical officer cited a number of documented accident cases from around the world where LNG spills had occurred and where there had been the fracture of tank cover plating of the storage tank and adjacent deck platting. Due to human error, there had been serious accidents in the U.S.A., Algeria, Indonesia, Quebec in Canada and Italy, where non-cryogenic materials had cracked and broken apart when exposed to liquid LNG.

Just then, a rating knocked on the door and, on being given the permission to enter, looked round the door, looked for the captain and handed him a number of messages from the admiralty.

"Excuse me a moment," the captain said to his assembled officers, as he quickly read the secret instructions from London.

After a few moments, he looked up and everyone was looking at him. He divulged what he could of this urgent information. The HMS *Freedom* had to continue to monitor the *Colossus*, stay within visual sight of the juggernaut, and that it was suspected that a Japanese gentleman called Judaire may be aboard. There was a physical description of the man and there were warnings that this vessel and the passenger were extremely dangerous and unpredictable and should be treated with extreme caution.

"Right, Stuart. What more have you to tell us? Please make it quick," the captain said, wishing to get the briefing finished so he could get back to the bridge.

Stuart explained two more dangerous features of LNG.

"When in liquid form and when there is a spill, LNG will start to evaporate and become gas and a combustible gas-to-air mixture such that when there is a source of ignition will cause a fire. Such fires burn with intense heat, at much higher temperatures than even oil fires, and these gas fires spread very rapidly. So the most worrying dangers of LNG are the dispersion characteristics it has, and the highly flammable nature of the evaporating gas."

To press these factual realities home to his crewmates, Stuart mentioned briefly the incident in Cleveland, Ohio in U.S.A. in 1944 when a LNG tank had ruptured, and its contents had spilt into the street and storm water drains, and the resultant explosion had killed a hundred and twenty-eight people. In Staten Island, New York, in 1973, there had been the collapse of the roof a LNG storage tank that caused an explosion that killed thirty-seven construction workers and in two thousand and four, in Skikda in Algeria, a LNG plant blew up, causing twenty-seven deaths and seventy-four seriously injured, with parts of the plant blown huge distances beyond the perimeter fence.

"As it evaporates, LNG can also cause gas clouds that, when ignited, will cause explosions with a tremendous force. In 2008 in Nigeria, a twenty-eight-inch LNG underground pipeline exploded, and the resulting fire engulfed an estimated twenty-seven square kilometres."

These were just a few of the many LNG incidents that had occurred and every one of these involved small amounts of LNG, certainly nothing vaguely approaching the huge two hundred thousand cubic metres floating nearby.

It was June in the Southern Atlantic, the winter in the southern hemisphere, and it was bitterly cold on deck. A few minutes before the meeting below decks finished, Brian Hardwick observed an extraordinary incident on the *Colossus*. As he watched through his binoculars, he observed a Japanese man of around five foot ten emerge from the side hatch door of the bridge, followed by three shorter Japanese men with one of them being restrained by the other two. There had been some gesticulating and then the taller man shot the restrained man through the head and Brian saw the victim fall dead onto the gangway beside the bridge.

What Brian Hardwick did not know was that the man with the gun was Judaire, who had summarily executed one of his senior technical team for misadvising him. Judaire was acting aboard the *Colossus* in an insane rage because of this British destroyer alongside wishing to come aboard.

How had the radio tracking agencies managed to locate the *Colossus*? How had his foolproof plan failed? Why had he not been advised correctly that the precise time he had broadcast would avoid detection? Judaire could not tolerate failure; he could never admit he himself was at fault and that his egotistical obsession and need for global recognition was what had actually started to bring his house of cards tumbling. He was taking sudden lunatic revenge on whoever was at hand. Even the Japanese captain of the *Colossus* had been threatened by Judaire to do crazy things should the British attempt to come close or come aboard. He was also frantically trying to work out a safe escape route away from the *Colossus*, now that he had been discovered. The most important matters were his pride, his dignity and that he would never allow himself to be taken alive. And he expected, indeed demanded, everyone on the *Colossus* to behave in the same way.

For the captain of the *Colossus*, a man in his mid-fifties who had been man and boy a merchant seafarer, the sudden ranting of a madman with a gun did not impress him too much. He was more fearful of the various other members of Judaire's guard who were aboard, wandering around with high calibre weapons next to the huge LNG storage tanks. The Japanese captain had sailed bulk LNG carriers for nearly twenty years, was highly experienced and had only joined the *Colossus* at the last moment since the regular skipper had been taken sick in Nigeria. Like all sea captains, to be instructed at the point of a gun on your own bridge is an act of piracy, something deeply repugnant to mariners. The captain had also been very angry to find that there were other secret activities going on aboard the vessel under his command, some days out to sea from Nigeria, when his life had been threatened first by some youngster, originally from Tokyo, touting a gun. The captain was from Osaka so there had been an immediate antipathy between these two men. When later, a tall half Japanese and European, surgically altered freak appeared with psychotic orders, the captain started to put a few things together in his mind. He had also lost a daughter in the bullet train derailment that had taken place some weeks earlier. If there was one person on the *Colossus* with the motivation and probably the resources to help the captain of the HMS *Freedom*, it was his opposite number on the bridge of the LNG super carrier.

As the captain of the Freedom walked onto the bridge, Brian Hardwick quickly told him of the incident he had witnessed, and as the captain looked across through his binoculars he asked, "How extraordinary. What do you think it means, Hardwick?"

Brian answered, "Not sure sir, but things do not look too happy over there. I also notice that many of the men on board are Japanese and do not look like regular sailors."

Just then, the captain exclaimed as he looked through his binoculars, "It's the captain, I can see him next to the bridge and he has just flashed 'Distract, I help'... and he has disappeared again onto the bridge."

The captain of the *Colossus* had quickly flashed a semaphore message, while the bridge was free of Judaire and his men. The captain then scribbled a massage to be sent by the radio room to London.

When he finished, he turned and said, "Brian, we have got to get onto the *Colossus* somehow, and soon. We are ordered to get the vessel intact, but the admiralty are worried that this Judaire may blow himself and the ship up. If the *Colossus* goes up, so will the Freedom, being where we are!"

It was a few minutes later when the answer from the admiralty came through and was delivered to the captain. After reading it he immediately started to give orders for various manoeuvres to distract Judaire and his men, while preparing to storm the *Colossus*.

Brian Hardwick turned to the captain and asked, "Captain, permission to accompany the boarding party; please, sir?"

The captain looked over at the young officer and there was a brief pause while he reflected on his request. "This is not usual Hardwick, but we need to find out what is on that vessel, so you had better get into your battle fatigues quickly. Permission granted."

The boarding plan was to send out two helicopters that would approach the Colossus from two different directions to provide further distraction to Judaire's men. They would not land, but would hover briefly over the stern and prow of the great vessel, enabling the marines to board quickly down two ropes dangling from each of the helicopters. It was a tricky manoeuvre, but one that the pilots and marines had executed many times before.

There was some low cloud ahead and the HMS *Freedom* was now steaming some distance away from the *Colossus*, and the boarding crews would fly east and then due north before flying west and then returning to approach the huge LNG vessel from the south-west and emerge suddenly from low beneath the clouds to deposit the marines and Brian Hardwick on the deck. With the helicopters rapidly approaching the Colossus from the west and the HMS *Freedom* sailing on the other side of them, it was hoped that this would further confuse and distract those on the LNG carrier. The boarding crews were soon aboard the two helicopters that flew away from the Freedom, in an easterly direction, flying fast and low, shielded from the sight of those on the *Colossus* by the destroyer. Looking through his binoculars, the captain of the Freedom could see men moving around on the bridge and decking of the *Colossus*, when suddenly, several of the crew on the LNG ship started to run around. The Japanese captain of the *Colossus* had triggered various safety-warning alarms on the ship and there were now sirens, hooters and lights flashing all across the decks and gantries of the ship. True to his word, the captain of the Colossus was trying to assist the *Freedom* crew to apprehend Judaire and his men.

The chopper that Brian Hardwick was on deposited him and six marines on the prow of the LNG tanker and they were soon down the ropes onto the deck taking cover as gun shots rang out and the helicopter quickly turned and zigzagged to avoid the hail of small arms fire and it was gone safely into the sky. As Brian looked down the massive deck beside the huge conical cylinder tops that lined the ship, he heard a hatch open behind him and, turning there before, him was a Japanese man with a handheld grenade launcher. They were soon struggling with each other and his adversary tried to hit Brian with the barrel of the weapon as he reached for a knife in the side of his battle fatigues. To use guns on such a vessel was plain madness and he wanted to disarm this fanatic quickly, but in the tussle the grenade launcher was fired and the grenade sped up over the nearby gantry and hit one of the LNG tanks mid-ship and there was a loud explosion. Momentarily distracted by the jolt of the weapon as it was fired, Brian stabbed the man in his left thigh and then in his shoulder and the man lay moaning and bleeding on the decking.

There was now close-combat fighting going on all over the ship and two marines from the aft boarding party had managed to get almost to the bridge when one of them was shot dead in the head at almost point blank range by a Japanese man who leant over the rail beside the door to the bridge. As the dead marine tumbled backwards, the remaining marine threw his knife upwards and watched it sank deep into the gunman's neck and his blood splashed onto the marines face as he quickly mounted the gantry and stormed onto the bridge. There were further gunshots and two Japanese, who were guarding the captain and his crew on the bridge, lay dead. The captain of the *Colossus* stood with one of the dead lying at his feet and he gave a slight smile toward the marine and then walked forward and opened a large red box on the side of the bridge, and carefully selected some buttons and switches. Within seconds there were tons of seawater being pumped over the decking to create a further distraction for Judaire's men.

Brian Hardwick had now entered the open hatch door near the front LNG tank and as he walked carefully along the corridor, followed by two marines, and after turning some corners he came to another closed hatch. The two marines stepped forward and leant heavily on the steel arms that were holding the door closed and released them, pushing the door back, and Brian stepped carefully over the doorframe into a large room. He was amazed to find a small television studio with two large cameras, lighting, and auto cue and various other pieces of equipment.

He felt something in his back and a voice said, "Do not turn round officer, I want you to accompany me onto deck, and help me get off this ship alive with one of your navy helicopters."

It was Judaire. As the door lay open, one of the marines started to gasp for air as hundreds of gallons of liquid natural gas poured from the two tanks ruptured by the grenade explosion and rapidly evaporated to become methane, natural gas. The methane-to-air mixture was becoming dangerous all over the ship, with very high concentrations of natural gas denuding the air of oxygen. In various spots on the Colossus crew and members of Judaire's guard were choking as they gradually began to suffocate.

Judaire, standing pointing his gun at Brian Hardwick, ordered another Japanese gentleman nearby to take his handgun and keep Brian and the two marines covered and the insane tyrant walked over to another door and disappeared. He had only been gone for a few minutes when the Japanese man holding the gun standing close to the open hatch door was visibly finding it hard to breath. Quickly covering is face, Brian Hardwick lunged at the man and after a brief struggle rescued the gun from his grasp and hit him to the ground and ordered one the marines to close the hatch door. Although they did not know it, there were thousands of gallons of liquid natural gas now pouring across the ship, into galleys and gangways and causing major damage in its path. Judaire appeared holding three metal cases about the size of a cigar box in one hand and a gun in the other hand. There was an immediate standoff as Brian Hardwick and Judaire pointed their weapons at each other. Spotting the door ajar, Judaire moved quickly to the hatch door facing the three men and pushed it open with his arm and then turned and stepped through. Immediately after doing so they heard him scream and Brian ran to the door to see him standing looking down at his legs turning solid as a stream of liquid natural gas that had filled the galley way rapidly froze him to death. Brian leant forward and grabbed the metal boxes from his hand and slammed the hatch door closed as Judaire dropped down and was immersed in the freezing liquid flooding the passageway.

The three boxes were the hard drives from Judaire's computers and Brian quickly stuffed them into the trouser pockets in the his battle fatigues and called to his comrades, "Come on, we have got to get out of here fast – the passage is flooding with LNG."

They frantically looked around for another way out, and Brian noticed some portholes beyond the door where Judaire had retrieved the computer components. There, to his relief, were four large square portholes that could be opened and he radioed for help. On the bridge of HMS *Freedom* they could see the damage being wrought by the escaping liquid natural gas to the plating and decking of the *Colossus*, and the captain ordered three helicopters to fly over the stricken ship to lift his men and any surviving members of the crew and Judaire's men.

The danger now was fire, as huge clouds of evaporated natural gas rose around the ship and from the waves. It was unusual weather as the helicopters flew over the *Colossus*; there was little wind and a mild swell as the rescue man lowered the hoop to winch men from below. One of the chopper pilots spotted Brian waving from the prow of the great ship and radioed to one of the other pilots to fetch him. Within a few minutes there, dangling by the side of the ship, was the safety harness and Brian helped his two mates through the porthole and they pushed themselves clear to be winched up to the helicopter. It took only a few minutes and some very skilful flying by the chopper pilot before all three of them were safely into the helicopter, which was now full with other marines, some badly injured, and two who were dead. Everyone was still tense and the adrenaline was flowing and the helicopter pilot swung his large machine up over the *Colossus* and flew fast back to the HMS *Freedom* where he landed on the aft helicopter pad and the door was thrown back and medical attendants came to remove the corpses and help the injured. Brian ducked low as he moved swiftly across the open deck to quarters below.

There were still two helicopters on duty over the *Colossus* when Brian reached the bridge of the *Freedom* and the captain was ordering the helmsman to steer the destroyer rapidly away from the *Colossus* that was now beginning to list and take on water. The captain ordered the helicopters to abort and get back to the Freedom and one of them had already turned and was heading back when Brian asked about the Japanese captain of the LNG juggernaut. The captain looked through his binoculars and as the third and last helicopter rose to retreat back to the Freedom, he saw the captain standing waving on the side of the bridge. Brian was now looking through his binoculars and he could see some of the few remaining Japanese members of Judaire's guard jumping into the sea, to certain death, and the huge slick of LNG that was now floating all around the ship.

The captain of the *Freedom* instantly gave an order to be relayed to the last retreating helicopter pilot to fetch the captain of the *Colossus* and he and Brian watched as the chopper swung back with the winch man standing by the open door already lowering the harness. Immediately, the Japanese captain was secure and free of the *Colossus*, the pilot moved away swiftly with him still being winched to safety. When the helicopter settled on the deck of the destroyer and the onboard crew had secured the machine, even before the rotor blades had stopped turning, the captain gave the order for full speed ahead and the destroyer listed as it veered swiftly away from the *Colossus* and the methane fumes that were now threatening to envelop even the HMS *Freedom*.

There on the bridge stood the Japanese captain of the Colossus, and both the captains shook hands and smiled at each other. The captain of the *Freedom* handed a pair of binoculars to the *Colossus* captain, who stood with oil on his clothes and blood on his face and arm. Everyone was looking at the *Colossus*, this vast ship with its five huge conical spheres, each containing fifty thousand cubic metres of liquefied natural gas that was now discharging across the tangled decking and superstructure of the vessel into the sea. Just one of these tanks contained some thirty million cubic metres of natural gas, and a huge methane cloud was forming around the vessel. It only needed the right air-to-gas mixture and a tiny spark to ignite the highly flammable cloud, which would then accelerate the vaporisation of the remaining LNG. In total, the vessel was carrying the equivalent of a hundred and fifty million cubic metres of natural gas, a vast amount of explosive and combustible methane.

The HMS *Freedom* continued to sail at full speed in an attempt to get clear, and the captain was asking for a welter of weather data, wind speeds and direction. The radar and radio room were monitoring other vessels in the vicinity and warning messages were being radioed to these ships and international authorities to advise aircraft in the vicinity. Someone was looking after the HMS *Freedom* that day, the mild weather conditions, and now there was a light wind that was beginning to move the methane cloud away from them, in the opposite direction. The *Freedom* captain had remembered one vital statistic from the LNG technical briefing earlier, the twenty-seven square mile inferno that had been caused in Nigeria some years earlier when a bulk LNG pipeline had exploded. They need to be miles away from this sinking hulk, as fast as possible.

The Japanese captain turned to the English captain and said that they had to sink the *Colossus* and explode the methane cloud and if he could study some charts. After a few minutes, he looked at the *Freedom* captain and gave him some coordinates and said once they were there they should fire on the *Colossus*. It was the final act of vital cooperation provided by the other brave seafarer, in the full knowledge that the *Colossus* and its discharging cargo were a lethal combination that had to be neutralised safely out of range of other shipping and countries that may lie in the path of the floating methane cloud. It was two hours later when the *Freedom* captain called his gunnery officer and ordered him to fire on the *Colossus*. Within a few minutes the great guns on the foredeck of the speeding destroyer turned, almost facing back at the bridge, and sent a volley of shells toward the *Colossus*.

There was an instant huge flash and a rush of wind across the decks of the destroyer and some minutes later a large wave rushed toward the HMS *Freedom* as it bobbed up over the crest and the wave continued its journey to the Namibian coastline. It was over, Judaire and his floating control centre destroyed, the computers evaporated together with everything else of the huge ship by the intense heat and magnitude of the explosion. Although the *Colossus* had been over the horizon from the *Freedom*, the size of the flash lighted up the whole sky, and was seen in parts of South America as well as along the coast of Namibia and South Africa.

It was then that the captain of the *Freedom* said to a colleague on the bridge, "Please, will you take captain…?" He paused before the Japanese gentleman said 'Isado', smiled, and continued, "… Captain Isado below and provide him with anything he needs?"

After they had left the bridge, the captain said, "Well, the admiralty will not be too pleased that we sunk her. Radio officer, will you please send this message to them," and he proceeded to dictate a brief message describing their engagement and the result.

On receiving the message, the admiralty advised the minister of defence, who instantly phoned the prime minister. Within an hour, the British prime minister stood at the lectern in Downing Street, briefing the media that a British naval destroyer had intercepted the vessel on which Judaire was sailing, and in the ensuing struggle, Judaire had died and the ship had sunk. Minutes later, this news was beamed across the world and there was jubilation.

42

The Last Villain

THE IMPACT OF THE LOSS OF ELECTRICITY SUPPLIES ACROSS South Africa had been dramatic. Most of the industrial and mining sector had shut down, as had the many shopping and commercial premises. Schools were already closed for the Soccer World Cup, but life in the shantytowns near the great cities had become particularly harsh for those living there. There was a surge in crime, particularly in the more affluent suburbs, with electronic and security equipment inoperable. With the loss of urban street lighting many people stayed within the safety of their homes and to protect their possessions from theft. Small businesses in the catering sector had been particularly hard hit, despite the many soccer tourists still in the country.

With the earlier electricity supply crisis in the country that had struck some four years earlier, all manner of contingency measures that had been introduced were now helping people through this unimaginable crisis. There were solar-powered traffic lights, thousands of standby generators and many hotels, bed and breakfast establishments and homes now heated their water with thermal solar systems and used bottled gas for cooking. Even the soccer media facilities and stadiums had emergency generators that were now in regular operation providing essential power. These provisions enabled the Soccer World Cup to proceed, but on a greatly reduced scale

Eskom had quickly identified the attack sites on the

transmission network with their fleet of Sapphire Air, Bell Helicopters now regularly patrolling the thousands of miles of high voltage lines. Repair teams had been airlifted to these sites and were busy making repairs, although it would still be some days before the whole system could be fully energised again and systematically brought back to full operation. A few areas in the country were, however, now receiving some electricity supplies. Even Neville on his farm in the Karoo had experienced limited impact of the sudden loss of grid electricity, since he simply switched to his standby generator for essential electricity for lighting, television, communications and his sophisticated music player. He had three months supply of diesel in his storage tanks on the farm and the lights around the homestead and the Xhosa farm worker's small community twinkled as usual.

Michelle Adler had been travelling, staying at a luxury hotel in Buenos Aires in Argentina with her youthful toy boy lover, when she was shocked to see the news on the television about the death of Judaire. After learning of his demise she had retired to her suite on her own to drink heavily, eventually falling asleep drunk, sprawled over the bed. When she awoke the following morning she began to panic and had quickly packed, spoken with her young lover and they had both caught a flight to Europe, continuing to travel under false identities.

Thomas was still staying at Himbledon with Liska and he had waited and checked the time difference before phoning Father Brendan in Sulphur Springs. When they spoke, Thomas asked him if he might know the local priest near the Milshner Castle in Bavaria, remembering that he had long established connections with that part of the world.

Louise had returned to the Hague and was already busy in her new office at the International Court studying various legal documents and previous court proceedings. Francesca had said goodbye to Joseph at Heathrow Airport the same day, before flying back to Rome to continue her work. When Joseph drove back and arrived at the Grange, Thomas was waiting for him and they met in the study. Thomas wanted Joe to travel with him the next day to Bavaria, since he had a strong feeling that this is where they would probably find Adler. Joseph also spoke fluent German and it had not taken Thomas long to convince him of the merit of his plan, to contact the local priest and then speak with the police before going to the castle. Joe and Thomas were determined to do whatever they could to try to help in apprehending Adler, and the information that Milshner had given to Thomas, just before his death, might just make all the difference.

They arrived in the small Bavarian village in the mountains late the following afternoon, having flown to Germany and hired a Mercedes at the nearby airport. Within two hours of arriving at the rectory and meeting the local priest, the local head of police joined them. Both the priest and the senior police officer knew the small castle, and the police had checked out the place just a few days before, and had found only a small staff there, but no sign of Adler. Nevertheless, it was agreed that early the next morning a small number of police officers, accompanied by Thomas and Joseph, would drive up to the castle and insist, with the necessary legal warrant, to search the whole of the premises. They booked into a small hotel, had a good supper and went to their rooms ready for an early start the next day.

It was a beautiful, clear sunny day the following morning as the police officer and his men met them, and they followed the police van out to the castle. It was a spectacular location with a good, tarred road that spiralled up to the small fairy tale castle set high on the mountainside. When they arrived at the large iron gates on the drive, two armed guards met them, an unusual development since the earlier visit by the police. Some resistance was given by the guards, who refused to open the gates, and when Joseph saw one of the guards starting to move back into the stone gate lodge he spoke quickly to one of the police officers, who immediately stepped over and restrained the man. It was to be a surprise visit and they did not want any warnings to be phoned up to the castle before they arrived unexpectedly at the front door.

The two guards were disarmed, handcuffed and left with one of the German police officers and the gates opened, and then the remaining group proceeded quickly to the castle. The driveway was the only way to reach the castle that was perched on the edge of the mountain with rock faces on three sides of the structure that was built into the mountain face.

The previous day the head of the local police had briefed Thomas and Joseph about the castle, its layout and the people they had interviewed when they had searched the premises. There was a limited staff complement of two chambermaids, two cooks, a handyman, gardener and head housekeeper making a total staff of seven. They lived at the castle in the staff quarters and they all wore a plain uniform and the ladies had small white hats. The police had photographed them all and these pictures had been shown to Thomas and Joseph and, apart from the gardener and the head housekeeper, all the staff were probably under thirty years of age. From a detailed inspection of the castle that included the vaults below, the head of the local police was confident that another thorough search would reveal if Adler and her boyfriend were there. The plan was simple: go to the front door and enter and then systematically search the premises.

When they drew up on the gravel area in the courtyard of the castle they were soon ringing the large iron bell pull by the main door. It was some time before the head housekeeper opened the door, just slightly, to enquire what they wanted, and there was a look of surprise on her face. Within seconds the head of police had entered the castle followed by two of his armed police officers and then Thomas and Joseph. It was a beautiful interior, luxuriously furnished with the most spectacular views across the valley and mountains beyond. Under instruction from the police chief, the housekeeper had gone to gather all the staff together, and as she did so the police officers climbed the impressive stone staircase to go up to the upper rooms to commence a systematic search. Under beds, inside the large solid wooden cupboards and in every nook and cranny, the diligent police officers searched. There was simply nowhere to hide, had they been there. When they arrived at one of the main bedrooms on the floor above the ground floor, it was locked and when they told the chief policeman he instantly alerted Thomas and Joseph and instructed the head housekeeper to come and unlock it. She became furtive, giving excuses that it always remained locked and that she did not have the key.

Without any further hesitation the police chief ordered that two of his men break open the door. This proved easier said than done, it was a large solid wooden door with heavy iron bolts and locks on the outside and it also appeared to be bolted on the inside.

“Is there any other way in or out of this room?” enquired Joseph, speaking German, and after further questioning the head housekeeper explained that there was a suite of rooms behind the door, bathrooms and bedrooms and that this door provided the only access. All the windows of these rooms looked out over the mountains and there was a vertical rock-face several hundred feet above the forest below.

After further discussion it was agreed that the only practical option was to use an explosive charge to get through the heavily bolted door. It was some fifteen minutes later when two further police vehicles arrived at the castle and among the new police arrivals were two explosive experts dressed in flack jackets, helmets and shields over their faces. After a prolonged discussion that Thomas could not understand and the explosive experts taking various measurements and putting up a special screen in front of the door to reduce flying debris, everything appeared ready. Everyone was told to wait outside, as the remote controlled detonators were placed within four explosive charges that had each been carefully positioned to release the door from its hinges. The policeman in control of this operation then appeared briefly in the courtyard, and called a warning and a head count was quickly taken to ensure everyone was outside. He stood with his back to the stonework beside the main door and triggered the explosion. There was a muffled thud sound before he and three of the policemen ran back into the castle, up the stone staircase and into the previously locked rooms. Thomas and Joseph had been asked to wait in the courtyard with the staff, and as they stood in the sunny morning air they heard a single gun shot.

A few minutes later, as some dust billowed from the doorway to the castle, the explosives expert emerged into the sunlight, smiling. He was followed by the two police officers, each covered in white dust and looking dishevelled, but holding two handcuffed people. One was Michelle Adler, covered in dust with some scratches on her face from some of the flying debris. The other was a tall athletic man in his mid-twenties with a large bruise appearing on his jaw and one of his eyes. It had been this young toy boy who had wildly fired the single shot, in a vain attempt to protect his ageing mistress, before he had been swiftly disarmed and punched in the face twice by one of the burly police officers. Adler said nothing; she simply stood with her head bowed while the young man was swearing in an American accent. The police quickly searched their two prisoners before turning them around and frogmarching them across to the police vehicles, and Adler was unceremoniously deposited in the rear seat of a police car, and the young American pushed into the back of the police van.

Two officers were left to take statements from all the staff and Thomas looked at Joseph, almost bemused at the speed and simplicity of their capture, before turning to the chief of police and asking, "What happens now with them both?"

The policeman answered Thomas with good English and explained they would be taken to the secure holding cells of the local police station, their rights would be read to them, and they would be interrogated and then charged.

"Perhaps you would also like to talk to them?" enquired the German, and Thomas smiled and nodded.

It was later the same day that Thomas came face to face with Michelle Adler. She was wearing a plain shirt and light grey unflattering trousers provided by her custodians as she sat in the interview room with bars on the windows. Even though she was now middle aged she had looked after her body and facial features, and with the aid of cosmetic surgery, looked some years younger than she actually was. There was a female police officer in the interview room as Thomas entered, but Adler sat motionless and did not look up at him. Thomas pulled out a chair and sat at the far end of the table looking at her from the side.

They sat there together for some moments before she

gradually turned and looked at this large man with a ruddy face sitting along the table from her.

"Who are you?" she asked in a defiant manner.

Thomas was calm and extremely restrained, answered, "I am Thomas Trimbledon, the uncle and brother of two innocent men that you and Judaire murdered in cold blood."

There was a pause as Adler looked away from him before she swivelled in her chair to face him, "What is that to me? I know nothing about such things."

Thomas quickly replied, "I think you do Michelle, together with the thousands of innocent people you have murdered with your personal campaign of terror."

There was a further long silence before Adler stood up, walked to the window and then turned to face Thomas with a slight smile on her face and said, "You can think those things, Thomas Trimbledon, but you will never prove it. I want a lawyer and I want to put a long distance call through to America, these are my rights."

Thomas sat for a few moments thinking about what she had said. He could feel a creepy sense of intense evil just being near this manipulative and highly sensuous woman. Her defiance and arrogance and whole manner was beginning to get to Thomas, and he knew he had to get out of this cell soon.

Thomas then asked, "Is it Hank you want to call in America?"

Adler suddenly looked surprised and, placing both her hands on the table, leant forward and said, "What is that to you, Trimbledon? It is none of your bloody business who I want to call in America."

She was trying to be deliberately provocative and to disarm this large, quiet man sitting near her.

Thomas quickly looked across at her and said, "Hank Milshner is dead. He will not be there to receive your call, or to help you out of trouble anymore, Michelle."

Momentarily, Thomas noticed his comment had hit Adler like a blow to the stomach, but she instantly concealed her feelings and started to laugh. "You are lying, Trimbledon. I spoke with Stanley just yesterday, and he told me Hank was sleeping, and Stanley never lies."

It was now time for Thomas to smile slightly as he said, "Quite right Michelle, Stanley does not lie; he is an honourable man and in a manner of speaking Hank is sleeping, he is sleeping in a cryogenic casket waiting to be buried with his parents, after you have been captured and brought to trial."

Feeling the ground slipping from beneath her, Adler turned away from Thomas and said, "Leave me alone and let me phone my lawyer."

Thomas was not going to stop now and he knew this conversation was being recorded and observed by Joseph and the chief of police standing in an adjacent room. "You have been read your rights, haven't you Michelle? You know that this conversation is being recorded and that anything you say may be used as evidence against you?"

"Yes, so what?" she retorted, and Thomas could see small beads of perspiration appearing on her forehead beneath her cropped blond head of hair.

Thomas stood up and stood opposite her, leaning his back on the heavy bars on the inside of the cell and continued. "There are just two more things I think you should know Michelle and trust me, I am not lying."

He told her about his meeting with Hank, how he had witnessed his death, how devastated Milshner had been by her betrayal and how he had taken all control from her of his family fortune and business interests. Thomas explained that Milshner had been entirely innocent of the atrocities, and that it had been her and Judaire who had carried out this evil campaign. He said it was unlikely any of Milshner's high-powered lawyers would ever be available to her again and that she would stand trial alone for the awful carnage she had committed. Judaire was also dead, her accomplice blown to pieces by the Royal Navy in the South Atlantic. Thomas then said, with heavy irony in his voice, that no doubt Judaire was planning to leave the Methane Colossus and travel to Argentina to meet her. Well, such plans were no more.

Adler had been listening with her head in her hands, and when Thomas paused she again looked straight into his eyes and sneered at him, saying, "Just try to prove it Trimbledon, try to prove it."

It was at this point, with deft precision, that Thomas calmly placed his trump card on the table, and before the listening audience next door he said slowly, "You see, Michelle, you made one grave mistake. You betrayed Hank Milshner, a man you thought mad, a man you could manipulate and use for your own evil desires. He loved you Michelle, probably more than any other man ever has ever loved you in your life. You thought you could treat him like all the other men you have used and abused, because you thought he was weak and under your spell. You were very wrong Michelle, and probably something you will never be able to understand is that it was his unconditional love for you that enabled you to manipulate him. When you betrayed that love, so carelessly, so ruthlessly, you finally destroyed Hank Milshner, but you also destroyed yourself."

Thomas stopped for a moment to let her fully grasp what he was saying and he noticed that the colour had drained from Adler's face, as she continued to sit motionless before him. He walked to the end of the table and leant forward where she was sitting and continued, "You completely underestimated Hank Milshner, he was from a noble good family, although you were always blind to the goodness in him, and this mistake is what will put you behind bars for the rest of your natural life, Michelle," and he stopped talking, waiting for her response.

Adler was now crying slightly in fear for herself, as she jutted out her chin toward him, in a further attempt at defiance, and said, "How's that? It still doesn't prove anything?"

"Oh, but it does, Michelle; you see, Hank wanted you to be caught, he wanted the carnage to end and he wanted you to be brought to justice. Although he loved you, he knew you and Judaire had to be stopped. That is why he gave me incontrovertible evidence that will convict you before a court of justice. He told me to look for you at the castle, he told me how he had tried to dissuade you and Judaire from those crazy ideas, all those years ago, about destroying the world, and he gave me documents in your handwriting and so much more. No Michelle, there will be no doubt whatsoever of your guilt."

Thomas slowly walked to the door of the cell and Adler tried to lunge at him from the other side of the table and then stood screaming at Thomas to get out.

Joseph, who had been watching the conversation between Thomas and Adler, felt the tension as Thomas ambled toward those gathered in the adjacent room and asked, "May I have a glass of water please?" The police chief reached for a glass and poured some water from the cooler and handed it to Thomas.

"Have you ever been a policeman, Thomas?" asked Joe.

Thomas smiled.

The tension of the situation gradually subsided and Joe offered to buy Thomas a beer across the street in a tavern and the police chief said he would keep them advised of developments.

As Thomas rose to his feet and placed the empty glass on the table he looked across at the policeman and said, with a determined look in his eye, "Just keep her alive, she must be brought to a public trial."

A few minutes later, as they crossed the village street, Joseph turned to Thomas and said, "That was quite some performance in there Thomas, I would not like to face you across a court of law."

Thomas chuckled and replied, "All in a day's work my dear boy, all in a day's work."

Much of the criminal justice system in Germany is Federal, and immediately it had been confirmed with the authorities that the local police had Michelle Adler in custody, special provisions were swiftly put into place. Although Germany has a system of criminal law geared toward restitution and rehabilitation of offenders, Adler was rightly regarded as a highly dangerous potential international terrorist. She also had a high flight risk, of suddenly disappearing and escaping a proper legal trial. The rail attacks, the loss of German citizens on one of the downed commercial aircraft; and the natural gas crisis earlier in the year in Germany, were all sound reasons for holding her. It was, however, certain evidence that Thomas was able to provide to the German legal authorities the following day that enabled a specially convened land court, with three judges and six lay judges, to subsequently convene a formal court hearing, during which Adler's full legal rights were protected, and a judgement was passed that she be jailed in a high-security facility pending further investigations and a further trial.

Hank Milshner had also provided Thomas with some confidential documents, signed by Adler, instructing various senior members of the cult to organise various resources for the planting of rogue devices for the high-speed train derailments. There were also other written documents that directly implicated her with many of Judaire's illegal activities. These, and some other items of evidence handed to Thomas by Hank Milshner at the mountain lodge in Montana, were to prove crucial in the months and years ahead in bringing Michelle Adler to justice.

Thomas had brought with him a selection of the evidence provided by Hank Milshner and the following day he was invited by a senior federal prosecutor and a small team of lawyers to share this information. When Thomas and Joseph met these legal professionals, some of them were incredulous at the story that Thomas told them about visiting Montana and the meeting with Hank Milshner. However, when Thomas opened his music satchel and produced some of this evidence they were convinced they had enough to convict her. There had been a series of legal procedures, Thomas had to give lengthy verbal evidence under oath and there had been the witnessing and certification of the documentary evidence. Thomas was certainly not going to leave any of the original documents out of his possession. A provisional date for the first hearing was set and Thomas was advised that he did not need to attend this, although he would be required to attend the full court hearing, when he would be called on to give evidence and be cross examined by Adler's defence lawyers.

Already the international media had got hold of the news of the arrest of Michelle Adler and had descended on the small Bavarian village. They were everywhere; with reporters, television cameras and intrusive behaviour, trying to elicit every scrap of news. The federal authorities had been quick to manage the situation, and had set up a news liaison team to keep the media properly briefed. Behind the scenes there were also frantic communications taking place between the German authorities, other countries, the European Union and global security agencies. Adler already had a small defence team provided under German legal arrangements and she had been quick to ask whether they still had the death penalty in Germany, and was visibly calmed when told they had abolished it some years earlier. Unbeknown to her, however, the American ambassador in Germany was already putting pressure on the government for extradition proceedings to start immediately, although the German government was resisting.

The last Thomas and Joseph saw of Michelle Adler in the small Bavarian village was when she was transported under heavy police guard in a convoy of vehicles away from the small village to a high security prison some miles away. The authorities were also careful to ensure that Adler was fully protected from the very real danger that someone might murder her for the alleged atrocities she had committed. Thomas and Joseph had watched the media circus on the opposite side of the street from where they were staying, as the convoy moved swiftly down the narrow street and away from the village with cameras flashing and a crowd being restrained behind temporary crowd control barriers. Adler had been brought out of the back of the small village jailhouse, together with her boyfriend, and deposited in two high-security police vehicles, unbeknown to the crowd in front of the police station. Taking their cue from this wise police behaviour, Thomas and Joe slipped down the rear stairs of the tavern and swiftly departed in the Mercedes to the airport.

* * *

IT WAS THE NEXT MORNING, BACK AT HIMBLEDON, that Joseph and Thomas had an opportunity to talk with Mark. There had been a message left by Stanley for Thomas to phone him and Mark had much information to also share with them both. After telling Mark precisely what had transpired in Germany, he advised them that the wheels of international policing were now turning very rapidly, and the various authorities had been busy rounding up people suspected of being part of Judaire's and Adler's psychotic activities. Many of these people working in commerce and industry had been dumfounded when they realised how they had innocently contributed to the chaos witnessed in recent months around the world. Most had been entirely innocent and had no idea of the bigger picture, where their small elements of technology or software fitted into the larger tapestry of Judaire's schemes.

Again, the information provided by Hank Milshner to Thomas had been invaluable and enabled the police authorities and other investigators to raid many companies, factories and industrial sites in many parts of the world. The fact that Judaire had died, his control centre, computers and transmitter destroyed, had filled the security bodies with confidence that they could now act with virtual impunity to round up the other members involved in this tyranny. Having identified the three rogue satellites, the space authorities had set up constant radio jamming to make them inoperable while they decided precisely what do with them. There had been some concern in certain quarters of the security establishment, that while Adler was also at large there may still be some risk of further attacks. Now that she was in custody, the way was clear and immediate dangers had been removed. There were, however, two final elements of risk that Mark had been particularly persistent in telling the prime minister's security advisors about.

The first was a possibility— remote, admittedly— that Judaire had set up some other destructive resources that would activate themselves in the event of anything happening to either himself or Adler. This scenario had been fully examined and although on balance it had been considered unlikely, it still remained a possibility and the intelligence and security agencies had been briefed to remain vigilant. The fact that Judaire's computers had been destroyed along with the Methane Colossus, was a disappointment to Mark since these might have provided the missing intelligence to enable him to completely close the loop on this whole ghastly affair.

The possibility of some destructive remnant being left behind by Judaire had been largely discounted by Mark after

Ruth had convinced him that Judaire's psychological profile indicated he was a man who could not tolerate failure or, even less, ever even contemplate it. With such a mentality, he would never have seen himself ever failing, so there would never be any thought of things to be left behind, if he did. It was a logic that appealed to Mark and when he had read the naval reports of what had happened a few days earlier, in the South Atlantic, Judaire's behaviour, before he died, appeared to fully correlate with these behavioural predictions. No, it was the second element of risk that concerned Mark more, the unidentifiable members of various independent cells still around the world, the remaining human, not technological, destructive resources, who may still spring into action. It was here that Uncle Thomas, following his extraordinary meeting with Hank Milshner and Stanley, was yet again to startle them.

"Have you phoned Stanley, Thomas?" Mark enquired, since it was now approaching the time when Stanley would be rising early at the mountain lodge in Montana.

"No, thanks for reminding me, I will do so," answered Thomas.

When Thomas managed to get through and heard the polite voice of Stanley on the other end, they quickly shared and confirmed all the recent news. Stanley then told Thomas that he was beginning to make preparations for Hank's funeral and they discussed some possible dates for when Thomas could get over to Sulphur Springs. Stanley said that he had some further information that Hank had left with him, and that he wished to testify against Michelle at her trial in Germany. It was, however, the last item of information that took Thomas by surprise, when Stanley said that the media should put out a global message that he would prepare, to be heard by the remaining cult members around the world. Many of these members had been recruited by Hank, and not Judaire, to the Christian cult, but had been hijacked by Judaire in subsequent years. Stanley was known by many of these people in earlier years, and he was sure they would respond, but there needed to be some form of armistice and a commitment that had they broken no laws, they would not be arrested.

This was all getting too complicated for Thomas over the phone, so he suggested that Stanley come immediately to Himbledon to assist with these final activities to bring the campaign of terror to an end. There was a brief pause before Stanley agreed and said he would come over in Hank's aeroplane and would phone Thomas back about where he would be landing and at what time, once he had made the arrangements. It was less than an hour later when they were speaking again, and Stanley said he would be arriving at Birmingham airport the following day, if someone could pick him up. He had arranged with Hank Milshner's personal pilots to fly him over in Hank's small Boeing jetliner.

When Thomas returned to the meeting room by the canal to explain the arrangements with Stanley, both Mark and Joseph were surprised at the suddenness of Stanley's arrival the next day.

As Thomas explained the need for a broadcast by Stanley to the remaining cult members, Mark burst out laughing and said, "Thomas, how do you do it? You have anticipated me; I wanted to speak to you both about this last possible threat?"

Thomas did not understand what Mark was talking about until he had explained. The three of them then looked at each other and nodded; this could be the final necessary action to bring the nightmare to a peaceful conclusion.

It had been a long and busy day as Mary walked into the meeting room and asked when they were finishing and be ready for supper. Thomas mentioned their American guest arriving tomorrow and they all walked upstairs. During supper, the phone continued to ring with messages and calls from all over the world. An Eskom helicopter pilot in South Africa had spotted some strange equipment in the Northern Cape that had led to the arrest and detention of one of the rogue live line crews who were now under cross examination by the local security police, who were confident that they would soon be on the trail of the remaining saboteurs. Neville had phoned from the Karoo.

Some weeks earlier, Brazil had won the Soccer World Cup and Bafana Bafana, the local South African national team, had also performed well, to the delight of local fans.

Global economic confidence had also risen sharply and the price of gold had dropped and equities, all around the world, had started to gently increase in value. The media were keeping the global population up to the minute with all these positive developments. Everywhere, among all people, there was a feeling of relief; people were smiling again and beginning to exchange jokes. A period of extreme darkness, anxiety and fear was beginning to lift all across the world.

Joseph was particularly brightened when Mark also said, "Ruth called yesterday to say that Anna is returning to her in Kensington shortly, since she is very much better. The possibility of her hurting herself has gone, she is sleeping well, coherent and although still on medication, appears to be well on the road to recovery."

Joe smiled broadly and looked across the kitchen table at Mary and Thomas and said, "Wonderful news; thanks, Mark. Mother, you must also be pleased."

Mary smiled and offered Thomas some more meat.

Just then Thomas said, "Have any of you heard the bells?" and Mark and Joe wondered for a moment what Thomas was referring to.

Mary smiled. It was Joseph who then suddenly remembered the many church bells that they had heard the previous day when they drove back to Himbledon from the airport.

"Yes, Thomas, rather like the end of the last war must have been" Joseph said.

43
Justice at Last

AT THE END OF WORLD WAR II THERE HAD BEEN A SCRAMBLE by the allies and the Russians to secure Nazi military technology. The Nazis were close to developing a nuclear weapon, they had rocket-powered military aircraft and rocket technology that was far advanced beyond anything else in the world. They had many more scientific developments and technologies that now proved to be of great interest to their victors. In the years that followed the end of the war, it was German rocket scientists who enabled the Americans to put the first man on the moon. There was more secret knowledge that the Germans had acquired during the war, often at huge human cost and the loss of lives with the use of slave labour. Much of the wartime technical advances laid the foundation for further discoveries and innovation in the decades that followed. As before, history was repeating itself.

Many politicians, military leaders and business people had started putting a similar big picture together, as the one Mark had described weeks earlier in his security briefings for the British prime minister. The Americans, Russians, Chinese and certain European countries were now eager to get their hands on some of the advanced technology that Judaire had developed over the previous twenty years. In remote mining complexes in Northern Canada, various research and development establishments scattered across the globe, in secret laboratories and in information technology incubators, an array of previously unseen technology was being discovered. It was extensive and diverse, ranging across a whole spectrum of scientific and technical achievements. There was a range of a completely new, more powerful and compact battery technologies, smart robots, tiny computer memory and data processing technology, a range of tiny electronic chips that had awesome processing capacities and much more. The developments with communication technology made even the cleverest of contemporary equipment appear archaic and there were discoveries being unearthed in a whole range of other disciplines. Energy and the creation of liquid fuels from plant material with new types of genetically modified plants, new types of photovoltaic panels for harnessing the sun, designs of entirely new rapid transit systems and many medical and pharmaceutical developments. In a small research and development facility in Ireland, a whole new range of battery-operated equipment was found for people with physical and other disabilities.

A global Aladdin's Cave was gradually being unearthed of technologies, scientific discoveries and other knowledge previously unknown, and it was often only when disparate elements, often thousands of miles apart in different establishments, were put together and connected, that it started to excite those with the knowledge to understand. The acquisition of this knowledge could enable those who had it in their possession to leapfrog competitors by many decades and gain huge commercial advantage. This also applied not only to commercial interests, but also to whole nations and political power blocks across the globe. An entirely new endeavour was beginning to crank up and the world was quickly returning to an unseemly dogfight to secure these treasures for the exclusive deployment by a few at the expense of the many.

Mark was one of those who often had the ability to connect the dots and see the bigger picture. He had always suspected that such looting would take place, although he had always hoped that this vast treasure trove of Judaire's creativity would now be put to good use for the benefit of civilisation, rather than its destruction. Little did Mark know that quite apart from the mad genius of Judaire, who had managed with the Milshner wealth to orchestrate such pioneering research on such a massive scale, that Hank had also inherited the entrepreneurial brilliance of his ancestors.

It was now the beginning of August, and Louise was to visit Himbledon from the Hague. Francesca and Achmed were due to arrive for a few days to discuss with Joseph further funding for extended field trials elsewhere in Africa. With Liska and Thomas also at the Grange, Mary was making preparations with a member of her staff about sleeping and catering arrangements. Stanley, from America, was to be accommodated in a single bedroom with en suite near Joseph's room, and Louise and Francesca were to sleep on the third floor in separate bedrooms while Thomas and Liska had their usual suite on the second floor. The scene was being set for a momentous few days at the Grange, although no single person had any idea of what lay ahead.

The German legal establishment had quickly started proceedings behind the scenes for the ultimate trial of Michelle Adler by the International Court of Justice. Her crimes against humanity had been global and with pressure mounting from the Americans and some other countries for her extradition, some senior pragmatic German politicians felt that her trial was beyond their jurisprudence and this was now being debated in legal circles in the country. Many in Germany also foresaw all manner of diplomatic, security and other problems arising in the future, the longer she remained in captivity on German soil.

There was a legal complexity, however, since Adler was American and the U.S.A. was not a signatory of the Rome Accord that provides the International Criminal Court with its jurisdiction to prosecute alleged criminals. Only those countries that have fully ratified this founding treaty come under the mandate of the ICC, so they cannot readily prosecute citizens of countries who have not signed the treaty. Behind the scenes, the U.S. government and diplomatic officials were flexing their muscles and trying to get her extradited to America for trial. Already within just a few short weeks of her arrest and detention, the wheels of international justice had become bogged down in needless complexities and international diplomacy.

To be able to keep Adler in custody under the German code of criminal law she also had to be convicted and found guilty of certain categories of crime. In view of this, the German political and legal establishment still intended to conduct a proper Federal trial and if she was found guilty, the intention was to imprison her until the broader international legal complexities could be resolved.

The substantive evidence that Thomas had provided to the German legal authorities appeared to provide them with a strong case, and arrangements were being made to prepare the prosecution and defence focussed on alleged crimes she had perpetrated within Germany. The derailment of the high-speed train on the Hanover line was the crucial allegation that had to be proved to keep her behind bars. Any weakness in the evidence or failure to prove a direct connection between Adler and the rail attack could jeopardise the prosecution case and could lead to her walking free.

Louise had taken a special interest in the case and had held lengthy discussions with some German lawyers now working at the ICC. If the U.N. Security Council decreed, then the ICC could also try Adler, although matters looked fragile with regard to proper justice being done. There was no agreement at the Security Council and now that the threat of global destruction had declined, many politicians and governments around the world were back to their customary behaviour, driven by self-interest.

The International Criminal Court came into being in 2002 when the founding treaty, The Rome Statute, came into force. Since this time, the ICC have received communications about alleged crimes in more than a hundred and forty countries and, after an initial review, the majority of these allegations were dismissed on the grounds of being beyond the jurisdiction of the court. To date, the court has opened just a few investigations with the major ones being Northern Uganda, the Democratic Republic of the Congo, the Central African Republic and Darfur. The court has indicted some fourteen people, seven of whom remain free, two have died, and just five are in custody. In the face of the continuing brutality and tyranny across the world, this is hardly a startling record, and justice frequently remains bogged down in legal and other technicalities. Sadly, the balance of power remains in the hands of the criminal rather than the just. Yet again, the actual evidence indicates a very different reality to the one most right minded people content themselves with.

As had been arranged over the phone, Thomas was at Birmingham airport to meet Stanley. Arrangements were made for the crew of the Boeing to stay in a small, comfortable hotel in a village outside the city. As Thomas drove Stanley through the English countryside, they discussed the funeral of Hank Milshner and both agreed that late September might be a good time to confirm the necessary arrangements. Stanley mentioned that there would be very few people at the funeral; Hank had no descendents and was the last of the Milshner family line. He had also wanted it to be a very small and modest affair. When they arrived at the Grange, Francesca and Achmed had already arrived and Joseph had driven to Heathrow to pick up Louise. Mary was the first to see Thomas drive up the drive and park the Aston Martin near the kitchen door and she walked and stood waiting to greet her guest from America.

Mary had no idea of what to expect, and as Stanley walked across the gravel dressed in a sports jacket she smiled and extended her hand in greeting.

"Welcome to Himbledon, you must be tired after your long flight." He shook her hand.

"Good to meet you, Mrs. Trimbledon, and good to be here."

She smiled and said, "Call me Mary."

He replied, "Sure, and I am Stanley."

It was not long before his bags had been deposited in his room and he had met Mark, Francesca and Achmed and they talked together with Thomas and Liska in the lounge.

Mary offered Stanley some tea or coffee and he took a mug of coffee before eventually sitting down. He was unaccustomed to being waited on and it took him a few minutes to orientate himself to this grand old English house and its occupants. Seeing an Arab gentleman in traditional dress had also thrown him momentarily, but after a few minutes conversation with Achmed, he began to relax. Thomas continued to make jokes and make everyone feel welcome and at home.

It was early evening when Joseph and Louise arrived from the airport and everyone had dispersed around the house. Mary greeted Louise with a kiss, and told her where she would be sleeping, that Francesca was in the room next to hers, and that dinner would be at 7:30 in the dining room. After she had dropped her bag in her room, Louise went to Francesca's room and they immediately started talking as Francesca changed for dinner. When they came down together to the lounge, Joseph was in conversation with Stanley and Thomas. Charlotte and Mark arrived and they looked rather preoccupied as Thomas served everyone with a pre-dinner drink. It was to be a rather momentous dinner this evening that went on late into the night with the most exceptional discussions around the large table.

As they made their way through to the dining room, Mark turned to his mother and said, "Charlotte and I have an announcement to make over dinner, Mother."

Mary nodded.

Stanley was a modest man, yet during the course of dinner those around the table were to discover there was more to this man than first appearances would ever suggest. Louise had come with matters on her mind from the International Court and various issues surrounding the criminal prosecution. Achmed and Francesca were excited about the success of some of their medical field trials and the opportunity to rapidly expand the programme, subject to more funding being found. Mark had on his mind the looting of the many technical and scientific developments flowing from Judaire's genius and what could be done about it. There was also the matter of dealing with the remaining cult cells and Stanley's message to be broadcast. Thomas was thinking about the funeral of Hank Milshner and the tribute that he was planning to the man. Joseph, Louise and Francesca also had another intimacy that would be revealed during the course of the evening, but it was Liska who set the tone for the evening.

As they sat down at the large table and soup was being served, Liska said that she and Thomas had an announcement to make.

"Oh, all right if you must, Liska," Thomas said, and then Liska said that she had asked Thomas to marry her and that he had agreed.

There were immediate congratulations and hugs and kisses and Mark stood up and proposed a toast to the happy couple. They were onto their main course when Charlotte nudged Mark and placed her hands in her lap as he gently knocked his wine glass to calm the conversation before standing up and looking at Charlotte and said, "I too have an announcement to make. Charlotte and I are engaged," and Louise and Francesca, who had already seen the ring, clapped and asked Charlotte to show everyone the ring on her finger.

Mark then proposed a toast to his future bride and Thomas proposed a toast to them both.

Mary had also noticed something going on between Francesca and Louise earlier in the meal and wondered if there were not to be further announcements, when during the dessert her curiosity was satisfied.

Francesca suddenly said, "I think Joseph also has something to tell everyone."

Joseph turned from his conversation with Achmed and said, "Oh, yes. Francesca and I have set a tentative date to get married," and Louise and Francesca smiled.

"When, then?" asked Mary, smiling.

Francesca said, "Next spring, here at Himbledon, if we may, Mary?"

Mary instantly replied, "Yes, of course; that will be wonderful."

Francesca got up and walked around and gave Mary a kiss on the cheek. There were further toasts and laughter.

When the meal was finished no one moved from the table. Cheese, fruit and chocolates were served and Mark passed around port glasses and offered all the ladies something to drink. Coffee was served on the dresser nearby and everyone settled down for more conversation. There was an air of contentment and calm as Thomas started to lead the conversation and referred to his meeting with Hank Milshner and how invaluable his help had been in bringing all the trouble to an end.

It was not long after some gentle coaxing from Louise, that Stanley started to talk. Louise had a suspicion that this man was more than a butler, having talked with him for lengthy periods throughout dinner. It was Louise who had slightly embarrassed Stanley by asking him directly about himself and how he had come to work for Hank Milshner. Talking slowly and very politely Stanley told them, as they sat listening intently, that he had known the Milshner family since he was a young man, from when he had been orphaned and he had been taken into a boy's home in Boston that was funded by the Milshner family. He had attended Harvard and read law and was an attorney and had benefited from a Milshner bursary. It had been some years later after practising corporate law that he had joined Hank and they had become friends. He had been involved in dealing with the roadhouse fire when Hank had been falsely implicated. The roadhouse owner, who was insolvent and was facing bankruptcy, had actually started the fire.

He had known Michelle Adler and her weird ways well in the early years and had often, at the instruction of Hank, got her out of trouble. Stanley was also a friend of Hank when he started his religious group with a small band of followers. Many were reformed drug users and others who "had few breaks in life before meeting Hank." They had enjoyed a few years of very happy times together, but then things had started to go wrong. Adler began to throw her weight around and there had been a major disagreement between her and Stanley, after which he moved away and went into his own legal practice. Hank, however, always kept contact with Stanley, and he continued to attend to some of Hank's personal legal affairs. They rarely saw each other for many years although Stanley had assisted Hank with some legal matters related to the purchase of the castle in Bavaria. It was at that time that he met Judaire briefly before the major rift between Adler and Hank.

Everyone around the table sat motionless, listening as the

gentle American spoke about his fascinating life. Stanley went on to say that Hank had altered his will a few months before he died and as his attorney there were some matters that he needed to talk to Thomas, Mark and Joseph about, but that could wait until tomorrow. Mark raised the issue of safeguarding Judaire's inventions from marauding governments and commercial interests.

Stanley smiled and said, "Do not worry Mark, everything is protected and is legally owned by the Milshner estate, Hank and I made sure of that over the last few years."

He went on to explain that although Adler had some control over some of Milshner's business interests— all a dreadful mistake, as things turned out— it had been he who advised Hank to retain legal ownership. Since he had joined Hank again, a few years earlier, Stanley had masterminded the protection of Milshner assets and had a global legal team under his personal direction. Louise sat, speechless at these extraordinary revelations.

It was Francesca who sensed something else about Stanley when she asked, "So you are not a butler, Stanley?"

There was a brief pause and Stanley looked a little embarrassed when he replied, "Well no, not strictly, although I looked after Hank in the last few years of his life. I was the only person he would trust. You see, I also loved Hank. He was rather like an older brother to me, from when I was a young guy."

Louise looked at Stanley and felt deep sympathy for him and to ease the sadness in the room she said, "It must have been hard for you when he died and all these terrible accusations that have been made against him?"

Stanley smiled slightly and said, "Yes, it was very hurtful for Hank, but now with the help of Thomas we are going to put that right, I hope."

Everyone nodded and Mary smiled kindly at Stanley, who swivelled on his chair and looked at Louise and said, "You were talking about the ICC earlier Louise, and Michelle being American."

"Yes, that's right; things all look horribly complicated and the U.S. authorities may get their wish and be able to extradite her," Louise answered.

Stanley smiled again gently, and said, "Michelle is not American, she is Canadian and Canada have ratified the Rome Accord, so the ICC have jurisdiction over her, providing the Canadian authorities agree. Since there were no attacks in Canada, they can hardly object to a trial at the ICC."

As he turned his napkin between his fingers Stanley continued, "Michelle was a runaway, ran away from her folks and crossed the border illegally into the States from Canada. She still holds Canadian citizenship."

Within a few seconds, the sharp legal brain of Stanley had clarified the legal situation concerning the future trial of Adler. Hank had made Stanley promise that he would ensure that Michelle Adler would receive a fair trial, be found guilty for her wrong doings and be put behind bars. He was in the process of fulfilling his promise.

Thomas then asked about Stanley's comment on the phone about wishing to testify at Michelle's trial in Germany.

"Yes that's right, Tom. I am going to Germany when we have finished our business here to meet the local prosecutors. I will act as a witness for the prosecution and have evidence that should readily convince the judges of her guilt."

44

The Boston Tribune

THE NEXT DAY AT THE GRANGE, STANLEY WAS UP EARLY and had taken a walk in the gardens before meeting Mary in the kitchen for some coffee before breakfast. Being on their own, Stanley said how sorry he was about Tim and John's deaths and said that the news of their murders had greatly distressed Hank. Mary found Stanley to be a kind and gentle man and she realised that he was a person who had been swept along by circumstances, an innocent bystander.

She laid her hand on his arm as they sat opposite each other at the breakfast table and said, "I feel for Hank Milshner, even though I never met the man. Thank you for coming here, Stanley, and for sharing what you did with us last night over dinner. When we can understand a little more about how things came about we can come to better accept them and forgive."

Stanley looked into her eyes and replied, "Yes, that's right Mary, you're right."

There were to be more surprises for Mark, Joseph and Thomas when they met with Stanley in the study. The first and urgent matter that Stanley wished to be attended to was the global broadcast to remaining cult members, and he handed them each a copy of a draft message he wished to record and have broadcast on international television networks. The matter of armistice had to be agreed with the prime minister and the U.S. president, however, before the message was to be transmitted and, after reading the draft and agreeing to its contents, Joseph said he would speak with the prime minister's office for the necessary arrangements to be agreed on and put into place. Mark said they had professional recording equipment at the Grange and could produce the necessary materials to be distributed to the media.

There was a lengthy discussion about the many things that Judaire had developed and that were now owned by the Milshner Estate. Stanley explained that a team of international patent lawyers had been working for the previous three years defining, describing and registering lists of technical and scientific matters. This had been done in conjunction with a thorough audit that Hank Milshner had ordered of all his business interests when he had rearranged the control and management of his companies. He and Stanley had assembled some of the best brains in the world to work with this audit team, so they would know exactly what they were dealing with and be able to protect the intellectual property.

Stanley said, "Many people may be at this moment pilfering some of these things, but if they ever try to use any of this material, they will immediately come up against Milshner patent protection, so for now I think we can relax. There are some other more important matters that I must discuss with the three of you."

Stanley held up a document and said it was the last will and testament of Hank Milshner that he had changed in the last few months of his life. The Milshner estate was worth trillions, plus all the intellectual property they had just discussed, and Hank had wanted all this wealth and knowledge to be managed by a Foundation for the benefit of mankind. Hank had no children or family to continue this important work, so three months before he died he had asked Stanley to set up a Foundation to manage these matters and he had stipulated just a few names of people he wanted involved, together with some key principles to guide the way in which the foundation would manage its affairs. Two of the names were in the room that day, Thomas and Joseph Trimbledon. The principles involved minimal regulation, the encouragement of competition and free enterprise, low operating overheads, vigilant monitoring of actual delivery, and transparency.

Stanley said, "Do you realise, guys, that between those of us in this room, we control a large slice of the global gross domestic product? It is a daunting responsibility and we are going to have to set up a range of checks and balances and ensure we do this job properly. Never again can we allow individuals, politicians or whoever else, to screw up. We have also got to help get the international economy up and running again, it is the only way we can properly start addressing the poverty and other needs of millions of people. We must thank God for this, another opportunity."

Mark, Joseph and Thomas looked at each other, trying to comprehend the significance of what Stanley had just said.

"Slow down a little Stanley, do you mean that Hank wanted us to work together?" asked Thomas.

"Yes. That is exactly what he wanted and we have some work to do in the next while, to meet his wishes."

There was a brief pause before Mark asked, "Forgive me Stanley, but I was always led to believe that Hank was mad, but from what you have just told us, he was far from insane."

Stanley then drew in his breath and said, "Let me answer you Mark, by saying that Hank had a bad mental breakdown at the time of the roadhouse fire. He had been dabbling in drugs and lost touch with reality. Shortly after the trouble in Colorado, I got him into treatment, and after getting the proper medical care he was fine. Then when he went to Germany he had another breakdown and began to have all manner of strange thoughts, and I blame Michelle for that. She claimed she was having dreams or some other nonsense and she got into Hank's head. When I got involved with them again with the legal transfer of the castle, I could see he was losing it again, so for the second time I got him into treatment. Michelle did not like that and we had a big fight over it, but Hank listened to me. To my knowledge, apart from those two incidents, Hank Milshner was one of the smartest and most far-sighted guys I have ever known."

Thomas looked at Stanley and asked, "So what Hank said to me at the lodge about wanting to try to help straighten out capitalism and the excesses of the rich world, were true Stanley?"

The American looked back at Thomas and replied, "Yep, they sure were true, because he could see what many of the rest of us couldn't, that the world is going to Hell. He could see the economic crash coming years before it started to happen, he lobbied against U.S. foreign policy, he reached out and invested in Arab and Moslem countries years back, he poured millions into education in the developing world, he was giving money to Aids relief at about the same time the Vatican got involved, he invested money into LNG long before the big oil companies got involved, because he saw this fuel as an interim step before other better energies are developed… I had better stop there, but listen guys, Hank Milshner was some man, but the old saying applies: give a dog a bad name and it sticks."

Joseph was busy trying to assimilate and think through what Stanley had been saying and he had a question. "So how did Judaire fit into all this, Stanley?"

There was a pause and Stanley raised his eyebrows slightly and replied, "That is a good question Joe, and I am not exactly sure. But again to the best of my knowledge what had excited Hank about Judaire was his brilliance and potential to develop new things that would help people, certainly never to destroy them. You know, while what has happened over the last few months is all dreadful; the loss of life and suffering, Hank felt responsible, he felt he had let it all happen. I know he was wrong thinking that, but he wanted to try to ensure nothing like it ever happens again and I think that is why he wanted you guys involved. He had read all the economic writings of your father, Joe, he knew how things are run here at Himbledon and he had a lot of time for the way you guys do things. Hank was also always more impressed with actual results on the ground than just talk and all the inspirational crap we get these days."

Thomas smiled and, looking at Mark and Joseph, said, "A man after my own heart; quite right, Hank."

Everyone chuckled and Stanley asked if anyone wanted more coffee before pouring himself some more from the hot coffee jug on the tray on the table.

Stanley continued to talk and he said that Hank Milshner had a completely new view of economics, and that some of his ideas were similar to those of John Trimbledon, particularly about good stewardship, and that there should be no shortage of food, education, proper shelter, and security for the world's population.

Stanley said, "Hank believed passionately that this is what the Creator wants for everyone, but the brokenness of man is what causes all the constraints and problems."

This was one of the foundational principles that Hank Milshner had been brought up with by his parents. When he had first met Judaire and when Stanley had helped with the purchase of the castle in Bavaria before Hank had his second breakdown, he was talking about the knowledge economy long before it became fashionable. He believed that a new knowledge economy, as John Trimbledon had postulated many times, which takes existing knowledge and technology and deploys it effectively, can create accelerating development and sufficient resources for everyone. Innovation and competitiveness and new ways of applying knowledge with technology can create enough for human needs, so concepts of scarcity should become obsolete. Hank was talking about concepts such as knowledge spirals, cognitive leadership and architecture, long before they appeared in academic textbooks. It was ideas such as these that had probably excited Hank about the brilliance of Judaire and that with the extraordinary list of developments and scientific breakthroughs that he achieved, Hank had been right.

It was Joseph who then raised a critical question when he asked, "You know, Stanley, the idea of 'enough for everyone' has been a focus of ours for many years. It is also about sufficiency rather than gluttony, it must be about being inclusive rather than exclusive, but how do we achieve this? The knowledge economy has already created plenty for many and can yield so much more although capitalism, particularly as we have witnessed it again in recent years, is failing. It simply enriches the few to the exclusion of the many. So the issue remains, having grown a rich harvest through the combination of knowledge and technology, the challenge is who controls this wealth and how to properly distribute it in an equitable way. This is where the world is failing."

Mark said, "Communism, democracy and even benign dictators have all failed mankind. Even today the U.N., the World Food Programme and other global efforts, although well meaning, are a huge disappointment."

Everyone nodded before Stanley said, "It is precisely with this issue that Hank Milshner has challenged us, just before his death, to focus our attention in working together and with others, to find sustainable governance and distribution principles. You know, philanthropy is a huge and growing part of the global economy and by working with other reputable bodies, whether they be private or state organisations, we can leverage our resources to try to bring about these changes. This is what Hank had dreamed about and lived for before Adler and Judaire stole his dream and defiled it."

Joseph thought for a moment before continuing to talk. He thought about his time in Cape Town, the work of Francesca and Achmed; and, the talent of his brother Mark with technology and the deployment of knowledge. He thought about the Trimbledon business empire and the thoughts that had entered his mind when at the Vineyard Hotel in Cape Town listening to Henry, the elderly Franciscan priest. Recent memories of Neville and his Karoo farm community also filled his mind.

He then said, "Hank Milshner was right. I agree, Stanley. We must think this whole thing through and in principle you have my support. We will need to have further discussions, bring in some of our people to start looking at the detail. While we will need to be clear about how we may be able to achieve these changes, there is already sufficient evidence and examples of better ways to manage these matters. In any event, the world is going to be a very different place as it recovers from the attacks and this depression. There is much to learn from these recent events and perhaps this will be a good time for fresh beginnings?" They all thought for a moment, looked at each other and nodded.

It was Thomas who had the last word before Stanley and Mark went off to make the recording, and Joseph went to phone the prime minister's office.

Not really understanding things like technology spirals or whatever they were called, he said, "While I do not understand all this clever language about technology, and prefer to leave that sort of thing to Mark, there are two essential ingredients that we are going to have to include in our thinking, if we are going to have any chance of success," and then he paused.

Joseph, Mark and Stanley sat looking at Thomas across the study as he continued, "Proper education and proper leadership. Education that will properly equip people to be able to make informed decisions and be able to fully participate in this brave new world you are talking about and assume their rightful responsibilities. For leadership, I am talking about selfless, visionary and charismatic leadership that serves rather than wanting to be served. If we can start to get these things right, then I am with you."

Stanley nodded and replied, "Exactly right Thomas, now you know why Hank wanted you as one of the founding members of this new Foundation that we spoke about earlier."

* * *

IT WAS LATE IN SEPTEMBER WHEN THOMAS, STANLEY, Joseph, Mark and Brendan Flynn stood with a small handful of other people, by Hank Milshner's graveside in Montana, as his coffin was lowered into the empty grave beside his mother. Strangely, there were no women present at the funeral; it had just worked out that way. It had been a simple funeral service, but deeply touching, particularly for Stanley and Thomas. Joseph and Mark had also been moved by the service of remembrance led by the local Lutheran Pastor and a Bible reading and brief eulogy that Brendan had been asked to give by Stanley. Thomas had remained behind, standing by the graves after the others had slowly walked away to go up to the lodge for some refreshments. He read the new inscription on the tombstone with Hank's name, date of birth and death and he prayed for him, his mother and his father, that they would soon be reunited in a happier place.

Thomas wanted to be alone for a while. After standing silently for several minutes by the graves, he then wandered across to the farmhouse and walked around the stables and empty paddocks and he imagined what it must have been like all those years ago when it was a bustling, happy farm with Hank's parents at the place. He sat on the edge of an empty water trough in the breeze, watching tumbleweed being blown across the empty paddocks, silent apart from the rustle of the wind, now a place of sorrow. He had tears in his eyes and felt like weeping at the sadness of it all, and he could also feel the grief of Tim's and John's deaths, almost overwhelming him. He remembered, when just a few short weeks earlier, he had come to this place with judgement in his heart, about the man whose mortal remains now lay nearby. He felt ashamed at himself and remembered the actual man, not the simplistic and wrong judgement the world had placed on Hank Milshner, but a very different person. He was reminded how quickly and all too readily we judge, and place labels on people when we should rather be reaching out to them, listening and befriending them.

He reflected that quite apart from the tragic circumstances of Hank's life, he had also become estranged from others because he thought differently, he had challenged accepted norms and he wanted to make a difference for the better. He remembered that so many good people had only ever received recognition after they were dead, when the busy world finally listened and understood their contribution.

Not that any of that actually really mattered, he thought, *it is not in this life we should seek reward.*

As he sat with some straw between his fingers, looking out across the huge landscape, his mind came to think about the tribute he and Stanley were now planning for Hank, and his sadness began to diminish when someone touching him lightly on the shoulder startled him.

"Are you okay, Tom?" Stanley asked, standing beside him. "We were getting worried about you down here all on your own, come on up to the lodge and have something to warm you up."

Thomas rose from the water trough and looked at Stanley and said, "Well, Stanley, Hank is now at rest and we must continue to pray that he will find peace with his parents."

Stanley looked up at Thomas and nodded, and they walked together between the empty farm buildings to join the others high above them in the mountain lodge.

Over the next few weeks, Thomas remained at the lodge with Stanley, making the preparations for the tribute to Hank to be held in Boston before the end of the year. The legal processes were continuing in Germany, and apart from Stanley having to fly to Europe for a few days to give evidence in the Federal trial of Michelle Adler, he remained at the lodge. Liska had flown over and was also staying at the lodge together with various members of Stanley's legal and business team. The place had become within just a few days of Hank's burial a bustling centre of activity with people coming and going. They had been joined by a friend of Thomas who was an impresario with a proven track record of staging large events and the order of music, different elements of the event continued to change. Thomas and Stanley wanted it to be simple, and not just a tribute to Hank, but an opportunity for the world to try to get some element of closure on the dreadful events of recent months. It was also to be a memorial to the many who had lost their lives and something that would enthral the ear and the eye to encourage reconciliation and unity.

Nothing like it had ever been attempted before. There were also to be dignitaries attending from across the globe, as well as the U.S. president, Russian, Indian and Chinese, and other political leaders, and also leaders of various religious communities, including the Pope. There were to be wounded and disabled ex-servicemen and women, many now using some of the new equipment developed by Milshner companies. Some of the crew of the HMS *Freedom* were to be present together with many Japanese dignitaries. They wanted this event to try to represent a watershed, a break with certain elements of the past and the announcement of new beginnings. It was to be televised in many languages and, between Thomas and Stanley; they had put together a large budget to cover all the costs. There was to be no element of commercialism, any government money or influence, and an independent professional media team had been assembled to ensure everything was done properly. While Thomas had the grand creative vision, it was Stanley's attention to detail and perfectionism that, when combined, would create a momentous event living in the minds of billions for years to come. That was the simple intention and that is what was achieved.

When the evening came for the tribute, held in the huge baseball stadium in Boston, everything was ready. The weather was also perfect, and it proved to be a wonderful evening of music, drama, comedy, speeches, tributes, and dance. There had been no political speeches and no religious eulogies, only some plain simple prayers, in Hebrew, Latin, English and from the Koran. The pope was there, as were the heads of all the other great churches. Liska's ballet company had danced, Thomas had played a brief piano farewell to Hank and there had been all of Hank's favourite music performed during the course of the evening.

There had been a staggering finale with fireworks, and a breathtaking performance by the Boston Symphony Orchestra of Aaron Copeland's "Fanfare for the Common Man". No better or more fitting an end could ever have been imagined.

However, for Joseph, Francesca and Louise, the heart-stopping highlight of the entire long evening was when the whole stadium went into darkness and the orchestra started to perform a medley of Copeland's music in a tribute to Abraham Lincoln, and Stanley walked slowly to the centre of the huge stage, a solitary figure standing under a single spotlight; he provided a deeply moving and haunting narration. It is worth repeating some of the timeless words of Abraham Lincoln that he quoted on that momentous night, before the hushed audience in the stadium and the billions of people who watched around the world.

Abraham Lincoln, the sixteenth president of the United States, said, "Fellow citizens we cannot escape history, fellow members of this Congress, we will be remembered despite ourselves. No personal significance or insignificance can spare one the fiery trials through which we will pass and will be judged by future generations. We, even we here, hold the power and responsibility…"

"The darkness of the quiet past is inadequate to destroy us; piled high with difficulty we must rise to the occasion, as our case is new, we must think and act anew, and then we shall save our country…"

"It is the eternal struggle between two principles, right and wrong throughout the world. No Matter where it comes from, whether from the mouth of a king who seeks to bestride his own nation to live by the fruits of their labour, or one man enslaving another, it is the same tyrannical principle."

"That we here highly resolve that these dead shall not have died in vain, but this nation, under God, will have a new thirst for freedom, and that government of the people, by the people, for the people, will not perish from the Earth."

45
The World Regains Its Dignity

IT WAS THE NEXT DAY AS MARY, JOSEPH, FRANCESCA, Louise, Mark and Charlotte were preparing to leave for the airport that Brian Hardwick phoned Mark on his mobile phone and asked about the three small boxes he had handed to him at Himbeldon a day before they had all flown to Boston for the Tribute. They spoke briefly and Mark asked when Brian would be back at Himbledon and he said within a few days for some further shore leave. Mark assured Brian the items were secure and that he would look at them immediately he had returned to the Grange. Logan airport was busy as they went through the various procedures for their flight back to Heathrow. It was some hours later after they had arrived back to the Grange and had rested that Mark went to the safe and removed the three computer hard drives.

It would soon be Christmas again and Louise had transited via Heathrow airport directly to The Hague and Francesca had caught a flight to Rome. Thomas had stayed in Boston for a few days with Liska, and Stanley staying with Charlie and Martha. Things would be a little less busy at Himbledon for the next few weeks leading up to Christmas, when the Grange would be full again as life everywhere gradually returned to a relative state of normality.

People were noticeably more friendly and polite. Many had received a terrifying jolt in recent months and appeared more appreciative of what they had, of each other and for the simpler pleasures of their freedom and life. Joseph liaised with the prime minister's office regarding the final remnants of the security clean-up operation that was now largely complete. He also liaised with Stanley and Thomas regarding the extensive work they had now embarked on to establish a joint Foundation.

It was almost a week after they had returned to Himbledon from Boston that Joseph noticed he had seen little of Mark since returning and that he had been embroiled in something below next to the canal. Little did he know that Mark had, after some initial difficulty with the advanced hardware, gained access to the three hard drives that Brian Hardwick had grabbed from the hands of the dying Judaire, in the final moments of the assault on the Methane Colossus. In almost a week Mark had only managed to study a fraction of just a single hard drive since it contained such a welter of information. They were very advanced pieces of hardware with an extraordinary memory capacity and they contained in three small boxes, each the size of a cigar box, everything that Judaire had developed, ever dreamed about and planned to inflict on the world.

For Mark, such material completely absorbed him and to have it all in a single small collection of silver boxes, such an array of futuristic knowledge, was almost overwhelming for him. It was when Joseph went looking for Mark and found him unshaven with flickering computer monitors set up all around the meeting room, that he became concerned about Mark.

"Are you okay, Mark?" asked Joseph.

Mark had replied, "Yes, perfectly, Joe."

Joseph continued, "But you do not look as though you have slept for a week; you look terrible, Mark. Can't all this wait?"

Mark stopped what he was doing and looked across at Joseph, then replied, "Yes, now it can, but I had to have some idea of what was on these hard drives and, Joe, we have everything here, all the things Stanley was talking about, and Judaire's intentions for further attacks and the 2012 Olympics in London."

They discussed some of the incredulous material on the hard drive that Mark had so far managed to interrogate, particularly the dramatic plans Judaire had for the build up to the Olympics. It was clear that Judaire had no intention of destroying the world, what he wanted was to dominate it. Had he not been stopped, it appeared he had all the means to have done just that. He had been holding back a whole range of cyber weapons that could have wrought wholesale damage and destruction, wherever and whenever Judaire wished. Mark stood up and walked to one of the computers and found a particular file and clicked it open. There on the screen were simulation images of some of what Judaire was yet to inflict and Joseph watched for a moment before burying his head in his hands and asking Mark to turn it off. They agreed that every thing on these hard drives needed to be catalogued and all the destructive material needed to be either destroyed or placed somewhere where it would be totally secure.

They sat for a moment in silence and it was Joseph who then asked, “Can you separate the good from the bad on these hard drives, Mark?”

Mark smiled rather wearily and replied, “Yes, I think I can, anyway we need all the good material for this Foundation that you and Thomas are getting excited about.”

Joseph smiled and said, “Precisely, Mark. Well, in that case I propose that all the bad parts on these Judaire drives you make secure, and that you then fly over to Luke and arrange for them to be put into the Vatican vaults, hopefully where they will never be required or seen again.”

Mark stood up and started to switch off all the computers in the meeting room and turned to Joe and said, “What a good idea Joe. That’s it then for today; I am going for a shave and then a beer with Charlotte. Please lock the room on your way up,” and Mark walked from the room, along by the canal bank and slowly up the stairs into the Grange.

It was some months later as Joseph and Francesca looked across the Zambezi from the veranda of the Royal Livingstone Hotel, near the Victoria Falls in Zambia, on the last leg of their honeymoon, that Francesca received a brief text message from Louise saying that Michelle Adler had been found guilty and the Federal German court had imprisoned her for a number of years.

Francesca instantly phoned Louise and they chatted and laughed together and Louise asked about the Karoo and whether Neville had kept his promise and taken her to the Owl House. He had, and Francesca told Louise that she must plan a visit to Neville at the farm. Louise also said that Adler would in all likelihood now be subject to a fuller trial by the International Court of Justice and that Stanley's evidence against her had been invaluable.

As they drew their conversation to an end Louise asked jokingly, "Any discussions yet about the name of our first child?" and they both laughed.

Francesca replied, looking across at Joseph with a glint in her eye, "No discussion yet, but it will either be John or Louise."

They both laughed and said goodbye.

"What was all that about Fran?" Joseph asked.

Francesca replied, "Oh nothing Joe. Louise sends her love."

The other ageless truth is that love and forgiveness conquer everything, even evil. Those who dismiss this fact as old fashioned or irrelevant in the world today, do so at their peril.

Lightning Source UK Ltd.
Milton Keynes UK
04 July 2010

156493UK00001B/130/P

9 781616 67083